Justice and Reconciliation in World Politics

Calls for justice and reconciliation in response to political catastrophes are widespread in contemporary world politics. What implications do these normative strivings have in relation to colonial injustice? Examining cases of colonial war, genocide, forced sexual labor, forcible incorporation, and dispossession, Lu demonstrates that international practices of justice and reconciliation have historically suffered from, and continue to reflect, colonial, statist, and other structural biases. The continued reproduction of structural injustice and alienation in modern domestic, international, and transnational orders generates contemporary duties of redress. How should we think about the responsibility of contemporary agents to address colonial structural injustices, and what implications follow for the transformation of international and transnational orders? Redressing the structural injustices implicated in or produced by colonial politics requires strategies of decolonization, decentering, and disalienation that go beyond interactional practices of justice and reconciliation, beyond victims and perpetrators, and beyond a statist world order.

CATHERINE LU is an Associate Professor in the Department of Political Science at McGill University. Her research intersects political theory and international relations, focusing on critical and normative studies of humanitarianism and intervention in world politics; justice, reconciliation, and colonialism; and cosmopolitanism, global justice, and the world state. She is the author of *Just and Unjust Interventions in World Politics: Public and Private* (2006) and has held research fellowships from the School of Philosophy at the Australian National University, the Alexander von Humboldt Foundation, and the Edmond J. Safra Center for Ethics at Harvard University, Massachusetts.

Cambridge Studies in International Relations: 145

Justice and Reconciliation in World Politics

Cambridge Studies in International Relations is a joint initiative of Cambridge University Press and the British International Studies Association (BISA). The series aims to publish the best new scholarship in international studies, irrespective of subject matter, methodological approach or theoretical perspective. The series seeks to bring the latest theoretical work in International Relations to bear on the most important problems and issues in global politics.

Justice and Reconciliation in World Politics

CATHERINE LU
McGill University, Montreal

CAMBRIDGE
UNIVERSITY PRESS

CAMBRIDGE
UNIVERSITY PRESS

University Printing House, Cambridge CB2 8BS, United Kingdom

One Liberty Plaza, 20th Floor, New York, NY 10006, USA

477 Williamstown Road, Port Melbourne, VIC 3207, Australia

314-321, 3rd Floor, Plot 3, Splendor Forum, Jasola District Centre, New Delhi - 110025, India

79 Anson Road, #06-04/06, Singapore 079906

Cambridge University Press is part of the University of Cambridge.

It furthers the University's mission by disseminating knowledge in the pursuit of education, learning and research at the highest international levels of excellence.

www.cambridge.org
Information on this title: www.cambridge.org/9781108413053
DOI: 10.1017/9781108329491

© Catherine Lu 2017

First published 2017
First paperback edition 2018

A catalogue record for this publication is available from the British Library

ISBN 978-1-108-42011-2 Hardback
ISBN 978-1-108-41305-3 Paperback

For Lorenz

Contents

Acknowledgments

This book represents over a decade of intellectual work that constituted a long and meandering journey of trying to understand problems of justice and reconciliation in political philosophy and contemporary world politics. Along the way, I have been fortified and sustained by the support of many people and institutions.

For their attentive and dynamic intellectual engagement, influence, and encouragement over various phases of this work, I would like to express deep gratitude to Arash Abizadeh, Pablo Gilabert, Jacob Levy, and Lea Ypi. Each of these scholar-friends has supportively engaged with my work and arguments over the years and pushed me gently and consistently to be more rigorous in argument, more clear in my thoughts, and more alive to their implications for the subject of this book. I am also especially thankful for David A. Welch, a stalwart mentor since the start of my academic career, who, in his usual, efficient fashion, promptly read and constructively commented on a penultimate draft of the manuscript. In addition, I am ever grateful to Robert E. Goodin for encouraging some of my initial work related to this project and, more recently, for reading the entire book manuscript and providing his typically candid criticism, sharp insights, and enthusiastic feedback. Words cannot express how indebted I am to these colleagues for their extraordinary intellectual, professional, and personal generosity and friendship.

This manuscript was markedly improved in its final stages by perceptive and constructive comments from two anonymous reviewers for Cambridge University Press. I would also like to thank the editors of the Cambridge Studies in International Relations series for including this work in their series, thereby continuing to promote deeper dialogue and intellectual engagement between scholars in political theory, international relations, and various other subfields.

Over the course of the book's transmutations, I have benefited the most from my colleagues in the Department of Political Science at

McGill University, as well as from those in History, Philosophy, and Law, who have created an intellectually and personally supportive environment for academic flourishing. My gratitude for their collegial engagement goes especially to Arash Abizadeh, Megan Bradley, Gaëlle Fiasse, Jacob Levy, Lorenz Lüthi, Victor Muñiz-Fraticelli, Frédéric Mégret, Alan Patten, Vincent Pouliot, René Provost, William Clare Roberts, Christa Scholtz, Hasana Sharp, Natalie Stoljar, Christina Tarnopolsky, Kristin Voigt, Daniel Weinstock, and Yves Winter. From the wider Montreal community, I am also indebted to Amandine Catala, Ryoa Chung, Peter Dietsch, Pablo Gilabert, and Cynthia Milton for their insights and support. Our many conversations over the years have been supported by numerous research communities, including the Research Group on Constitutional Studies (RGCS) of McGill's Yan P. Lin Centre for the Study of Freedom and Global Orders in the Ancient and Modern Worlds; the Montreal-wide Groupe de Recherche Interuniversitaire en Philosophie Politique (GRIPP); the Centre for International Peace and Security Studies (CIPSS); McGill's Centre for Human Rights and Legal Pluralism (CHRLP); and the Centre de Recherche en Éthique (CRÉ) at the Université de Montréal.

I have appreciated greatly the diverse and stimulating insights of many postdoctoral fellows as well as graduate and undergraduate students who took my seminars, wrote research papers and master's theses, or participated in workshops and seminars on themes related to this book project. Among the many postdoctoral fellows and graduate students, I am especially grateful to Daniel Silvermint, Mohamed Sesay, Aberdeen Berry, Lou Pingeot, Derval Ryan, Benjamin Thompson, Raphaëlle Mathieu-Bédard, Yann Allard-Tremblay, Briana McGinnis, Robert Sparling, Tim Waligore, and Caleb Yong for their critical feedback and discussions that helped to refine and improve some of the book's main arguments. I would also like to thank, in chronological order, Kristin Rawls (2007), Raphaëlle Mathieu-Bédard (2014), Robert Creamer (2015), and Mohamed Sesay (2015) for providing valuable research assistance. In addition, I am very grateful to two undergraduate students, Nayla-Joy Zein and Kelsey Brady, who were especially helpful with more mundane tasks related to producing the final manuscript. For their steady and prompt technical assistance with computer issues, I must also thank Marc Desrochers and Mark Grant.

I was able to complete the bulk of this book project while on sabbatical leave in 2015–2016, as a visitor with the Government Department at the London School of Economics and Political Science. I am grateful to the political theory group – Katrin Flikschuh (my official host), Leigh Jenco, Chandran Kukathas, Christian List, Anne Phillips, Kai Spiekermann, Laura Valentini, and Lea Ypi, as well as fellow visitor Peter Niesen, from the University of Hamburg – for a thoroughly welcoming, stimulating, and intellectually productive year. I am especially indebted to Laura for organizing a workshop on the manuscript in June 2016 and to all the participants who engaged so thoughtfully and helpfully with the book, especially Katrin Flikschuh, Mollie Gerver, Jakob Huber, Kimberly Hutchings, Nimrod Kovner, Carmen Pavel, Kai Spiekermann, Laura Valentini, Anahi Wiedenbrug, and Lea Ypi. In addition, I would like to thank the people and institutions that provided me with further opportunities to present and discuss parts of this work during my year in the UK: Lorenzo Zucca and Ori Herstein (King's College London), Leigh Jenco and Lea Ypi (London School of Economics), Jeff Howard (University College London), Chandran Kukathas and Tom Poole (London School of Economics), David Miller (Nuffield College), Clare Chambers and Duncan Bell (University of Cambridge), Martin O'Neill (University of York), Lynn Dobson and Kieran Oberman (University of Edinburgh), and Anthony Lang (University of St. Andrews). While I am sorry not to be able to identify all the participants of the seminars and workshops where I presented my work, I would like to express my appreciation for all the constructive discussions, including with Duncan Bell, Chris Brown, Daniel Butt, Sarah Fine, Mervyn Frost, Amanda Greene, Simon Hope, Mathias Koenig-Archibugi, Margaret Kohn, Matthew Kramer, Terry Macdonald, Mihaela Mihai, Jeanne Morefield, Peter Niesen, Robert Nichols, Alasia Nuti, Cornelia Navari, Avia Pasternak, Massimo Renzo, Andrea Sangiovanni, Robbie Shilliam, Ashwini Vasanthakumar, Leif Wenar, and Robin Zheng.

I have also incurred debts from other institutions that have significantly supported my intellectual journey. Thanks to a research fellowship from the Alexander von Humboldt Foundation, I was able to spend the 2010–2011 academic year with the Center for Transnational Relations, Foreign and Security Policy, of the Otto Suhr Institute for Political Science, at the Freie Universität Berlin. I am grateful to

Thomas Risse and Ingo Peters for supporting my application and making possible my first visit with German academia. In 2012 and 2014, I was also able to spend a few weeks as a visiting fellow with the Justitia Amplificata research group, while located at the Forschungskolleg Humanwissenschaften, an Institute for Advanced Studies of the Goethe Universität Frankfurt am Main. I owe great thanks to Rainer Forst and Stefan Gosepath not only for their own intellectual support during these visits but also for providing an ideal environment in which I had the opportunity to benefit from conversations with many talented postdoctoral and visiting faculty fellows during those two summers. For making my visits so carefree, I am grateful to the excellent staff at the Forschungskolleg in Bad Homburg, especially Ingrid Rudolph and Beate Sutterlüty. For two months in 2013, I also made progress on parts of this manuscript while on a visiting Research School of Social Sciences fellowship with the School of Philosophy at the Australian National University. I would like to thank Christian Barry and Bob Goodin for making that visit possible, which enabled me to enjoy the company of another vibrant community of scholars, including Toni Erskine, Seth Lazar, and Nicholas Southwood. In addition to these research fellowships, I am indebted to the Social Sciences and Humanities Research Council of Canada (SSHRC) for providing generous research funding throughout the course of this book project.

Several conferences contributed greatly in pivotal stages of this book project. Thanks to a Connection Grant from the Social Sciences and Humanities Research Council of Canada, Lea Ypi and I were able to bring together a stellar group of scholars for a conference on "Global Justice after Colonialism" at McGill University in May 2014. The conference bridged discussions about global justice, historical colonialism and its legacies, and contemporary practices of settler colonialism, and I am especially grateful to Senator Murray Sinclair (Mizanagheezhik Onaakonigewigimaa), Chief Commissioner of the Truth and Reconciliation Commission of Canada, for his reflections on the challenges of reconciliation in settler colonial states such as Canada. I also benefited enormously from the rich discussions generated at a conference organized by Katrin Flikschuh and Martin Odei Ajei, "Normative Disorientation and Institutional Instability," which took place at the University of Ghana, Legon, in March 2015. Stefan Gosepath and Rainer Forst of the Justitia Amplificata Centre for Advanced Studies at the

Goethe Universität Frankfurt am Main also made a significant contribution by supporting a conference on "Historical Injustice," held at the Wissenschaftskolleg zu Berlin in July 2015. I would like to thank them for funding the conference, Tamara Jugov and Lea Ypi for organizing it, and all the participants for the engaging conversations. Finally, I am grateful to the Yan P. Lin Centre at McGill University for making possible the inaugural conference of the Research Group on Global Justice in September 2016. I have presented ideas and arguments in this book at many diverse workshops, conferences, and seminars over the past fifteen years in Canada, the US, Germany, India, Japan, Australia, Ghana, and the UK, and while I cannot identify everyone, I would like to thank all the participants who took the time to engage with my ideas and help me to think through the problems in this book. In addition to those already mentioned, I would like to thank Farid Abdel-Nour, Ashok Acharya, Caesar Atuire, Paige Digeser, David Estlund, Volker Heins, Pablo Kalmanovitz, Jonathan Lear, Dvora Levinson, Robert Meister, Sankar Muthu, Jiewuh Song, Anna Stilz, Richard Vernon, Laurel Weldon, Melissa Williams, and Reinhard Wolf for illuminating discussions on themes related to this work.

I am grateful to John Haslam for his prompt enthusiasm about the book project in August 2015, which spurred me to seek its conclusion, and for being a good shepherd of this manuscript as it worked its way through the review process. In addition, I am indebted to Saleema Nawaz Webster for her sharp editorial assistance on the fictional prelude, and I am very thankful to Anamika Singh and Holly Monteith, who provided assistance with the production process and copy editing of the entire book.

Some portions of this book are drawn from previous publications, which provide partial representations of various stages of my thinking about the problems addressed in this book. I would like to express my thanks to the editors of the journals or edited volumes in which these publications appeared and to the publishers for allowing me to include them in this book, as well as to all those who gave me valuable feedback in the production of those works. Parts of Sections II and III of Chapter 1 are drawn from "Justice and Moral Regeneration: Lessons from the Treaty of Versailles," *International Studies Review* 4, 3 (2002): 3–25, and "Reparations and Reconciliation," in *The Oxford Handbook of Ethics and War*, eds. Helen Frowe and Seth Lazar (2015), Chapter 28, reproduced by permission of Oxford University Press;

and Section V of Chapter 1 is drawn from "Shame, Guilt and Reconciliation after War," *The European Journal of Social Theory* 11, 3 (August 2008): 367–83. The previous publication that most substantively launched this book project was "Colonialism as Structural Injustice: Historical Responsibility and Contemporary Redress," *The Journal of Political Philosophy* 19, 3 (September 2011): 261–81, which makes up over half of Chapter 4 and a small portion of Chapter 8 of this book. Small sections of Chapters 6 and 7 stem from "Reparations and Reconciliation," in *The Oxford Handbook of Ethics and War*, eds. Helen Frowe and Seth Lazar (2015), reproduced by permission of Oxford University Press, Chapter 28; and "Justice and Reparations in World Politics," in *Reparations: Interdisciplinary Inquiries*, eds. Rahul Kumar and Jon Miller (2007), reproduced by permission of Oxford University Press, 193–212.

It is impossible to thank enough the people who have sustained me over the course of this book project. My gratitude goes most deeply to Lorenz for his abiding attention, love, and support, through struggles personal and intellectual, which proved decisive in making this book, and many other gems in my life, a reality.

Prelude

The Dream of Astyanax's Nurse*
(circa thirteenth century BCE)

The dream is the same every time.

With Astyanax clinging to her neck, she is on one of the city's high towers, surrounded by Achaean soldiers. Some have fear in their eyes, others, indifference. Or maybe just the weariness of war. She gazes searchingly at each of them, specimens of shattered humanity. She threatens and curses. She glares. Pleads. Cries. Begs.

It's of no use.

Astyanax is the only one affected, and his wailing pierces the battlements. Then, the soldiers close in. Overwhelming her with their fists and sweat, they pry Astyanax from her grasp. What has this infant ever done to them, other than be the son of Hector? How could this poor babe frighten anyone – he who was so afraid of his father's plumed helmet and spear that he could only hide in his nurse's bosom?

She lunges for him, but catches only his last wail. And then he is thrown –

These high and steep walls that were meant to protect! His cry is no more.

"O what a nurse am I!" she wails.

Who did it? Was it the son of Achilles, or Odysseus? Or was it Calchas, the prophet? Who gave the orders? Later, it was rumored that Astyanax leapt off the walls by himself. If only that were so.

In the dream, there is no time to settle accounts. She watches in horror as the priceless treasure, falling, dissolves. Then the world

---

* In Greek mythology, Astyanax, "protector of the city," was the infant son of the Trojan warrior Hector and Andromache. During the sack of Troy, the Achaeans (Greeks) threw Astyanax off the high battlements of the city to avoid the possibility of future revenge. See Homer, *The Iliad of Homer*, trans. Richmond Lattimore (Chicago: University of Chicago Press, 2011), 6.390–502; and Euripides, *The Trojan Women*, trans. Nicholas Rudall (Chicago: Ivan R. Dee, 1999). Thanks to Saleema Nawaz Webster for her editorial assistance with this prelude.

dissolves – the soldiers, the towers, the city's walls – all fall away, their ashes scattering far and wide.

Only, the nurse remains, amidst a lonely vault of sand. O calamity! Is nothing left? As she peers upwards through the dense cloud of dust, a voice breaks through. Could it be Andromache?

"Dig, and look for the gems," the voice commands.

"Impossible!" she cries, grasping at the boundless sea of sand.

Always, at this point, the nurse is startled awake. There is sand underneath her fingernails. Did she see gleams, or was that part of the dream?

"Come," she says, struggling to stand. "We must dig."

Introduction

What evil slavery breeds! Once conquered by violence, one must endure injustice.

– Chorus, in *Hecuba*[1]

I Faces of Colonial Injustice

With a Union Jack draped over his coffin, the paramount chief of the Herero, Samuel Maherero, returned from exile in Bechuanaland (Botswana), to be buried alongside his ancestors in Okahandja, South West Africa (Namibia), on August 23, 1923. The Herero honor guard who met his train consisted of 150 mounted men and 1,500 infantry-men; most wore German military uniforms and ranks, and subscribed to the pan-African modernizing vision of Marcus Garvey's Universal Negro Improvement Association. Nearly two decades earlier, in 1904, Maherero had led a dispersed alliance of Herero in a war over deteriorating conditions of Imperial German colonial rule. The conflict culminated in the genocide of the Herero and, a year later, of the Nama. The defeated lost all their rights to own land or cattle, to practice their own religion, and to have their own chiefs – a set of conditions that effectively destroyed their traditional economic livelihoods, culture, and political self-determination. The survivors, mainly women and children, were subjected to mass incarceration in death-inducing forced labor "concentration camps." Within four years, up to eighty thousand members, or nearly 80 percent of the Herero community, and ten thousand Nama, about half of its members, perished.[2]

---

[1] Euripides, *Hecuba* (or *Hekabe*), lines 332–33. Thanks to Lynn Kozak for her assistance with this translation.

[2] General Adrian Dietrich Lothar von Trotha, the German colonial troop commander who issued the infamous genocidal edict in October 1904, was ordered by the Kaiser and Chancellor von Bülow to rescind the extermination order in December but, in January 1905, was instructed by the Chancellor to

During World War I, fighters from Herero and Nama communities allied with British-led South African forces that invaded German South West Africa, defeating their German oppressors and effectively ending German colonialism in the territory in 1915. In the immediate aftermath, the British Parliamentary "Blue Book" that documented their mistreatment under German colonial administration, including genocide and mass incarceration, served as the basis for stripping Germany of all its colonial claims. Postwar and postgenocide justice for the Herero and Nama, however, did not translate into independence from all colonial rule, punishment of the perpetrators of genocide, cattle and land restitution, or reparations to the survivors.³ Instead, in 1920, the fledgling new world order heralded by the League of Nations declared South West Africa to be a Class C mandate territory, "inhabited by peoples not yet able to stand by themselves under the strenuous conditions of the modern world." The League's Permanent Mandate Commission appointed the Union of South Africa, led by a white-minority government, as the "civilized" mandatory power to uphold the "sacred trust of civilisation" to administer the territory according to the "well-being and development" of the indigenous population.⁴ By 1926, the

establish "concentration camps" (*Konzentrationslager*): "the surrendering Herero should be ... put under guard and required to work." See David Olusoga and Casper W. Erichsen, *The Kaiser's Holocaust: Germany's Forgotten Genocide* (London: Faber and Faber, 2010), 161. On the rise and fall of Samuel Maherero, his collaborations with Imperial Germany, and the eventual formation of a united Herero identity, see Jan-Bart Gewald, *Herero Heroes: A Socio-Political History of the Herero of Namibia 1890–1923* (Oxford: James Currey, 1999). On the funeral, see also Wolfram Hartmann, "Funerary photographs: the funeral of a chief," in *The Colonizing Camera: Photographs in the Making of Namibian History*, Wolfram Hartmann, Jeremy Silvester, Patricia Hayes, eds. (Athens: Ohio University Press, 1999), 125–31.

³ Under the military administration of the Union of South Africa between 1915 and 1920, some prosecutions were mounted in a "Special Criminal Court," but "there were no detailed investigations into specific allegations contained in the Blue Book ... and certainly no attempt to put German officers on trial for war crimes." On this point, as well as the postwar contestation of the Blue Book as a piece of English and South African war propaganda against Germany, see the introduction in Jeremy Silvester and Jan-Bart Gewald, *Words Cannot Be Found: German Colonial Rule in Namibia: An Annotated Reprint of the 1918 Blue Book* (Leiden: Brill, 2003), xviii. The volume contains a reprint of the Blue Book, officially named *The Report on the Natives of South-West Africa and Their Treatment by Germany*.

⁴ League of Nations, *Covenant of the League of Nations*, April 28, 1919, www.refworld.org/docid/3dd8b9854.html.

solidarity forged by the doctrine of white supremacy between existing German settlers and new Afrikaner settlers from South Africa led to a political reconciliation that included an official policy to expunge the Blue Book from government records. In this way, the Herero, the Nama, and other Africans in the territory came to endure internationally supervised colonial subjection under white settler rule for another seventy-five years.[5]

Thus, when Samuel Maherero's son, Friedrich, who also lived in exile from Herero lands, died in 1952, the return of his remains to the same grave site as his father was initially challenged by the Okahandja municipality, which claimed that enlarging the burial ground would contaminate the village's water installations. Eventually, Friedrich's remains were permitted to be buried at the grave site, but only on the condition that no other descendants of Maherero would be buried there after Friedrich. In an official communication, the municipal authorities asked, "Why should the public interests of whites be left behind in the interests of native traditions *which will inevitably die out?*"[6]

Neither the Herero nor their traditions died out. Following Namibian independence, the Herero mounted a legal case in 2001 against the German state as well as German corporations for the 1904–1907 genocide.[7] The postcolonial Namibian state, dominated by another major social group, the Ovambo, refused to support the Herero demand for reparations until 2007, when the Namibian National Assembly resolved that "the government should be an interested party in any discussion between its nationals and the German government on the issue of reparation."[8] The motion stated that "reparation seeks to identify and redress those wrong doings so that the countries and people who suffered will enjoy full freedom to continue their own development on more equal terms."[9]

---

[5] See Susan Pedersen, *The Guardians: The League of Nations and the Crisis of Empire* (Oxford: Oxford University Press, 2015), 114–20.

[6] Gewald, *Herero Heroes*, 283, emphasis mine. By the 1980s, Herero chiefs were buried once again at the gravesite in Okahandja.

[7] *Deutsche Welle*, "Germany urges Herero to drop lawsuit," August 5, 2004.

[8] *New Era*, "Ovaherero, Nama weigh into government on reparation stance," February 18, 2016.

[9] National Assembly of Republic of Namibia, "Motion on the OvaHerero genocide," September 19, 2006, http://genocide-namibia.net/wp-content/uploads/2015/02/2006_09_Motion_Genocide_nam_parliament-1.pdf.

The hundredth anniversary of the end of German colonialism prompted a petition demanding Germany to "finally face the truth and recognise its own historical responsibility for the genocide of the Ovaherero and Nama: there should be no unequal treatment for African victims of genocide or their descendants!" The petition, "Genocide is Genocide," was delivered to the office of the German president, Joachim Gauck, by a delegation from Namibia, led by the Herero Paramount Chief and former attorney-general of Namibia, Vekuii Rukoro, on July 9, 2015. The petition called on the German president, parliament, and government to recognize "the genocide against the Ovaherero and Nama" and to declare Germany's "unconditional willingness to participate in an open dialogue with the descendants of the victims, as well as with the Namibian government concerning measures which can be taken to achieve reconciliation."[10] One year later, in July 2016, the German government of Angela Merkel announced that it would formally recognize the genocide and apologize to *Namibia*.[11] The interstate efforts by the Namibian and German governments, however, have been criticized by some Herero and Nama leaders and activists for excluding their representatives and leaders as well as the most affected communities in the structures the two states have set up to negotiate a joint interstate response to the 1904–1907 Herero/Nama genocide.[12] Dissatisfaction over the interstate process has moved representatives of the minority Herero and Nama communities to lodge a class action lawsuit against Germany, under the Alien Tort Statute, with the US District Court in Manhattan.[13]

---

[10] The German President did not receive the group personally. Petition, "Genocide is genocide!," July 9, 2015, English translation available at: http://genocide-namibia.net/wp-content/uploads/2015/06/appeal-genocide-is-genocide-English.pdf.

[11] J. Huggler, "Germany to recognise Herero genocide and apologise to Namibia," *The Telegraph*, July 14, 2016.

[12] German Bundestag, "Press statement on reparation for the 1904–1908 genocide committed by Imperial Germany on the Herero and Nama people/nation," February 17, 2016, English translation available at: http://genocide-namibia.net/wp-content/uploads/2015/03/PRESS-CONFERENCE-17-FEBRUARY-2016.pdf. In 2015, Namibia appointed Dr. Zed Ngavirue and Germany appointed Ruprecht Polenz as special envoys to discuss reparations. See also N. Onishi, "Germany grapples with its African genocide," *New York Times*, December 29, 2016.

[13] The Herero today comprise 8 percent of the Namibian population, and the Nama approximately 5 percent. *BBC News*, "Herero and Nama groups sue Germany over Namibia genocide," January 6, 2017.

The struggles of the Herero and the Nama for justice and reconciliation over the devastations of colonial rule are shared by many others. In June 2013, the British government concluded a "full and final settlement" of a high court action that awarded £19.9 million to 5,228 Kenyans for the torture and other mistreatment they endured during the Mau Mau uprising and ensuing state of emergency declared by the British colonial administration in its attempts to thwart an anticolonial insurgency in Kenya between 1952 and 1960.[14] A further legal claim has been launched against the British Foreign and Commonwealth Office (FCO) by a group of more than forty-four thousand Kenyans for physical abuse, false imprisonment, forced labor, and other deprivations suffered in the same period.[15] The Mau Mau reparations case has also inspired a lawsuit by the families of thirty-three people who were killed by British colonial forces while peacefully demonstrating against the detention of pro-independence activists during a state of emergency declared in the spring of 1959 in Malawi.[16] Meanwhile, a group of 1,104 Koreans have formed the largest class action lawsuit against seventy Japanese firms for forced labor in Japanese munitions factories during World War II, claiming 100 billion won (US$90 million) for unpaid wages and damages.[17] Furthermore, in March 2014, fourteen Caribbean countries agreed on a comprehensive plan that calls upon "the former slave-owning nations of Europe – principally Britain, France, Spain, Portugal, the Netherlands, Norway, Sweden and Denmark – to engage Caribbean governments in reparatory dialogue to address the living legacies of these crimes."[18] In the US, scholars and social activists have called for a congressional commission to study

---

[14] Press Association, "UK to compensate Kenya's Mau Mau torture victims," *The Guardian*, June 3, 2013.

[15] O. Bowcott, "Mau Mau rebellion victims claim parliament was misled over torture," *The Guardian*, May 23, 2016.

[16] G. Mapondera, "Malawians seek compensation for Nyasaland massacre during British rule," *The Guardian*, April 20, 2015.

[17] See S. Miou, ed., "100 S. Korean victims of Japan's wartime forced labor join lawsuits against Japanese firms," *Xinhuanet*, February 2, 2016. For an overview of transitional justice issues in South Korea, both international and domestic, see Hun Joon Kim, "Transitional Justice in South Korea," in *Transitional Justice in the Asia-Pacific*, Renée Jeffery and Hun Joon Kim, eds. (Cambridge: Cambridge University Press, 2014), 229–58.

[18] Sir H. Beckles, "Reparations Commission press statement," the Caribbean Community (CARICOM), December 10, 2013.

"reparation" proposals for African Americans, in light of slavery and its legacies.[19]

In addition, indigenous peoples in settler colonial states have pursued projects of justice and reconciliation for policies of cultural devastation, genocide, forced displacement and assimilation under settler colonial rule.[20] The Canadian government, for example, apologized in 2008 for the Indian residential schools system, which involved the separation, and often forced removal, of more than 150,000 indigenous children from their families and communities between the 1880s and 1980s. The rationale of the system – "to kill the Indian in the child" – amounted to a civilizing strategy based on assumptions about the inferiority of indigenous peoples and their need to be domesticated into civilization.[21] The 2015 Truth and Reconciliation Commission of Canada found that, instead of achieving any civilizational aims, residential schools were "part of a conscious policy of cultural genocide," exposing indigenous children to widespread physical and sexual abuse and systemic deprivations of food, housing, and clothing, resulting in

[19] For moral, legal, and strategic analysis of the case for redress, as well as sources on the long history of activism on this issue, see Michael T. Martin and Marilyn Yaquinto, eds., *Redress for Historical Injustices in the United States: On Reparations for Slavery, Jim Crow, and Their Legacies* (Durham, NC: Duke University Press, 2007); Ta-Nehisi Coates, "The case for reparations," *The Atlantic*, June 2014.

[20] See Penelope Edmonds, *Settler Colonialism and (Re)conciliation: Frontier Violence, Affective Performances, and Imaginative Refoundings* (Basingstoke: Palgrave Macmillan, 2016); Glen Sean Coulthard, *Red Skin, White Masks: Rejecting the Colonial Politics of Recognition* (Minneapolis: University of Minnesota Press, 2014); Elazar Barkan, *The Guilt of Nations: Restitution and Negotiating Historical Injustices* (New York: W. W. Norton, 2000).

[21] On June 11, 2008, then Prime Minister of Canada Stephen Harper made a Statement of Apology to former students of Indian Residential Schools, on behalf of the Government of Canada. See Prime Minister Stephen Harper, "Statement of apology to former students of Indian Residential Schools," Indigenous and Northern Affairs Canada, June 11, 2008. The Indian Residential Schools Settlement Agreement, the largest class action settlement in Canadian history, provided for CAN$1.9 billion to more than seventy-eight thousand former students of the residential schools system; CAN$3.024 billion for settling more than thirty-five thousand claims of sexual abuse and serious physical and psychological abuse; CAN$60 million for the Canadian Truth and Reconciliation Commission; CAN$20 million for commemorative projects; and CAN$125 million for the Aboriginal Healing Foundation to assist with providing mental and emotional health services to affected individuals and communities.

the documented deaths of more than six thousand children.[22] In addition to the compensation and victim assistance programs provided to survivors, the Truth and Reconciliation Commission issued ninety-four recommendations, including calls on "federal, provincial, territorial, and municipal governments to fully adopt and implement the [2007] United Nations Declaration on the Rights of Indigenous Peoples as the framework for reconciliation."[23]

II Fundamental Questions

The emerging prominence of these and other cases associated with the history and practice of colonial war, oppression, and atrocity raises critical but also perplexing questions about justice and reconciliation as moral/political projects in contemporary international and transnational relations. Why has it taken more than one hundred years for the Herero and Nama genocides to be widely and publicly acknowledged?[24] Why are these other cases of colonial atrocity only being litigated or settled now? Are contemporary agents obliged to apologize or make any reparations for the acts of previous generations and governments? Why is the Namibian state reluctant to support the demands for justice and reconciliation launched by the Herero? Why is the pursuit of justice and reconciliation for colonial injustice limited to cases of genocide, torture, and other egregious human rights violations? What response is still required of international institutions, given that international endorsement of colonialism officially ended in 1960 with the United Nations Declaration on the Granting of Independence to Colonial Countries and Peoples? Why should struggles for justice and reconciliation by indigenous peoples in settler colonial and "post-colonial" states be considered pertinent to the study of these themes

---

[22] *The Final Report of the Truth and Reconciliation Commission of Canada,* vol. 1, *Summary* (Toronto: James Lorimer, 2015).
[23] See Calls to Action 43–44 in Truth and Reconciliation Commission of Canada, *Calls to Action,* 4, www.trc.ca/websites/trcinstitution/File/2015/Findings/Calls_to_Action_English2.pdf.
[24] Despite heightened awareness in Africa and Germany, in April 2015, Pope Francis called the Armenian genocide by Ottoman Turkish forces during the First World War "the first genocide of the twentieth century." See David Olusoga, "Dear Pope Francis, Namibia was the 20th century's first genocide," *The Guardian,* April 18, 2015.

in international relations? Such questions reveal that struggles to settle accounts for colonial injustices have not only been historically and
politically contentious but also morally controversial. Answering these
questions will involve a critical examination of the historical development of practices and institutions of justice and reconciliation in modern international relations and open up a challenging array of normative issues for scholars engaged with these concepts in political theory,
international relations, human rights, transitional justice, legal studies,
and postcolonial studies.

Whose responsibility is it to redress and address colonial injustices,
given the historical legality of colonial international order? Which
agents should participate in redress and reconciliation processes – individuals, states, other corporate agents, or other social groups such as
indigenous peoples? How do contemporary agents incur any responsibility to redress injustices of the distant past? How is redress for
colonial injustice related to theorizing and realizing contemporary
global justice? Under what conditions might agents be reconciled to the
social/political institutions that enabled or produced social and political injustices and that still may constitute so many of the options and
limits of their lives? What implications does the pursuit of justice and
reconciliation in response to colonial injustice have for the development and transformation of international and global order?

This book is a study in normative and critical political theory of
how to conceptualize practices of justice and reconciliation that aim
to respond to colonial and structural injustice in international and
transnational contexts. The objective is to improve our normative
descriptions and diagnoses of interactional and structural injustices
associated with colonial rule in modern international relations, with
a view toward developing more plausible and normatively constructive orientations for understanding, analyzing, and evaluating contemporary international and transnational political efforts to redress and
address such injustices. In pursuing this aim, this book builds on and
integrates extensive and diverse literatures in political theory, transitional justice, and international relations and history.

Political theorists have become increasingly engaged with both the
global contexts of justice[25] and dimensions of rectificatory justice in

---

[25] See Charles Beitz, *Political Theory and International Relations* (Princeton, NJ:
Princeton University Press, 1999 [1979]); John Rawls, *The Law of Peoples*

historical and transitional contexts.[26] There is still work to do, how-ever, to connect these literatures and to clarify the relationship between theories of justice that seek to redress historic and transitional contexts, and more general theories of political, social, and global justice. Some philosophical work has focused on individual moral psychology and reactive attitudes as the bases for conceptualizing justice and reconcili-ation in the framework of repairing interpersonal moral, civic, and sen-timental relations.[27] A large body of theoretical work has engaged in analyses of principles and practices of rectificatory, corrective, restora-tive, or transitional justice, such as acknowledgment, apology, retribu-tion, amnesty, reparation, and forgiveness,[28] as well as of institutions of

(Cambridge, MA: Harvard University Press, 1999); David Miller, *National Responsibility and Global Justice* (Oxford: Oxford University Press, 2007); Laura Valentini, *Justice in a Globalized World: A Normative Framework* (Oxford: Oxford University Press, 2011); Lea Ypi, *Global Justice and Avant-Garde Political Agency* (Oxford: Oxford University Press, 2012); Mathias Risse, *On Global Justice* (Princeton, NJ: Princeton University Press, 2012).

[26] See Janna Thompson, *Taking Responsibility for the Past: Reparation and Historical Injustice* (Malden, MA: Polity Press, 2002); Jeff Spinner-Halev, *Enduring Injustice* (Cambridge: Cambridge University Press, 2012); Daniel Butt, *Rectifying International Injustice: Principles of Compensation and Restitution between Nations* (Oxford: Oxford University Press, 2009); Manfred Berg and Bernd Schaefer, eds., *Historical Justice in International Perspective* (Cambridge: Cambridge University Press, 2009).

[27] See Jeffrie G. Murphy and Jean Hampton, *Forgiveness and Mercy* (Cambridge: Cambridge University Press, 1988); Jeffrie G. Murphy, *Getting Even: Forgiveness and Its Limits* (Oxford: Oxford University Press, 2003); Margaret Urban Walker, *Moral Repair: Reconstructing Moral Relations after Wrongdoing* (Cambridge: Cambridge University Press, 2006); Charles L. Griswold, *Forgiveness: A Philosophical Exploration* (Cambridge: Cambridge University Press, 2007); Nyla R. Branscombe and Bertjan Doosje, eds., *Collective Guilt: International Perspectives* (Cambridge: Cambridge University Press, 2004).

[28] See Martha Minow, *Between Vengeance and Forgiveness: Facing History after Genocide and Mass Violence* (Boston: Beacon Press, 1998); P. E. Digeser, *Political Forgiveness* (Ithaca, NY: Cornell University Press, 1994); Mihaela Mihai and Mathias Thaler, eds., *On the Uses and Abuses of Political Apologies* (Basingstoke: Palgrave Macmillan, 2014); Melissa Nobles, *The Politics of Official Apologies* (New York: Cambridge University Press, 2008); Jon Miller and Rahul Kumar, eds., *Reparations: Interdisciplinary Inquiries* (Oxford: Oxford University Press, 2007); Anthony Duff and David Garland, eds., *A Reader on Punishment* (Oxford: Oxford University Press, 1994); Robert Meister, *After Evil: A Politics of Human Rights* (New York: Columbia University Press, 2011); Bronwyn Leebaw, *Judging State-Sponsored Violence, Imagining Political Change* (Cambridge: Cambridge University Press, 2011).

accounting and accountability, such as truth commissions and criminal tribunals.[29] Some theoretical discussions have also contributed to conceptual clarification and theoretical innovations in understanding the meaning and value of reconciliation in contexts of political transition from authoritarian to democratic rule.[30] Political theorists have also extended visions of responsibility for political injustices and harms, investigating the notions of complicity, corporate and collective wrongdoing, and responsibility for structural injustice.[31]

In addition, contemporary strategies of redress for injustices from the colonial era have relied on practices that developed in response to atrocities committed in contexts of interstate war or in contexts of political transition after domestic repression. Such practices have been the subject of a vast interdisciplinary field of "transitional justice,"[32] which primarily examines principles, institutions, and practices of dealing with politically induced mass atrocities and serious human

[29] Judith Shklar, *Legalism* (Cambridge, MA: Harvard University Press, 1964); Carlos Santiago Nino, *Radical Evil on Trial* (New Haven, CT: Yale University Press, 1996); Robert I. Rotberg and Dennis Thompson, *Truth v. Justice: The Morality of Truth Commissions* (Princeton, NJ: Princeton University Press, 2000); Gary Jonathan Bass, *Stay the Hand of Vengeance* (Princeton, NJ: Princeton University Press, 2000); Mark A. Drumbl, *Atrocity, Punishment, and International Law* (Cambridge: Cambridge University Press, 2007); Mark J. Osiel, *Making Sense of Mass Atrocity* (Cambridge: Cambridge University Press, 2009); Mihaela Mihai, *Negative Emotions and Transitional Justice* (New York: Columbia University Press, 2016).

[30] Andrew Schaap, *Political Reconciliation* (New York: Routledge, 2005); Linda Radzik, *Making Amends: Atonement in Morality, Law, and Politics* (Oxford: Oxford University Press, 2009); Colleen Murphy, *A Moral Theory of Political Reconciliation* (Cambridge: Cambridge University Press, 2010); Daniel Philpott, *Just and Unjust Peace: An Ethic of Political Reconciliation* (Oxford: Oxford University Press, 2012).

[31] Larry May, *Sharing Responsibility* (Chicago: University of Chicago Press, 1992); Christopher Kutz, *Complicity* (Cambridge: Cambridge University Press, 2000); Tracy Isaacs, *Moral Responsibility in Collective Contexts* (Oxford: Oxford University Press, 2011); Tracy Isaacs and Richard Vernon, eds., *Accountability for Collective Wrongdoing* (Cambridge: Cambridge University Press, 2011); Iris Marion Young, *Responsibility for Justice* (Oxford: Oxford University Press, 2011); Robert E. Goodin and Chiara Lepora, *On Complicity and Compromise* (Oxford: Oxford University Press, 2013).

[32] On the contested and political nature of "transitional justice" as a distinct interdisciplinary field of research stemming from practice, see Christine Bell, "Transitional justice, interdisciplinarity and the state of the 'field' or 'non-field,'" *International Journal of Transitional Justice* 3, 1 (2009): 5–27. For a new theoretical treatment, see Colleen Murphy, *The Conceptual Foundations of Transitional Justice* (Cambridge: Cambridge University Press, 2017).

rights violations, typically in contexts of political transition following periods of repression, civil conflict, or war.[33] While rich and varied, the dominant normative approaches in this field identify justice
in terms of individual criminal accountability for atrocities and serious human rights abuses, or through the lens of "restorative justice,"
which saliently attempts to connect justice to reconciliation, typically
leaving space open for other accountability practices, such as lustra-
tion, as well as for amnesty, reparations, and other measures to promote victim restoration and societal "healing."

The paradigmatic cases studied in literatures on transitional justice
and/or reconciliation are thus the International Military Tribunal at
Nuremberg, widely viewed as the foundation of the development of
institutions and practices of individual legal accountability for atrocities and serious human rights violations, and the South African Truth
and Reconciliation Commission, renowned for introducing notions of
healing and forgiveness as legitimate political responses to atrocities
committed in contexts of intrastate racialized oppression. While some
have criticized the accounts of justice and reconciliation that claim to
have been inspired by these cases, hardly anyone has questioned that
these are the appropriate historical reference points for thinking about
these issues.[34]

Nuremberg is also the historical starting point for most scholars
in international relations, human rights, and international law interested in the theme of justice as accountability for wrongdoing. Liberal

[33] See Pablo de Greiff, "Theorizing transitional justice," in *Transitional Justice*,
Melissa Williams, Rosemary Nagy, and Jon Elster, eds. (New York: New York
University Press, 2012), 31–77; Ruti G. Teitel, *Transitional Justice* (New York:
Oxford University Press, 2000). Some have also noted the application of
transitional justice frameworks to deal with issues of redress in "mature" or
"stable" democracies. See Leebaw, *Judging State-Sponsored Violence*, 173; and
Stephen Winter, *Transitional Justice in Established Democracies: A Political
Theory* (Basingstoke: Palgrave Macmillan 2014). For an excellent account of
revising transitional justice to deal with the structural injustices associated with
harms to indigenous peoples from settler colonialism, see Jennifer Balint, Julie
Evans, and Nesam McMillan, "Rethinking Transitional Justice, Redressing
Indigenous Harm: A New Conceptual Approach," *The International Journal of
Transitional Justice* 8 (2014): 194–216.
[34] See Leebaw, *Judging State-Sponsored Violence, Imagining Political Change*,
who criticizes the depoliticized conceptions of justice and reconciliation
grounded in these cases. In her own reexamination of these cases, she recovers
more critical conceptions of legalism and restorative justice in response to
state-sponsored violence.

institutionalists, international jurists, and human rights scholars have
endorsed the institutionalization of international criminal justice, in
the form of prosecutions of individuals who have committed genocide,
war crimes, or crimes against humanity, as a progressive force of institutional and political change in international relations toward a liberal
culture of respect for the rule of law and individual human rights.[35]
Critics from realists to progressivists to Marxists, however, have questioned the effectiveness of such transitional justice strategies, raising
the question of whether "justice leads and politics follows" or whether
"politics leads and justice follows."[36] There is therefore much empirical
dispute in the political science literature on transitional justice about
the kinds of political conditions necessary for successful transitional
justice or reconciliation processes and strategies. Empirically, the effectiveness of criminal prosecutions and truth commissions in terms of
deterring or preventing future atrocities or strengthening the establishment of human rights–respecting democracies is highly variable.

While the literature in transitional justice does have some historical
reference points, it generally has not yet incorporated historical and
sociological studies in international relations that expose the imperial
and colonial origins of modern international law and order, and their
effects on postcolonial conditions.[37] These works open new normative
challenges to scholars in international relations and international law

[35] See Kathryn Sikkink, *The Justice Cascade: How Human Rights Prosecutions
Are Changing World Politics* (New York: W. W. Norton, 2011).
[36] See Leslie Vinjamuri and Jack Snyder, "Law and politics in transitional
justice," *Annual Review of Political Science* 18 (2015): 303–27 at 305; Leslie
Vinjamuri, "The International Criminal Court and the politics of peace and
justice," in *The Law and Practice of the International Criminal Court*,
Carsten Stahn, ed. (Oxford: Oxford University Press, 2015); Victor Peskin,
*International Justice in Rwanda and the Balkans: Virtual Trials and the
Struggle for State Cooperation* (New York: Cambridge University Press, 2008);
Jelena Subotic, *Hijacked Justice: Dealing with the Past in the Balkans* (Ithaca,
NY: Cornell University Press, 2009).
[37] Edward Keene, *Beyond the Anarchical Society: Grotius, Colonialism and
Order in World Politics* (Cambridge: Cambridge University Press, 2002); Barry
Buzan and George Lawson, *The Global Transformation: History, Modernity
and the Making of International Relations* (Cambridge: Cambridge University
Press, 2015); Antony Anghie, *Imperialism, Sovereignty and the Making of
International Law* (Cambridge: Cambridge University Press, 2005); Jean
Comaroff and John L. Comaroff, eds., *Law and Disorder in the Postcolony*
(Chicago: University of Chicago Press, 2006).

to interrogate how the colonial history of international order and relations ought to affect or inform theories and practices of justice and reconciliation in world politics. Indeed, one contribution of historicizing the development of modern international order is to reveal quite different starting points for thinking about problems of justice and reconciliation at the international and transnational levels.[38]

Constructivists in international relations have done much work to illuminate practices and structures of hierarchy that pervade the historical development of modern international order, to the point where Vincent Pouliot has observed that "today there is arguably nothing particularly controversial in stating that world politics is less about anarchy than it is about hierarchy."[39] Ayşe Zarakol has detailed how normative expectations embedded in the "standard of civilization" generated "exclusionary figurations and status hierarchies," placing a social stigma on those whose normative universes were declared "backward," "barbaric," "uncivilized," or in other ways failing to live up to a culturally specific and parochially Western version of modernity.[40] Such studies are in accord with the work of theorists of the "English School," who have embarked on revising their traditional conception of international order.[41] Edward Keene, for example, has shown that Hedley Bull's classic concept of an "anarchical society" does not adequately capture the historical development of international society and needs to be supplemented with an account

---

[38] In Buzan and Lawson's account of global transformation, "*Western-colonial* international society" spanned from the late eighteenth century until the end of the Second World War, followed by "*Western-global* international society," lasting from 1945 to the first decade of the twenty-first century. Whereas both of these stages represented globalism centered on a small group of Western states, the authors characterize the third current stage of global modernity as "decentred globalism," where the mode of power "is both less unevenly concentrated and more combined than in previous stages." See Buzan and Lawson, *The Global Transformation*, 273–74. See also Neta C. Crawford, *Argument and Change in World Politics: Ethics, Decolonization, and Humanitarian Intervention* (Cambridge: Cambridge University Press, 2002), for a historical overview of the normative struggle for decolonization in historical contexts that span the past five hundred years.

[39] Vincent Pouliot, *International Pecking Orders: The Politics and Practice of Multilateral Diplomacy* (Cambridge: Cambridge University Press, 2016), ix.

[40] Ayşe Zarakol, *After Defeat: How the East Learned to Live with the West* (Cambridge: Cambridge University Press, 2011), 15.

[41] The traditional formulation is from Hedley Bull, *The Anarchical Society: A Study of Order in World Politics* (London: Macmillan, 1977).

of how international order developed in relations between European and non-European peoples. According to Keene, two different structuring principles came to be operationalized in the historical development of international order: "Within Europe, international order was supposed to provide for peaceful coexistence in an anarchic and plural world by encouraging toleration... Beyond Europe, international order was intended to promote civilization."[42] With similar appreciation of the historical origins of international order, Andrew Hurrell has concluded, "our major international social institutions continue to constitute a deformed political order, above all because of the extreme disparities of power that exist within both international and world society and the consequent degree to which this privileges the imposition of particular understandings of what constitutes global justice."[43] Postcolonial and critical theorists of international relations have also criticized the discipline for its Eurocentrism and for failing "to study the weak and the strong together, as jointly responsible for making history."[44] While these and other international relations scholars have provided compelling interpretations of international hierarchical order and practice, examined their historical development through centuries of imperialism and colonialism, and even identified their moral failings, there has been little connection made between their insights and normative theorizing about justice or reconciliation in global or transitional contexts.[45]

---

[42] Edward Keene, *Beyond the Anarchical Society*, 145 and 147. Of course, the civilizing rationale also coincided with imperial nation-building projects within Europe, entailing the suppression of minority or peripheral cultural groups. For an example, see J.S. Mill on the eventual absorption of Welsh and Scottish nations into the British nation which he deemed superior, in his *Considerations on Representative Government* [1861] in *On Liberty and Other Essays* (Oxford: Oxford University Press, 2008), 431.

[43] Andrew Hurrell, "Order and justice in international relations: what is at stake?," in *Order and Justice in International Relations*, Rosemary Foot, John Lewis Gaddis, and Andrew Hurrell, eds. (Oxford: Oxford University Press, 2003), 48.

[44] Tarak Barkawi and Mark Laffey, "The postcolonial moment in security studies," *Review of International Studies* 32 (2006): 329–352 at 333.

[45] The field of International Relations does include some significant literature that highlights social structures, including "structural violence" (John Galtung, "Violence, peace, and peace research," *Journal of Peace Research* 6, 3 [1969]: 167–91) and "world-system theory" (Immanuel Wallerstein, *The Modern World-System: Capitalist Agriculture and the Origins of the European World-Economy in the Sixteenth Century* [Berkeley: University of California

This book aims to work out the normative issues and implications that stem from taking structural injustice and alienation into account in thinking about global justice, international hierarchy, transitional justice, historic injustice, and political reconciliation in international and transnational relations. The project is partly an argument to mainstream scholars in political theory and international relations, as well as several subfields of inquiry, about why structural injustices revealed in colonial international history, and reproduced in contemporary structures of international hierarchy, should be fundamental topics of concern to anyone interested in justice and reconciliation as moral/political projects in international and transnational relations.

III Toward a New Orientation

In developing conceptions of justice and reconciliation appropriate for understanding and evaluating contemporary strategies and practices of responding to political catastrophes in international and transnational contexts, this book will highlight some enduring conceptual problems that pervade some literatures in international relations, political theory, and transitional justice. First, there are divergent views on which concept to privilege in defining the moral tasks involved in responding to political wrongdoing and injustice. Related to this dispute is a disagreement about the relationship between justice and reconciliation as moral/political projects. Some view justice and reconciliation to be conflictual or mutually exclusive strivings in conditions of political catastrophe. International realists, for example, tend to view the pursuit of justice as a morally or politically contentious and dangerous endeavor that is counterproductive if one's desired end is peaceful reconciliation. In contrast, the pursuit of reconciliation, for critical and progressive theorists, is inherently politically conservative and morally contestable, as it entails problematic compromises of justice.

Alternatively, theorists and practitioners of "transitional justice," while generally choosing justice as their organizing concept, typically forward conceptions of justice as "restorative" and conceptions of reconciliation as "moral repair" that make justice and reconciliation not

Press, 2011 (1976)]). I have chosen "structural injustice" over the term "structural violence" in order to emphasize the centrality of questions of justice to understanding, explaining, and evaluating practices of war, violence, and peace in international and transnational relations.

only complementary, but sometimes indistinguishable, moral/political goals. Daniel Philpott, for example, has posited that reconciliation "equals justice" and the restoration of right relationships, making reconciliation equal to a wide notion of "restorative justice."[46] Colleen Murphy has noted that in general, there is little consensus in the transitional justice literature about the relationship between justice and reconciliation: "Is there a tension between these ideals, or are they fundamentally compatible? If reconciliation and justice do conflict, which moral value should be pursued? Should reconciliation be sacrificed for the sake of justice, or justice for the sake of reconciliation?"[47] The vast literature on transitional justice thus has not settled the question of whether both justice and reconciliation are necessary, how they may be analytically distinct, or how they are related to each other as responses to social and political injustice in diverse political contexts.

Second, existing conceptions of justice and/or reconciliation, especially in the transitional justice literature, focus primarily on interactional accounts of wrongdoing and harm, usually between victims and perpetrators of serious human rights violations. Justice typically refers to a settling of accounts in which culpable agents are punished and victims of wrongdoing are repaired, balancing and closing the moral books. Reconciliation typically refers to measures that aim to reduce individual or collective sentiments of fear, resentment, anger and hatred, or to repair ruptured and damaged social and political relationships in order to return to or establish some normatively ideal model of social unity. As Bronwyn Leebaw has critically argued, the frameworks of "human rights legalism" and "restorative justice" both tend to emphasize the victim–perpetrator relationship in contexts of political violence. Both depoliticize the project of transitional justice in ways that are normatively and politically obscuring.[48] In focusing on victims and perpetrators of mass atrocities and the transitional contexts of regime change from repressive or authoritarian to democratic

---

[46] Referring to Jewish, Christian, and Islamic traditions, Philpott argues that "in the foundational texts of our source traditions and schools, the meaning of reconciliation turns out to be virtually the same as the meaning of justice in this comprehensive, relational sense...Put more simply, reconciliation is a concept of justice – the justice of comprehensive right relationship." See Philpott, *Just and Unjust Peace*, 54.

[47] Colleen Murphy, "A reply to critics," *Criminal Law and Philosophy* 10 (2016): 165–177 at 166.

[48] Leebaw, *Judging State-Sponsored Violence, Imagining Political Change*.

rule as definitive of the field or *problématique* of transitional justice, these literatures also face difficulties explaining and incorporating the rise in calls for justice and reconciliation in purportedly "stable," "mature," or "established" democracies.[49]

Third, the majority of scholarly analysis of justice and reconciliation in international contexts begins with or implies statist premises. Literature in the study of international relations on postwar justice, reconciliation, and international order, for example, has tended to focus predominantly on major states and major interstate wars.[50] This statist bias is most obvious when considering that the concept of war that occupied the central place in the study of international relations largely excluded uses of force in colonial contexts such as the 1904 Herero–German war.[51] Although recent literature in international relations has begun to incorporate a greater diversity of colonial injustices in analyzing problems of justice and reconciliation in international contexts,[52]

---

[49] Colleen Murphy, for example, argues that "differences in the damage found in transitional contexts versus stable democratic contexts impact the necessity of pursuing societal political reconciliation as an objective of public policy in each case ... [A]n explicit commitment to and pursuit of political reconciliation may not be as imperative in stable democratic contexts, given that the scale of damage is smaller and that the social and moral conditions on which relationships structured by law, trust, and capabilities depend are basically unaffected." This view, however, does not seem to provide sufficient acknowledgment of the pervasively, even constitutionally, distorting features of settler colonial states, which may account for why some "well-established" democracies, such as Canada and Australia, have embarked on reconciliation projects with respect to indigenous peoples. See Murphy, "A reply to critics," 169–70.

[50] See G. John Ikenberry, *After Victory: Institutions, Strategic Restraint, and the Rebuilding of Order after Major Wars* (Princeton, NJ: Princeton University Press, 2001).

[51] Most wars of colonial subjection were referred to as "uprisings" or were called "small wars." See Charles E. Callwell, *Small Wars: Their Principles and Practice* (Champaign, IL: Book Jungle, 2009 [1896]). According to Tarak Barkawi, "'small wars' have been seen as simply derivative of what was happening in the First World, denying the global South its own dynamics and agency." See Barkawi, "On the pedagogy of 'small wars,'" *International Affairs* 80, 1 (2004): 19–37. Chapter 7 engages further with this problem.

[52] See Manfred Berg and Bernd Schaefer, eds., *Historical Justice in International Perspective*; Christopher Daase, Stefan Engert, Michel-André Horelt, Judith Renner, and Renate Strassner, eds., *Apology and Reconciliation in International Relations: The Importance of Being Sorry* (London: Routledge, 2016).

the statist bias is perhaps more apparent in the field of normative political theory, where those working on justice beyond borders have also
tended to take the modern-day state and states system as givens in
the international context when developing theories of human rights or
of international rectificatory or distributive justice.[53] While there has
been a burgeoning literature on the agency and responsibility of group
agents, including nonstate group agents such as corporations as well
as international organizations and nongovernmental organizations,[54]
there has been relatively less attention paid to the structural dimensions of injustices, which may transcend national or statist frameworks
of agency and responsibility. The effect of the focus on agent wrongful
conduct – whether the agent is an individual, state, or corporate entity –
is a relative obscuring of a wider sense of agents' moral and political
responsibility for the defective structural conditions that shape, enable,
produce, or reproduce different faces of colonial injustice.

This book seeks to address these conceptual problems and challenges
in its construction of normative accounts of justice and reconciliation,
and their relationship, that are appropriate for responding to international and transnational injustices associated with colonial international order and its legacies. First, the book makes the case that justice and reconciliation are analytically distinct concepts and cannot
be reduced to each other. Justice and reconciliation respond to distinct but related challenges arising from conditions of political injustice. While justice aims to rectify or redress wrongdoing and injustice,
reconciliation responds to various kinds of alienation that produced or
were produced by wrongdoing and injustice. Understood in this way,
it becomes clearer why unjust political acts or conditions generate calls
for both justice and reconciliation. Measures that instantiate justice in
the form of settling accounts between agents for a wrong, for example,
may not respond to the alienating conditions that produced the wrong,

[53] See Charles Beitz, *The Idea of Human Rights*; Daniel Butt, *Rectifying
International Injustice: Principles of Compensation and Restitution between
Nations* (Oxford: Oxford University Press, 2009); Mathias Risse, *On Global
Justice*.
[54] On state and other forms of group agency, see Alexander Wendt, *Social Theory
of International Politics* (Cambridge: Cambridge University Press, 1999); Toni
Erskine, ed., *Can Institutions Have Responsibilities? Collective Moral Agency
and International Relations* (New York: Palgrave Macmillan, 2003); Christian
List and Philip Pettit, *Group Agency: The Possibility, Design, and Status of
Corporate Agents* (Oxford: Oxford University Press, 2011).

or redress the alienation produced by the wrong. From this perspective, notions of "restorative justice" that attempt to fold reconciliation into a more expansive conception of justice and notions of reconciliation that equate it with achieving justice are conceptually confusing and indicate that some long-standing debates about justice and reconciliation may be misguided.

Second, both justice and reconciliation should be analyzed and conceptualized in interactional and structural terms. *Interactional justice* refers to the settling of accounts between agents for wrongful conduct or unjust interactions and for undeserved harms and losses or injuries. In its backward-looking function, interactional justice is a form of corrective and rectificatory justice between agents involved in the wrong. Instead of broadening our conception of justice to include reconciliation, we should instead broaden the relevant task of justice beyond this interactional account. The task of doing justice in response to social and political injustices must also respond to problems of structural injustice, which refer to the institutions, norms, practices, and material conditions that played a causal or conditioning role in producing or reproducing objectionable social positions, conduct, or outcomes. Rectifying or correcting such structural injustices has both backward-looking and forward-looking functions. In its backward-looking function, rectifying structural injustices is part of the task of repudiating the wrongs they enabled or generated. The forward-looking aim of redressing structural injustice is to eliminate any continuing unjust effects that structural injustices may produce or reproduce. In addition, eliminating structural injustice is a powerful way of preventing future interactional injustices that are conditioned by social and political structures. Thinking about the requirements of *structural justice* takes our view of rendering justice in contexts of political catastrophes beyond victims and perpetrators and toward the institutional, normative, and material conditions in which they interact.

In addition, the book understands the task of remedying such injustices as deeply related to the political struggle for reconciliation. I understand reconciliation to be a response to various types of social and political alienation that pervade conditions of political catastrophe. As a regulative ideal, reconciliation is defined not only by the moral quality of agents' interactional relations but also by the relevant agents' mutual affirmation of the relevant social/political structures at domestic and international levels that organize and mediate their activities and relations. Indeed, the book argues that the project of *structural reconciliation* is normatively fundamental and necessary for guiding genuine communication between agents about the terms of *interactional reconciliation*. Furthermore, reconciliation as a political project that responds to colonial injustice must also confront the challenge of *existential reconciliation*, or the disalienation of agents whose subjective freedom has been distorted by such injustice.

Third, this book demonstrates, through an engagement with the historical record, that in an international context, a narrow focus on statist political agency and responsibility is problematic. Such a perspective distorts the historical record of how colonialism as an international practice was produced and how it operated, as well as the differential patterns of victimization that it generated. While statist accounts may capture the structured nature of colonial injustices that were mediated by state institutions and agents, the concentration on interstate interactional injustice misses other consequent structural injustices, located at the international or transnational levels, and based on socially oppressive constructions of civilization, modernity, race, class, and gender, that marked colonial injustices of the twentieth century. A statist bias obscures, for example, the colonial nature of the decolonization process of the mid twentieth century, especially as it entrenched the inferior status of indigenous peoples vis-à-vis the settler colonial states into which they were forcibly incorporated.

In forwarding a structural perspective on colonial injustices, the book seeks to complicate the normative picture of responsibility for colonial injustice and to leave behind simplistic dichotomies that rest on implausibly idealized forms of individualist and statist political agency and responsibility. With respect to colonial injustices, these arguments respond to conventional biases in political and theoretical discussions about justice and reconciliation that obscure the complicity and responsibility of some colonial elites, and the role of structural injustices shared by colonizer and colonized societies, as well as those embedded in international order, in producing many colonial injustices. Highlighting the responsibility of contemporary agents to redress the reproduction of structural injustices, as well as to construct a mutually affirmed and affirmable social/political order, helps to clarify the grounds on which contemporary agents far removed in time from historic injustice may come to bear any responsibilities for addressing injustices of the distant past.

Taken together, the arguments of this book mark an attempt to show why we must think beyond some conventional conceptions of justice and reconciliation, beyond victims and perpetrators, and beyond a statist framework when conceptualizing the moral/political projects of justice and reconciliation in response to political catastrophes in modern international and transnational relations. By focusing on structural injustices implicated in colonial injustices, and through an engagement in particular with the historical record on a variety of colonial conflicts of the twentieth century, the book reveals that quests for justice and reconciliation in world politics are unfinished political projects that foretell potentially radical transformations of domestic and global orders.

IV The Plan of the Book

The chapters proceed as follows. Chapter 1 analyzes the 1919 Versailles peace process that concluded World War I, widely viewed as a spectacular case of failed postwar reconciliation due to the harsh pursuit of justice. I argue that the neglect of Versailles by scholars of justice and reconciliation is unfortunate since it marked the first international attempt to redress some of the atrocities committed in contexts of colonial rule. My analysis reveals that the difficulty of attaining a "peace of justice" can be attributed to the failure of the Allied powers to commit to various components of structural and distributive justice. First, they did not achieve justice in the distribution of war costs among themselves, which exacerbated the interactional justice issue of war reparations to be paid by Germany. To the extent that the architects of Versailles failed, it was in their inability to agree on, and effectively implement, terms of structural and distributive justice that would have enabled the economic recovery of Europe in a way that could check a defeated, but unreconciled, Germany.

Second, a related structural defect of Versailles was its architects' shallow commitment to reform the international order to accommodate demands for equality and inclusion by colonized peoples. While US president Woodrow Wilson and other Allied leaders proclaimed that the new international order would be based on the principle of self-determination, and while German colonial atrocities in South West Africa served as a justification for depriving the country of colonies, Versailles left a structurally unjust colonial international order intact.

In perpetuating a derogatory status to colonized peoples as inferior agents in the process of constructing a new world order, Versailles and its institutional product, the League of Nations, were, in a significant sense, failures in terms of correcting a fundamental structural injustice of the international system.

Conceptually, the chapter introduces the theoretical framework of the book, outlining interactional and structural accounts of both justice and reconciliation and discussing their relationship. Justice as settling accounts refers to the duties of accountability and reparation for wrongful interactions, as well as other strategies of redress for structural injustice, and reconciliation as nonalienation refers to a regulative ideal characterized by agents' mutual affirmation of the social/political order that organizes and mediates their interactions.

Chapter 2 begins by examining how disputes about accountability and responsibility for political catastrophes can exacerbate political conflict and engender further violence, oppression, and atrocity. Key to this dynamic is the problematic discourse of victimhood that states or groups typically use, not to acknowledge but to deny claims of victimhood, especially of their opponents. Denial can be effected through idealized notions of victimhood as well as the transformation of personal experiences of victimhood into political claims of victimhood by collectives and states. Idealization, collectivization, and instrumentalization of victimhood in ideological disputes are problematic when they enable those who claim to be victims, or those who claim to be acting on their behalf, to absolve themselves of responsibility for the suffering they inflict on others.

As the wars over official narratives and history textbooks attest, the pathologies of victimhood can pervade historical narratives of political catastrophes, which typically entail an account of historical responsibility. This issue is salient in contemporary debates about who can claim victimhood in contexts of colonial or imperial rule that provoked violent anticolonial resistance, as well as in debates about responsibility for the devastations of war. The chapter concludes by focusing on the war between the North Vietnamese Communists and the US (1964–1973) and considering the implications of constructing historical narratives that acknowledge victim agency and responsibility in the context of a complex and devastating political catastrophe.

Mindful of the political pathologies of victimhood, Chapter 3 examines criminal tribunals as institutional mechanisms that aim to discipline the quest for accountability against those responsible for political catastrophe. A rich body of philosophical discussion exists that interrogates the justificatory principles and purposes that ground practices of legal retribution within modern states. Sociological and historical analyses are an important corollary to the normative enterprise if one is concerned to devise appropriate normative frameworks for the development of accountability practices and institutions in actual societies. Focusing on the International Criminal Court (ICC), this chapter finds that the instrumentalization of institutions of accountability by dominant states to buttress the political status quo is not confined to the level of international politics. The self-referrals by African states indicate that such states may also attempt to exploit the ICC for their own advantage in domestic power disputes by stigmatizing through criminalization their domestic opponents.

More broadly, the determination of individual legal liability for wrongful conduct in contexts of political catastrophe is morally difficult and often inadequate as a way of conceptualizing responsibility for such catastrophes. This chapter examines problematic prosecutorial strategies for assigning individuals liability for participating in *structured* injustices, such as fighting in an unjust war of conquest and annexation as a member of a state's military apparatus. Furthermore, if *structural* injustices are central to the production of political catastrophes, then confining practices of accountability and responsibility to the individual "crime-and-punishment" model will be wholly inadequate. A more normatively robust and comprehensive settling of accounts for political catastrophes must go beyond settling accounts between individual victims and perpetrators.

Chapter 4 argues that the interactional framework for describing the nature of international and transnational injustices, and for conceptualizing responsibilities generated by such injustices, is incomplete. The interactional framework misses the structural bases of unjust interactions and thus also misconceives the nature and scope of responsibilities for justice in response to international and transnational injustices. This chapter outlines the role of structural injustices in producing many types of international and transnational wrongs and harms, raising a different kind of corrective or remedial justice in addition to and distinct from the accountability we typically seek of individual perpetrators of direct wrongdoing. By characterizing colonial international order as an international structural injustice, I go against the classic structural characterization of international relations as an anarchical state of nature, a staple tenet of both realist and liberal international relations theory. Indeed, from a historical political perspective, the depiction of modern international order as an anarchical system of self-help is a normatively obscuring myth.

Focusing on the case of Japanese colonialism in Korea, and the Japanese military system of sexual forced labor and slavery in particular, the chapter demonstrates that colonial injustices relied on social structural processes that enabled and even encouraged individual or state wrongdoing and produced and reproduced unjust outcomes. In this sense, the field of responsible agents for colonial structural injustices goes beyond direct perpetrators of wrongdoing. In addition, a structural approach identifies the contributory role of structural injustices within colonized societies in the production of some colonial injustices, thus raising questions about responsibility *of and among* colonized peoples. Acknowledging colonial injustices as structural injustices generates a moral and political responsibility to effect structural reforms that ought to be shared by colonizer and colonized, as well as by the international society of states.

Chapter 5 examines how we should think about the responsibility of contemporary agents – as individuals, peoples, and states – in cases of international or transnational historic injustices of the distant past, such as slavery and historical colonialism spanning four hundred years. Although calls for redress of a variety of historic injustices are common today, shifting the burden of responsibility for redressing historic injustice to contemporary agents is controversial because it appears to violate standard principles of determining moral accountability and responsibility for wrongdoing.

This chapter evaluates interactional and structural approaches to conceptualizing justice in terms of redressing historic international and transnational injustices of the distant past (where the agents responsible for producing the original wrong, relationally or structurally, are dead). These approaches differ in how they address three particularly contentious kinds of connections that need to be established. First, how do past injustices relate to or become contemporary injustices? Second, how are past agents to be connected to contemporary agents, as victims, perpetrators, or otherwise contributors to injustice? Third, what is the relationship that contemporary agents have toward the past injustices or their legacies? The chapter identifies problematic ways that the interactional approach attempts to answer these questions and develops an argument for a structural approach that is focused not on rectifying the distribution of holdings between contemporary agents but on rectifying the historically developed structurally unjust institutions, discourses, and practices that produce and reproduce contemporary unjust processes and outcomes.

Wrongful conduct and harms generate not only the sense of moral injury that underlies the demand for justice but also alienation. Chapter 6 argues that the challenge of reconciliation arises as a response to the alienation revealed or produced by political catastrophes. The chapter distinguishes between three related forms of reconciliation: (1) *interactional reconciliation*, which responds to alienation arising between agents through their interactions; (2) *structural reconciliation*, which responds to the alienation that arises from the social and political practices and structures that mediate agents' activities and relations; (3) and *existential reconciliation*, which responds to the internal or self-alienation of agents that typically accompanies both interactional and structural forms of alienation. Reconciliation should be understood as a regulative ideal that aims not only to reconcile parties relationally to each other but, more fundamentally, to create a mutually affirmable and affirmed social/political order that can support the flourishing of nonalienated agents. Using Frantz Fanon's suggestion of the need for a genuine communication to take place between colonizers and the colonized about the terms of reconciliation, the chapter addresses two specific challenges that reveal how structural and existential alienation complicate the quest for reconciliation involving reparatory dialogue. The problem of structural alienation denotes defects of the social/political structure that hamper the ability of the appropriate agents to engage in reparatory dialogue. The problem of existential alienation denotes an agent's anxiety and uncertainty about what constitutes authentic agency, a condition precipitated by the disruption and collapse of social and moral frames by which agents were socialized and engaged in the activity of self-realization.

Chapter 7 examines contemporary legal and political struggles to redress political catastrophes through reparations. I trace the development of reparation as a concept and practice in international relations, mainly in response to interstate war, noting that historically, such a concept has only come to prominence as states came to devise and endorse various forms of international law and international institutions attempting to regulate the use of force in their external and internal relations. The framework for reparation that developed following the two world wars was essentially interactional or trans-actional, in which states deemed culpable for wrongful conduct were obligated to make reparations to their victims and for war damages. While this interactional model of reparation is morally powerful, it is not sufficient in many contexts of political catastrophe, such as war. Thus, if the redress of harms and losses is a natural corollary of the redress of wrongful conduct, then proper redress of political catastro-phes requires going beyond the interactional model of reparation if victims are to receive redress for their losses and damages.

The structural account of reparation is pertinent not only for repa-rations between states after major interstate wars but also for repara-tions for individuals who suffer losses and harms in contexts of interna-tional and transnational political catastrophes. This chapter analyzes the increased standing of the individual as a subject of international law and the effects on international practices of reparation in circum-stances of armed conflict. Mass reparations programs in response to political catastrophes rely on grounds other than moral responsibility for wrongdoing. Proper redress of victims' injuries and losses, as a mat-ter of structural justice, must entail going beyond the interactional duty of direct perpetrators to provide reparations to their victims and can obligate the victim's state, a liable external state, as well as the society of states and global civil society as a whole.

Chapter 8 focuses on the rise of colonial reparative claims, and argues for a need to think beyond standard forms of reparation in order to redress adequately structural injustices that enabled various colonial injustices and that may still permeate the social stratifications of international and transnational relations. To the extent that such structural injustices, organized around race, class, gender, majority-minority, or core-periphery distinctions, continue to pervade our social structures and relations at international and transnational levels, the moral and political responsibility to eliminate them constitutes the unfinished work of the political struggles for structural justice and rec-onciliation in international and transnational relations, especially as they relate to the legacies of empire, slavery, and colonialism.

Acknowledging the responsibility to redress structural injustices that continue to pervade international order requires new normative and political reorientations. In closing, this final chapter highlights three strategies involved in this reorientation: decolonization, decentering, and disalienation. These strategies, when pursued competently and simultaneously by variously situated agents, can contribute to the overturning of structural injustice and create new avenues and opportunities for constructive transformations of international and transnational relations and order, both between and within states, and both with respect to the internal and external constitutive rules and practices of states and international order. Paradoxically, the greater contestation prevailing practices of justice and reconciliation provoke, the more potential they may engender for disalienating the agency of the oppressed; decentering knowledge, institutions, and practices of governance; and decolonizing the normative, social, and political structures of international and transnational order.

1 | *Justice and Reconciliation*
Versailles, 1919

I have never dreamed of the good luck to see the formation of a League of Nations in my own days... The impossible is about to happen. You can't imagine my happiness.

– Kang Youwei, Chinese political reformer, 1919[1]

I Introduction

Nearly one century ago, burdened by the pall of more than four years of war that devastated millions of lives, French premier Georges Clemenceau opened the Versailles peace process with Germany on May 7, 1919: "It is neither the time nor the place for superfluous words... The time has come when we must settle our account."[2] In the self-understanding of the architects of the peace process, the political task in the face of a brutal war was not only to do justice, understood as a settling of accounts for the war's devastations, but also to create a robust "basis upon which the peoples of Europe can live together in friendship and equality."[3] The aim of constructing a "peace

---

[1] Quoted in Erez Manela, *The Wilsonian Moment: Self-Determination and the International Origins of Anticolonial Nationalism* (Oxford: Oxford University Press, 2007), 108.

[2] Quoted in George A. Finch, "The peace negotiations with Germany," *American Journal of International Law* 13, 3 (1919): 536–667 at 536. The Paris Peace Conference opened on January 18, 1919, but the process to restore peace with Germany took place in May and June at Versailles. The Paris Peace Treaties (1919–1923) encompassed the Treaty of Versailles (with Germany); the Treaty of Saint-Germain-en-Layne (Austria); the Treaty of Neuilly (Bulgaria); the Treaty of Trianon (Hungary); the Treaty of Sèvres (Ottoman Empire); and the Treaty of Lausanne (Turkey).

[3] "Reply of the Allied and Associated Power to the observations of the German delegation on the conditions of peace, and ultimatum [May 1919]," in *The Treaty of Versailles and After: Annotations of the Text and the Treaty* (Washington, DC: US Department of State, 1947), 54.

of justice"[4] implied a necessary and compatible relationship between a just accounting of the war and the possibility and desirability of future peace.[5]

Although Clemenceau's statement invokes a simple business-like image of accounting in commercial affairs, settling accounts after a political catastrophe such as a major war is far from straightforward.[6] Indeed, the Treaty of Versailles, which concluded the terms of peace with Germany and established the League of Nations, is popularly perceived as one of the most spectacular failures of settling accounts in international history. Even at the time, some commentators warned that the victorious Allied powers – mainly Britain, France, and the US – were pursuing a harsh justice at the expense of future reconciliation.[7] What went wrong with the Versailles peace settlement? And what lessons might it contain for thinking about justice and reconciliation as moral/political projects in international and transnational relations?

In the literatures investigating justice and reconciliation by scholars of human rights, transitional justice, political theory, and international law, Versailles is a neglected case. More typically, it is the International Military Tribunal at Nuremberg after the Second World War that serves as the historical starting point for understanding the development of norms, practices, and institutions of justice and reconciliation in international relations. The neglect of Versailles is unfortunate, however, since it marked the first international attempt to redress some of the atrocities committed in contexts of colonial rule. Given the 1904–1907 Herero and Nama cases of war and genocide under German colonial rule, described in the Introduction, the Versailles peace process ought not to be overlooked by those who seek to understand contemporary struggles for justice and reconciliation in international and transnational relations.

---

[4] See "German observations on the conditions of peace," May 29, 1919, in *The Treaty of Versailles and After*, 39.

[5] See also David Hunter Miller, ed., *The Drafting of the Covenant*, vol. 1 (New York: Putnam, 1928), 148.

[6] Of course, accounting for economic transactions is, in reality, quite complex, involving a host of ethical issues as well. See Ronald F. Duska, Brenda Shay Duska, and Julie Anne Ragatz, *Accounting Ethics*, 2nd ed. (Malden, MA: Wiley-Blackwell, 2011).

[7] See, e.g., John Maynard Keynes, "Proposals for the reconstruction of Europe (1919)," in his *Essays in Persuasion* (New York: W. W. Norton, 1963), 17–18.

Prominent scholars of international relations who have paid attention to the settlement of 1919 have tended to neglect the implications of redressing colonial injustice for the development of international order, leading to a blind spot in understanding contemporary trends in struggles for justice and reconciliation in world politics. John Ikenberry, for example, does analyze the 1919 peace process, focusing on the US as the victorious power, and President Wilson's ambitious liberal institutionalist agenda "to create a stable and legitimate postwar order organized around democratic countries that operate within liberal institutions and uphold collective security." His analysis, however, neglects Versailles's impact on the question of the legitimacy of colonialism in the postwar international order. In failing to acknowledge and problematize the compatibility of Wilson's liberal institutional agenda with the continuation of a colonial international order, Ikenberry forgoes an examination of its implications for the stability and legitimacy of liberal international order.[8]

The relative neglect of Versailles also means that scholars have not substantially revised the realist account of Versailles as a paradigmatic failure of postwar reconciliation caused by the Allied powers' harsh pursuit of justice against defeated powers. According to this view, far from doing "justice," Versailles "humiliated" Germany and became the focal point of deep resentments in the defeated nation, laying the groundwork for a more devastating world war. The pursuit of justice in the form of a punitive settling of accounts compounded the shame of defeat and inspired projects of violent revenge in Germany that became instrumental in Hitler's rise to power. As the historian Gordon Martel has described this assessment, after World War II, "it seemed even more apparent that Versailles had been fundamentally flawed, that it led to Nazism, the war, and the Holocaust."[9] Thus, Elazar Barkan has noted that Allied leaders took this lesson from Versailles and, rather

---

[8] See G. John Ikenberry, *After Victory: Institutions, Strategic Restraint, and the Rebuilding of Order after Major Wars* (Princeton, NJ: Princeton University Press, 2001). For correctives, see Jeanne Morefield, *Covenants without Swords: Idealist Liberalism and the Spirit of Empire* (Princeton, NJ: Princeton University Press, 2004), and Jeanne Morefield, *Empires without Imperialism: Anglo-American Decline and the Politics of Deflection* (Oxford: Oxford University Press, 2014).

[9] Gordon Martel, "A comment," in *The Treaty of Versailles: A Reassessment after 75 Years*, ed. Manfred F. Boemeke, Gerald D. Feldman, and Elisabeth Glaser (Cambridge: Cambridge University Press, 1998), 624.

than impose harsh reparations on Germany in 1945, embarked on the Marshall Plan: "Rather than hold to a moral right to exploit enemy resources, as had been done previously, the victor underscored future reconciliation and assisted its defeated enemies to re-establish themselves. In hindsight the policy is widely celebrated."[10]

From Versailles, realists have posited that justice and reconciliation are incompatible strivings in the aftermath of major domestic and international political catastrophes. More generally, realists have argued that the pursuit of justice as a matter of accountability for wrongdoing, far from deterring future transgressions, may only foster resentment and continued communal conflict, undermining the prospects for domestic or international reconciliation.[11] If conflict pervades the landscape of politics after war, atrocity, and oppression, the politics of settling accounts seems all too frequently only to compound or intensify political conflicts. In this interpretation, justice resembles the vengeful Furies, who threaten to wreak cyclical havoc on social and political order; future peace seems to require a more conciliatory approach.[12]

This realist view of the conflictual relationship between justice and reconciliation, however, has been challenged by liberal institutionalists, international jurists, and human rights scholars, who have endorsed the pursuit of justice as accountability, especially through prosecutions of individuals who have committed genocide, war crimes, or crimes against humanity, as a progressive force of institutional and political change in international relations toward a liberal culture of respect for the rule of law and individual human rights.[13] Rather than viewing such forms of justice as conflicting with the goal or value of

[10] Elazar Barkan, *The Guilt of Nations: Restitution and Negotiating Historical Injustices* (New York: W. W. Norton, 2000), xxiii.

[11] Jack Snyder and Leslie Vinjamuri, "Trials and errors: principle and pragmatism in strategies of international justice," *International Security* 28, 3 (2003–2004): 5–44; Jack Goldsmith and Stephen Krasner, "The limits of idealism," *Daedalus* 132, 1 (2003): 47–63; Stover Eric and Harvey M. Weinstein, *My Neighbor, My Enemy: Justice and Community in the Aftermath of Mass Atrocity* (Cambridge: Cambridge University Press, 2004).

[12] Aeschylus, *The Eumenides*, in *Oresteia*, trans. Richmond Lattimore (Chicago: University of Chicago Press, 1953), 135–71.

[13] See Anne-Marie Slaughter, *A New World Order* (Princeton, NJ: Princeton University Press, 2004); Kathryn Sikkink, *The Justice Cascade: How Human Rights Prosecutions Are Changing World Politics* (New York: W. W. Norton, 2011); Payam Akhavan, "The rise and fall, and rise of international criminal justice," *Journal of International Criminal Justice* 11, 3 (2013): 527–36.

political reconciliation, liberals tend to view them as complementary or causally connected tasks. In this light, the uncritical adoption of the realist interpretation of Versailles by a vast array of scholars needs to be revisited. Indeed, contemporary historical scholarship since the 1970s shows that the terms of Versailles, while flawed, did not lead to excessively harsh or punitive demands on Germany.[14]

The historical record on Versailles raises normative complexities about both justice and reconciliation that have not received adequate attention. Identifying and analyzing these complexities will illuminate the nature of the moral and political tasks that conditions and experiences of political catastrophe produce, an important step to understanding the promise and limits of various practices of justice and reconciliation and for formulating appropriate remedies. This chapter reopens the peace settlement of 1919 and examines its conceptions and measures to realize justice and reconciliation. First, the chapter frames the issue of German reparations in the context of disputes among the Allied powers about responsibility for the economic reconstruction of Europe. Second, the chapter assesses the accounting of German colonial atrocities in South West Africa against a background of continued endorsement of colonialism as an internationally legitimate form of intersocietal political relation and structure of rule. A thorough normative analysis that is historically informed can show that the relationship between the demands of justice and reconciliation in response to contexts of international and transnational injustice and catastrophe is more complex than either the realist or liberal model suggests.

II Justice and Reconciliation: Interactional and Structural

When the guns finally fell silent on November 11, 1918, the world had endured an unexpectedly long period of unrelenting war. It is unlikely that any of the belligerents could have known in 1914 how much carnage they had unleashed by their decisions to go to war. At the war's end, all European belligerents were economically depleted and had suffered devastating losses in human life, totaling nearly 10 million. Incontrovertibly, World War I was a "political catastrophe."

---

[14] Marc Trachtenberg, *Reparation in World Politics: France and European Economic Diplomacy, 1916–1923* (New York: Columbia University Press, 1980); Sally Marks, "The myths of reparations," *Central European History* 11 (1978): 231–55.

While political catastrophe can be defined by events or episodes of widespread patterns of wrongful or harmful social and political conduct, outcomes, and/or relations, such catastrophes are typically produced or coproduced by a confluence of human social and political agents and structures that express morally objectionable or defective social norms, institutions, and practices.[15] In such contexts, endemic to war, oppression, and atrocity, injustice and alienation abound. And it is in response to these common features of political catastrophe – injustice and alienation – that we can understand calls for both justice and reconciliation.

In this section, I advance the claim that justice and reconciliation ought to be conceptualized as distinct but related normative challenges arising in contexts of political catastrophe and injustice. While justice and reconciliation are analytically distinct concepts and cannot be reduced to each other, the normative aims and political struggles over justice and reconciliation should be analyzed and formulated together.

In the course of this book, I develop two ways to conceptualize both justice and reconciliation – interactional and structural – and their interrelationship. The pursuit of justice is a response to the injustices and wrongs that attend conditions of political catastrophe. Injustice in such contexts may consist of wrongs, harms, and injuries that are committed in interactions between agents, whether these agents are individual or corporate. The notion of corrective justice typically addresses such forms of interactional injustice.[16] *Interactional justice* refers to the settling of accounts between agents for wrongful conduct or unjust interactions, and for undeserved harms and losses or injuries arising from wrongful conduct or interactions. Settling accounts in

---

[15] "Catastrophe" as a dramatic term in classical tragedy refers to sudden terrible outcomes or reversals of fortune involving human action. While ancient Greek tragedians located the cause of catastrophes often partly outside human comprehension and control, my understanding of "political catastrophes" is more Aristotelian in trying to understand them as the consequences of a long and complicated backstory of human agents, actions, and structures that exhibit the many dimensions of human fallibility and frailty. See Aristotle, *Aristotle's Poetics*, trans. Stephen Halliwell (Chicago: University of Chicago Press, 1998). For a discussion of Aristotle's "philosophical reinterpretation of tragedy" as a genre, see Stephen Halliwell, "Plato and Aristotle on the denial of tragedy," *Proceedings of the Cambridge Philological Society* 30 (1984): 49–71.

[16] Aristotle, *Nicomachean Ethics*, ed. Roger Crisp (Cambridge: Cambridge University Press, 2000), Book V, distinguishes between distributive justice and corrective justice.

interactional terms involves determining whether or not a wrong has occurred; whether or not someone has suffered an injury; who is responsible or accountable for the wrong or injury; and what measures are appropriate for settling accounts between the parties involved. Interactional justice is a common aim of practices of settling accounts in response to political catastrophes and involves practices of accountability, punishment, compensation, and reparation between parties that are identifiable victims and perpetrators of wrongdoing. In an interactional frame, states responsible for internationally wrongful conduct may incur liabilities to make reparation to parties – individual, corporate, or collective – that suffer injuries or losses from the wrong, just as individuals who commit wrongs may incur various forms of liability, including punishment and reparations to their victims. The kinds of agents that can participate in interactional injustice may be individual natural persons, corporate entities such as states, and less formally constituted groups whose members nevertheless share joint intentions and are capable of joint action.[17] In all these cases of individual, joint, and corporate agents, interactional justice relates to what the agents involved in unjust interactions can demand from each other for wrongs committed or suffered.

In contexts of political catastrophe, however, the concept of justice cannot be confined to interactional wrongs or injustices. In addition, objectionable types of conduct may have their source or engine in unjust domestic or international institutions, norms, policies, and practices that organize, direct, incentivize, and facilitate wrongful conduct. Objectionable harms and losses may also be the outcomes of the working of social background structural processes that condition the contexts in which agents interact. Political catastrophes may thus involve a combination of interactional injustices (between individual or structured group agents) and structural injustices. Structural injustices broadly refer to institutions, norms, practices, and material conditions that play a causal or conditioning role in producing objectionable conduct or outcomes. The structures in question encompass institutionalized, formal, or informal rules or norms, practices, or conditions. My conception of structural injustice relies on the account of social structures and processes developed by the late American

---

[17] See Tracy Isaacs, *Moral Responsibility in Collective Contexts* (Oxford: Oxford University Press, 2011), 27.

political philosopher Iris Marion Young. Social structures consist of "the confluence of institutional rules and interactive routines, mobilization of resources, as well as physical structures such as buildings and roads" and provide "background conditions for individual actions by presenting actors with options; they provide 'channels' that both enable action and constrain it."[18] The concept of *structural injustice* focuses not on unjust acts or interactions between agents but on the social structures and processes that condition their interaction, embodied in "institutions, discourses, and practices."[19]

Structural injustices place individuals and groups in social positions or socially produced categories that entail vulnerability to unjust treatment, structural indignity, or objectionable social conditions. These vulnerabilities and injustices can include marginalization from the structures and benefits of social cooperation, exclusion from universes of moral obligation and the social bases of dignity and respect, exploitation of productive labor, denial or distortion of social and political appropriative agency, and unjustified regulatory coercion and arbitrary violence.[20] In social and political contexts, structural injustices work to condition in morally objectionable ways the social positions, identities, agency, roles, aspirations, and potential and actual achievements of persons and groups. When structural injustices inform laws and norms, shape the design and purposes of institutions and social practices, and produce material effects, they enable, legitimize, normalize, and entrench conditions under which structural and interactional injustice may persist on a regular and predictable basis.

The pursuit of justice that responds to structural injustices is fundamentally corrective, not of an agent or an interaction, but of the conditions in which agents interact and relate to themselves, each other, and the world. In this form, corrective structural justice responds to

---

[18] Iris Marion Young, "Responsibility and global justice: a social connection model," *Social Philosophy and Policy* 23, 1 (2006): 102–30 at 111–12. For her posthumous book that provides a more comprehensive account of her view of social structures, and structural injustice, see Young, *Responsibility for Justice* (Oxford: Oxford University Press, 2011), 53–74.

[19] Iris Marion Young, "Taking the basic structure seriously," *Perspectives on Politics* 4 (2006): 91–97 at 95.

[20] For a related but somewhat different description of five faces of (structural) oppression – exploitation, marginalization, powerlessness, cultural imperialism, and violence – see Iris Marion Young, *Justice and the Politics of Difference* (Princeton, NJ: Princeton University Press, 1990), 39–65.

structural injustices or defects that enabled or produced objectionable harms and losses or that placed some agents in objectionable social positions of vulnerability or privilege that made unjust interactions or objectionable conditions systemically possible or even probable. Whereas interactional corrective justice pertains to the conduct of agents and the settling of accounts between agents in accordance with their moral responsibility in unjust interactions, structural corrective justice pertains to the moral qualities of the social positions produced by the social and political structures that mediate and organize agents' activities and relations. Manifestations of structural injustice require forms of corrective justice that are distinct from those that are standard to the idea of corrective interactional justice, which presupposes agent wrongdoing under fairly just or decent background conditions. In addition, structural corrective justice expands the field of agents that can bear moral and political responsibility to repair the harms and damages resulting from political catastrophes.

In an interactional framework, only perpetrators or culpable agents may bear such responsibilities toward their victims, given that the aim of interactional corrective justice is to rectify an interpersonal (or inter-agent) moral relation specific to the agents involved. But in addition to the obligations of perpetrators, others who participate in or contribute to structural injustice have responsibilities to redress such injustice. This task may involve assisting and empowering victims of wrongdoing, as well as groups placed in social positions of vulnerability to victimization, to achieve the conditions necessary for structural dignity and structural justice in their various social and political relations. Thinking about the requirements of *structural justice* takes our view of rendering justice in contexts of political catastrophes beyond victims and perpetrators of wrongful conduct and toward the institutional, normative, and material conditions of their past, present, and future interactions. Structural corrective justice is predicated on an acknowledgment of defects in the background conditions produced by previous accounts of political and distributive justice and is thus connected to the revision of those terms.

While justice aims to respond to wrongdoing by agents as well as redress structurally unjust processes and background conditions that mediate agents' interactions, reconciliation responds to various kinds of alienation wrought by political catastrophe. Alienation denotes the denial, distortion, or disruption of an agent's appropriative powers, which form the agent's capacity to experience subjective freedom as a participant in the social world that organizes the agent's identities, activities, roles, and aspirations.[21] An example of alienation in international relations can be found in Ayşe Zarakol's analysis of how various powers – the Ottoman Empire after World War I, the Japanese Empire after World War II, and the Soviet Union after the end of the Cold War – came to experience, through defeat, major disruptions of their internal frameworks of socialization and appropriation of the social and normative universes that would define them and their social positions in the world. In Zarakol's terminology, Turkey, Japan, and Russia came to be stigmatized as inferior, while developing "a self-negating position of an outsider" in an international system dominated by the West and Western constructions of modernity.[22] Reconciliation as a response to alienation is concerned with the subjective freedom of agents as makers of their social world, which is related to, but distinct from, questions of justice regarding agents' rights and duties in a social order or their claims in the distribution of social primary goods given a particular social world. As a regulative ideal, reconciliation focuses on agents' mutual and nonalienated affirmation of the social/political order.

Three related forms of alienation and reconciliation will be examined in this book: (1) *interactional reconciliation*, which responds to alienation arising between agents through their interactions; (2) *structural reconciliation*, which responds to the alienation that arises from the social and political practices and structures that mediate agents' activities and relations; (3) and *existential reconciliation*, which responds to the internal or self-alienation of agents that typically accompanies both interactional and structural forms of alienation.

Interactional reconciliation responds to alienation between agents and leads us to ask what agents involved in a damaging or harmful interaction may require of each other to make good their relationship. Typically, interactional reconciliation focuses on the rights and needs of victims and the obligations of perpetrators to provide remedies to restore their damaged relationship. On this view, apology, punishment, compensation, reparations, and forgiveness constitute measures to repair the damaged relationship between agents; the

---

[21] See Rahel Jaeggi, *Alienation*, trans. Frederick Neuhouser and Alan E. Smith (New York: Columbia University Press, 2014).

[22] See Ayşe Zarakol, *After Defeat: How the East Learned to Live with the West* (Cambridge: Cambridge University Press, 2011).

responsible agents are those who were involved in the damaging interaction; and the forms of remedy should respond to agent-specific
sources and effects of damage or injustice. After war and genocide,
reparations programs that involve individual perpetrators repairing
victims' losses aim at interactional reconciliation. In international relations, the agents may be states, and interactional reconciliation focuses
on what warring states can require of each other in order to affirm their
relationship.

Structural reconciliation aims to remedy agents' alienation from
the social institutions, norms, practices, and structures that mediate
relations between agents. The construction of a mutually affirming
social/political order has objective and subjective components. Objectively, structural reconciliation involves constructing a social/political
order that establishes rights and duties that allow agents to exercise
their moral and political agency, in a set of background conditions that
ensure the social bases of respect and dignity in their institutional relations and structural conditions. Structural reconciliation also has a subjective component: agents' nonalienation from the rules, norms, practices, relations, and conditions of the domestic and/or international
social/political order.

This subjective component of structural reconciliation entails *existential reconciliation*, or the resolution of agents' alienation from themselves, a legacy often precipitated by the disruption or collapse of
social frames that grounded and oriented agents' capacities for self-
realization in the social world. In conditions of structural injustice,
reconciliation involves processes of disalienation that aim to establish
or recover the subjective freedom of agents, or their capacity to integrate and appropriate the social conditions they inhabit in a nonalienated way. Reconciliation in response to political catastrophe should be
understood as a regulative ideal that aims not only to reconcile parties
relationally to each other but, more fundamentally, to create a mutually affirmable and affirmed social/political order that can support the
flourishing of nonalienated agents.

While this theoretical framework will be developed in the rest of
the book, this chapter will begin to reveal a basic account through an
analysis of the ways in which the Versailles peace process attempted,
and failed, to produce a "peace of justice." The case demonstrates the
extent to which the efforts of the architects of Versailles to resolve the
tasks of interactional corrective justice between belligerent states were

closely tied to their commitment to a wider account of their responsibility for the structural justice of international order. Furthermore, the case illustrates that their defective resolution of conflicts of justice was often predicated upon, as well as reinforcing of, defective visions of political reconciliation, evaluated especially in terms of their moral blindness and deafness to the claims of colonized peoples in the construction of the postwar world order.

The first theme that reveals the interconnectedness of interactional and structural accounts of justice includes the issues of (1) what the Allied powers would demand from Germany and other defeated powers in the way of reparations for war costs and damages and (2) how the Allied powers would settle accounts with each other with respect to the distribution of total war costs, as well as those associated with the economic reconstruction of a devastated Europe. Reparations from the defeated powers, mainly consisting of civilian damages resulting from the war, constituted a primary measure of interactional justice between victors and vanquished. This interactional issue, however, was closely tied to the structural issue of how to deal with the economic consequences of the war. The Allied delegation at Versailles had to formulate a plan for the economic reconstruction of Europe, which raised questions of distributive justice among the victors. It is partly because the victorious Allied powers diverged on a solution to the structural consequences of the war that the politics of exacting reparations from Germany became so vexed.

Second, Versailles marked the first time that a European "great power" was held to account for the mistreatment of colonial subjects and resulted in a rudimentary international system of oversight – the mandates system – for populations and territories formally controlled by defeated empires. In the interactional settling of accounts with Germany, the architects of Versailles effectively ended German colonialism, but this endeavor also raised deeper, structural questions about the justice of a colonial international order. For this reason, many people outside of Europe looked to the Versailles peace process with heightened expectations of a great transformation in world order. The Allied powers, however, attempted to uphold a distinction between civilizing colonialism – a basically sound political project of great powers – and barbaric colonialism, exemplified by Germany's treatment of the peoples in German South West Africa. As believers in the civilizing mission of colonialism, this distinction allowed the framers of the Versailles peace process to argue consistently in favor of depriving Germany of its colonies, while endorsing the continuation of a colonial international order, but their stance ensured the growing alienation of the colonized from the postwar international order.

The case of the peace settlement of 1919 demonstrates that disputes among agents about how to settle accounts between them for war's devastations were deeply related to their disputes about the terms of an acceptable international order. These conflicts lie at the root of disagreements and conflicts over justice and reconciliation in the aftermath of major political catastrophes in international relations. In this light, the failure of Versailles can be viewed as a failure of both justice and reconciliation, not only interactionally, but more fundamentally, in structural terms.

III Reparations and the Economic Reconstruction of Europe

In its accounting of interactional rectificatory justice, the Treaty of Versailles assigned responsibility for paying the losses and damages incurred in the war to Germany and its allies (Part VIII, Article 231), called for trials to punish transgressions against the laws of war by defeated powers (Part VII), and set up a commission to determine the extent of reparations (Part VIII). Were these terms of interactional justice in the Treaty of Versailles too harsh?[23]

In fact, the interpretation and enforcement of the interactional terms of justice in the Treaty of Versailles were rather modest, ineffectual, and selective. Although Part VII of the Versailles Treaty called for punishing the Kaiser (Article 227) and those among the defeated powers who were responsible for transgressing laws of war (Articles 228–30), no real punishment was ever effected. Kaiser Wilhelm II, charged with "a supreme offence against international morality and the sanctity of treaties," lived out his life in Holland without ever facing prosecution. The vast majority of those German soldiers charged with war crimes escaped a guilty verdict or were allowed to escape from prison.[24] Gary

---

[23] This section is drawn from "Justice and moral regeneration: lessons from the Treaty of Versailles," *International Studies Review* 4, 3 (2002): 3–25.

[24] See Geoffrey Robertson, *Crimes against Humanity: The Struggle for Global Justice* (New York: New Press, 1999), 210–11; Gerd Hankel, *The Leipzig Trials: German War Crimes and Their Legal Consequences after World War I* (Republic of Letters, 2014). According to Hankel, the Leipzig Trials became a

Bass has noted that leaders such as British prime minister Lloyd George were worried that the fledgling Weimar Republic would fall if too many Germans were subjected to the trials: he "only wanted to make an example. Trying very large numbers would create great difficulties for the German Government, which he believed to be better than either a Bolshevist Government or a Militarist Government."[25] The largely ineffectual measures of accountability explain why it is Nuremberg after World War II, rather than Versailles, that is considered a historical turning point for the development of principles of accountability for war and war conduct in international relations.

Versailles's reparations scheme was the main point of political contention, and was almost immediately portrayed as a vindictive imposition of victor's justice on a defeated Germany and its allies. In tune with an interactional account of justice that sought to hold Germany responsible for the war, leaders of the Allied and Associated powers asked, somewhat sharply and rhetorically, "Somebody must suffer for the consequences of the war. Is it to be Germany, or only the peoples she has wronged?" The legitimacy of exacting reparations from Germany was premised on the Allies' judgment of Germany's moral responsibility for initiating the war, and it is in the framework of interactional justice that we may understand their argument at Versailles that "reparation for wrongs inflicted is of the essence of justice."[26] Earlier in August 1918, Lloyd George characterized reparations as a punitive deterrent, arguing that "Germany had committed a great crime ... and it was necessary to make it impossible that anyone should be tempted to repeat that offence. The Terms of Peace must be tantamount to some penalty for the offence."[27] Under Versailles, reparations constituted a means of holding accountable German leaders and the German people for throwing the world into the abyss of a devastating world war.

Historian Sally Marks has pointed out, however, that charges of exorbitant reparations being imposed on Germany were unfounded. Although Article 235 of the Versailles Treaty required Germany to pay

venue through which the German military established legal justifications for their war crimes rather than be held accountable for them.

[25] See Gary Jonathan Bass, *Stay the Hand of Vengeance: The Politics of War Crimes Tribunals* (Princeton, NJ: Princeton University Press, 2002 [2000]), 79.

[26] "Reply of the Allied and Associated Powers," in *The Treaty of Versailles and After*, 48.

[27] Quoted in Trachtenberg, *Reparation in World Politics*, 51 and 48.

20 billion gold marks by May 1, 1921, Germany paid only about 8 billion.[28] German obligations to make reparations to the Allies were premised on a condition of the armistice reached in November 1918, which required Germany to pay "for all damage done to the civilian population of the Allies and their property by the aggression of Germany by land, by sea and from the air." During the Paris Peace Conference, the payment of reparations referred specifically to the "restoration of the devastated areas," and especially of Belgium and northern France, which were ravaged by German forces. As historian Marc Trachtenberg has shown, German troops destroyed important French coal mines while retreating in 1918, an act that had no military purpose but served the economic one of crippling French competition in order to ensure "a postwar market for German exports." While Article 231 of the Versailles Treaty does not mention "war guilt" at all, it does specify "the responsibility of Germany and her Allies for causing all the loss and damage to which the Allied and Associated Governments and their nationals have been subjected as a consequence of the war imposed upon them by the aggression of Germany and her allies," and Article 232 limited German liability to civilian damages.[29]

While there were disputes between the Allied powers about what counted as part of civilian damages and, therefore, part of Germany's reparative obligations, the system of reparations established in 1921 was based on an Allied assessment of Germany's capacity to pay, and did not expand based on Allied claims. France suffered the most direct devastation, but Britain had assumed the greatest war costs. France favored privileging reparation payments for direct devastation over other war costs, but this meant that it could claim the greatest share of German reparation payments, and Britain the least, since Britain had suffered little direct civilian damage. The UK succeeded in enlarging

---

[28] According to Trachtenberg, half of the 8 billion was credit granted to Germany for purchases of food and raw material. See Trachtenberg, *Reparation in World Politics*, 205. Sally Marks notes that "20 billion marks is approximately what Germany paid during the entire history of reparations." See Marks, "The myths of reparations," 233.

[29] Article 231, Versailles Treaty. According to Sally Marks, "The myths of reparations," the same clause was incorporated into the treaties with Austria and Hungary, "neither of whom interpreted it as a declaration of war guilt" (232). Furthermore, "Austria became so impoverished that she paid no reparations beyond credits for transferred property, while Hungary paid little" (234).

the portion of the reparation pie that it was due by insisting on the inclusion of pensions and separation allowances as part of civilian damages; but whatever increases it received would be at the expense of France, since "inclusion of pensions and allowances increased the British share of the pie but did not enlarge the pie."[30] France initially claimed a distribution whereby it would receive 70 percent of German payments and Britain would receive 20 percent, with the rest going to Belgium, Italy, and Serbia. The British proposed in April 1919 a proportion of 56:28. Negotiations over these percentages continued until 1920, when it was finally agreed that the French–British ratio of German payments would be 52:28.[31]

Ultimately, disagreements about how to distribute the total financial burdens of the war made it impossible to fix a final reparations sum for the treaty, heightening German fears, often manipulated for political reasons, that the "German people would thus be condemned to perpetual slave labour."[32] According to Marks and other historians, the economic disagreements between the Allied powers "played to the advantage of Germany, which effectively resisted paying reparations" as its expression of rejection of the terms of peace. Politically, the battle over reparations in the interwar years was "a struggle for dominance of the European continent and to maintain or reverse the military verdict of 1918."[33]

Historical evidence suggests that influential members of the German business elite expressed their resentment of the moral judgment against Germany by effectively resisting compliance with the reparation demands.[34] But concern for the stability of the political transition

[30] Marks, "The myths of reparations," 232.

[31] Margaret MacMillan, *Paris 1919: Six Months That Changed the World* (New York: Random House, 2001), 192. Trachtenberg claims that the percentage set at the Spa Conference in mid 1920 was 52:22. See Trachtenberg, *Reparation in World Politics*, 72.

[32] MacMillan, *Paris 1919*, 192.   [33] Marks, "The myths of reparations," 255.

[34] According to Marks, the German government delayed tax reform and currency stabilization measures, intentionally mismanaging Germany's economic affairs "in hopes of obtaining substantial reductions in reparations." See Marks, "The myths of reparations," 239. Jon Jacobson argues, however, that the German government did not pursue "a contrived and coordinated policy of deliberately promoting inflation to avoid reparation payment . . . Internal political and economic weakness rather than foreign ambition determined German reparation policy." See Jacobson, "Is there a new international history of the 1920s?," *The American Historical Review* 88, 3 (1983): 617–645 at 638.

in Germany led Allied leaders, such as Lloyd George, "to take an indulgent attitude toward Germany [on the issue of reparations], to be flexible regarding the treaty, to be generous in allowing time for compliance." The failure of Allied powers to maintain political solidarity on enforcing the terms of Versailles enabled German denial of responsibility to persist and intensify. For example, the lack of substantial payment of reparations could be explained in one of two ways: either Germany was unable to pay, or it was unwilling to do so. The British were more persuaded by German claims of inability to pay, while the French viewed the lack of payment as an indication that "defeat and revolution had not really transformed the German spirit."[35] While French leaders were not willing to be indulgent, they lacked the means to enforce compliance. Jacques Seydoux for the French Foreign Ministry concluded, "Through threats alone, France had been unable to force Germany to make a serious effort; on the other hand, to go in and reorganize all of Germany, he later wrote, was 'beyond our power.'"[36] As Jacobson has put the dilemma, "The potential cost of the fulfillment of the Versailles Treaty . . . was either the end of democratic conditions in Germany or its loss of economic and territorial sovereignty."[37] In a world exhausted by war and increasingly reluctant to employ force to obtain compliance, a militarily defeated but unrepentant Germany effectively evaded the terms of accountability set out in Versailles. This combination of factors meant that the mechanisms of settling accounts laid out in the Treaty of Versailles – trials and reparations – were largely ineffectual rather than overly harsh in their effects on Germany. Indeed, the incongruence between the punitive terms of Versailles and their lack of punitive effects on Germany is striking.

The case of Versailles shows that the moral and political efficacy of terms of interactional justice, including reparations as a mechanism of accountability, depends on several critical factors. For one thing, the imposition of reparations against defeated parties can easily look like self-aggrandizement or a continuation of domination if exacted by the victors in the absence of an authoritative framework that reflects a

---

[35] Trachtenberg, *Reparation in World Politics*, 99.   [36] Ibid., 103 and 273.
[37] Jacobson, "Is there a new international history of the 1920s?," 638.

wider communal judgment of the moral entitlements and responsibilities of the victors and the vanquished. This is to say that in international relations, the viability of justifying reparations as a component of interactional justice depends on the comprehensiveness and content of the terms of structural justice that mediate and organize agents' relations and activities, and whether these terms provide for judgments of responsibility and accountability of the parties involved in the practice of war. In this way, the terms of interactional corrective justice are dependent on the terms of structural and distributive justice; to the extent that the terms of structural and distributive justice are contested, ambiguous, incomplete, or absent, the terms of interactional justice will be more conditional.

Practices of interactional corrective justice typically depend on the terms of structural and distributive justice that produce certain background conditions and a spectrum of available social positions, from which agents derive their rights and responsibilities. Accountability in the forms of retributive and reparative (or compensatory) justice may be important requirements of structural justice (without which a social structure may place victims in an intolerable social position), but what victims can demand in the way of accountability, compensation, or reparation must also be limited or conditioned to a significant extent by considerations of structural and distributive justice.

A clear accounting of what was required of Germany in the way of reparations as a matter of interactional justice was thus hampered by a failure of justice of a different kind. In the aftermath of World War I, with an unrepentant Germany stalling on reparation payments, the political necessity of reconstructing the devastated areas and resolving the payment of general war costs raised the problem of distributive justice between the victorious Allies. Reparations from the defeated powers for civilian damages constituted only a subset of the total "war costs" incurred by the belligerents in the war.[38] Although the framework of interactional justice might demand that Germany pay for postwar reconstruction, an alternative framework that focused on structural justice might have generated a moral duty of the international community as a whole to restore areas devastated by Germany. On this view, Germany was not the only state that had obligations to help

---

[38] Trachtenberg, *Reparation in World Politics*, 43.

the victims of the war. This is indeed how the French hoped to recover economically from the war: "French leaders looked not to Germany but to their allies for a solution." The French minister of commerce in 1918, Étienne Clémentel, envisaged a global fund to restore the ravaged areas, the creation of an Allied economic bloc strong enough to restrain German ambitions, and the eventual development of an "economic union of free peoples" into which Germans could ultimately be integrated.[39] Unfortunately, the community of sacrifice that had been forged in war failed to persist in peace.

The history of the negotiations between the Allied and Associated powers over the economic reconstruction of Europe reveals little sense of communal obligation between them. The US remained aloof from its European allies, and while it contributed militarily to Germany's defeat and was willing to fund the Allied war effort through loans, "America expected to be paid back." Instead of exhibiting economic confidence in its allies and promoting economic solidarity, American officials were motivated by mistrust of European economic management skills and by a sense of Anglo-American economic rivalry. American abandonment of the wartime system of economic cooperation meant a denial of the French view of distributive justice during the period of economic reconstruction, which involved the pooling of war costs, and the reapportionment of inter-Allied debt, with "each nation paying according to its ability."[40] Without American cooperation with these proposals, the economic recovery of the European belligerents came to rely more on the payments that could be extracted from Germany.

A redistribution of war costs would have enabled the economic regeneration of France and Belgium, and a strong Allied economic union could have protected everyone even from an unrepentant Germany, and in time may have provided the material basis for political reconciliation.[41] Instead, "the net effect of World War I and the peace settlement was the effective enhancement of Germany's

[39] Ibid., 1 and 17.

[40] Ibid., 21 and 54. Albert Rathbone, an Assistant Secretary of the US Treasury, wrote in a letter of March 1919, "The Treasury . . . will not assent to any discussion at the peace conference, or elsewhere, of any plan or arrangement for the release, consolidation or reapportionment of the obligations of foreign governments held by the US. The Treasury would discontinue advances to any government that supported such schemes" (54–55).

[41] Jacobson, "Is there a new international history of the 1920s?," 633.

relative strength in Europe, particularly in regard to her immediate neighbours."[42]

IV Versailles and the Colonial International Order

In the course of the war, some old orders collapsed – including the Russian, Ottoman, German, and Austro-Hungarian empires – and in their wake arose new political demands. When the Russian empire folded, its revolutionaries called for "the establishment of permanent peace on the basis of the self-determination of peoples." The Russian Bolsheviks who would lead the October 1917 revolution gave the right of national self-determination a radical interpretation that translated into a right of the colonized to overthrow their colonial masters. The new world order envisaged by Lenin and the Russian revolutionaries heralded "the liberation of all colonies; the liberation of all dependent, oppressed, and non-sovereign peoples." Although Russia was in turmoil from civil war in 1919, colonized peoples around the world held great hope that the Paris peace process would herald a new, more just world order. Surendranath Banerjee, a prominent moderate leader, noted at the 1916 Indian National Congress that the enormity of the war meant that the world was "on the eve of a great reconstruction."[43] The expectations of an improved international order gripped not only anticolonial political elites but also civil society. One group of Chinese students in Britain, for example, established a League of Nations society, stating that the new world order must not be "a League of great Nations and smaller Nations as satellites, but a League of all Nations with equality of rights before the Law."[44]

US president Woodrow Wilson had a somewhat less radical interpretation of the right to self-determination, which did not explicitly entail the dissolution of empires. Rather, Wilson's account of self-determination involved a requirement that imperial governance conform to a standard of political legitimacy based on the consent of the governed. According to historian Erez Manela, the "Wilsonian moment" in international relations promised an international order based on "equality among legitimate polities governed by popular consent." Wilson's congressional speech known as "The Fourteen Points"

---

[42] Marks, "The myths of reparations," 255.
[43] Manela, *The Wilsonian Moment*, 37 and 82.   [44] Ibid., 117.

included the call that a lasting peace required "a reordering of international society on the basis of the principles of government by consent, the equality of nations, and international cooperation."[45] As Manela has explained, Lenin and Wilson posed two different conceptions of self-determination as a prerequisite for overturning the structural injustice of the existing international system. According to the Bolsheviks, the principle of "national" self-determination was a "call for the revolutionary overthrow of colonial and imperial rule through an appeal to the national identity and aspirations of subject peoples." Wilson tied self-determination not to national independence but to self-government, consent of the governed, popular sovereignty, and an international order based on democratic forms of government. While Lenin saw self-determination as a "revolutionary principle" that would aid in the overthrow of an imperial capitalist world order, Wilson saw self-determination as a potential "antidote" to the communist "revolutionary impulse" by aligning colonial administration more closely with the basic autonomy and welfare interests of subject populations.[46]

This dispute about what the principle of self-determination entailed represents a political struggle over the terms of international structural justice. Is structural justice at the international level compatible with a colonial international order that establishes a hierarchy among states and peoples based on a standard of civilization, designating some as civilized, and others as dependent, backward, or insufficiently civilized to govern themselves? Or does structural justice at

---

[45] Quoted ibid., 16. Wilson's speech to Congress, the "Fourteen Points," was delivered on January 8, 1918. Although Wilson did not actually use the term "self-determination" until February 1918, Point 5 did assert that colonial claims would be settled in a "free, open minded, and absolutely impartial manner, based upon a strict observance of the principle that in determining all such questions of sovereignty the interests of the populations concerned must have equal weight with the equitable claims of the government whose title is to be determined" (40).

[46] Manela, *The Wilsonian Moment*, 42–43. Communist parties were not immune from the racialized prejudices and hierarchies of white-dominated labor unions in this period. The tendency of the American Communist movement, founded in 1919, was initially to reduce the "Negro question" to "an economic or class question to be settled when the general rights of labour were established through revolution." For a history of the relationship between communist parties of South Africa and the US with the black working class from the end of World War I to 1950, see Edward Johanningsmeier, "Communist and Black Freedom movements in South Africa and the US: 1919–50," *Journal of Southern African Studies* 30, 1 (2004): 155–80 at 159.

the international level require the repudiation of colonial international order, and the establishment of a global order that forsakes the standard of civilization as a criteria for self-determination, thereby opening the way to full and equal recognition of the right of all peoples to self-determination?

The architects of the Paris Peace Conference had to engage with the issue of colonialism, and the peace settlements of 1919–1923 did represent the "most far-reaching and widest-ranging system of treaties made up to that time."[47] With respect to colonialism, Versailles was unusual for acknowledging and implementing a settling of accounts for colonial atrocities. In particular, the Allied powers were adamant that Germany would lose its colonies. To that end, in 1917, the British government commissioned Major Thomas Leslie O'Reilly to draft a report on German colonial misdeeds in South West Africa. Known as the "Blue Book" (a term for all British Parliamentary Reports),[48] the report described the policy of settlement, and the deterioration of relations between German settlers and the indigenous peoples of the territory, mainly the Herero and Nama peoples. In the wake of the 1904 "uprising" by the Herero, the report details the policy of extermination pursued by German colonial forces, led by General Lothar von Trotha, who gave the following order on October 2, 1904: "I, the Great General of the German troops, send this letter to the Herero people. Hereros are no longer German subjects. All Hereros must leave the land. If the people do not want this, then I will force them to do so with the Big Gun. Any Herero found within the German borders, with or without a gun, with or without cattle, will be shot. I shall no longer receive any women and children. I will drive them back to their people, or I will shoot them. This is my decision for the Herero people."[49] The report's thorough account of the ensuing genocide of the Herero included photographic evidence and sworn statements of survivors, as well as witnesses, including members of the Nama tribes who had helped the German colonial military, the

[47] "Preface," in *The Treaty of Versailles and After*, iii.
[48] The full title of the report was "Union of South Africa – report on the natives of South-West Africa and their treatment by Germany." See Jeremy Silvester and Jan-Bart Gewald, eds., *Words Cannot Be Found: German Colonial Rule in Namibia: An Annotated Reprint of the 1918 Blue Book* (Leiden: Brill, 2003).
[49] Quoted in Uazuva Kaumbi, "Namibia: official support for Herero reparation struggle," *New African*, December 2006, 47.

Schutztruppe, to track the Herero. The 212-page report also provided details of the subsequent German campaigns against the Nama and the institution of "concentration camps" in Lüderitz, and on Shark Island, between 1904 and 1907, that served as forced labor and extermination camps for Herero and Nama prisoners from the "uprisings," most of whom were women and children.[50] In addition, the report also documented everyday brutalities of German colonial administration and disciplinary practices, including photographs of floggings and hangings. It is estimated that in Germany's campaign to colonize South West Africa, over three-quarters of the entire Herero population (up to eighty thousand out of a population of one hundred thousand), as well as half of the Nama people, were killed, either in battle or due to harsh conditions imposed by German troops. As David Olusoga and Casper Erichsen note, "The Blue Book stands almost entirely alone as a reliable and comprehensive exploration of the disinheritance and destruction of indigenous peoples."[51]

At Versailles, the German atrocities in South West Africa were compared with those committed by the German army in Europe, especially against Belgian civilians. Germany's record of genocide and atrocities against the peoples of South West Africa was given as evidence of Germany's inability to realize colonialism as a civilizing mission. According to Allied leaders, in their justification of placing most German colonies under the mandates system of the League of Nations, Germany's initiation of the war constituted "the greatest crime against humanity and the freedom of peoples that any nation, calling itself civilized, has ever consciously committed." In addition, atrocities committed under German colonial rule made it impossible "to entrust to her the responsibility for the training and education of their inhabitants."[52] Unlike Lenin, however, Wilson was not prepared to challenge colonial

---

[50] According to existing records, of the 2,400 Nama prisoners from the war against the Germans that began in 1904 who were sent to the concentration camps, only 500 were alive when the camps were closed in April 1907, and only 248 of those remained alive by 1909. The Herero who were imprisoned earlier, starting in 1904, died in similar numbers, although official statistics did not begin to be recorded until April 1906. See David Olusoga and Casper W. Erichsen, *The Kaiser's Holocaust: Germany's Forgotten Genocide* (London: Faber and Faber, 2010), 229–30.

[51] Ibid., 264.

[52] Quoted in Susan Pedersen, *The Guardians: The League of Nations and the Crisis of Empire* (Oxford: Oxford University Press, 2015), 33.

international order completely; thus he supported the idea of gradual reforms, instituting mandates over colonial territories, with "advanced powers" serving as trustees.

On the subject of colonies, then, Versailles "dealt only with colonial issues that arose directly from the war, largely those related to former German and Ottoman possessions outside Europe." With respect to these territories in Africa (such as South West Africa), the Middle East, and the Pacific, the League of Nations instituted a Permanent Mandates Commission, which was "to receive and examine the annual reports of the Mandatories and to advise the [League of Nations] Council on all matters relating to the observance of the mandates."[53] Article 22 of the Covenant of the League of Nations gave "advanced nations" the power to govern colonies and territories that were relinquished by the defeated – Germany and the Ottoman empire – and that were deemed to contain "peoples not yet able to stand by themselves under the strenuous conditions of the modern world."

The mandate system that dealt with colonies and territories from the defeated powers was a part of the most significant institutional instrument of international structural justice that came out of Versailles – the Covenant of the League of Nations – and this institutional innovation certainly enjoyed pride of place in the Treaty of Versailles (Part I), establishing the terms of international order following World War I. Leaders of the colonized expected that their grievances could be taken to the League of Nations for international adjudication, a hope not supported by the colonial powers that dominated the Versailles peace process, and eventually the operation of the League. For example, while a British commission to investigate "colonial disturbances" in Egypt in December 1919 viewed such matters to be "an imperial issue" to be negotiated between colonized and colonizer, Egyptian activists expected their conflict with Britain to be recognized as "a conflict between equals that should be adjudicated by the international community [at the League of Nations] on the basis of Wilsonian principles."[54] The final text of the Covenant of the League of Nations, however, did not include the term "self-determination" and offered little of substance to colonized and subjugated populations seeking

[53] The Mandates Commission was very much "an imperialists' club," containing many retired colonial governors, ministers, or high officials. Ibid., 61.
[54] Manela, *The Wilsonian Moment*, 156.

mutually affirmable terms of international political association. The Paris Peace Conference thus failed to redress one of the most constitutive and consequential structural injustices in the international system.

These emerging terms of international structural justice set the terms of interactional justice between agents. Article 22 classified mandate territories into three separate groups according to their degree of advancement; thus, under the terms of Versailles, South West Africa became a Class C mandate and was placed under the control of the Union of South Africa.[55] As Robbie Shilliam has noted, this decision at Versailles involved a rejection of another proposal that, if adopted, might have kick-started the decolonization of international order. The rejected proposal was made by Marcus Garvey's Pan-African Universal Negro Improvement Association (UNIA), which petitioned the League of Nations in 1922 to place the mandated German colonies in Africa under its control.[56] The settling of accounts for the Herero and the Nama in South West Africa thus did not result in their independence from all colonial powers or racial domination, only from German colonial rule. The solidarity forged by a doctrine of white supremacy also ensured that the transfer of power from Berlin to Pretoria protected the German settler colonial population and the influx of Afrikaners by maintaining "the standing of the white race."[57] Thus, in less than a decade, in 1926, the British and South African governments ordered that the Blue Book be destroyed as part of a postwar reconciliation

---

[55] For a thorough critique of the mandate system and the imperial origins of international law, see Antony Anghie, *Imperialism, Sovereignty and the Making of International Law*, 115–95.

[56] Robbie Shilliam, "What about Marcus Garvey? Race and the transformation of sovereignty debate," *Review of International Studies* 32, 3 (2006): 379–400 at 380. The UNIA represented a potential path toward decolonizing international and transnational social structures, although Garvey acknowledged that there were internal tensions in the Pan-African political project, proclaiming that "Black capitalists could be as exploitative of the 'menu peuple' as their white counterparts." Ibid., 398.

[57] Olusoga and Erichsen, *The Kaiser's Holocaust*, 258; and Pedersen, *The Guardians*, 116. Another example of the assertion of white supremacy in shaping the League of Nations occurred early on, in February 1919, when the League framers rejected a "racial equality clause," proposed by Japan, the only nonwhite country recognized as a "great power" at Versailles. At the same time, it should be acknowledged that imperial Japan was not motivated by any commitment to a contemporary notion of universal racial equality but primarily by its insecurity as a great power in a Eurocentric international order. See Naoko Shimazu, *Japan, Race and Equality: The Racial Equality Principle of 1919* (New York: Routledge, 1998).

effort to integrate better the German-speaking white settler population of the territory within the new South African mandatory colonial
project.

The League Covenant envisaged the mandate system to institute
international oversight of colonial administrations, as a way of guaranteeing "the principle that the well-being and development of such
peoples form a sacred trust of civilisation" (Article 22). Yet as historian Susan Pedersen documents in her thorough examination of the
mandate system, "mandatory oversight was supposed to make imperial rule more humane and therefore more legitimate; it was to 'uplift'
backward populations and – so its more idealistic supporters hoped –
even to prepare them for self-rule. It did not do these things: mandated
territories were not better governed than colonies across the board and
in some cases were governed more oppressively; claims by populations
under League oversight for political rights were more often met with
repression than conciliation."[58] Thus, while the "mandate principle"
for the governance of colonial possessions of the defeated powers held
possibilities for independence, "with the league controlled by imperialist powers, the mandate system became not much more than a shadow
of what it was intended to be."[59] Not surprisingly, the disappointing
outcomes of Versailles fed "a growing sense of estrangement from the
Western-dominated international society."[60]

V German Alienation from the Postwar International Order

Faced with the devastation wrought by the First World War, cynicism
about societal values as well as political and social institutions –
domestic and international – was pervasive.[61] The experience of
world war not only produced alienation between warring parties but
also agents' structural alienation from domestic and international
social/political orders, from the domestic patriarchal family to the
"family of nations."[62] According to some international relations
scholars, the alienation between belligerents produced by a brutal

---

[58] Pedersen, *The Guardians*, 4. On the miserable plight of the Bondelswarts
(Nama) under South African mandatory rule, see her Chapter 4 (112–41).
[59] Manela, *The Wilsonian Moment*, 25 and 61.   [60] Ibid., 186.
[61] This section is drawn from my "Shame, guilt and reconciliation after war," *The
European Journal of Social Theory* 11, 3 (August 2008): 367–83.
[62] Martel, "A comment," in *The Treaty of Versailles: A Reassessment after 75
Years*, 635.

and lengthy war explains why the architects of Versailles pursued hard-hearted justice at the expense of reconciliation: "There was little sentiment among the victors for reconciliation with the beaten foe. The impulse was rather to punish him, to place burdens upon him that would prevent his recovery or delay it for an indefinite period . . . Too many of the participants were unreconciled and bent solely upon the most Draconian forms of punishment against the Germans or the Austrians or the Turks."[63] But were the architects of Versailles irreconcilable with Germany and bent on its destruction?

Marc Trachtenberg has documented that while strict justice might have dictated that Germany should pay to rebuild the areas it had devastated, French leaders understood that this "would completely crush [Germany] and reduce her to a state of economic bondage which would strip away from humanity all hope of a lasting peace." French leaders posited that French security would best be achieved through "economic collaboration" with Germany, and that "the surest way of re-establishing between the two countries a peace worthy of the name is by working to join together their material interests."[64] No matter how devastating the consequences of war, then, reparative claims against Germany had to be limited, not only practically but also morally, by considerations of a future international order that included both Germany and France.

While French policy makers ultimately conceived of reparations as part of a conciliatory project, Germans at the time were uniformly convinced of the injustice of Versailles.[65] One source of alienation was the Versailles peace process itself. No direct oral discussions were admitted between the Allied and German delegations, and at the signing of the treaty, the two German delegates, denied seats at the table, were "ushered in and out of the hall like criminals escorted to and from the dock."[66] E. H. Carr wrote of the "unnecessary humiliations" of the process, which "fixed in the consciousness of the German people the conception of a 'dictated peace'; and they helped to create the

---

[63] Gordon A. Craig and Alexander L. George, *Force and Statecraft: Diplomatic Problems of Our Time*, 2nd ed. (Oxford: Oxford University Press, 1990), 50–51.

[64] Trachtenberg, *Reparation in World Politics*, 18, 100, and 158.

[65] Eric D. Weitz, *Weimar Germany: Promise and Tragedy* (Princeton, NJ: Princeton University Press, 2007), 38.

[66] David A. Welch, *Justice and the Genesis of War* (Cambridge: Cambridge University Press, 1993), 128.

belief, which became universal in Germany and was tacitly accepted by a large body of opinion in other countries, that the signature extorted from Germany in these conditions was not morally binding on her."[67] Indeed, it was not the old imperial regime but representatives of the new democratic German government who, on June 23, 1919, declared that "yielding to superior force and without renouncing in the meantime its own view of the unheard of injustice of the peace conditions . . . it is ready to accept and sign the peace conditions imposed" by the Allied delegation at Versailles.[68] Neither the process nor the terms of interactional justice set out in Versailles fostered feelings of guilt and shame among the vanquished about Germany's role in precipitating the war; instead, feeling victimized at Versailles, Germans became preoccupied with expressing their rejection of the peace.

This story about Versailles precipitating the failure of reconciliation, and causing subsequent violent political conflict, however, is too simple. Such an interpretation obscures the deep political divides and contestations that pervaded German postwar politics. Between 1918 and 1933, political conflict within Germany included differences in political responses to the perceived injustices of Versailles. Eric Weitz's study of the Weimar Republic reveals that Germany at war's end was teeming with calls for radical political and social transformation. The revolution of 1918–1919, started by sailors in Kiel, gained popular momentum in its call "for an immediate end to the war, the removal of the Kaiser and his generals, and a new, democratic government." The experience of defeat after a brutalizing war that killed 2 million German men and wounded 4.2 million more created the political conditions for great transformations.[69]

The Weimar democratic revolution, however, was incomplete as it left in place entrenched conservative elites who remained stalwart enemies of the fledgling democracy.[70] The revolution in Germany exposed deep political divisions among the vanquished that promised to precipitate a thorough and critical self-examination, but influential parts

---

[67] E. H. Carr, *International Relations between the Two World Wars (1919–1939)* (London: Macmillan, 1965), 5 and 46.

[68] Finch, "The peace negotiations with Germany," 554. Finch was assistant technical advisor to the American delegation at the peace conference.

[69] Weitz, *Weimar Germany*, 18.

[70] See also Hans Mommsen, *The Rise and Fall of Weimar Germany*, trans. Elborg Forster and Larry Eugene Jones (Chapel Hill: University of North Carolina Press, 1996), 76.

of the conservative elite were able to subvert this politically painful
and potentially transformative process by uniting Germans against
Versailles. Any account of the reasons for the failure of reconciliation
after World War I thus must include the established conservative elite's
denial of defeat and hostile attitude toward the democratic republic;
it was the self-serving strategy of this conservative elite to magnify the
flaws of Versailles and popularize the interpretation of Versailles as a
"ritual of humiliation." In this light, the flaws of Versailles served as a
convenient excuse for conservatives to resist the painful examination
and repudiation of Germany's authoritarian and militarist traditions.

It is also important to remember that although Germans of the entire
political spectrum considered Versailles to be deeply unjust, they differed on how to respond politically to the "humiliation." By 1925,
for example, the Weimar government under the conservative Gustav
Streseman had chosen a policy of "fulfillment": Germany would meet
its treaty commitments while negotiating their revision. By September
1926, Germany had gained admission to the League of Nations, and
in August 1928, Germany became part of the initial group of states to
sign the Kellogg–Briand Pact, renouncing war as a means of resolving
political conflicts.[71] Ultimately, however, the failure of established conservatives to relinquish their dreams of empire and great-power status
fed their illusions of a betrayed military and their permanent hostility
toward the "traitorous" democracy.

Weitz argues that the mistake made by the Social Democrats in the
revolution after World War I was "their refusal to challenge the social
and economic bases of elite power in the army, churches, economy, universities and state bureaucracy." In pandering to the political right, the
Weimar democrats chose a strategy that would yield dire antidemo-
cratic consequences in the 1930s when political, social, and economic
conditions deteriorated with the onset of the Great Depression. While
the National Socialist and other radical movements were politically
marginal in the 1920s, Nazi propaganda about rectifying the "national
shame" started to achieve significant political results only with the aid
of two other factors: "the support of the established Right and the
Depression."[72]

Conservative elites sought to displace the pain of a shameful
defeat by vilifying the Weimar Republic and exploiting contemporary

---

[71] Weitz, *Weimar Germany*, 205 and 109.   [72] Ibid., 349 and 359.

political and economic crises to effect its overthrow. The hideous transformation of German politics by the National Socialists thus required
the complicity of the reactionary conservative elites who continued to
aspire to "an authoritarian system domestically and a revival of Germany's great-power status internationally." In this vein, Weitz argues
that the rise of National Socialism was "a counterrevolution" against
the postwar democratic transformations effected under the Weimar
Republic. With the help of reactionary conservatives, the National
Socialists thus effected another kind of internal revolution that spelled
permanent irreconciliation with the postwar international order.[73]
In this sense, Germany's estrangement was primarily structural and
directed at the international status order that deprived it of one of the
major markers of great-power status.[74] The historical record thus significantly refutes assessments of Versailles as a punitive and humiliating peace imposed by irreconcilable victors on the vanquished. The
problems of the war's estrangements also lay elsewhere.

VI Anticolonial Struggle: From Interactional to International Structural Reconciliation

The case of Weimar Germany shows that agents may be alienated not
only from each other but also from the social and political institutions and orders that accord their status and rights and mediate their
activities. Problematic structures and practices of international organization may also contribute to sustaining some agents' problematic
views of what ambitions they can legitimately pursue and what constraints merit respectful compliance. While German colonial ambitions
had various internal drivers,[75] German conservative elites did not continue to dream of empire *despite* the postwar international order but
partly because of it. As Shogo Suzuki has explained, European international society was "Janus-faced" and, even after Versailles, required
cordial relations based on respect for international law between

---

[73] Ibid., 357–58.
[74] On the significance of status-respect in international relations, see Reinhard
Wolf, "Respect and disrespect in international politics: the significance of
status recognition," *International Theory* 3, 1 (2011): 105–42.
[75] See Bradley Naranch and Geoff Eley, eds., *German Colonialism in a Global
Age* (Durham, NC: Duke University Press, 2014).

"civilized" states and the "adoption of coercive policies towards 'uncivilized' states as an inherent part of a 'civilized' state's identity."[76]

Many subjugated peoples in the colonial international order of the early twentieth century hoped that the terms of Versailles which dealt with the defeat or collapse of empires by recognizing the independence of Poland, Ireland, and Czechoslovakia, for example, would be applied more generally to all subjected colonies and territories.[77] Chinese political reformer Kang Youwei praised Wilson's plan for a League of Nations, believing it to be a fulfillment of the Confucian ideal of *datong*, or universal peace.[78] But Versailles did not establish an international order that would vindicate these aspirations. Despite the March First protests against Japanese colonial rule that took place in Seoul and, subsequently, the entire peninsula, in 1919, the question of Korea, and the validity of its annexation by Japan in 1910, did not even get raised at the official peace negotiations, given the decision by the victorious great powers to limit the peace conference to dealing with "only questions emanating directly from the war."[79]

Even within that limit, however, Chinese aspirations for self-determination were effectively eclipsed at Versailles. The most prominent test of the principle's application in Asia was in the case of Shandong Province, a German-controlled territory that was captured by Japan early in the war. China sought the province's return to Chinese sovereignty, but the British and French governments were committed to honoring their secret wartime agreements with Japan to recognize the latter's seizure of Shandong as legitimate, in return for its participation in the Allied war effort. The decision of the Big Three – Lloyd George, Clemenceau, and Wilson – to accept the Japanese claim to Shandong at the end of April 1919 sparked the May Fourth student demonstration in front of Tiananmen (the Gate of Heavenly Peace) that became a mass protest movement against the terms of the postwar colonial international order. Thus, China became the only represented state at the Paris Peace Conference not to sign the treaty, when its two delegates were prevented from attending the official signing ceremony

---

[76] See Shogo Suzuki, "Japan's socialization into Janus-faced European international society," *European Journal of International Relations* 11, 1 (2005): 137–64 at 139.

[77] For Korean aspirations, see Manela, *The Wilsonian Moment*, 207.

[78] Ibid., 108–9.   [79] Ibid., 166.

on June 28, 1919, by Chinese students outraged about the Shangdong decision.[80]

As discussed earlier, although the victorious powers did not overtly adopt a policy of annexation of the colonies and territories in Africa, the Middle East, and the Pacific that had been under the sovereignty of the defeated powers, they also did not institute an international regime that recognized the self-determination claims of such groups.[81] The League of Nations Permanent Mandates Commission that was to supervise these colonies and territories came to exhibit deep contestations and contradictions over the terms of international structural reconciliation. This was most apparent in the petition process established in 1923 by the League of Nations Council, which enabled populations subjected to mandatory rule to protest the conduct of countries that were mandatory powers, and to assert their claims as peoples entitled to political independence.[82] Such protests and petitions from the mandated territories were subject to discussion by the Mandates Commission, distributed to all state members of the League of Nations, and publicly accessible to the world.[83] The mandate system, however, was structurally limited as a mechanism for fostering any conciliatory dialogue between subject populations and their mandatory power, since according to the mandatory powers and the Mandates Commission, the system "was a contract between the mandatory power

---

[80] Ibid., 181. In fact, Japan did return the territory to China in 1922, under pressure from the US (216).

[81] One exception was the Mandate for Palestine, made effective in September 1923. The Mandate incorporated Britain's Balfour Declaration of 1917, which obligated the mandatory power to "secure the establishment of the Jewish national home" as well as "the civil and religious rights of all the inhabitants of Palestine." This dual but uneven obligation, toward establishing Jewish nationhood in Palestine, but only recognizing the civil rights of Palestinian Arabs in the territory, "reflected the great disparity in political leverage between the two populations." Not surprisingly, Palestinian Arabs, who made up 89 percent of the population in Palestine in the 1920s, came to be alienated from the new international order that adjudicated their claims in these unequal terms. See Natasha Wheatley, "Mandatory interpretation: Legal hermeneutics and the new international order in Arab and Jewish petitions to the League of Nations," *Past and Present: A Journal of Historical Studies*, 227, 1 (2015): 205–48 at 215–16. Thanks to Laila Parsons for her assistance with this reference.

[82] A case of North American indigenous peoples attempting to assert their claims to international standing at the League of Nations is discussed in Chapter 6.

[83] Pedersen, *The Guardians*, 83.

and the League, not between the League and the local population."
While key figures of the Mandates Commission tried to uphold mandate principles as a check against France and Great Britain, the two
main mandatory powers, their efforts were ultimately limited by these
imperial powers that were deeply resistant to international oversight
on their plans.[84] Through the various conflicts that arose over the interwar years, "the Commission, the mandatory powers, and the mandated
populations struggled to shape the principles and character of the new
mandates regime. The programme that emerged was at once paternalistic and authoritarian, rhetorically progressive and politically retro-
grade – a programme perfectly tailored to the task of rehabilitating the
imperial order at its moment of greatest disarray."[85]

According to the argument forwarded in this chapter, these political
struggles were not only struggles for justice, and not merely struggles
for interactional reconciliation between the subjugated and their colonizers, but they also represent emerging struggles by agents about the
terms of their reconciliation with the emerging international and global
order. As Pedersen has noted, petitioning allowed petitioners "to enter
and speak in a multi-vocal, international arena" and "was one of the
key mechanisms (publicity being another) through which a previously
binary relationship – colonizer, colonized – was triangulated."[86] This
"internationalization" of colonial conflicts exposed the international
structural foundations of colonial relations and practices. Through various conflicts brought to the Mandates Commission and the League
of Nations in the 1920s and 1930s, subjected populations expressed
their rejection of the colonial structures of international order. At the
same time, dissident political movements in the colonies, while varied
in their view of the political alternatives, were typically led by many
who were educated and socialized in the West, and therefore sympathetic with Western, democratic, liberal, as well as imperial and racist
values.[87] Yet in failing to address the fundamental structural injustice

[84] Petitions had to be submitted through government channels of the mandatory
power and were considered "receivable" only if they did not call the terms
of the mandate itself into question. Although "between 1925–1939 the
Commission submitted some 325 separate reports" to the League Council,
most petitions "did not normally win the petitioner redress." See ibid., 85–86
and 91.
[85] Ibid., 111.   [86] Ibid., 94.
[87] In discussing Egyptian, Indian, Chinese, and Korean anticolonialists, Manela
observes, "The notions of racial and civilizational hierarchies that served as a

and source of structural alienation of the colonial international system, Versailles ensured another century of international and transnational political conflict over the terms of justice and reconciliation between peoples in international relations. Indeed, although anticolonial struggles failed in 1919, "political programs and organizations committed to self-determination became more powerful and more pervasive than before."[88]

VII Conclusion

In the aftermath of World War I, a defeated but intransigent Germany was not so much relationally unreconciled to the victor states, as structurally unreconciled to the terms of the new international order that, while depriving Germany of its colonies, continued to validate colonialism as a marker of great-power status. As the historical record shows, the main failure of the architects of Versailles with respect to justice was not in being too harsh on demanding German accountability; rather, it was in the failure of the Allied powers to commit to various components of structural and distributive justice. First, they failed to achieve justice in the distribution of war costs among themselves, which exacerbated the interactional justice issue of war reparations to be paid by Germany. The lack of commitment by the victors to structural justice and reconciliation in Europe resulted in a continent that was unprepared to defend against an unrepentant Germany that was increasingly unreconciled to its status in the international order. To the extent that the architects of Versailles failed, it was in their inability to agree on, and effectively implement, terms of structural and distributive justice that would have enabled the economic recovery of Europe in a way that could check a defeated but unreconciled Germany.

Second, a related structural failure of Versailles was its architects' shallow commitment to transform the international order in response to demands for equality, inclusion, and self-determination by colonized

central legitimating tenet of the imperial order in international affairs were not at the time limited to Europeans alone." See Manela, *The Wilsonian Moment*, 153. On anticolonial politics based on equality and inclusion in the French empire, see Adria K. Lawrence, *Imperial Rule and the Politics of Nationalism: Anti-Colonial Protest in the French Empire* (Cambridge: Cambridge University Press, 2013).

[88] Manela, *The Wilsonian Moment*, 221–24.

peoples. While US president Woodrow Wilson and other Allied leaders proclaimed that the new international order would be based on the principle of self-determination, and while German colonial atrocities in South West Africa served as a justification for depriving the country of colonies, Versailles left a structurally unjust colonial international order intact. In denying equal standing to make claims of self-determination or inclusion to the colonized, Versailles and its institutional product, the League of Nations, were, in a significant sense, failures in terms of correcting a fundamental structural injustice of the international system. This failure continued and deepened the alienation of colonized groups and peoples from the interstate order established and dominated by Western powers and provoked and shaped the course of anticolonial and anti-imperial political struggles that occupied much of world politics in the twentieth century and that continue to shape contemporary trends in global political conflict in the twenty-first century.

The conclusion of World War II heralded the development of liberal institutions of settling accounts, focused predominantly on victims and perpetrators of internationally wrongful conduct, including aggression, war crimes, and crimes against humanity. Justice as settling accounts involves two principles: accountability of those responsible for wrongdoing and reparation of those who suffered undeserved harms or losses. But who can claim to be a victim? And what does it mean to give victims their due? The next chapter tackles these thorny questions as they relate to conditions and experiences of international and transnational political catastrophe, including those that involve violent anticolonial and anti-imperial conflict.

2 | *Pathologies of Victimhood*

Blood speaks with a terrible voice!

– Luu Doan Huynh[1]

I Introduction

In political conditions that have culminated in war, oppression, or atrocity, attention turns to the urgent but confounding task of settling accounts. Those harmed in such contexts, as well as their supporters, typically seek ways to have their status as victims recognized and to ensure that perpetrators are held to account. In a normative sense, the task of justice as a matter of settling moral accounts between agents presupposes a deep concern for the plight of victims. The concept of victimhood relies on a normative framework from which judgments of guilt and innocence, justice and injustice, transgression and responsibility, can be derived. In law-governed societies, agents typically look to the law for an answer to the question of who can claim to be a victim of injustice. From a legalistic perspective, victims are those who suffer breaches of the law or do not receive their legal entitlements. Legal-normative claims of victimhood, in a functional sense, depend on their embeddedness or institutionalization in a system of law. For example, in a society where there are legally institutionalized rules of property that validate certain individual entitlements to personal property, individuals who have personal property taken from them without their consent can legitimately claim to be victims of theft. In the absence of

---

[1] Luu Doan Huynh (1929–2010) was a Senior Researcher at the Institute for International Relations, Ministry of Foreign Affairs, Hanoi. He was also a participant in the diplomacy of the US–Vietnam War. Quoted in Robert S. McNamara, James G. Blight, Robert K. Brigham, Thomas J. Biersteker, and Herbert Y. Schandler, *Argument without End: In Search of Answers to the Vietnam Tragedy* (New York: Public Affairs, 1999), 87.

such a legal rule, claims of victimhood related to property theft would lack a normative foundation and become normatively untenable.[2]

The necessity of embedding victimhood within a rule-based institutionalized order is articulated in Aeschylus's dramatic trilogy the *Oresteia*. In the last installment, Orestes, son of Agamemnon, is being hounded by the Furies, the spirits of retribution, for having killed his mother, Clytaemnestra. In the *Eumenides*, Orestes has fled to Athens, where the goddess Athena institutes a court to hear the dispute between Orestes and the Furies. Orestes justifies his act as fit vengeance against the perpetrator responsible for killing his father, while the Chorus that represents Clytaemnestra asserts her victimhood and condemns Orestes for having committed the "unendurable wrong" of shedding kindred blood.[3] In the end, Athena's judgment saves Orestes while assuaging the Furies, ending the cycle of civil violence. While Aeschylus's play reveals the necessity of public institutions of settling accounts, it also exposes the tentative and fragile nature of such institutions. Athena's impartiality is suspect, her reasons for judging in favor of Orestes are less than convincing, and the Furies only give up their claim on his life after the goddess offers them various positive enticements, including a place of honor in the city. The settling of accounts effected by Athena's court and the ensuing reconciliation of the Furies are highly contingent and do not assuage our terror of the Furies; thus Brian Vickers has commented that "reading the *Oresteia* makes one afraid for one's life."[4]

Aeschylus shows that lurking beneath our institutionalized forms of settling accounts for injustice is a raw and emotionally ferocious subjective experience of injustice that can rise to test and overwhelm established normative orders. Jeffrie Murphy has highlighted the

---

[2] See Thomas Hobbes, *Leviathan: Or the Matter, Forme and Power of a Commonwealth Ecclesiasticall and Civil* (New York: Collier Books, 1962), Chapter 13. Of course, there is significant cultural, political, and historical variation in property regimes.

[3] Aeschylus, *The Eumenides* in *Oresteia: Agamemnon, The Libation Bearers, The Eumenides*, trans. Richmond Lattimore (Chicago: University of Chicago Press, 1953), line 146.

[4] Brian Vickers, *Towards Greek Tragedy: Drama, Myth, Society* (New York: Longman, 1973), 425. Quoted in Peter Euben, *The Tragedy of Political Theory* (Princeton, NJ: Princeton University Press, 1990). See also Bronwyn Leebaw, *Judging State-Sponsored Violence, Imagining Political Change* (Cambridge: Cambridge University Press, 2011), 108–16.

subjective occurrent experience of victimhood as consisting of "certain feelings of anger, resentment, and even hatred that we typically (and *perhaps* properly) direct towards wrongdoers, especially if we have been *victims* of those wrongdoers."[5] Although our subjective experiences of suffering injustice may be shaped by conventional legal and moral norms, Judith Shklar insists that victimhood "has an irreducibly subjective component that the normal model of justice cannot easily absorb."[6] This subjective experience of victimhood spawns what social psychologists have called the "justice motive," which is "a reaction to a perceived discrepancy between entitlements and benefits."[7] More than power, more than security even, it seems, people – individually and collectively – seek not to be unavenged victims of injustice.[8]

As David Welch explains, the occurrent experience of injustice "triggers a unique emotional response. It engages powerful passions that have the effect of increasing the stridency of demands, amplifying intransigence, reducing sensitivity to threats and value trade-offs, increasing the willingness to run risks, and increasing the likelihood of violent behavior."[9] Welch's analysis of the role of the justice motive in causing interstate war leads him to observe that the pursuit of justice between self-governing communities is especially fraught with moral and political danger. In political contexts in which agents disagree on the principles of justice, or where such principles do not specify clearly agents' entitlements and obligations, as well as in contexts where agents have not affirmed the relevant principles and do not behave in conformity with them, or lack institutions and

[5] Jeffrie G. Murphy, "Introduction: The retributive emotions," in *Forgiveness and Mercy*, Jeffrie G. Murphy and Jean Hampton, eds. (Cambridge: Cambridge University Press, 1988), 2.

[6] Judith N. Shklar, *The Faces of Injustice* (New Haven, CT: Yale University Press, 1990), 37.

[7] David A. Welch, *Justice and the Genesis of War* (Cambridge: Cambridge University Press, 1993), 19. See also M.J. Lerner and S.C. Lerner, eds., *The Justice Motive in Social Behavior: Adapting to Times of Scarcity and Change* (New York: Plenum Press, 1981), 12–13.

[8] Plato, Hobbes, and Rousseau have all referred to this motive. See Hobbes, *Leviathan*, Chapter 15; Jean-Jacques Rousseau, *Project of Perpetual Peace*, trans. Edith M. Nuttall (London: Richard Cobden-Sanderson, 1927), 57; Plato, *The Republic of Plato*, trans. Allan Bloom, 2nd ed. (New York: Basic Books, 1991), Book IV, 440c, 120.

[9] Welch, *Justice and the Genesis of War*, 20.

procedures for resolving conflicts about them,[10] the normative functions of the discourse of victimhood become more vulnerable to corruption and perversion.

   Some might argue that in such contexts, it would be better to bypass
the concept of victimhood altogether. This worry about focusing on
victims and victimhood arises from observations of the problematic
role played by disputes about victimhood in exacerbating political conflict. Contemporary observers and scholars of domestic and international conflict have identified perceptions of victimhood as central to
fueling political violence.[11] Oliver Ramsbotham and Tom Woodhouse
have observed in their study of intrastate wars that "nothing is more
characteristic of [such conflicts] than mutual perceptions of injustice
and victimization...Past outrage, resentment, unrequited desire for
revenge and a deep sense of injustice swell the stream of public memory,
ready to break out again and fuel future conflict if the circumstances
arise."[12] The tensions and disputes related to how accounts are settled
may perpetuate grievances and resentments that may serve only too
well to pave the road to further political injustice and catastrophe.

   Worries about "the cultivation of victimhood" as a political pathology lead to a more fundamental suspicion that the very *idea* of justice as settling accounts is itself ultimately misguided. Might the peaceful regeneration of societies actually proceed more smoothly if people
were *not* encouraged to focus on claims of victimhood, moral injury,
and rectification? I do not think this can be the right answer, nor is
it likely to be a realistic one. But it is clear that the pursuit of justice
as a matter of settling accounts in response to political catastrophe is
not simply a matter of taking "the victim's view."[13] Put another way,
even if settling accounts is about taking the victim's view, how to go
about fulfilling this task is far from transparent or straightforward. To
understand properly the idea of justice as settling accounts, it will be
essential to clarify how we are to think about victims, how we even

[10] Ibid., 212. See also David A. Welch, "The justice motive in East Asia's
   territorial disputes," *Group Decision and Negotiation* 26, 1 (2017): 71–92.
[11] Chris Hedges, *War Is a Force That Gives Us Meaning* (New York: Anchor
   Books, 2003 [2002]), 64.
[12] Oliver Ramsbotham and Tom Woodhouse, *Humanitarian Intervention in
   Contemporary Conflict: A Reconceptualization* (Cambridge: Polity Press,
   1996), 100–101.
[13] Shklar, *The Faces of Injustice*, 126.

determine who they are, what it means to take their view, and what is involved in giving victims their due.

This chapter examines how disputes about accountability and responsibility for political injustices can exacerbate political conflict and engender further violence, oppression, and atrocity. Key to this dynamic is the problematic discourse of victimhood that states or groups typically use, not to acknowledge but to deny claims of victimhood, especially of their opponents. Denial can be effected through idealized notions of victimhood, as well as the transformation of personal experiences of victimhood into political claims of victimhood by collectives and states. Idealized notions of victimhood typically highlight the connection between victims and moral innocence or blamelessness. When such idealization is linked to the collectivization and instrumentalization of victimhood in ideological disputes, it enables those who claim to be victims, or those who claim to be acting on their behalf, to absolve themselves of responsibility for the suffering they inflict on others.

The paradigmatic image of victims as helpless also obscures their capacity for agency. The chapter concludes by considering the implications of acknowledging victim agency and responsibility in contexts of complex political catastrophes. A study of the war between the Democratic Republic of Vietnam (DRV) and the US (1964–1973) shows that responsibility for the devastations of the American Vietnam War challenges both American and North Vietnamese ideological frameworks for understanding and evaluating responsibility for the decade-long militarized conflict.

II Victimhood as Political Pathology

Despite the centrality and ubiquity of the concept of victimhood in political discourse, it has remained "an intractable notion." Provocatively, Judith Shklar continues, "For all our wealth of historical experience, we do not know how to think about victimhood. Almost everything one might say would be unfair, self-serving, undignified, untrue, self-deluding, contradictory, or dangerous."[14] The salience of the concept of victimhood in the construction of political identities, claims,

[14] Judith N. Shklar, "Putting cruelty first," in *Ordinary Vices* (Cambridge, MA: Harvard University Press, 1984), 17 and 22–23.

conflict, and political catastrophe makes the task of critical engagement and normative analysis more urgent than ever. Who can claim
to be a victim? Why do answers to that question generate so much
controversy? Can the question be answered definitively, and by whose
authority? Shklar is skeptical, noting, "We are often not even sure who
the victims are. Are the tormentors who may once have suffered some
injustice or deprivation also victims? Are only those whom they tor-
ment victims? Are we all victims of our circumstances? Can we all be
divided into victims and victimizers at any moment? And may we not
all change parts in an eternal drama of mutual cruelty?"[15]

Existing legal and normative accounts of victimhood in domestic
and international societies may reflect ideological biases stemming
from the unequal distribution of power rather than any objective or
sound moral theory. In this vein, Makau Mutua has criticized the
global human rights regime for privileging certain kinds of injustice
while ignoring others: "The human rights movement recognizes only a
particular type of victim. The term 'victim' is not deployed popularly
or globally but refers rather to individuals who have suffered specific
abuses arising from the state's transgression of internationally recognized human rights. For example, the human rights movement regards
an individual subjected to torture by a state as a victim whereas a person who dies of starvation due to famine or suffers malnutrition for
lack of a balanced diet is not regarded as a human rights victim. The
narrow definition of the victim in these instances relates in part to the
secondary status of economic and social rights in the jurisprudence of
human rights."[16] Limiting recognition of victimhood to conventional
normative accounts may thus prove to be an inherently conservative
strategy. We would be expressing unjustified faith in existing models
and institutions of domestic or global justice to think that they can
ever completely take into account "the extent, variety, and durability
of human injustice."[17]

[15] Ibid., 17.
[16] Makau Mutua, "Savages, victims, and saviors: the metaphor of human rights,"
Harvard International Law Journal 42, 1 (2001): 201–45 at 203n11. See also
Mutua, *Human Rights: A Political and Cultural Critique* (Philadelphia:
University of Pennsylvania Press, 2002). Philosophers have engaged with the
problem of global poverty from diverse perspectives, including human rights
and global justice. See Pablo Gilabert, *From Global Poverty to Global Equality:
A Philosophical Exploration* (Oxford: Oxford University Press, 2012).
[17] Shklar, *Faces of Injustice*, 37 and 126.

The Latin origin of the word *victima* refers to live animals offered in sacrifice during religious rites.[18] The first human victim of the Trojan War was Iphigenia, killed like "a goat for sacrifice"[19] by her father, Agamemnon, reportedly in order to appease an angry goddess preventing his fleet from setting sail for Troy. To be victimized is to suffer a wrong or injustice, to be placed in a position of inferiority or subordination where one is incapable of asserting, defending, or enjoying one's legitimate and rightful entitlements, interests, and claims. Because the status of victimhood entails powerlessness or inferiority, instances of victimization are likely to be underreported, since at the personal level, at least, "most people hate to think of themselves as victims; after all, nothing could be more degrading. Most of us would rather reorder reality than admit that we are the helpless objects of injustice."[20] Yet, ironically, victimhood is a common political claim. Being a victim can empower and elevate the claimant, as victims stand on a moral high ground compared to the perpetrators of wrongdoing: from a moral perspective, it is not victims but their perpetrators who are disgraced and inferior.

This paradoxical combination of power and powerlessness in the status of victimhood helps to explain how claims of victimhood can serve to exacerbate conflict in conditions of political catastrophe. Although the moral function of the status of victimhood is to acknowledge suffering and moral responsibility, certain assertions of the status in politics can corrupt its moral function so that it becomes instrumental to the denial of suffering and moral responsibility. Ironically in political discourse, claims of victimhood that fuel violent conflict are typically about the denial rather than the acknowledgment of victimhood, especially to one's opponents. Mutual denial of claims of victimhood, rather than their mutual acknowledgment, thus fuels the political pathology of victimhood to destructive proportions.

Idealized Victimhood and the Problem of "Dirty" Victims

The quintessential victim is not only powerless like a sacrificed animal but, by implication, also morally blameless or innocent. Idealized

---

[18] *Oxford English Dictionary.*
[19] Aeschylus, *Agamemnon* in *Oresteia: Agamemnon, The Libation Bearers, The Eumenides*, line 234.
[20] Shklar, *Faces of Injustice*, 38.

notions of victimhood typically highlight this connection between victims and moral innocence, and even virtuousness. Euripides portrays the sacrificed Iphigenia not only as an innocent but as a paragon of moral virtue, facing her impending death with quiet courage and dignity.[21] The expectation of the moral perfection of victims powerfully shapes accounts of the victims and perpetrators of political catastrophes. Shklar has observed that the idealization of victims is an understandable reaction to atrocity and a common strategy to heighten the moral rebuke against perpetrators' misdeeds as well as to salvage a kind of moral faith in humanity: "It is…a perfect way to shame the cruel, but more significantly it is the only way to avoid the nausea of misanthropy. The victims must redeem mankind."[22] In a historical example, Adam Hochschild notes that in the struggle against Belgian king Leopold II's brutally exploitative regime in the Congo, the leading white human rights advocate Edmund Dene Morel tended to idealize its victims: "The picture Morel gives in his writings of Africans in the Congo before whites arrived is that of Rousseau's idealized Noble Savage: in describing traditional African societies he focuses on what was peaceful and gentle and ignores any brutal aspects."[23] If such idealization can help to mobilize popular and political support for a morally progressive cause, why does Shklar warn that "even at the cost of misanthropy, one cannot afford to pretend that victimhood improves anyone in any way"?[24]

One problem with idealizing victims is that it can obstruct acknowledgment of actual victims. For what about those humans who are not so passive or virtuous? Can they still claim to be victims? One answer is offered in Zhang Yimou's *The Red Sorghum*, a film that details the life of Chinese villagers in the 1920s who fall victim to Japanese aggression a decade later.[25] In one scene, the Japanese invaders have captured the local mobster, who previously caused hardships to the villagers. The Japanese commander orders the village butcher to flay the mobster alive. Interestingly, although it is the mobster who is threatened with and ultimately suffers this atrocious act, he does not come across as the

---

[21] Euripides, *Iphigenia at Aulis*, http://classics.mit.edu/Euripides/iphi_aul.html.
[22] Shklar, "Putting cruelty first," 15.
[23] Adam Hochschild, *King Leopold's Ghost: A Story of Greed, Terror, and Heroism in Colonial Africa* (New York: Houghton Mifflin, 1998), 210.
[24] Shklar, "Putting cruelty first," 15.
[25] Zhang Yimou (director), *The Red Sorghum – Hong Gao Liang* (China: Xian Film, 1987).

main victim of the scene. Instead, our sympathies focus on the butcher, who is first given the order and must decide to save his own life by committing the deed or refuse and be shot, as well as the butcher's apprentice, who does finally carry out the deed but loses his sanity as a result. Compared to the morally upright butcher and his vulnerable young apprentice, it is difficult to think of the mobster as a victim, because he does not fit into the stereotypical image of virtuous victimhood. We know too much about his sordid past deeds to consider him morally virtuous or innocent. Furthermore, he does not seem to possess any redeeming skill or knowledge that would make his death a social loss. It is precisely because he lacks virtue and any other kind of excellence that it is difficult to acknowledge him as a victim; indeed, in other circumstances, his suffering in the form of criminal punishment would hardly meet with disapproval.

There is no room in an idealized account of victimhood for such moral complications as unvirtuous victims or victim-perpetrators. By such a standard, "authentic" victimhood typically consists of innocent and powerless women and children who need to be comforted, rather than driven young men and women who become armed rebels or insurgents. Mainstream media portrayals of victims often emphasize their powerlessness, loss, and confusion rather than their sense of injustice and capacity for resistance and vengeance. For those engaged in ideological conflict, when opponents do not measure up to the saintly image of victimhood, they do not deserve to be acknowledged as "real" victims. The problem with this politics of "real" victimhood is that it creates a morally arbitrary hierarchy of victims that can then be used to justify the worst moral transgressions against the "other." Marie Smyth has noted in her observations of the Northern Ireland peace process that inclusive definitions of victimhood "relying on human suffering as the qualification for victim status ... posed challenges to those who had to countenance the inclusion of those from the community that had harmed them in the same 'victim' category as themselves ... The terms 'innocent' and 'real' were used by some groups as a means to exclude others from the category of genuine victimhood."[26] Ironically, idealized notions of victimhood enable belligerents to mobilize support, justify, or excuse their own transgressions and deny responsibility

[26] Marie Smyth, "Putting the past in its place: issues of victimhood and reconciliation in Northern Ireland's peace process," in *Burying the Past: Making Peace and Doing Justice after Civil Conflict*, Nigel Biggar, ed. (Washington, DC: Georgetown University Press, 2003), 125–54 at 128.

for any suffering their actions may inflict, especially against their opponents, whose unjust cause or counterviolence renders them incapable
of being "real" victims.

But if only the morally pure and innocent can claim to be victims,
then, aside from babies and young children, there will be few adult
humans who can claim to be "real" victims. Auschwitz survivor Primo
Levi notes, in the context of the Holocaust, that

> the prisoners of the Lagers, hundreds of thousands of persons of all social
> classes, from almost all the countries of Europe, represented an average, un-
> selected sample of humanity. Even if one did not want to take into account
> the infernal environment into which they had been abruptly flung, it is illog-
> ical to demand – and rhetorical and false to maintain – that they all and
> always followed the behavior expected of saints and stoic philosophers.[27]

The morally simplistic image and expectation of victims as wholly
innocent, passive, and helpless must inevitably clash with the complexity of victims in the flesh, creating the problem of "dirty" victims. In
this vein, Makau Mutua has complained that contemporary human
rights discourse assumes an idealized image of victimhood that makes
it difficult to acknowledge some victims:

> The victim must also be constructed as sympathetic and innocent. Otherwise
> it is difficult to mobilize public outrage against the victimizer. Moral clarity
> about the evil of the perpetrator and the innocence of the victim is an essen-
> tial distinction for Western public opinion, for it is virtually impossible to
> evoke sympathy for a victim who appears villainous, roguish, or unreceptive
> to a liberal reconstructionist project.[28]

In the current legal case mounted by the families of thirty-three
unarmed protesters who were killed by British colonial forces during a state of emergency declared on March 3, 1959, in Nyasaland
(now Malawi), the defenselessness of the protesters makes them viable
victims deserving of financial compensation. This legal case, however, makes no indication that the political activists of the Nyasaland
African Congress who engaged in violent protests in their fight for
independence, and whose harsh detention on a passenger ship was the
subject of the peaceful protest, ought also to be considered victims of

---

[27] Primo Levi, *The Drowned and the Saved*, trans. Raymond Rosenthal (New
York: Vintage International, 1989), 49.
[28] Mutua, "Savages, victims, and saviors," 230.

colonial injustice. Adhering to an idealized conception of victimhood makes the concept inaccessible to many human victims, who, although they may not be saints, nevertheless have been wronged or exposed to objectionable treatment or conditions. If we want to retain the concept of victimhood for human beings, we must recognize that victims may be difficult, disagreeable, misguided, morally imperfect, or unvirtuous, and even, in some circumstances, perpetrators, who nevertheless have suffered some setback or injury to their legitimate claims, rights, or interests.

Victims, Agency, and Responsibility

The assumption of moral innocence or blamelessness attached to idealized victimhood also serves to obscure the misdeeds of those who are cast as victims. Hochschild's account of the horrors suffered by the Congolese under King Leopold's reign provides a stunning example. Between 1880 and 1920, outright brutality through murder, as well as forced labor conditions leading to starvation, exhaustion, exposure, disease, and lowered birthrates, claimed approximately 10 million lives from the Congo.[29] Belgium's responsibility for this brutal period of oppression and atrocity, however, was quickly forgotten by August 1914, when the neutral country was invaded by Germany and suffered heavy civilian casualties. As Hochschild notes, "the process of forgetting the killings of Leopold's Congo received an unexpected boost when [because of Germany's unprovoked invasion] Belgium itself *was seen as victim* instead of conqueror."[30] Indeed, while the atrocities committed by Imperial Germany in South West Africa served as the justification for revoking Germany's colonial claims, Ruanda-Urundi (present-day Rwanda and Burundi) in German East Africa fell under Belgian colonial administration, first as a League of Nations Class B Mandate between 1924 and 1945, then as a United Nations trust territory from 1945 to 1962.

Similarly, Japanese claims of victimhood arising from the atomic bombings of Hiroshima and Nagasaki served to obscure the country's moral misdeeds during the Second World War. According to historian John Dower, "remembering Hiroshima and Nagasaki . . . easily became a way of forgetting Nanjing, Bataan, the Burma-Siam railway, Manila,

---

[29] Hochschild, *King Leopold's Ghost*, 233.   [30] Ibid., 295, emphasis mine.

and the countless Japanese atrocities these and other place names sig-
nified to non-Japanese."[31] In a fascinating study, James Orr also traces
"the origins of an amnesia over Japanese war aggressions by revealing the emergence of victim consciousness as the major mechanism to
that amnesia."[32] Precisely because the idealization of victimhood can
be used in this way to deflect responsibility, according to Ian Buruma,
"German liberals, scholars as well as artists, have shied away from German victimhood...The bombing of Dresden, for example, has long
been a favorite topic of German revanchists and guilt-deniers on the
extreme right."[33] The point is not that the claims of victimhood by the
Belgians in 1914, or by the Japanese and Germans in 1945, are not
legitimate because of their culpability in other contexts. Rather, these
claims of victimhood become problematic when used to deny, dissolve,
or deflect moral responsibility for those other contexts.

The language of victimhood can serve as an escape route from moral
accountability not only when victims are idealized but also, ironically,
when they are diminished, especially their capacity for agency. For the
condition of powerlessness attributed to victims renders them morally
blameless, since those who are deprived of agency are also divested of
responsibility. The problem is that the tendency to conceive of victims
as helpless and thereby blameless diffuses the blame and responsibility of perpetrators who themselves can claim to be subjects of past
victimization.[34] The claim of being a powerless and damaged victim,

---

[31] John Dower, "The bombed: Hiroshimas and Nagasakis in Japanese memory,"
in *Hiroshima in History and Memory*, Michael J. Hogan, ed. (Cambridge:
Cambridge University Press, 1996), 116–42 at 123.

[32] James J. Orr, *The Victim as Hero: Ideologies of Peace and National Identity in
Postwar Japan* (Honolulu: University of Hawaii Press, 2001), 173. Orr argues
that "the amnesia was intermittent and often only partial. In fact, there have
always been voices of conscience, just as there have always been incidences of
inadvertent and willful neglect of Japan's aggressive past. Rather than dwell
on this amnesia, one needs also to trace the selective and manipulated
remembrance of those aggressions."

[33] Ian Buruma, "The Destruction of Germany," *The New York Review of Books*
51, 16 (October 21, 2004): 8–12 at 9. See also W. G. Sebald, *On the Natural
History of Destruction* (New York: Modern Library, 2004), who argues that
Germans themselves chose to remain largely silent on the subject of German
victimhood because raising the claim itself would open up the issue of their
own moral culpability.

[34] See Robert Nisbet, "Victimology," in *Prejudices: A Philosophical Dictionary*
(Cambridge, MA: Harvard University Press, 1982), 304 and 306. See also
Shklar, *Faces of Injustice*, 33.

more acted upon than acting, amounts to the claim that one is not a morally responsible agent.[35]

While those who seek to deflect responsibility for their own actions or inactions may invoke the image of the powerless victim, many who have been victimized often find such a self-image intolerable. Shklar thus argues that even the victims of National Socialist oppression and atrocity ought not to be viewed as entirely powerless and blameless.[36] She considers a critical and frank accounting of the role of individuals and groups to be important because we ought not "to absolve them of all responsibility. To do so would be to remember them as less than human, as beings without will or intelligence. As long as they were alive they had responsibilities, and to deny that, or to ignore their errors and to speak only of those who did act heroically, would be unjust to the dead and to the survivors. If the victims could not fail, they were not human, and one might as well call them sheep."[37]

Doing justice to victims does not involve denying their agency while holding unrealistic assumptions about the agency of perpetrators but entails recognizing and evaluating the agency of both and holding consistent views about the responsibility of both victims and perpetrators. Raising the issue of victim responsibility may sound to some like blaming the victim, opening another avenue for perpetrators to escape responsibility. This would be true only if one held a zero-sum account of the moral responsibility of victims and perpetrators, which is implied by the idealized account. There is no reason, however, to assume that perpetrators automatically bear less responsibility for their misdeeds just because victims also bear responsibility for their own actions and inactions. For example, the fact that various Congolese groups practiced a form of slavery before European arrival does not absolve the Europeans who participated in the slave trade of their moral culpability for establishing a far more brutalizing slave trade.[38] Rather than

[35] See also Smyth, "Putting the past in its place," 126–27.
[36] For an account of the trials faced by Shklar's family escaping from National Socialist Europe, see Judith N. Shklar, "A life of learning," Charles Homer Haskins Lecture, American Council of Learned Societies Occasional Paper No. 9, April 1989, www.acls.org/Publications/OP/Haskins/1989_JudithNShklar .pdf.
[37] Shklar, "Putting cruelty first," 18.
[38] See Hochschild, *King Leopold's Ghost*, 10: "the fact that trading in human beings existed in any form turned out to be catastrophic for Africa, for when

undermining the status of agents who were enslaved as victims, recognizing the agency of the victimized can facilitate a deeper appreciation of their full humanity and the moral gravity of diverse practices of slavery as major social and political injustices.

The Political or Ideological Instrumentalization of Personal Victimhood

Another dimension of claims of victimhood in contexts of political catastrophe that we should approach with caution involves the transformation or co-optation of individual experiences of victimhood into political claims of victimhood by collectives and states. In one sense, politicization and collectivization might be said to help individuals escape the isolating consequences of victimization.[39] In modern contexts, it is conventionally the state's duty to acknowledge when its citizens have been harmed or wronged and to seek their vindication by bringing the perpetrators to justice. In this function, the state expresses a moral solidarity with the victims that helps to reaffirm the disrupted social bond between victim and community. Thus, Jean Hampton has argued that "how society reacts to one's victimization can be seen by one as an indication of *how valuable* society takes one to be, which in turn can be viewed as an indication of how valuable one really is."[40] Similarly, collectives, whether they are revolutionary movements or social groups, take up the grievances of their individual victimized members partly as a way to express group solidarity. Psychologist Brendan Hamber claims, "Those affected by political violence need, above all else, to feel part of their community again and to share their grief and suffering with others in it." According to this view, official and communal acknowledgment helps to mitigate the psychological suffering of individual victims.[41]

Europeans showed up, ready to buy endless shiploads of slaves, they found African chiefs willing to sell."

[39] Judith Lewis Herman, *Trauma and Recovery: The Aftermath of Violence – From Domestic Abuse to Political Terror* (New York: Basic Books, 1997), 51–52.

[40] Jean Hampton, "The retributive idea," in *Forgiveness and Mercy*, Jeffrie G. Murphy and Jean Hampton, eds. (Cambridge: Cambridge University Press, 1988), 141.

[41] Brandon Hamber, "Does the truth heal? A psychological perspective on political strategies for dealing with the legacy of political violence," in *Burying*

While the collectivization of individuals' suffering may shore up internal group cohesion and solidarity, it may also serve to exacerbate the conditions for unjust and alienating relations between groups. Governments and collectives embroiled in political and ideological conflict can attempt to deflect their own moral and political responsibility for deteriorating political conditions by appropriating the undisputed moral innocence of some victims, especially children, women, and unarmed civilians. The innocence and vulnerability of these individuals is projected onto the collective or the governing authorities, obscuring whatever responsibility they may bear for perpetuating the political and social conditions for ongoing conflict or violence. Collectivizing victimhood can thus exacerbate political conflict between groups by providing either governments or groups who claim to be acting on the victims' behalf with an escape route from moral and political accountability, while obscuring their own political failures to resolve the conditions that enabled, encouraged, or provoked wrongful interactions. In the case of the start of the 1904 Herero-German war, for example, a steady stream of inaccurate and distorted news of the killing of settlers by "a savage race" fueled the Kaiser's and the German public's nationalist response: "few people dared to challenge the accuracy of the reports from the colony" or to inquire about the reasons behind the rebellion.[42]

Furthermore, the ideological instrumentalization of victimhood may have little to do with acknowledging or meeting the needs and concerns of actual individuals who have suffered direct pain, injury, loss, or destruction from the violence. For example, although Japan's postwar national identity of victimhood is based on the suffering of those affected by the atomic bombings of Hiroshima and Nagaski, historian John Dower notes that both the Japanese government and populace did little to aid the recovery of the survivors. The Japanese government did not extend special assistance to bomb victims until after American occupation ended in 1952; meanwhile, survivors had to depend on local resources that had been practically annihilated by the bombings. The Japanese populace also had an ambivalent relationship with the victims of Hiroshima and Nagasaki: "all initially were

the Past: Making Peace and Doing Justice after Civil Conflict, Nigel Biggar, ed. (Washington, DC: Georgetown University Press, 2003), 155–76 at 168.

[42] David Olusoga and Casper W. Erichsen, *The Kaiser's Holocaust: Germany's Forgotten Genocide* (London: Faber and Faber, 2010),130–31.

presumed to carry the curse of the bombs in their blood. Hibakusha were not welcome compatriots in the new Japan. Psychologically if not physically, they were deformed reminders of a miserable past. Given the unknown genetic consequences of radiation, they were shunned as marriage prospects. The great majority of Japanese, overwhelmed by their own struggles for daily survival, were happy to put them out of mind."[43] The Japanization of victimhood from Hiroshima and Nagasaki also obscured acknowledgment of the actual record of victims, which included American and Japanese-American deaths, as well as an estimated forty thousand to fifty thousand Korean deaths.[44] Between 1967 and 1999, Japanese officials refused the request of a group of Korean-Japanese living in Hiroshima to erect a memorial stone to Korean victims of the atomic bombings in the Hiroshima Peace Memorial Park. Only in 1999 did Japanese authorities give permission to move the memorial inside the sacred grounds of the peace park.[45]

It is not only governments that instrumentalize victims' experiences in the service of ethnonationalist political rivalries. In another example described by Maki Kimura, a Korean woman, Zheng Shunyi, survived the Japanese military system of forced sexual labor and slavery but remained in China after the war, marrying and raising a family. In 1997, Zheng expressed a wish to see her homeland one more time, and a victim support group fulfilled her wish. When she became ill, however, the victim support group "prevented her from returning to China," then "refused to return her remains to China, despite her family's repeated request that they should send them back." The support group claimed that "only South Korea could restore her dignity." As Kimura argues, "the support group seems to focus too much on nationalistic discourse, claiming Zheng Shunyi as a 'Korean comfort woman' victim and neglecting her other identities and aspects of her life . . . The problem seems to arise partly because women's experiences are treated

[43] Dower, "The bombed," 126 and 128.
[44] Dower explains, "As a Japanese colony, Korea was a source of extensively conscripted and heavily abused labor in wartime Japan . . . Such laborers were, in effect, double victims – exploited by the Japanese and incinerated by the Americans. By the same token, the Japanese were revealed as being simultaneously victims and victimizers. Indeed, as the story unraveled, it was learned that even in the immediate aftermath of the nuclear holocaust, Korean survivors were discriminated against when it came to medical treatment and even cremation and burial." See Dower, "The bombed," 140.
[45] On the history of exclusion, see Dower, "The bombed," 140.

not as something individual or personal, but as a collective national memory."[46]

Not surprisingly memoirs of survivors often contain complex narratives that raise difficult issues of complicity, collaboration, and internal betrayal. Thus, as Wolf Biermann has observed about Wladyslaw Szpilman's memoir recounting his struggle for survival in war-ravaged Warsaw, "the *nomenklatura* of Eastern Europe in general were unable to tolerate such authentic eyewitness accounts as this book. They contained too many painful truths about the collaboration of defeated Russians, Poles, Ukrainians, Latvians and Jews with the German Nazis."[47] Sarah Song also raises the challenge of "countermemories" of Korean women whose experiences of sexual exploitation in the Japanese military's "comfort women" system did not match the standard narrative of Korean nationalist human rights activists.[48] In the political battle to co-opt victimhood for one's own side or group, the complicated truths of individual suffering, and of intragroup moral responsibility for complicity and collaboration, are lost. Victims may even face persecution within their own communities for failing to tell the ideologically correct story about their experiences.[49]

III Settling Accounts for War: Implications of Victim Agency and Responsibility for the American Vietnam War

Judith Shklar argued that "the best intellectual response" to political catastrophes "is simply to write the history of the victims and victimizers as truthfully and accurately as possible."[50] The intellectual

---

[46] Maki Kimura, *Unfolding the "Comfort Women" Debates: Modernity, Violence, Women's Voices* (Basingstoke, UK: Palgrave Macmillan, 2016), 212.

[47] Wolf Biermann, "Epilogue," in Wladyslaw Szpilman, *The Pianist: The Extraordinary Story of One Man's Survival in Warsaw, 1939–45*, trans. Anthea Bell (Toronto: McArthur, 1998), 211–12. The memoir was first published in Polish in 1946.

[48] See C. Sarah Soh, *The Comfort Women: Sexual Violence and Postcolonial Memory in Korea and Japan* (Chicago: University of Chicago Press, 2008). Chapter 4 discusses this case in more detail.

[49] See, for example, the difficulties encountered by Jerzy Kosinski after publication of his fictionalized memoir, *The Painted Bird*. See "Afterword" in Kosinski, *The Painted Bird*, 2nd ed. (New York: Grove Press, 1976 [1965]), ix–xxvi.

[50] Shklar, *Ordinary Vices*, 23.

and political task of constructing a historical narrative of the causes, development, and consequences of political catastrophes may offer a corrective to the pathological discourses of victimhood that pervade such contexts, often well after outright hostilities have ended. As the wars over official narratives and history textbooks attest, however, this task can be fraught with complication and requires certain social and political conditions to obtain that guarantee public access to information and protection from state or social sanctions in order to yield forthright examinations as well as open public debate of the historical evidence.[51] What implications does the historical research enterprise have for the normative evaluation of responsibility for complex political catastrophes that have culminated in atrocity or in enduring oppression or violence? And how does being mindful of the pathologies of victimhood discourse, expressed through idealization, collectivization, and ideological instrumentalization, allow us to recognize and resist historical or political narratives that fuel the political pathologies of victimhood?

These questions are salient in contemporary debates about who can claim victimhood in contexts of colonial rule that provoked violent anticolonial resistance, as well as in debates about responsibility for the devastations of war. In the case of South Africa, for example, the amnesty provision of the Truth and Reconciliation Commission (TRC) was controversial among some members of the African National Congress who believed that they should not have to apply for amnesty for any acts of violence they committed in their just war against apartheid. The South African TRC commissioner Alex Boraine rebuked this view, stating, "Unjust acts can be committed within the framework of a just war, no less than just acts in an unjust war."[52] Indeed, the frameworks of humanitarian law and just war theory provide the theoretical resources for evaluating both the justice of causes

---

[51] On the "history wars" in Australia over its settler colonial history, see Stuart MacIntyre and Anna Clark, *The History Wars* (Melbourne: Melbourne University Press, 2004). On the battles in history textbooks in a number of cases, see Elizabeth A. Cole, ed., *Teaching the Violent Past:* History Education and Reconciliation (Lanham, MD: Rowman and Littlefield, 2007). On the difficulties of carrying out this intellectual task, see the American Historical Review Forum, "Truth and reconciliation in history," *American Historical Review* 114, 4 (2009): 899–977.

[52] See Antjie Krog, *Country of My Skull: Guilt, Sorrow, and the Limits of Forgiveness in the New South Africa* (New York: Three Rivers Press, 1998), 152.

to go to war and issues of justice in the conduct of war. Thus John Rawls criticized the Allied bombing of Dresden in February 1945, the fire-bombing of Tokyo and other Japanese cities in the spring of 1945, as well as the atomic bombings of Hiroshima and Nagasaki in August as grave wrongs that violated principles of just conduct in war, despite the undisputed justice of waging war against German and Japanese aggression.[53] Even the idea of a "supreme emergency exemption" presupposes that victims or those who are resisting injustice bear responsibility for following principles of just conduct in their resistance and can only justify departures from such principles in contexts of extreme emergency or necessity.[54]

As Robert Stover has observed, however, settling historical accounts for political catastrophes involving war and oppression requires normative evaluations that go beyond the standard criteria of just war theory or humanitarian law. In his account of judging historical responsibility for the Cold War, Stover finds that parties' actions can be judged in terms of their responsibility for their war aims, for initiating war, for perpetuating or prolonging war, for negotiating in bad faith, for objectionable acts during war, and for consequences their actions in war produce, as well as for failing to respond adequately to such acts and consequences.[55] Such evaluations of political responsibility for war cannot be adequately captured through just war theoretical frameworks, but a more comprehensive settling of accounts is necessary for understanding past political catastrophes and preventing their repetition. The Second Vietnam War or the American Vietnam War (1964–1973) is one of the most vexed twentieth-century conflicts that grew out of anticolonial, nationalist struggles in the political context of the Cold War.[56] In the course of the war, the US dropped more bombs in Vietnam than were used by all sides in World War II.[57] Some 3.8 million Vietnamese, North and South, military and civilian, were killed in the conflict. Fifty-eight thousand Americans lost their lives.

---

[53] See Rawls, *The Law of Peoples*, 95–99.

[54] Michael Walzer, *Just and Unjust Wars: A Moral Argument with Historical Illustrations* (New York: Basic Books, 1977), 251–68.

[55] Robert Stover, "Responsibility for the Cold War – a case study of historical responsibility," *History and Theory* 11, 2 (1972): 145–78.

[56] The Indochina conflict includes three wars, the First Indochina/French war (1946–54), the Second American war, and the Third Indochina war of 1978–1979.

[57] Donovan Webster, *Aftermath: The Remnants of War* (New York: Vintage Books, 1998), 166.

The historiography on the war over the past four decades is characterized by raging debates between orthodox, revisionist, and neoconservative interpretations over the reasons for US military involvement in the Indochina conflict in the 1950s, the escalation in the 1960s, and the eventual withdrawal by 1973. These debates, suffused with Cold War ideological divisions, entail moral and political judgments about the legitimacy of the reasons for American involvement and about the soundness of military intervention, as well as of the strategies for conducting the war and negotiating the peace. While the historiography in the 1970s and 1980s relied mainly on Western sources, since the 1990s, the historiography has come to include communist perspectives from Vietnamese, Chinese, and Russian sources.[58]

While no official international criminal tribunals sanctioned by the community of states held any leaders to account for the devastating war, in an unusual strategy, Robert S. McNamara, US secretary of defense from 1961 to 1968, initiated a project of truth seeking two decades after the American withdrawal from Saigon. The critical oral history project, conducted between 1995 and 1998, involved a series of discussions, held in Hanoi, between Vietnamese and US scholars and former officials. The process yielded the conclusion that the war was a tragedy born of "mutual misperception, misunderstanding, and misjudgment by leaders in Washington and Hanoi."[59] McNamara's view accords with the traditional revisionist perspective in the historiographical literature, which interprets the war as tragedy that could have been averted had American leaders only been more knowledgeable of Vietnam's history and leaders and more prudent in its policy choices.[60] McNamara's exercise in truth finding yielded insightful views of the misperceptions and misunderstandings that played a role in the militarization of the conflict. Contrary to the beliefs of the North Vietnamese leadership, the US did not want to dominate Vietnam like an imperial power; the US was "not opposed to an independent, unified

---

[58] See Lien-Hang T. Nguyen, *Hanoi's War: An International History of the War for Peace in Vietnam* (Chapel Hill: University of North Carolina Press, 2012).

[59] Robert S. McNamara, James G. Blight, Robert K. Brigham, Thomas J. Biersteker, and Herbert Y. Schandler, *Argument without End: In Search of Answers to the Vietnam Tragedy* (New York: Public Affairs, 1999), 6.

[60] See Stanley Karnow, *Vietnam: A History* (New York: Viking Press, 1983); William J. Duiker, *US Containment Policy and the Conflict in Indochina* (New York: Oxford University Press, 1994).

Vietnam."[61] The discussions convincingly show that US policy makers were driven by fear of communism rather than by imperialistic ambition. In April 1950, precipitated by the Sino-Soviet alliance, signed on February 14, and its possible impact on Korea and Indochina, a National Security Council report, NSC-68, declared a national emergency in the face of the communist threat: "The issues that face us are momentous, involving the fulfillment or destruction not only of this Republic but of civilization itself."[62] Most prominent in this context was the perception of the "loss of China" in 1949 to Mao Zedong's Communists. The connection is made clear in July 1956, when US Secretary of State John Foster Dulles spoke about "the loss in Northern Vietnam."[63]

Fear of losing the battle against communism, and fear of the implications this would have on the security of the West, made the struggle in Vietnam part of a worldwide conflict that became the Cold War. At the same time, US policy makers were wrong to assume that the southern Vietnamese National Liberation Front hid a thinly disguised "unified communist drive for hegemony in Asia" run by communist China.[64] If US participants had known anything about Vietnam's history of struggle against Chinese domination, they would not have bought the fallacious assumption that the North Vietnamese regime was a mere instrument or extension of Chinese and Soviet communist power.[65]

Indeed, the domino theory that provided the justification for American military intervention after French withdrawal presupposed that the North Vietnamese had no agency and were merely a Soviet or

[61] McNamara, *Argument without End*, 56–57.
[62] "NSC-68," April 14, 1950, in *Foreign Relations of the United States*, 1950, vol. I (Washington, DC: Government Printing Office, 1977), 234–92 at 238.
[63] McNamara, *Argument without End*, 67.   [64] Ibid., 41.
[65] As Luu Doan Huynh stated, "Vietnam a part of the Chinese expansionist game in Asia? For anyone who knows the history of Indochina, this is incomprehensible." Quoted ibid., 81. On the history of Vietnamese resistance to Chinese domination from the tenth century onward, see "The Vietnamese Emperors," in *In Search of Southeast Asia: A Modern History*, David Joel Steinberg, ed. (Honolulu: University of Hawaii Press, 1985), 69–67; Zhai Qiang, *China and the Vietnam Wars* (Chapel Hill: University of North Carolina Press, 2004); Pierre Asselin, *Hanoi's Road to the Vietnam War 1954–65* (Berkeley: University of California Press, 2013). US President Eisenhower articulated the original version of the domino theory in 1954.

Chinese pawn in a global contest for hegemony between the superpowers. A neoconservative interpretation of the war that came to prominence in the 2000s similarly endorses the validity of the domino theory, arguing that the fear of the spread of communism by American policy makers was essentially valid, that the US intervention had positive consequences for noncommunist countries in Southeast Asia, and that the counterinsurgency campaign pursued by the US could have succeeded.[66] Current historical scholarship, however, shows that this interpretation fails to acknowledge that rather than being puppets of Moscow or Beijing, the Vietnamese Communists were primarily their own political masters. Their objectives, however, were closely aligned with Beijing's policies under Mao, and could be framed in terms of their belief and commitment to a loose global alliance of like-minded anti-imperialist movements.[67] Still, despite the legitimate reasons that the US may have had to support anticommunist nationalist forces in Vietnam, these reasons arguably did not entitle it to use military force to attempt to control the course of nationalist anticolonial struggle in Vietnam to suit its own ideological agenda. In this sense, the American decision to intervene militarily was not only a failure of rationality, as McNamara acknowledged, but also a failure of morality. In addition, even if US fears were legitimate, the conduct of the war was still unjust, because it was "carried on in so brutal a manner that even had it initially been defensible, it would have to be condemned, not in this or that aspect but generally."[68]

In the critical history project that McNamara instigated, General Vo Nguyen Giap, a former defense minister during the American Vietnam War, challenged McNamara's reading of the conflict as a tragedy, in their first meeting: "You are wrong to call the war a 'tragedy' – to say that it came from missed opportunities. Maybe it was a tragedy for you, because yours was a war of aggression, in the neocolonial 'style,' or fashion, of the day for the Americans. You wanted to replace the

---

[66] Michael Lind, *Vietnam, the Necessary War: A Reinterpretation of America's Most Disastrous Military Conflict* (New York: The Free Press, 1999); Mark Moyar, *Triumph Forsaken: The Vietnam War, 1954–1965* (Cambridge: Cambridge University Press, 2006).

[67] See Lorenz Lüthi, "Vietnam's world revolution," in *The Cold War beyond the Superpowers* (forthcoming).

[68] Michael Walzer, *Just and Unjust Wars*, 299.

French; you failed; men died; so, yes, it was tragic, because they died for a bad cause. But for us, the war against you was a noble sacrifice."[69] For the Vietnamese Communists, despite the heavy costs, the war against the US was a just war against an imperial aggressor. This radical interpretation "depicts the United States as a global hegemon, concerned primarily with its own economic expansion, and reflexively opposed to communism, indigenous revolution, or any other challenge to its authority."[70] The official Vietnamese history of the war is titled *The Long Resistance: 1858–1975* and begins with the struggle against French imperialism, followed by the fight against Japanese aggression during World War II, French attempts to recover colonial control between 1945 and 1954, and then the American military intervention until 1975.[71] The American intervention, in this narrative, reflected American commitment to global hegemony, which made the US logically irreconciled to revolutionary nationalist movements in the Third World. This was also the basic verdict of the international war crimes tribunal set up in December 1967 by the British philosopher Bertrand Russell, a civil society initiative involving prominent writers, politicians, scientists, and lawyers that aimed to condemn and end the military involvement of the US in Vietnam's struggle for independence.[72] A corollary to this radical view is that South Vietnam was a nonentity, largely a creature of the US, and therefore lacked autonomy.

Tarak Barkawi has argued for scholarship that recognizes the Global South with "its own dynamics and agency," noting that many actors in the Global South, including Vietnamese nationalists, were involved in struggles beyond the East–West conflict between superpowers, including struggles "for political independence and autonomy, for the right to determine their own fate and manage their own affairs, and for a

[69] McNamara, *Argument without End*, 25.
[70] Robert J. McMahon, "Vietnam War (1960–75): changing interpretations," in *The Oxford Companion to American Military History*, John W. Chambers, ed. (Oxford: Oxford University Press, 1999), 767. For a thorough analysis of the war from a radical view, see Gabriel Kolko, *Anatomy of a War: Vietnam, the United States, and the Modern Historical Experience* (New York: The New Press, 1994).
[71] Nguyễn Khắc Viện, *The Long Resistance: 1858–1975*, 2nd ed. (Moscow: Foreign Languages, 1978).
[72] See Marcos Zunino, "Subversive Justice: the Russell Vietnam War Crimes Tribunal and transitional justice," *International Journal of Transitional Justice* 10 (2016): 211–29.

just share of resources and distribution of wealth and opportunity."[73] Decentering agency, however, yields even greater normative complexity and complication. Decentering historical analysis of the American Vietnam War away from the Cold War superpower contest has yielded historical scholarship on South Vietnam that has refuted assumptions about the puppet status of South Vietnam, showing that its leaders were independently minded and had their own anticolonial and anti-communist views of a unified Vietnam's postcolonial future.[74]

Similarly, recognizing the agency, especially of North Vietnamese Communist leaders, reveals that they were driven by more than an anticolonial, nationalist agenda. Historical research has found that the North Vietnamese Communist leadership, especially Le Duan in the early 1970s, was committed to establishing Vietnamese hegemony over all of Indochina and a communist agenda for world revolution.[75] While the Democratic Republic of Vietnam (DRV) initially engaged in war with the US in an anti-imperial struggle, acknowledging the agency of North Vietnamese leaders means giving up assumptions that they could only have subscribed to anticolonial and nationalist goals and values. While Barkawi poses alternative ways to understand the motivations or aims of Vietnamese nationalists, he does not conceive that they may also have illegitimate or morally defective motivations and aims. Historical excavation, however, may confirm that while the Vietnamese Communists were victim to an unjust and disproportionate military assault by the US, they were also responsible historical agents in their own right, especially in the latter phase of the war with respect to their war aims. First, the North Vietnamese Communists were unjust in mounting a violent insurgency in order to settle their disputes with anticommunist nationalists in South Vietnam about the trajectory of the Vietnamese anticolonial struggle, to which they were *both* committed. Second, motivated by hegemonic aspirations over all of Indochina, the DRV pursued a maximalist strategy during the Paris peace negotiations with the Nixon administration in the early 1970s, resulting in

[73] See Tarak Barkawi, "On the pedagogy of 'small wars,'" *International Affairs* 80, 1 (2004): 19–37 at 22.

[74] Edward Miller, *Misalliance: Ngo Dinh Diem, the United States, and the Fate of South Vietnam* (Cambridge, MA: Harvard University Press, 2013); Jessica M. Chapman, *Cauldron of Resistance: Ngo Dinh Diem, The United States, and 1950s Southern Vietnam* (Ithaca, NY: Cornell University Press, 2013).

[75] See Lorenz Lüthi, "Beyond betrayal: Beijing, Moscow, and the Paris Negotiations, 1971–1973," *Journal of Cold War Studies* 11, 1 (2009): 57–107.

two more years of war before it acceded to "a deal it essentially could have had in the spring of 1971."[76] To the extent that Vietnamese Communist expansionist war aims prolonged the war from 1971 to 1973, the radical demands, especially of the DRV leader Le Duan, were coresponsible for the deaths of millions in Vietnam, Laos, and Cambodia in the 1970s. In this light, the American Vietnam War cannot be considered a "noble sacrifice" for either the Americans or the Vietnamese but mainly a tragedy for the Vietnamese and the Indochinese, for which the US and the North Vietnamese Communists were, to a significant degree, coresponsible.

IV Conclusion

This chapter has revealed the ways in which victimhood discourse can operate as a political pathology, by simplifying and distorting responsibility for political catastrophes by idealizing, collectivizing, or instrumentalizing victimhood discourse in ideological contests. These strategies fuel often mutual denials of moral and political responsibility and pave the road to political conditions that yield and sustain political catastrophes. The next chapter examines how institutions of justice that have developed to redress political injustice and alienation respond to the challenges posed by the pathologies of victimhood. Institutions of settling accounts, such as criminal tribunals as well as truth commissions, typically justify their work as contributing to the vindication or fulfillment of victims' needs, rights, or interests. Yet, such institutions that aim to settle accounts for wrongful interactions between agents encounter difficulties in fulfilling their normative objectives in contexts of structural injustice. The contribution of such institutions to deterring, preventing, or accounting for political injustice thus depends on the structural conditions that enable and mediate their operation.

[76] Lüthi, "Beyond betrayal," 107.

3 | *Settling Accounts*

My seventh proposition goes further: once the Spaniards have demonstrated diligently both in word and deed that for their own part they have every intention of letting the barbarians carry on in peaceful and undisturbed enjoyment of their property, if the barbarians nevertheless persist in their wickedness and strive to destroy the Spaniards, they may then treat them no longer as innocent enemies, but as treacherous foes against whom all rights of war can be exercised, including plunder, enslavement, deposition of their former masters, and the institution of new ones... Furthermore, as the doctors explain in their discussions of war, the prince who wages a just war becomes *ipso jure* the judge of the enemy, and may punish them judicially and sentence them according to their offence.

– Francisco de Vitoria, *On the American Indians – De Indis* (1539)[1]

I Introduction

In the aftermath of political catastrophes such as major war, criminal tribunals are institutional attempts to cope with and discipline the task of justice as settling accounts. The development of a social/political order, with authoritative institutions and practices of conflict resolution that can impartially adjudicate responsibility for wrongful conduct and implement accountability measures against wrongdoers, points to one ideal type of institutional response to the demand to settle accounts for conflicts of justice in domestic and international relations. This chapter examines the development of international legal

---

[1] Excerpt reproduced in "Francisco de Vitoria: just war in the age of discovery," in *The Ethics of War: Classic and Contemporary Readings*, G. Reichberg, H. Syse, and E. Begby, eds. (Malden, MA: Blackwell, 2006), 288–332 at 303–4.

institutions that aim to hold various agents accountable for wrongful conduct recognized by international law. While general rationales for the establishment of legal institutions of accountability may be the desire to discipline the retributive emotions and to promote the rule of law, historical and sociological analyses of institutions and mechanisms of accountability yield important insights for understanding and assessing their social, political, and normative functions and effects. Focusing on the International Criminal Court (ICC), this chapter finds that its instrumentalization by powerful and weak states occurs at both international and domestic levels, and for reasons and objectives that may contradict or hinder the normative justifications for developing such institutions.

More broadly, this chapter aims to highlight normative difficulties encountered by individual-based interactional models of settling accounts for wrongdoing in contexts of structured and structural political injustice. The determination of individual legal liability for wrongful conduct in contexts of political catastrophe is morally difficult and often inadequate as a way of conceptualizing responsibility for such catastrophes. In such contexts, individual actions may contribute to *structured* injustices, where wrongful acts or objectionable outcomes committed or produced by individuals can be attributed to their roles within corporate agents or highly organized and/or purposive social groups. This chapter examines problematic prosecutorial strategies for assigning individual liability for participating in structured injustices, such as fighting in an unjust war of conquest and annexation as a member of a state's military apparatus. Individual actions may also contribute to *structural injustice*, consisting of unintended, generalized, or impersonal harms or wrongs that result from social structural processes in which many individual and corporate agents may participate. If structural injustices are central to the production of political catastrophes, then confining practices of accountability and responsibility to the individual "crime-and-punishment" model will be wholly inadequate. A more normatively robust and comprehensive settling of accounts for political catastrophes must go beyond the interactional view between individual victims and perpetrators in a way that also avoids a descent into pathological political narratives, discourses, and practices of settling accounts that involve collective stereotyping and vilification.

II Power, Authority, and Punishment: The Politics of the International Criminal Court

A rich body of philosophical discussion exists that interrogates the justificatory principles and purposes that ground practices of legal retribution within modern states.[2] Punishment may serve as a form of incapacitation of belligerents who can rekindle conflict, and thus deter or prevent future conflict. Some view punishment as part of a legal or moral order that expresses a commitment to, or vindication of, the rule of law. Punishment may also be pivotal for satisfying the retributive emotions of victims, or rehabilitating offenders,[3] establishing the basis for improved social relations. Punishment of the guilty may be intrinsic to the notion of retributive justice, as well as instrumentally valuable for the ends of peace and reconciliation. In this sense, punishment as a measure of interactional justice may serve to advance structural objectives. At the same time, structural justice and reconciliation may also justify not punishing in certain cases or contexts of wrongful interactions. Empirically, peace, justice, and reconciliation may come to be established without the institution of punishment, and sometimes the desired transformation of social structures does not materialize despite practices of punishment.

To understand how practices of settling accounts, including punishment, may constitute a remedy in the form of a cure, or a poison, in different contexts,[4] it is important to note, as suggested by Antony Duff and David Garland, that the practice of punishment is not an "abstract ahistorical structure, but a social institution which takes different forms in different social contexts."[5] Debates about criminal justice in domestic contexts have benefited from sociological and historical analyses of the social meanings and effects, as well as historical development, of practices of punishment. Sociological and historical

---

[2] See Antony Duff and David Garland, eds., *A Reader on Punishment* (Oxford: Oxford University Press, 1994).

[3] Plato identifies two goals of punishing those guilty of violating the laws: "to make the one who receives the judicial punishment either better or less wicked." See Plato, *The Laws of Plato*, trans. Thomas Pangle (Chicago: University of Chicago Press, 1988), 854e.

[4] See Danielle S. Allen, *The World of Prometheus: The Politics of Punishing in Democratic Athens* (Princeton, NJ: Princeton University Press, 2000), 85.

[5] Duff and Garland, "Introduction: thinking about punishment," in *A Reader on Punishment*, 23.

analyses are an important corollary to the normative enterprise if one is concerned to devise appropriate normative frameworks for the development of accountability practices and institutions in actual societies. While general rationales for the establishment of legal institutions of accountability may be the desire to discipline the justice motive and retributive emotions, or to establish the rule of law, it is important to examine the political and historical development of such institutions with a view to understanding and assessing their social, political, and normative functions and effects. As Thomas Franck has observed, law among mortals is "a system of norms constantly engaged in a process of challenge, adaptation, and reformulation."[6] The content and function of law and legal systems are inextricably wedded to issues of power and extralegal ideas and contestations about justice in any society, domestic, international, and global. As Frédéric Mégret has observed, "focusing on holding states accountable for reneging on their obligations (customary or conventional) does not tell us whether these obligations were just in a deeper way."[7]

Similarly, institutions that focus on holding individuals accountable for violations of international law, such as the International Criminal Court, are not only legal institutions with legalistic objectives; their purposes and operation should also be understood and assessed in moral and political terms.[8] While law is a distinct realm of practice, it cannot be understood or evaluated in isolation from its normative and political contexts. As Judith Shklar has argued, "law is a form of political action, among others, which occasionally is applicable and effective and often is not. It is not an answer to politics, neither is it isolated from political purposes and struggles... The question is

---

[6] See Thomas Franck, "Interpretation and change in the law of humanitarian intervention," in *Humanitarian Intervention: Ethical, Legal, and Political Dilemmas*, J. L. Holzgrefe and Robert O. Keohane, eds. (Cambridge: Cambridge University Press, 2003), 204–31 at 204.

[7] See Frédéric Mégret, "International Justice," in *Fundamental Concepts of International law*, J. d'Aspremont and S. Singh, eds. (New York: Edward Elgar, forthcoming).

[8] See Lu, "The International Criminal Court as an institution of moral regeneration: problems and prospects," in *Bringing Power to Justice: The Prospects of the International Criminal Court*, Joanna Harrington, Michael Milde, and Richard Vernon, eds. (Montreal: McGill-Queen's University Press, 2006), 191–209; and Lu, "The politics of legal accountability and genocide prevention," in *Confronting Genocide*, René Provost and Payam Akhavan, eds. (Dordrecht: Springer, 2011), 295–303.

not, 'Is law politics?' but 'What sort of politics can law maintain and reflect?'"[9] This acknowledgment of the inseparability of law from politics and morality should not be read as an endorsement of a cynical interpretation that law is inevitably (or ought to be) a mere servant to power. Rather, it should lead us to interrogate the politics of accountability, and the political conditions that shape the interpretation, application, and outcome of legal rules and practices of holding agents to account for wrongdoing. The key question to ask, then, is not whether international legal institutions of criminal justice, such as the ICC, are political – they inescapably are. But what kinds of politics can such institutions support, maintain, and reflect?

In his provocative study, Antony Anghie asserts that the historical development of international law cannot be divorced from its imperial and colonial context of power and ideas. Referring to Francisco de Vitoria, a "brave champion of Indian rights," Anghie notes that "the vocabulary of international law, far from being neutral, or abstract, is mired in this history of subordinating and extinguishing alien cultures."[10] Anghie shows how a critical reading of the history of international law can reveal the "underlying dynamic of racialized power and the role it plays in reproducing colonialism" in contemporary international relations and law. Racialized power disparities inform not only past colonial practices based on the civilizing mission but also contemporary political agendas of "good governance," both of which focus on "the irreproachable ambition to better human well-being." In showing how international law became an instrument of imperial domination against "Third World" peoples, Anghie argues that in the operation of contemporary international law, the "colonial history of international law is concealed even when it is reproduced."[11] Indeed, it was not until 1970 that the United Nations General

---

[9] Judith N. Shklar, *Legalism: Law, Morals, and Political Trials* (Cambridge, MA: Harvard University Press, 1964), 143–44.

[10] Antony Anghie, "Francisco de Vitoria and the colonial origins of international law," *Social and Legal Studies* 5, 3 (1996): 321–36 at 332–33. In Vitoria's work, "European practices are posited as universally applicable norms with which the colonial peoples must conform if they are to avoid sanctions and achieve full membership" (332).

[11] Antony Anghie, *Imperialism, Sovereignty and the Making of International Law* (Cambridge: Cambridge University Press, 2004), 268. See also Anghie, "Decolonizing the concept of 'good governance,'" in *Decolonizing International Relations*, Branwen Gruffydd Jones, ed. (Toronto: Rowmand and Littlefield, 2006), 109–30 at 113.

Assembly passed Resolution 2621 declaring that "the continuation of colonialism in all its forms and manifestations is *a crime*"
(Article 1).[12]

Although the legitimacy of colonialism, based on a civilizing rationale, has been formally repudiated in international law, and contemporary international society consists of formally equal sovereign states,
in reality, international relations continue to be marked by vast disparities in power that inhere in a socially stratified, hierarchical international order.[13] These disparities and hierarchies matter especially
to understanding and evaluating the quality, scope, nature, and function of regimes of punishment that have developed in international
and transnational relations. Danielle Allen has noted that "the practice of producing and executing punitive judgments rests on a society's
conceptualization of authority and desert."[14] In contemporary international relations, the problem of establishing authority beyond borders
in a world of formally sovereign states leads to the charge that any settling of accounts between states is better characterized as "victor's justice." Furthermore, recognition of the reproduced structural injustices
that continue to ground hierarchical international society calls into
question the desert-basis of international institutions of accountability.

The International Court of Justice (ICJ) is a legal institution that
aims to settle conflicts between states based on international law,
including holding states accountable for violating their obligations
under international law. The ICJ, however, cannot compel states to submit their disputes to the Court, or enforce compliance with the Court's
judgments, so in practice, states may escape international legal responsibility for violations of international law. For example, in the June
1987 ICJ judgment of the case between Nicaragua and the US, the
ICJ ruled that the US was under an obligation to make reparation to
Nicaragua for breaches of the international legal principles of nonuse
of force and nonintervention, as well as aspects of humanitarian

---

[12] Resolution 2621 (XXV), "Programme of action for the full implementation of
the Declaration on the Granting of Independence to Colonial Countries and
Peoples," see https://documents-dds-ny.un.org/doc/RESOLUTION/GEN/NR0/
348/86/IMG/NR034886.pdf?OpenElement.

[13] See Vincent Pouliot, *International Pecking Orders: The Politics and Practice of
Multilateral Diplomacy* (Cambridge: Cambridge University Press, 2016). Social
stratification also marks global civil society.

[14] Allen, *The World of Prometheus: The Politics of Punishing in Democratic
Athens*, xi.

law.[15] The US, however, remained of the view that the ICJ was without jurisdiction and that the Nicaraguan application to the Court was inadmissible.[16]

The development of interstate human rights courts in the latter half of the twentieth century means that international legal justice has, in addition to facilitating the settlement of interstate disputes, moved toward adjudicating state accountability for violations of human rights and humanitarian law.[17] Following the ad hoc International Criminal Tribunal for the former Yugoslavia (1993) and the International Criminal Tribunal for Rwanda (1994), the establishment of the International Criminal Court (ICC) in 2002 can be viewed as another example of the increased standing of individuals in international law, and international legal recognition of the importance of obligations to respect basic humanitarian and human rights law.[18] As a novel international institution of criminal law and justice, the ICC pursues accountability of individual persons for their role in producing genocide, war crimes, and crimes against humanity. By holding individual perpetrators accountable for such serious violations of humanitarian law, the ICC seeks to contribute to deterring or preventing future violations, delivering justice by upholding the rule of law, and promoting societal reconciliation.[19]

[15] The case pertained to the US's involvement in mining Nicaragua ports and waters without warning or notifying Nicaragua and in supporting the *contras*, a mercenary rebel force, which conducted military and paramilitary activity in and around Nicaragua. See www.icj-cij.org/docket/files/70/6505.pdf.

[16] www.icj-cij.org/docket/files/70/10081.pdf. In September 1991, Nicaragua renounced all further right of action based on the case and requested a discontinuance of the proceedings. The case was then removed from the Court's list. See www.icj-cij.org/docket/files/70/10231.pdf.

[17] Regional human rights courts, such as the European Court of Human Rights and the Inter-American Court of Human Rights, have developed into authoritative legal systems that can order legally binding judgments.

[18] There are also hybrid criminal courts, which are mixtures of domestic and international criminal legal processes and institutions that try particular cases, including in East Timor, Sierra Leone, Kosovo, and Cambodia. See Laura A. Dickinson, "The promise of hybrid courts," *The American Journal of International Law* 97, 2 (2003): 295–310. The African Union also supported the institution of a court in Senegal to try the ex-ruler of Chad, Hissene Habre, for crimes against humanity committed between 1982 and 1990. He was convicted by the court at the end of May 2016. See *BBC News*, "Hissene Habre: Chad's ex-ruler convicted of crimes against humanity," May 30, 2016.

[19] The Preamble to the *Rome Statute of the International Criminal Court*, July 17, 1998, UN Doc. A/CONF. 183/9, 2187 UNTS 90, reprinted in *International*

Since its inception, however, enduring structural disparities between states have raised the question of whether the International Criminal Court risks becoming an International *Colonial* Court,[20] or an instrument for already dominant states to teach manners to the weak and marginalized, while remaining largely immune to such judgments in their own cases. Significantly, although three of the five permanent members of the United Nations Security Council (UNSC) – the US, Russia and China – have not themselves signed or ratified the Rome Statute, the UN Security Council has referred to the ICC situations in two countries that have not signed the Rome Statute.[21]

As of the start of 2017, the Office of the Prosecutor of the ICC had twenty-four cases in ten "situations." Four States Parties to the Rome Statute – Uganda, the Democratic Republic of the Congo, the Central African Republic, and Mali – have referred situations occurring on their own territories to the Court. Pretrial chambers granted the prosecution authorization to open an investigation proprio motu in the situation of Kenya (2010), Côte d'Ivoire (2011), and in and around South Ossetia, Georgia, between July 1 and October 10, 2008 (2016). All but one of the situations – Georgia – are located on the African continent. To date, since 2002, the ICC has six individuals in custody and thirteen individuals at large. In terms of judgment, as of February 2017, the ICC has made nine convictions and one acquittal.[22]

In response to several indictments, including against the president of Sudan, Omar al-Bashir, on two counts of war crimes, five counts of crimes against humanity, and three counts of genocide, Sudanese government representatives have accused the ICC and UN Security Council of basing justice on "exploitation of crises in developing countries and bargaining among major Powers," and argued that the UNSC resolution "exposed the fact that the ICC was intended for developing and weak countries and was a tool to exercise cultural superiority."[23]

Legal Materials 37, 5 (1998): 1002, italics mine. See also United Nations, *Rome Statute of the ICC Overview*, www.un.org/law/icc/general/overview.htm.

[20] Mwangi S. Kimenyi, "Can the International Criminal Court play fair in Africa?," *Africa in Focus*, Brookings Institute, October 17, 2013.

[21] The UN Security Council has referred the situation in Darfur, Sudan, and the situation in Libya – both non-States Parties.

[22] www.icc-cpi.int/. The 2016 budget for the ICC was €130.67 million. The Court cost US$1 billion in its first thirteen years of existence.

[23] UNSC Resolution 1593 (2005), adopted by vote of eleven in favor to none against, with four abstentions (Algeria, Brazil, China, US), March 31, 2005,

Although a self-serving response by the Sudanese government, it does highlight the fact that in current global political conditions, the ICC is a nonuniversal institution of criminal justice, incapable of holding the most potentially egregious violators to account, given the veto powers of members of the UN Security Council, which can block prosecutions. In February 2016, at a meeting of the African Union, member states backed a Kenyan proposal to study withdrawal from the ICC. Although not a binding decision on member states, the move indicates a perception among African elites that the Court has unfairly targeted Africans for prosecution.[24] A major test for the ICC, in terms of its ability to promote a global rule of law through a universalized and impartial system of international criminal justice, will be whether it can hold the world's most powerful to account.[25]

The instrumentalization of institutions of accountability by dominant states to buttress the political status quo is not confined to the level of international politics. Despite Sudan's protests about victimization by "major powers," some of the other situations before the Court indicate that weak states may also attempt to exploit the ICC for their own advantage in domestic power disputes.[26] Somewhat unexpectedly, three of the current cases were self-referrals from the African continent, where the ruling government in question referred its own conflict to the ICC. For example, the Ugandan government's self-referral has led to indictments against key leaders of the rebel Lord's Resistance Army (LRA) – the first warrants to be issued by the ICC in October 2005. Mark Drumbl has noted, however, that the Ugandan government was itself involved in committing atrocities. Bringing in the ICC thus becomes one strategy that ruling governments can employ to "consolidate power and avoid enfranchising the policy preferences of

www.un.org/News/Press/docs/2005/sc8351.doc.htm. For a fuller discussion, see Lu, "The politics of legal accountability and genocide prevention."

[24] *The Guardian*, "African Union members back Kenyan plan to leave ICC," February 1, 2016. Under new political leadership, Gambia canceled its intended withdrawal from the ICC in February 2017. See Merrit Kennedy, "Under new leader, Gambia cancels withdrawal from International Criminal Court," *National Public Radio*, February 14, 2017.

[25] See William A. Schabas, "The banality of international justice," *Journal of International Criminal Justice* 11, 3 (2013): 545–51.

[26] See Sarah Nouwen and Wouter Werner, "Doing justice to the political: the International Criminal Court in Uganda and Sudan," *European Journal of International Law* 21, 4 (2010): 941–65.

afflicted local populations."[27] As Paola Gaeta has put it, "by request-ing ICC intervention, that state could be using the Court as a politi-cal weapon in the hope that its intervention could assist it in achiev-ing its domestic political and military aims."[28] This use of the Court becomes apparent in situations where the cooperation of governments with the investigations of the ICC is limited to the pursuit of cases against rebel or antigovernment factions. Given that self-referring gov-ernments such as Uganda are themselves parties to the political vio-lence and conflict, self-referral can undermine the actual and perceived impartiality of the ICC. As Drumbl observes, "in local eyes, the fact that the ICC was invited by the Ugandan government spoils its putative impartiality."[29]

Retributive and expressivist theories of punishment posit a back-ground condition of largely law-abiding members of a community of shared values; punishment is a debt owed by the offender to the law-abiding community, or punishment expresses the moral censure of a community bound by shared values. In conditions of political catastrophe such as civil war, state repression, or collapse, however, there is no unified community of shared values or no ideally lawful political community. States embroiled in ongoing violent political con-flicts and marked by severely contested or corrupted political author-ity structures thus lack the authority to punish in the name of com-munity, on retributive or expressivist grounds. For one party involved in an ongoing conflict to utilize the apparatus of international crim-inal justice in such conditions amounts to waging war by legalistic means.

Indeed, abolitionists of punishment are critical of the concept of "crime" and prefer to view many crimes as indications of "conflict" between members in a community. Procedurally, abolitionists favor civil law's dispute resolution mechanisms as ways to resolve "crime" rather than criminal law's system of adversarial trials that determine guilt and lead to the incarceration of individuals. Institutionally, abo-litionists are also concerned that the affected parties or communi-ties own the process of redress and conflict resolution, rather than

---

[27] Mark A. Drumbl, *Atrocity, Punishment, and International Law* (Cambridge: Cambridge University Press, 2007), 144–46.

[28] Paola Gaeta, "Is the practice of 'self-referrals' a sound start for the ICC?," *Journal of International Criminal Justice* 2, 4 (2004): 949–52 at 952.

[29] Drumbl, *Atrocity, Punishment, and International Law*, 145.

professionalized institutions such as criminal courts. Finally, abolition-ists emphasize that the purpose or end of responding to conflicts should not be "just deserts" but reconciliation, involving the restoration of vic-tims and the rehabilitation of offenders to the community.[30] Abolition-ist Herman Bianchi has located the European origins of the criminal justice system and the role of the prosecutor in the medieval Inquisi-tion. Criminalizing heretics had a "stigmatizing power" that enabled the church to defeat dissidents and inflict infernal punishments on them. Bianchi makes the striking claim that in militating against con-flict resolution, "criminal law is like war."[31]

The ICC represents the approach of international criminal law and justice, which presupposes a fairly well-ordered and lawful interna-tional community with legitimate authority to punish. An alternative strategy to international criminal law is international conflict reso-lution, which presupposes a fairly divided or socially stratified inter-national community, whose institutions cannot presuppose universal legitimate authority but must operate in ways that avoid reproducing entrenched status hierarchies and that promote more positive struc-tural transformations of international order. Refraining from using the stigmatizing power of criminalizing political enemies, negotiating a peace settlement between warring parties, giving rebel groups a share in political power, providing amnesties, focusing on victim rehabilita-tion rather than the punishment of perpetrators, and so on, may all be crucial to changing catastrophic political conditions into minimally tolerable or decent ones. The application of international criminal law, however, is not foreclosed by adopting a conflict resolution approach. Indeed, successful conflict resolution may ultimately serve to establish the necessary international and domestic political conditions and struc-tures under which the principles of corrective and retributive justice may become more morally meaningful and operational.

---

[30] Duff and Garland, *A Reader on Punishment*, 333. For a vivid portrayal of how the operation of criminal justice favored by the modern bureaucratic state can militate against local needs for more conciliatory conflict resolution, see Zhang Yimou's film about a peasant woman's case against a village chief, *QiuJu Goes to Court* (China/Hongkong: Sony Pictures, 1992).

[31] Herman Bianchi and R. van Swaaningen, *Abolitionism: Towards a Non-Repressive Approach to Crime* (1986), 113–26; reprinted as Bianchi, "Abolition: assensus and sanctuary," in Duff and Garland, *A Reader on Punishment*, 336–51 at 336 and 338.

III Individual Responsibility for Structured Wrongs

The International Criminal Court holds individual persons accountable, making them liable to punishment and paying reparations, for
their contribution to internationally wrongful acts, including genocide, war crimes, and crimes against humanity. Bronwyn Leebaw has
noted that criminal tribunals attempt to depoliticize conflict by placing
blame on individuals.[32] Social and political catastrophes that culminate
in atrocities, however, are practically never produced by individuals
acting alone. As Judith Shklar described the crimes of the National
Socialists in Germany that produced World War II and the Holocaust, "one is not dealing here with a handful of deviants, but with a
social movement, and this makes the relationship between the causes of
and responsibility for these acts exceptionally problematic."[33] Shklar's
account of the political catastrophe of National Socialism highlights
the role of social structures that mediate and organize the agency of
many individuals.

We can make a broad distinction between two different categories
of social structures, and the injustices to which they may give rise. One
may be more appropriately called *structured* injustices, where wrongful acts or objectionable outcomes committed or produced by individuals can be attributed to their roles within corporate agents or highly
organized and/or purposive social groups.[34] Individuals who enact
repressive policies in their capacity as state leaders or functionaries may
be considered morally responsible for participating in *structured* injustices. So may individuals who jointly share a goal and pursue it through
collective action, even if their structured cooperation does not amount
to a corporate agent.[35] For political leaders, individual criminal liability may be based on their role as leaders of a corporate agent responsible for internationally wrongful conduct, or on their contribution to
a joint criminal enterprise or common purpose. Military leaders may

---

[32] Bronwyn Leebaw, *Judging State-Sponsored Violence, Imagining Political Change* (Cambridge: Cambridge University Press, 2011).

[33] Shklar, *Legalism*, 192.

[34] Tracy Isaacs distinguishes between "organizations and goal-oriented collectives," which nevertheless "share a common feature in virtue of which they have agency; a collective intentional structure that gives rise to collective intention and collective action." See Tracy Isaacs, *Moral Responsibility in Collective Contexts* (Oxford: Oxford University Press, 2011), 27.

[35] Isaac's example is the perpetrators of the 1994 Rwandan genocide.

also bear liability based on their superior responsibility for crimes committed by their subordinates. More generally, forms of international criminal responsibility include direct and indirect perpetration, coperpetration, instigation, ordering, soliciting, inducing, planning, aiding and abetting, and complicity in the commission of recognized crimes in international law.[36] Membership in a culpable corporate agent, such as a state, can also lead to reparative liabilities for individual members, through their participation in a structured injustice.[37]

Another form may be called *structural injustice*, consisting of unintended, generalized, or impersonal harms or wrongs that result from social structural processes in which many individuals and corporate agents may participate. Tracy Isaacs has characterized such injustices as "wrongful social practice" and includes among them "racist, sexist, homophobic, and other discriminatory practices that perpetuate oppression or lead to the exploitation of groups of people."[38] Colonial racialized ideologies of civilization and good governance, for example, constitute structural injustices that may distort the social relations between and within individuals, nations, and states. Such structural injustices may produce intentional interactional wrongs, such as the imposition of colonial rule, as well as unintentional harms, such as the devaluation and marginalization of indigenous systems of knowledge.

How does taking structures into account affect how we should think about individual responsibility and accountability for wrongdoing? By taking structures into account, I do not mean to endorse the version of structuralism in which "social-structural regularities cause individuals to act by overriding their intentional dispositions."[39] If the overriding thesis (collectivism) were correct, then individuals would be functionaries but not agents capable of moral agency and responsibility.

---

[36] See Elies van Sliedregt, *Individual Criminal Responsibility in International Law* (Oxford: Oxford University Press, 2012).

[37] This topic is covered in Chapters 7 and 8.

[38] Isaacs, *Moral Responsibility in Collective Contexts*, 157. Iris Marion Young's account of structural injustice involves examining how the actions of many contribute "to structural processes that produce vulnerabilities to deprivation and domination for some people who find themselves in certain positions with limited options compared to others." See Young, *Responsibility for Justice* (Oxford: Oxford University Press, 2011), 73.

[39] William Clare Roberts, "Who's afraid of structuralism? Prospects for structuralist explanation in the social sciences," unpublished manuscript with the author.

The validity of structural causal explanations does not undermine the workings of normal human intentional psychology.[40] At the same time, assessing individual moral responsibility (and especially accountability) for wrongful acts or objectionable outcomes becomes more complicated when the structured and structural contexts of individual agency are taken into account. As Iris Marion Young has observed, what usually "counts as a wrong for which we seek a perpetrator and for which he or she might be required to compensate, is something we generally conceive as a deviation from a baseline."[41] This standard model of wrongdoing assumes a just or morally acceptable baseline, against which individuals' wrongful actions constitute aberrations. But in cases of structured or structural injustice, individuals' wrongful actions typically conform to, rather than deviate from, a morally defective baseline.

In this section, I explore how to think about individuals' participation in wrongful acts or objectionable outcomes produced through their participation in structured injustices, specifically those injustices arising from the corporate agency of a political community organized in the form of a state.[42] Individual members may be connected to these wrongs in different ways. An individual or group of individuals in a position of authority and power in the state may be directly responsible for turning the state as a corporate agent into a structure/agent of injustice. For example, the Japanese annexation and colonization of Korea in 1910 resulted from the coordinated and intentional policies of the Japanese government. Not only can responsibility for this act be attributed to the Japanese state as a corporate agent, individual members of the executive or government may each jointly share responsibility for this corporate act.[43] Individual members of the Japanese government of that time may each and jointly also bear moral responsibility for their state's colonial and imperial policies that culminated

---

[40] In making this argument, Roberts criticizes the conflation of structuralism with collectivism in Philip Pettit, *The Common Mind: An Essay on Psychology, Society and Politics* (Oxford: Oxford University Press, 1993).

[41] Iris Marion Young, "Responsibility and global justice: a social connection model," *Social Philosophy and Policy* 23 (2006): 102–30 at 120.

[42] How to think about responsibility for structural injustices is the focus of the rest of this book.

[43] According to List and Pettit, "group agents may nest within one another: the members of a larger entity like the state may also form smaller group agents like the executive." See Christian List and Philip Pettit, *Group Agency: The Possibility, Design and Status of Corporate Agents* (Oxford: Oxford University Press, 2011), 40.

in fifteen years of war and devastation in Asia and the Pacific (1931–1945). Individuals who participate intentionally and in a coordinated manner to commit an act share responsibility for that act.[44]

Participating in structured injustices, such as fighting in an unjust war of conquest and annexation as a member of a state's military apparatus, raises two complicated types of questions about individual responsibility: (1) Can individuals be morally responsible, and accountable, for the acts of others, or acts produced by joint activity with others?[45] (2) If responsibility is attributable to the state as a corporate agent, are all members of the state (and not just the executive) liable for the acts (or the consequences of acts) that are done in their collective name?[46]

Responsibility is a complex and "slippery" concept.[47] Most theorists of responsibility agree that to hold an agent responsible in a moral sense is to make an assessment of blame or praise about an agent. "Whodunit" mysteries are not literally about who caused a death in a physical, empirical sense but who is guilty or deserves blame for causing a wrongful death. There are different ways in which we may judge an agent responsible in the blameworthy, and not just (or necessarily causal), sense. First, an agent's responsibility can be based on an assessment of her character, her virtues or vices. For example, although it is Othello who kills Desdemona in Shakespeare's tragedy, one may plausibly argue that Iago is the most blameworthy character, whose malicious manipulations of Othello's insecurities and vulnerabilities deserves the audience's indignation.[48] We may judge (think and hold) Iago morally responsible for Desdemona's death even though no

---

[44] See Christopher Kutz, *Complicity: Ethics and Law for a Collective Age* (Cambridge: Cambridge University Press, 2000). See also Isaacs's account of moral responsibility for joint intentional agency, *Moral Responsibility in Collective Contexts*.

[45] Shane Darcy, *Collective Responsibility and Accountability under International Law* (Leiden: Transnational, 2007).

[46] See John M. Parrish, "Collective responsibility and the state," *International Theory* 1, 1 (2009): 119–54; Anna Stilz, "Collective responsibility and the state," *The Journal of Political Philosophy* 19, 2 (2011): 190–208; Richard Vernon, "Punishing collectives: states or nations?," in *Accountability for Collective Wrongdoing*, Tracy Isaacs and Richard Vernon, eds. (Cambridge: Cambridge University Press, 2011), 287–306.

[47] See David Miller, "Distributing responsibilities," *The Journal of Political Philosophy* 9, 4 (2001): 453–71 at 455.

[48] William Shakespeare, *The Tragedy of Othello* (New York: Signet Classics, 1998).

court would succeed in holding him accountable or criminally liable for it.

Second, agents typically acquire responsibility and are held accountable for what they do (or fail to do), in particular for their voluntary (uncoerced) and intentional acts. We praise agents when we consider their actions (or omissions) to be good and right, and we blame agents when we consider their actions to be bad or wrong.[49] An agent may be blameworthy in this sense, even if the motives underlying the action do not point to a blameworthy character trait. To take an example of corporate agential responsibility, although the US was in a just war against Imperial Japan, and although its objectives to save lives and end the war in the Pacific were good ones, one may still evaluate the US fire bombings of Tokyo and atomic bombings of Hiroshima and Nagasaki in 1945 to be wrongful acts that violated the laws of war, for which the US deserves, not moral praise, but blame.

Third, in addition to being based on an agent's character and acts, responsibility may also be based on the consequences of agents' actions. For David Miller, an agent is "outcome responsible" when she is "responsible for the consequences of her action, and the resulting benefits and burdens should fall to her, including liability to compensate harms that befall others." Outcome responsibility is distinct in that an agent may not be blameworthy in a morally culpable way for the outcome: "outcome responsibility does not require attribution of moral fault to agent." While moral culpability is based on an assessment of the agent's intentions and mental state in committing an act, outcome responsibility is based on the reasonably foreseeable consequences of an agent's uncoerced acts.[50]

When agents are found to be responsible in a morally relevant sense, the question of what consequences or social responses should flow from that fact arises. Christian List and Philip Pettit argue that group agents can be held responsible in the same way as individual agents, but

---

[49] See List and Pettit, *Group Agency*, 154.
[50] Miller gives the example of the clumsy person who, although not morally responsible, is outcome responsible for the items he breaks. Outcome responsibility is based on some causal connection between an agent's acts and the outcome. See David Miller, "Holding nations responsible," *Ethics* 114, 2 (2004): 240–68 at 246. Miller also discusses other grounds on which agents may incur "remedial responsibility" to put a "bad situation right" that are not based on an agent's direct connection (in terms of their causal, moral or outcome responsibility) to the bad situation. See Miller, "Distributing responsibilities."

"how they can be best regulated, penally or instrumentally," is a separate question.[51] This means that the question of moral responsibility is distinct from questions of regulation. Questions of moral responsibility have to do with the blameworthiness of an agent's character, (intentional and uncoerced) actions, or the consequences of such actions. Questions of accountability have to do with the appropriateness of various methods of holding agents accountable in light of justified social aims or ends.

To hold an agent accountable, then, is to assign blameworthiness or praise to an agent (usually for his or her actions or omissions), with a view to assessing the appropriateness of punishing or rewarding the agent, or some other measure that would be effective in regulating an agent's conduct. As Christopher Kutz has explained, standard notions of individual moral agency and accountability are based on three principles, which he terms "the individual difference, control and autonomy principles": "I am only accountable for a harm if something I did made a difference to its occurrence"; "I am only accountable for events over which I have control, and whose occurrence I could have prevented"; and "I am not accountable for the harm another agent causes, unless I have induced or coerced that agent into performing an act."[52] Iris Marion Young understands this account as the liability model of responsibility, used in legal and moral reasoning about responsibility, "for the purposes of sanctioning, punishing, or exacting compensation or redress" from liable parties.[53]

How does the structured nature of individual acts (or omissions), involving coordinated and joint activity with others, affect the questions of individual responsibility and accountability for wrongdoing? The notion that individuals may be responsible for the actions of others is quite commonplace. As members of families, social groups, nations, states, religious orders, and humanity, individuals typically *feel* responsible for the acts of others. If my estranged family relative commits a crime and harms others, I may still feel ashamed and a special responsibility, not only to help him do the right thing, but also to express my disapproval of his actions – by helping his victims, for example – especially if he does not choose to do the right thing. As Farid Abdel-Nour has observed, individuals may incur national responsibility "for actions performed by others (dead or alive)" by virtue of imaginative

---

[51] Ibid., 157.   [52] Kutz, *Complicity*, 3.
[53] Young, *Responsibility for Justice*, 98 and 104.

identification with past acts and achievements of conationals, and feeling shame or pride for the acts and achievements of their nation.[54] Although taking one's sense of national belonging seriously makes one a candidate for incurring national responsibility, including an appropriate sense of shame for one's nation's morally objectionable acts and achievements, Abdel-Nour also makes it clear that such national responsibility "cannot meaningfully lead to punishment."[55] Indeed, one bedrock principle of individual accountability is that "I am not accountable for the harm another agent causes, unless I have induced or coerced that agent into performing an act."[56] Individuals are accountable for their direct or otherwise culpable contribution to a wrong or harm. To hold individuals liable for the acts of others violates a principle of criminal law: *nulla poena sine culpa*.[57]

In the context of political catastrophes, however, the development of international criminal law has led to prosecutorial strategies that make individuals not only responsible but also criminally liable for the acts of others. In one form, individuals who are superiors in a chain of command may incur liability for the wrongful acts of their subordinates that they failed (by culpable omissions) to prevent, repress, or punish. Superiors may not just be military commanders but also civilian political leaders. In the Tokyo Trial, for example, the foreign minister of the Japanese Imperial cabinet, Hirota Koki, was given the death penalty, based on the concept of cabinet responsibility, for the gross maltreatment of prisoners of war under the care of the Japanese military:

A member of a Cabinet which collectively, as one of the principal organs of the Government, is responsible for the care of prisoners is not absolved from responsibility if, having knowledge of the commission of the crimes in the sense already discussed, and omitting or failing to secure the taking of measures to prevent the commission of such crimes in the future, he elects to continue as a member of the Cabinet.[58]

---

[54] Farid Abdel-Nour, "National responsibility," *Political Theory* 31, 5 (2003): 693–719 at 694.

[55] Ibid., 703.   [56] Kutz, *Complicity*, 3.

[57] Darcy, *Collective Responsibility and Accountability under International Law*, 198. As Darcy notes, shared responsibility (where individuals have each intentionally participated in committing an act) is distinct from collective responsibility (where individuals may not have made any culpable contribution to the commission of an act).

[58] Quoted in Yuma Totani, *The Tokyo War Crimes Trial: The Pursuit of Justice in the Wake of World War II* (Cambridge, MA: Harvard University Press, 2008), 139.

A "civilian with a respectable professional background," Koki's membership in the Japanese Imperial war cabinet was enough to establish his legal culpability under the cabinet/superior responsibility doctrine, even though the treatment of prisoners of war was not part of his cabinet portfolio. The Tokyo Trial's application of the superior responsibility doctrine, however, seems to have been an exception; currently, the doctrine has been interpreted much more restrictively, so that superiors must exhibit a guilty intention, in having knowledge of the particular details of the offense, but culpably omitting to exercise their effective control over subordinates to prevent the offense, and failing in their duty to prevent, repress, or punish subordinates for the offense.

The Charter of the International Military Tribunal for the trial and punishment of major war criminals from defeated states in World War II also included a provision to hold individuals accountable for the acts of others: "Leaders, organizers, instigators and accomplices participating in the formulation or execution of a common plan or conspiracy to commit any of the foregoing crimes [including crimes against the peace, war crimes and crimes against humanity] *are responsible for all acts performed by any persons* in execution of such plan."[59] In addition to cabinet responsibility and the superior responsibility doctrine, individuals participating in a joint criminal enterprise or a common plan become liable for the acts of other participants, even if those acts were not expressly part of the common plan.[60]

Mark Osiel has pointed to the problematic judgments of legal guilt produced by these prosecutorial strategies: the common enterprise participation law makes the conviction of high-level perpetrators too easy, while current interpretations of the doctrine of superior responsibility make it too difficult. These problems reveal the difficulty of making judgments about individual guilt, responsibility, and accountability in the context of structured injustices.[61] While legal judgment of

---

[59] *Charter of the International Military Tribunal*, Article 6, Nuremberg Trial Proceedings, vol. 1, online at: http://avalon.law.yale.edu/imt/imtconst.asp#sec1, emphasis mine.

[60] See Darcy, *Collective Responsibility and Accountability under International Law*, on the reliance on "joint criminal enterprise" in prosecutions of International Criminal Tribunal for the former Yugoslavia (227–37).

[61] For a thorough analysis of how international law attributes criminal liability to individuals, and the array of possible defenses, see Elies van Sliedregt, *Individual Criminal Responsibility in International Law*.

individual accountability should track individual responsibility in a plausible and legitimate way, the enterprise has difficulty assessing individual responsibility for structured wrongs that involve organized and joint activity with many others, at the same time that the gravity of the wrongs motivates an urgent necessity to hold someone accountable for the sake of social aims such as effective deterrence, prevention of future conflict, and social peace.[62] For these reasons, historically, the practice of punishing individuals for political catastrophes can become a form of scapegoating, unfairly burdening individual agents with a greater share of responsibility than warranted, or a form of whitewash that lets other more culpable agents off the moral hook or obscures deeper institutional and structural failings.

Such concerns about the potential dysfunctions of institutions of settling accounts are worrisome because the concept of "just deserts" that grounds retributive justice is sensitive to nonideal background conditions of extreme inequity or pervasive structural injustice that would undermine any notion of individual desert. Jeffrie Murphy's exposition of Marx's critique of punishment is particularly instructive. Murphy notes that the picture of the criminal in retributive theory is of "an evil person who, of his own free will, intentionally acts against those just rules of society which he knows, as a rational man, benefit everyone including himself."[63] A Marxist analysis of crime, however, views the criminal as having ordinary, socially conditioned motivations rather than being aberrantly evil, and as "alienated" by oppressive structural conditions rather than enabled by them to be an autonomous agent.[64] More generally, while retributive theory views institutions of punishment as correlates of corrective justice, a sociological approach may lead to a view of institutions of punishment themselves as "structural injustices" that target the politically or socially weak or

---

[62] Mark Osiel, *Making Sense of Mass Atrocity* (Cambridge: Cambridge University Press, 2009), 24.

[63] J. G. Murphy, "Marxism and retribution," *Philosophy and Public Affairs* 2 (1973): 217–43. Reprinted in Duff and Garland, *A Reader on Punishment*, 44–70 at 64.

[64] In using a Marxist approach to exemplify a structural analysis of punishment, I do not mean to reduce all criminality to their economic bases. Rather, I mean to highlight Marx's insight about the importance of the social structures and conditions that motivate crime, and the implications of structural alienation for theories of accountability that presuppose autonomy.

vulnerable.[65] In studies of crime and punishment within liberal democracies, "a massive research literature ... traces the operation of bias, of discrimination of [sic] grounds of race, gender, or social class, in the official treatment of suspects and offenders from disadvantaged or less powerful sections of the community."[66] The biased administration of international criminal justice in a nonideal context of vast institutionalized disparities among states should be a source of deep concern to anyone who seeks to ground the ICC on principles of retributive justice. If retributivism merely provides a "transcendental sanction" to the status quo,[67] it may perversely become a handmaiden to the perpetuation of structurally unjust social hierarchies within states, as well as between states in contemporary world politics.

If we understand war crimes, genocide, and crimes against humanity not only as individual, corporate, or collective acts but as outcomes of agents operating within fundamentally unjust political and social structures, different accounts of moral and political responsibility need to be developed that go beyond the individual liability model of responsibility associated with theories of retributive justice and the work of international criminal tribunals. If structural injustices are central to the production of political catastrophes, then confining practices of accountability and responsibility to the individual "crime-and-punishment" model will be wholly inadequate.

Individual Responsibility and Liability Derived from Corporate Wrongdoing

Another set of questions about individual responsibility for structured injustices relates to how individuals stand in relation to the accountability of corporate agents. If responsibility is attributable to the state

---

[65] Bernard Harrison, "Violence and the rule of law," in *Violence*, Jerome A. Shaffer, ed. (New York: McKay, 1971), 139–76. See also Murphy, "Marxism and retribution," 50.

[66] Duff and Garland, "Introduction: thinking about punishment," in *A Reader on Punishment*, 26. According to the Office of the Correctional Investigator of Canada, the "incarceration rate for Aboriginal adults in Canada is estimated to be ten times higher than the incarceration rate of non-Aboriginal adults." See www.oci-bec.gc.ca/cnt/rpt/oth-aut/oth-aut20121022info-eng.aspx.

[67] Marx quoted in Murphy, "Marxism and retribution," 47.

as a corporate agent, are all members of the state (and not just the executive) liable for the acts (or the consequences of acts) that are done in their collective name?[68] As Anna Stilz has noted, "it makes sense to treat states as moral persons, since they are incorporated groups with an internal constitution that allows them to form collective intentions, grasp moral reasons, exercise deliberative control, and act voluntarily." At the same time, not all states are structured in the same ways, thus Stilz concludes that there should be "multiple principles for distributing state responsibility, according to the type of political constitution at stake."[69] Both Stilz and John Parrish argue that members of democratic states bear more responsibility than citizens of nondemocratic states for state wrongdoing.[70]

It should be noted that in these discussions of liability for state corporate wrongdoing, no theorist justifies any form of violent collective punishment on the members of a perpetrator state, although such practices were quite common in intergroup and international relations, especially in contexts of war, where hostage takings and reprisals against innocent civilians were regular occurrences.[71] In contexts of war, accountability measures against defeated states have taken the forms of regime change, occupation, territorial transfers, colonial dispossession, military and economic incapacitation, and reparations for war damages. I discuss state responsibility for reparations in more detail in Chapter 7. For now, one may note that accountability for corporate wrongdoing in contemporary international law and practice is limited partly by the individual and collective interests of its members. Reparations thus should not be conceived or justified as punitive measures against the population of a culpable state. Partly, this restriction is based on some acknowledgment that the populations necessarily

---

[68] For pioneering work on this theme, see Peter A. French, *Collective and Corporate Responsibility* (New York: Columbia University Press, 1984); Toni Erskine, ed., *Can Institutions Have Responsibilities? Collective Moral Agency and International Relations* (New York: Palgrave Macmillan, 2003); and Toni Erskine, "Kicking bodies and damning souls: the danger of harming 'innocent' individuals while punishing delinquent states," in *Accountability for Collective Wrongdoing*, Isaacs and Vernon, eds. (New York: Cambridge University Press, 2011), 261–86.

[69] Stilz, "Collective responsibility and the state," 19.

[70] See Parrish, "Collective responsibility and the state."

[71] See the first half of Darcy, *Collective Responsibility and Accountability under International Law*.

bearing the reparative burden of states typically are largely "morally blameless."[72] Even in the case of democratic regimes, accountability in the form of punishment for wrongful state conduct should be limited to individual political and military leaders, although the responsibility to pay for damages to others resulting from such conduct becomes a liability of the population, along with the political responsibility for any related institutional and structural reforms. Such liability is thus not based on a collectivized notion of moral responsibility and, whatever the regime type, nothing may justify a level of material reparations that would incapacitate a state from fulfilling its domestic obligations of ensuring domestic security, the effective administration of justice, the provision of a basic and universal level of health care and education, and the maintenance of functional and sustainable economic structures.[73]

If it is true that most individual members of a culpable nondemocratic state are morally blameless, however, what can justify the distribution of the state's liability to them? One interesting answer to explore would be whether holding citizens of nondemocratic states responsible for "their" state's wrongdoing can serve a "developmental rationale." As List and Pettit explain, "by finding the group responsible, we make clear to members that unless they develop routines for keeping their government or episcopacy in check, they will share in member responsibility for what is done by the group and may also have a negative form of enactor responsibility for allowing it to be done . . . We are naturally disposed to ascribe responsibility, it appears, not just to fully responsible agents but also to 'responsibilizable' entities; not just to agents that are already fit to be held responsible but also to entities that are capable of being made fit to be held responsible."[74] In contrast, however, one might argue that the subjects of such a regime are as much victims as the external parties who suffer from the state's culpable conduct. From this point of view, the liabilities of the culpable state may be more appropriately transferred to the society of states, which may

---

[72] James Crawford and Jeremy Watkins, "International responsibility," in *The Philosophy of International Law*, Samantha Besson and John Tasioulas, eds. (Oxford: Oxford University Press, 2010), 283–98 at 290.

[73] See also Avia Pasternak, "Limiting states' corporate responsibility," *The Journal of Political Philosophy* 21, 4 (2013): 361–81; and Avia Pasternak, "Sharing the costs of political injustices," *Politics, Philosophy and Economics* 10, 2 (2011): 188–210.

[74] List and Pettit, *Group Agency*, 168–69.

have different reparative responsibilities to both the internal and external victims of such regimes.

IV Conclusion

Settling accounts for political catastrophes through individual criminal prosecutions entails determining the guilt or innocence of individual parties, for the purpose of assigning punishment for wrongdoing and reparation for victims of wrongdoing. The political effects of such international institutions and norms of accountability on domestic processes of justice and reconciliation have, in fact, been quite varied.[75] Jelena Subotic has found that Serbia, Croatia, and Bosnia reacted to international pressures to engage in "transitional justice" measures by instrumentalizing them for "ulterior political motives: to get rid of domestic political opponents, to obtain international financial aid, or to gain admission to the European Union."[76] Depending on international and domestic social structures, practices, and conditions, interactional processes of settling accounts between agents for political catastrophe can yield outcomes that range from having some remedial effect to being largely ineffectual in establishing human rights–respecting regimes, to even having a pernicious effect on domestic political developments. In general, the historical and structural complexities of many political injustices that have yielded catastrophes require richer and more complex moral vocabularies and categories of response than either the criminal justice model of determining individual guilt and innocence, or the international law model of states' international responsibility, can provide.

The pursuit of justice, understood as a settling of accounts for political catastrophe, is a fraught task, but not all conflicts arising from such struggles are necessarily morally and politically unconstructive. If Judith Butler is right – that "disorientation" is "at the heart of moral deliberation"[77] – various institutions and practices of settling accounts can serve the useful function of unsettling and repudiating

---

[75] Thanks to Maria Popova for her assistance in developing this insight.

[76] Jelena Subotic, *Hijacked Justice: Dealing with the Past in the Balkans* (Ithaca, NY: Cornell University Press, 2009).

[77] Judith Butler, *Giving an Account of Oneself* (New York: Fordham University Press, 2005), 110.

old norms, beliefs, and justifications that led to political catastrophe.[78] In this vein, proponents of international criminal law have claimed, rather ambitiously, that criminal tribunals serve an "expressivist" function in the long term, including "the crafting of historical narratives, their authentification as truths, and their pedagogical dissemination to the public."[79] Criminal trials "can turn tragedy into a teaching moment . . . Prosecution and punishment in response to extraordinary crimes can thereby serve a broader didactic purpose that meets the interests of history and memory." At the same time, pointing to the Tokyo Trial, Mark Drumbl acknowledges that the "didactic value of international proceedings is not preordained."[80] Indeed, Jan-Werner Müller has observed that rather than stimulating probing soul searching and moral transformation, "detailed studies have demonstrated how punishment [after the Second World War] contributed to a myth of expiation and rebirth."[81] In this chapter, I have argued that practices of settling accounts that focus on individual criminal liability for political catastrophes remain highly controversial and morally problematic, mainly for structural reasons.

More fundamentally, given the structural dimensions of political catastrophes, any expressive or educative value of criminal trials will be partial and incomplete. This is so because their exclusive focus on determining individual liability for wrongdoing cannot address the issue of political responsibility for the structural dimensions of political catastrophes. Even if practices of international criminal law and justice were effective at holding individual perpetrators to account, they obscure recognition of different kinds of responsibility for structurally organized or conditioned harms and injustices. Recognizing this fact about political catastrophes ought to lead to greater humility about any expressive or didactic functions attributed to systems of criminal justice in domestic and international contexts.

A more normatively robust and comprehensive settling of accounts for political catastrophes must go beyond the reckoning of moral debts

---

[78] See also Mihaela Mihai, *Negative Emotions and Transitional Justice* (New York: Columbia University Press, 2016), who identifies the importance of "negative emotions," such as resentment and indignation, and their expression through judicial review of transitional justice bills or criminal trials, for establishing the value of respect and concern for all in democratic transitions.

[79] Drumbl, *Atrocity, Punishment and the Law*, 173.   [80] Ibid., 175.

[81] Jan-Werner Müller, ed., *Memory and Power in Post-War Europe: Studies in the Presence of the Past* (Cambridge: Cambridge University Press, 2002), 6.

between individual victims and perpetrators in a way that also avoids a descent into pathological political narratives, discourses and practices that involve collective stereotyping and vilification. Furthermore, it is the structural transformations that aim toward a more comprehensive account of structural and distributive justice in international relations that will determine whether the ICC operates effectively from a normative point of view. Contemporary violence in Africa, for example, may very well be produced by culpable agents operating in deficient social structures, but if these phenomena of flawed agents and structures are themselves at least partially a "consequence of long histories of colonial and postcolonial interaction with the West,"[82] then internationally supported institutions and practices of accountability will need to be designed in ways that do not reproduce the structural conditions that enable such wrongs. The long-term moral significance of the work of the International Criminal Court, in terms of whether it can serve retributive, deterrent, expressive, or educative functions, thus ultimately depends on great structural transformations in regional and world politics. In this way, the legitimacy and sustainability of institutions that aim to deliver justice in interactional terms depend on progress toward redressing structural injustice in world politics.

---

[82] See Tarak Barkawi and Mark Laffey, "The postcolonial moment in security studies," *Review of International Studies* 32 (2006): 329–52 at 347.

4 Agents, Structures, and Colonial Injustice[1]

During the battle, which lasted about fifty days, I did not see any women at all. I knew that as a result of (being without access to women), men's mental condition ends up declining, and that's when I realized once again the necessity of special comfort stations. This desire is the same as hunger or the need to urinate, and soldiers merely thought of comfort stations as practically the same as latrines.

– Japanese Eleventh Army Signal Corps officer, 1945[2]

I Introduction

Colonialism was officially repudiated as an international practice at the 947th plenary meeting of the United Nations General Assembly in its 1960 Declaration on the Granting of Independence to Colonial Countries and Peoples. The Declaration equated the "subjection of peoples to alien subjugation, domination and exploitation" to "a denial of fundamental human rights"; affirmed the principle of self-determination for all peoples in their political status and economic, social, and cultural development; and condemned the "standard of civilization" rationale for colonial rule by asserting that "inadequacy of political, economic, social or educational preparedness should never serve as a pretext for delaying independence."[3] This Declaration

---

[1] Over half of this chapter is a modified version of "Colonialism as structural injustice: historical responsibility and contemporary redress," *The Journal of Political Philosophy* 19, 3 (2011): 261–81. A shorter, earlier version appeared in a Korean language translation: "Colonialism as structural injustice and implications for responsibilities of repair," *The Journal of Asiatic Studies*, 53 (2010): 33–54.

[2] Quoted in Yoshiaki Yoshimi, *Comfort Women: Sexual Slavery in the Japanese Military during World War II*, trans. Suzanne O'Brien (New York: Columbia University Press, 2000), 199.

[3] United Nations, "Declaration on the granting of independence to colonial countries and peoples," Resolution 1514 of the United Nations General

constituted an official rejection by the society of states of the colonial history of international and transnational relations as it had been practiced and developed for more than four hundred years.[4]

Although over half a century has passed since the Declaration, the colonial past is still a raw and corrosive ingredient in contemporary international relations between former colonizing countries and their colonial subjects. In particular, fractious interstate politics over issues of acknowledgment and redress raise questions about historical responsibility for colonial injustice and how contemporary agents should respond to that past. Contemporary theories and politics of redress in international relations are dominated by a state-centric approach that frames all questions about historical responsibility, rectificatory justice, and political reconciliation in terms of interactions *between* former colonizer and colonized peoples or states. Daniel Butt, for example, conceives of the problem of "international" rectificatory justice to be concerned only with "justice between, not within, modern-day self-governing communities." Thus, the problem of international "historical rectification" only pertains "if the people of one modern day state have duties to persons who are members of other states."[5] Because colonialism involved states as perpetrating agents and peoples as subjects of alien domination, it is typical to "think of colonialism first and foremost as a wrong done by the colonizer to the colonized."[6]

Assembly, 1960, www.un.org/Depts/dpi/decolonization/declaration.htm. See Gerrit Gong, *The Standard of "Civilization" in International Society* (Oxford: Clarendon Press, 1984). For a more recent study that examines contemporary manifestations of imperial civilizational discourse, see Brett Bowden, *The Empire of Civilization: The Evolution of an Imperial Idea* (Chicago: University of Chicago Press, 2009).

[4] For a description of colonialism and its historical variants, based on settlement, economic and resource exploitation, and a religious or "civilizing mission," see Margaret Kohn, "Colonialism," *The Stanford Encyclopedia of Philosophy*, Spring 2014 ed., Edward N. Zalta, ed., http://plato.stanford.edu/archives/spr2014/entries/colonialism/.

[5] Daniel Butt, *Rectifying International Injustice: Principles of Compensation and Restitution between Nations* (Oxford: Oxford University Press, 2009), 23. By definition, then, Butt's theory of rectificatory justice for international historical injustices excludes any claims that indigenous peoples may make against settler colonial states or international institutions. The problematic nature of this limit is explored in more detail in Chapter 6.

[6] Lea Ypi, Robert E. Goodin, and Christian Barry, "Associative duties, global justice, and the colonies," *Philosophy and Public Affairs* 37 (2009): 103–35 at 133.

Historical forms of colonialism, of course, did entail colonizer states imposing objectionable social and political relations and conditions on those they colonized, enabling governments, militaries, corporations, churches, settler groups, as well as other social elites to engage in various forms of inequitable and oppressive acts and practices. Colonialism thus manifested in practices such as military conquest and political subjugation, extermination, enslavement and exploitation of subjugated populations, the annexation of territories, expropriation of property, resource extraction, as well as knowledge and cultural destruction.[7]

A state-centric interactional approach that focuses only on the responsibility of perpetrator states or nations, however, cannot tell the whole story about responsibility for many colonial injustices. In this chapter I explore the implications of analyzing colonial injustices in the framework of social structures at various levels that organize and mediate such injustices.[8] Like most political, social, and economic injustices that affect large groups of people, colonial injustices involved not simply wrongful acts by state perpetrators. They also relied on social and political norms, institutions and structural processes that enabled and even encouraged individual or state wrongdoing, and produced and reproduced injustice.

An interactional approach obscures the transnational structural bases of wrongful agent conduct, such as the progressive narrative that justified the establishment of colonial international order in the nineteenth century. Based on "scientific racism," nineteenth-century ideas of progress recast the chain of being according to racialized ascriptive characteristics, installing an untransferrable right to rule over "lesser" and "inferior races" by "superior races." As Barry Buzan and George Lawson have noted, "racism was not something exclusive to [Nazi

---

[7] For a compelling account of the distinctive wrong of a variety of colonialisms, including settler, commercial, and civilizing versions, as "the embodiment of an objectionable form of political relation," see Lea Ypi, "What's wrong with colonialism," *Philosophy and Public Affairs* 41, 2 (2013): 158–91.

[8] For development of the concept of structural injustice, I draw mainly from the work of Iris Marion Young, "Responsibility and global labor justice," *The Journal of Political Philosophy* 12 (2004): 365–88; "Responsibility and global justice: a social connection model," *Social Philosophy and Policy* 23 (2006): 102–30; "Taking the basic structure seriously," *Perspectives on Politics* 4 (2006): 91–97; "Structural injustice and the politics of difference," in *Contemporary Debates in Political Philosophy*, T. Christiano and J. Christman, eds. (Malden, MA: Wiley-Blackwell, 2009), 362–83. Much of this work is restated in Young, *Responsibility for Justice* (Oxford: Oxford University Press, 2011).

Germany and Imperial Japan]. It was part of a wider set of experiences and attitudes that underpinned *Western-colonial* international society."[9] The discussion of the peace settlement of Versailles in 1919 in Chapter 1 points to the importance of international law and order in producing the wider structural context for interactional colonial injustices and should lead to questions about international responsibility for redressing such injustices. In addition, structural injustices within colonized societies may also contribute to the production of colonial injustices or account for differential patterns of victimization among the colonized. Acknowledging colonialism as structural injustice does not displace assessments of individual agents' or states' liability for wrongful actions but identifies other contributory agents and structures in the production of colonial injustices and raises the question of the responsibilities of those other contributory agents, including *of international society, as well as of and among* colonized peoples.

II Legal Colonialism and International Structural Injustice

Humans are by nature political animals, according to Aristotle, meaning not only that we are social beings that need to live with others but also that we realize a distinctive human excellence through our participation in well-ordered political communities. We do not need to adopt fully Aristotle's account of human excellence or the good life to appreciate the centrality of social organization, despite imperfections, to shaping the form, range, and content of individual members' pursuits of worthy lives. In extreme cases of dysfunctional social and political organization, however, a human is "the worst of all animals."[10] Aristotle's account of the human animal reveals a simple but difficult truth about the human condition: as individuals, we cannot flourish properly or fully without a supportive social structure that can only be created and sustained through joint purposive action with others. Yet it is also through our participation in social/political structures and

---

[9] Barry Buzan and George Lawson, *The Global Transformation: History, Modernity and the Making of International Relations* (Cambridge: Cambridge University Press, 2015), 124. See also Edward Keene, *Beyond the Anarchical Society: Grotius, Colonialism and Order in World Politics* (Cambridge: Cambridge University Press, 2002), 118–24.

[10] Aristotle, *The Politics*, trans. Carnes Lord (Chicago: University of Chicago Press, 1984), 1253a32–3. See also Richard Kraut, *Aristotle: Political Philosophy* (Oxford: Oxford University Press, 2002), Chapter 7.

the great power of organized human agency that the individual human being can become "the worst of all animals."

As discussed in the previous chapter, the most potent forms of injustice are thus not interactional between lone individual human beings, but *structured*, through or by organized social groups, and *structural*, mediated and conditioned by social structures and processes in which many participate. We can make a broad distinction between two different categories of structurally based injustices. One may be more appropriately called *structured* injustices, where wrongful acts or objectionable outcomes committed or produced by individuals can be attributed to their roles within corporate agents or highly organized and purposive social groups. Individuals who, as members of such groups, enact willfully repressive policies in their capacity as state leaders or functionaries may be considered morally responsible for producing a *structured* injustice. Another form of *structural injustice* consists of unintended, generalized, or impersonal harms or wrongs that result from social structural processes in which many may participate. Structured and structural injustices can produce a variety of wrongs, from oppression and domination to exploitation and marginalization, when they enable agents, individual or corporate, to exercise power inappropriately over others, or without due regard for others' legitimate rights, interests or needs, alienating their agency, hindering their autonomy, and undermining their well-being. There are different ways that different kinds of social structures mediate, condition, enable, or constrain individual, collective, and corporate agency, and taking them into account adds a new dimension to discussions about responsibility for social and political injustices.

As demonstrated in Chapter 1, by 1919 and the establishment of the League of Nations, many among the colonized had come to view their particular struggles beyond interactional terms, rejecting the move of imperial powers such as Britain to render conflicts between colonizer and colonized as domestic problems of empire to be resolved "internally," or bilaterally.[11] The internationalization of efforts to redress colonial injustice is exemplified by the petition filed in 1923 by Chief

---

[11] As Erez Manela noted, Egyptian activists in 1919 did not want the British to set up a commission to investigate "colonial disturbances," but they wanted their conflict with Britain to be recognized as "a conflict between equals that should be adjudicated by the international community [at the League of Nations] on the basis of Wilsonian principles." Manela, *The Wilsonian Moment*, 156.

or Deskaheh of the Iroquois Confederacy, Levi General, against Canadian settler colonialism,[12] as well as by the League's Permanent Mandates system that was responsible for handling cases of misconduct by mandatory powers, such as the 1922 Bondelswarts affair in South West Africa.[13] In these and other cases that arose in the interwar period, colonial conflicts and grievances were not only interactional between the colonizers and the colonized but also mediated and adjudicated by international structures and institutions.

Viewing colonial injustices as partly products of a colonial international order that produced and relied on various structural injustices goes against the classic structural characterization of international relations as an anarchical state of nature, a staple tenet of both realist and liberal international relations theory. Realists in particular emphasize that there is no single agent such as a world state, or a dominant state, that has the power, authority, and responsibility to formulate the rules, or determine the interpretation, application, and enforcement of principles of justice of any kind – distributive, retributive, reparative – among the various agents that participate in international and transnational relations. According to this interpretation, the international order is fundamentally a system of self-help in which all claims of justice and injustice are subjective and unilateral and therefore not enforceable against others in any authoritative way. The realist corollary to this view is that the satisfaction of whatever justice-related claims may arise in international relations is subject to the arbitrary vagaries of a self-help system of enforcement. In practical terms, this means the power politics produced by an anarchical international structure either eclipses or substitutes for assessments of justice or injustice in international relations.

[12] See Chapter 6 for a fuller elaboration of this case. See also Audra Simpson, *Mohawk Interruptus: Political Life across the Borders of Settler States* (Durham, NC: Duke University Press, 2014), 134–37.

[13] See Susan Pedersen, *The Guardians: The League of Nations and the Crisis of Empire* (Oxford: Oxford University Press, 2015), 112–41. Despite the League's condemnation of South Africa and the South West African administration for its cruel treatment of the Bondelswarts, William Rappard of the Permanent Mandates Commission Secretariat lamented that "history ... showed that it was a *misfortune* for natives to inhabit a white man's country" (130, emphasis mine). For a discussion of the arbitrariness of the distinction between misfortune and injustice, and its contingency on technology, ideology, and interpretation, see Judith N. Shklar, *The Faces of Injustice* (New Haven, CT: Yale University Press, 1990), 1–8.

Liberal normative theorists have criticized the realist assertion that international anarchy necessitates skepticism about the possibility of moral action and judgment in international relations, while constructivists in international relations theory have challenged the realist conclusion that anarchy necessitates a system of self-help dominated by competitive power politics.[14] Liberal international relations scholars build on the constructivist insight to argue that while "still anarchic," international institutions "can be established that provide some measure of restraint on states," making it possible for "international political order to operate with some measure of constitutionalism."[15] From a historical perspective, however, the depiction of modern liberal international order as a modified anarchical system of self-help is a normatively obscuring myth.[16] In particular, the long-standing image of international anarchy has obscured the recognition of international structured and structural injustice. Given the palpable and patterned hierarchies of domination produced in contexts of colonialism and empire, the international order more closely resembles a predatory system, forged by competition as well as cooperation between the great powers and other elites that came to dominate international and transnational relations over the course of the past two centuries.[17] Far from anarchical, modern international order reflects the consequences of interactional injustices and the operation of deep structural injustices. Acknowledging that structural injustices have organized and mediated the historical and ongoing development of international order allows us to view the challenges raised by

---

[14] The realist skeptical view was criticized by Charles Beitz, *Political Theory and International Relations* (Princeton, NJ: Princeton University Press, 1979). For the classic constructivist critique, see Alexander Wendt, "Anarchy is what states make of it: the social construction of power politics," *International Organization* 46, 2 (1992): 391–425.

[15] See G. John Ikenberry, *After Victory: Institutions, Strategic Restraint, and the Rebuilding of Order after Major Wars* (Princeton, NJ: Princeton University Press, 2001), 30.

[16] See also Beate Jahn, *The Cultural Construction of International Relations: The Invention of the State of Nature* (Basingstoke: Palgrave, 2000); and Keene, *Beyond the Anarchical Society*.

[17] According to Sandra Halperin, "a predatory European worldview was evident from the first conquests made outside Europe." See Sandra Halperin, "International relations theory and the hegemony of western conceptions of modernity," in *Decolonizing International Relations*, Branwen Gruffydd Jones, ed. (Toronto: Rowman and Littlefield, 2006), 43–63 at 47.

contemporary struggles for justice and reconciliation as central political and normative questions for contemporary world politics.

Despite the historic development of international mechanisms of
accountability for war crimes and crimes against humanity following
World War II, the relative lack of accounting for similar injustices committed in contexts of colonial rule in the twentieth century is striking.
The settling of accounts after World War II was aimed mainly at crimes
against the peace and war crimes. Both the Nuremberg and Tokyo Trials focused on repudiating wars of aggression between states as the
most serious violations of international law and order, and although
the trials saw the introduction of the category of "crimes against
humanity," only such crimes committed in the context of interstate
war were acknowledged. As Judith Shklar observed about Nuremberg,
the Tribunal "decided to interpret crimes against humanity restrictively, limiting itself to those committed after 1939, and so assimi-
lating them to the less controversial charge of war crimes."[18] Yuma
Totani's comprehensive study of the Tokyo Trial shows that contrary
to popular belief, the Trial recognized a wide variety of wrongful conduct by Japan in the war, constituting twenty "particular patterns of
atrocities" for which the Tribunal held the Japanese government at
the highest level to be accountable. Totani's examination of actual
trial records also shows unambiguously that Allied prosecutors at the
Tokyo Trial, especially the Dutch representative, Sinninghe Damste,
presented evidence of "the Japanese commission of various forms of
sexual violence including sexual slavery, targeted in principal at the
Asian female population."[19] While there was some accountability for
Japanese mistreatment of the colonial subjects of other colonizer states
in the context of war, the Allied prosecutors did not pursue an accounting of Japanese mistreatment of its own Korean or Taiwanese colonial subjects. Evidently, Japan's treatment of its own colonial subjects
was excluded from the mandate of the Tokyo Trial, which focused on
Japan's war of aggression and war crimes against other colonial powers and *their* colonial subjects.

---

[18] Judith N. Shklar, *Legalism: Law, Morals, and Political Trials* (Cambridge, MA:
Harvard University Press, 1964), 165.
[19] Yuma Totani, *The Tokyo War Crimes Trial: The Pursuit of Justice in the Wake
of World War II* (Cambridge, MA: Harvard University Press, 2008), 184 and
179.

Resistance against acknowledging responsibility for injustices committed in the context of colonial rule, that were distinct from the injustice of aggressive war and crimes against humanity committed in contexts of war, has persisted. Thus, even in the case of the undisputed 1904 genocide of the Herero people in the context of Germany's colonization of German South West Africa (today's Namibia), the former German president Roman Herzog, in 1998, cited the absence of international legal reparative provisions for colonialism in the early twentieth century to support his government's decision not to pay reparations to Herero descendants.[20] As Sidney Harring has perceptively noted, the German politician framed the Herero genocide in the context of colonialism, and "for Herzog, colonialism was 'legal' in 1905 under international legislation, therefore ending the discussion of Herero reparations."[21] It is estimated that in Germany's campaign to colonize South West Africa, over three-quarters of the entire Herero population, as well as half of the Nama people, were killed, either in battle or due to harsh conditions imposed by German troops.[22] Although Germany has acknowledged, and is planning to apologize for the genocide, it has consistently refused to accept liability, and hence reparative obligations, to Herero descendants, "since the international rules on the protection of combatants and civilians were not in existence at the time that war crimes were being committed in Namibia."[23]

While the historical legality of colonialism cannot constitute an adequate moral defense of colonial practices, legal colonialism does not fit

[20] Jeremy Sarkin and Carly Fowler, "Reparations for historical human rights violations: the international and historical dimensions of the Alien Torts Claims Act genocide case of the Herero in Namibia," *Human Rights Review* 9 (2008): 331–60 at 355.

[21] Sidney L. Harring, "German reparations to the Herero nation: an assertion of Herero nationhood in the path of Namibian development?," *West Virginia Law Review* 104 (2002): 393–417 at 406.

[22] Sarkin and Fowler, "Reparations for historical human rights violations," 333. For a thorough history, see David Olusoga and Casper W. Erichsen, *The Kaiser's Holocaust: Germany's Forgotten Genocide* (London: Faber and Faber, 2010). I discussed the treatment of South West Africa in the Versailles peace process of 1919 in Chapter 1.

[23] Allan D. Cooper, "Reparations for the Herero genocide: defining the limits of international litigation," *African Affairs* 106 (2006): 113–26 at 117. At the time of writing, a controversial interstate process between Germany and Namibia is expected to conclude in 2017, and include an apology, as well as some targeted development assistance. Redress for this case is discussed in further detail in Chapter 8.

into a typical way of thinking about the nature and circumstances of wrongdoing, as an aberrant and willful violation of shared communal norms, laws, or practices. As Iris Marion Young has observed, the type of wrongdoing that triggers processes by which we seek perpetrator accountability and victim reparation is generally conceptualized "as a deviation from a baseline."[24] This standard model of wrongdoing assumes a just or morally acceptable baseline, against which individuals' wrongful actions constitute aberrations. Contemporary redress politics typically assume this model with states as the relevant moral agents. Colonial injustices are thus constituted by a state's wrongful acts against another state or nation, for which the perpetrator state ought to be held accountable through punishment of its leaders as well as through compensation to those victimized.

This approach to accounting for colonial injustices, however, is vulnerable to the criticism that it inaccurately portrays the nature and circumstances of wrongdoing in the colonial case. Colonizer states' actions were typically not aberrant violations of international norms, customs, or laws. The state-centric interactional approach has difficulty acknowledging the legal basis of many colonial injustices because its underlying model of wrongdoing and responsibility cannot grasp the nature of wrongs that are constituted in part by unjust baselines. In such circumstances, individuals' or states' wrongful actions typically conform to, rather than deviate from, a morally defective baseline.

Japan, for example, sought to negotiate its entry into a colonial international system characterized by European domination of non-European peoples in a way that would avoid the insecurity and vulnerability of all non-Europeans to be branded inferior – a prospect which rendered "a nation ripe for colonization."[25] According to Japanese leaders at the time, there seemed no better way of achieving recognition as a member of the family of civilized nations than to acquire colonial subjects and build a colonial empire.[26] As Shogo Sukuki has argued, the rise of Japanese expansionist policies was strongly

---

[24] Young, "Responsibility and global justice: a social connection model," 120.
[25] Alexis Dudden, *Japan's Colonization of Korea: Discourse and Power* (Honolulu: University of Hawai'i Press, 2005), 1.
[26] Disastrously, Japanese colonial and imperial politics culminated in fifteen years of war and devastation in Asia and the Pacific (1931–1945). On Japan's insecurities about its great-power status, see Naoko Shimazu, *Japan, Race and Equality: The Racial Equality Principle of 1919* (New York: Routledge, 1998).

correlated with its entry in the Western society of states in 1853.[27] The sociological reality was that in a colonial international system, Japan was not behaving like a deviant state but was acting in accordance with prevailing international norms, if not international law, when it annexed and colonized Korea in 1910.[28] A compelling normative assessment of the injustice of colonialism must be able to acknowledge this fact of *internationally legitimated* (to be distinguished from morally *legitimate*) colonization prior to the 1960 Declaration, and also explain in what way a legally sanctioned or socially legitimized practice can be considered wrongful or morally objectionable.

In their development of such an account, Jeppe von Platz and David Reidy have put forward a type of injustice characterized by "social contexts that are in some sense completely or pervasively unjust." In such forms of injustice, "a system of entitlements may be predicated on, may track and express, a morally corrupt or unacceptable desert- or value-basis." Colonialism as it developed in the nineteenth and early twentieth centuries, premised on an entitlement to conquer and subjugate other peoples based on a notion of racial or civilizational superiority, was such a structural or systemic historical wrong, in which there is a "manifestly unacceptable or morally corrupt desert- or value-basis underlying a rule-governed social practice, institution or system of entitlements."[29]

The work of von Platz and Reidy builds on an illuminating examination of structures and structural injustice developed by Iris Marion Young. Young defines "structures" as "the confluence of institutional

---

[27] Subsequently, Japan "sent troops to Taiwan in 1874, and went to war with China in 1894–1895, followed by war with Russia in 1904–1905. Taiwan was annexed in 1895, and so was Korea in 1910." See Shogo Suzuki, "Japan's socialization into Janus-faced European international society," *European Journal of International Relations* 11, 1 (2005): 137–64 at 138; and his *Civilisation and Empire: China and Japan's Encounter with European International Society* (New York: Routledge, 2009).

[28] Although the legality of the annexation is hotly disputed, there is no question that the dominant Western powers of the international system accepted Japan's annexation of Korea in 1910, having themselves engaged in similar practices (the US in the Philippines, Germany in East Africa, Britain in Egypt, France in Madagascar). See E. Taylor Atkins, *Primitive Selves: Koreana in the Japanese Colonial Gaze, 1910–45* (Berkeley: University of California Press, 2010), 14; Dudden, *Japan's Colonization of Korea.*

[29] Jeppe Von Platz and David Reidy, "The structural diversity of historical injustices," *Journal of Social Philosophy* 37 (2006): 360–76 at 364 and 366.

rules and interactive routines, mobilization of resources, as well as physical structures such as buildings and roads." Structures provide "background conditions for individual actions by presenting actors with options; they provide 'channels' that both enable action and constrain" agency. The concept of structural injustice refers to social structures and processes – embodied in "institutions, discourses, and practices" – that are based on morally unacceptable values or belief systems.[30] The existence of structural injustice in a society perverts systems of norms and entitlement; enables, legitimizes and normalizes individual wrongdoing; and, depending on the social structures affected, may produce unjust outcomes ranging from unfair distributions of the burdens and benefits of social cooperation to mass violations of human rights against socially vulnerable groups. According to Young, "structural injustice exists when social processes put large categories of persons under a systematic threat of domination or deprivation of the means to develop and exercise their capacities, at the same time as these processes enable others to dominate or have a wide range of opportunities for developing and exercising their capacities."[31] Structurally unjust social processes based on class, disability, race, and gender, for example, produce and perpetuate different types of social vulnerabilities for some, as well as certain kinds of advantages or privileges for others.[32]

Young has also employed a structural injustice approach to account for inhumane or unjust labor conditions that result from transnational unjust structural processes of the global apparel industry; the harms produced by such structural injustices have "no isolatable perpetrator, but rather result from the participation of millions of people in institutions and practices." It is not the case, however, that the concept of structural injustice is only pertinent in cases of harms or injustices where there is no determinate perpetrator. In her reference to the Holocaust, Young observes that "the makers of genocidal policies and those that directly implement them are enabled and supported by wider social structures in which many participate." Structural injustice is thus an important constitutive component in the production of some flagrant injustices which have identifiable perpetrators and/or

---

[30] Young, "Taking the basic structure seriously," 95.
[31] Young, "Responsibility and global justice: a social connection model," 110 and 111–12; Young, *Responsibility for Justice*, 52.
[32] See Young, "Structural injustice and the politics of difference."

direct causal relationships between an agent and a harm. Most cases of social and political injustice, from inhumane labor conditions to sexual exploitation to genocide, should therefore "be analyzed on these two levels."[33]

While structural injustices are analytically distinct from "the wrongful action of an individual agent" (individual wrongdoing) and "the willfully repressive policies of a state" (what I have called structured injustices), structurally based injustices can involve all of these types of wrongs. Colonial injustices, like most political, social, and economic injustices that affect large categories of people, involve not simply wrongful acts by individual or state perpetrators but rely on social structures and structural processes that enable and even encourage individual or state wrongdoing, and produce and reproduce unjust outcomes. A state-centric interactional approach that focuses only on guilty states or guilty individuals thus cannot tell the whole story about historical responsibility for structurally based injustices. A structural account of colonial injustice can acknowledge the legalization and normalization of colonial practices and, indeed, views colonial legality as a hallmark of the structural nature of colonial injustice, since typically, structural injustices occur "as a consequence of many individuals and institutions acting in pursuit of their particular goals and interests, *within given institutional rules and accepted norms*." A structural injustice approach highlights the contributory role of those who participate in making, implementing, and enforcing the rules, institutions, and social practices at various levels that enable, encourage, and produce "widespread and repeated" violations.[34]

Structural injustices in the colonial system of international law, for example, made Korean women more vulnerable to being recruited, often deceptively or forcibly, into Japan's military comfort system. Japan had signed international treaties banning traffic in women and girls in 1925, but Article 14 of the International Convention for the Suppression of Traffic in Women and Children allowed member states to exempt colonies from the application of the convention, and Japan, like many other colonial powers, exempted its colonies of Korea and

---

[33] Young, "Responsibility and global labor justice," 377.
[34] Young, "Responsibility and global justice: a social connection model," 112 (my emphasis), 114, 115.

Taiwan, as well as Kwantung (Manchuria).[35] While Japanese leaders were anxious about the recruitment of Japanese women for the "comfort women" system, they showed little prudential or normative regard for the recruitment of non-Japanese women. Thus Yoshiaki Yoshimi has documented that a notice distributed in February 1938 by the Japanese Home Ministry's chief of the Police Bureau to each prefecture and metropolitan district in Japan contains the admonishment that recruiting Japanese women to serve as prostitutes for Japanese military personnel may be "contrary to the spirit of international treaties relating to the traffic in women and girls," but this admonishing notice was not distributed to the government-generals of Korea or Taiwan.[36] Just as international practice permitted the annexation and colonization of Korea, it also provided a legal loophole for Japan to mistreat some of its most vulnerable colonial subjects.

According to a structural injustice approach, moral responsibility for wrongful acts can certainly be attributed to the colonizing state and culpable individuals, but some share of historical responsibility should also be attributed to all states, especially the dominant ones, that contributed to perpetuating the unjust social structures of a colonial international system. Acknowledging colonialism as structural injustice does not displace assessments of agents' liability for wrongful actions but identifies other agents that contribute to the production of colonial injustices and raises the question of their remedial responsibilities. If colonizer states bear duties of redress for those who suffered harms and damages from their colonial injustices, a structural injustice approach should lead us to inquire about the different types of responsibilities that all participants in international structural injustice may have toward individual victim-survivors as well as toward groups targeted by or made vulnerable to victimization by colonial structural injustices. The role of the international legal and political order that justified and enabled colonial acts, policies, and practices thus raises the question of responsibility for international structural injustice, as well as what redress of such structural injustice may entail on the part of differentially situated agents.

[35] United Nations, "International Convention for the Suppression of Traffic in Women and Children," 1921, http://untreaty.un.org/English/CTC/CTC_04.asp.
[36] Yoshimi, *Comfort Women*, 155.

III Domestic Structural Injustices under Colonial Rule: The Case of the Japanese Military "Comfort" System

In this section, I will be concerned primarily to develop an account of colonial structural injustices through an examination of the experience of Japanese colonialism in Korea (1910–1945) and the divisive politics of redress that has marked contemporary Korean–Japanese relations. Upon its annexation of Korea in 1910, Japan's colonial injustices include subjecting large numbers of Koreans, mainly men, to forced labor in mines and factories or to conscription in the Japanese Imperial army. It is estimated, for example, that between sixty-five hundred and ten thousand Korean forced laborers were killed in the atomic bombings of Hiroshima and Nagasaki.[37] During the Asia–Pacific war, Japan used women, the majority of whom were colonial subjects from Korea, to provide sexual services to Japanese soldiers.[38] The military system of forced sexual labor and slavery involved an estimated two hundred thousand women of Korean, Chinese, Taiwanese, Filipino, Indonesian, Malaysian, Burmese, Dutch, and Japanese origin. Under Japanese colonial rule, Koreans not only lost political autonomy but also faced an attempt by Japan to obliterate their cultural identity, through measures such as forcing Koreans to adopt Japanese names, imposing Japanese as the official language of education, and requiring Koreans to take an oath as Imperial subjects.[39]

With the normalization of political relations through the 1965 Treaty on Basic Relations between the Republic of (South) Korea and Japan, leaders of both countries voiced hopes of establishing "future-facing permanent and friendly relations on which [they] can build a new respectful and prosperous history." Despite this common desire, and while the 1965 treaty "declares that all issues involving compensation and reparations claims are settled by the treaty, disavowing the

---

[37] See John W. Dower, "The bombed: Hiroshimas and Nagasakis in Japanese memory," in *Hiroshima in History and Memory*, Michael J. Hogan, ed. (Cambridge: Cambridge University Press, 1996), 140.

[38] See C. Sarah Soh, *The Comfort Women: Sexual Violence and Postcolonial Memory in Korea and Japan* (Chicago: University of Chicago Press, 2008), xii; Pyong Gap Min, "Korean 'comfort women': the intersection of colonial power, gender, and class," *Gender and Society* 17 (2003): 938–57.

[39] Typically, Korean comfort women were assigned Japanese names upon arrival at a military comfort station. See Yoshimi, *Comfort Women*, 153.

possibility of future claims," the presence of an unsettled past is observable in several aspects of contemporary Japanese–Korean relations.[40] The politics of redress has been especially rancorous. In particular, since the early 1990s, South Korean and transnational human rights activists have pursued official redress for survivors of Japan's military system of sexual forced labor and slavery.[41] In response, Japanese officials started to issue routine apologies on several aspects of Japan's twentieth-century imperial and colonial record, including for the case of "comfort women."[42] Activists in South Korea, however, more sensitive to efforts by Japanese conservatives to evade and displace liability for Japan's transgressions, have rejected such statements of apology as "lip-service," and continue to press the Japanese government to offer a "clear-cut" apology and compensate victims.[43] In 2011, a statue of a Korean girl in traditional dress, financed by citizens' donations, was installed across from the Japanese embassy in Seoul, a monument buttressing the protests that have occurred there weekly since 1992, often including eighty- and ninety-year old victim-survivors of the military "comfort" system and their supporters.[44]

How should we think about responsibility for Japanese colonial injustices and, in particular, for the military system of sexual forced labor and slavery? In all societies, including those under colonial rule,

---

[40] Alexis Dudden, *Troubled Apologies among Japan, Korea and the United States* (New York: Columbia University Press, 2008), 44 and 94.

[41] The first publicly identified Korean "comfort woman" was Kim Hak-sun, who testified about her experience at the Korean Church Women United office on August 14, 1991, and eventually filed a lawsuit with two other women in December that year. See Maki Kimura, *Unfolding the "Comfort Women" Debates: Modernity, Violence, Women's Voices* (Basingstoke, UK: Palgrave Macmillan, 2016), 3.

[42] See, for example, "Statement by the Chief Cabinet Secretary Yohei Kono on the result of the study on the issue of 'comfort women,'" Ministry of Foreign Affairs of Japan, August 4, 1993, www.mofa.go.jp/policy/women/fund/state9308.html.

[43] For an account of the struggle between conservative and progressive forces in Japan over collective memory of the imperial and colonial past in postwar Japan, see Kiyoteru Tsutsui, "The trajectory of perpetrators' trauma: mnemonic politics around the Asia-Pacific war in Japan," *Social Forces* 87 (2009): 1389–422.

[44] Choe Sang-hun, "Statue deepens dispute over wartime sexual slavery," *New York Times*, December 15, 2011. From 234 Korean women in the 1990s, there are now, in 2017, 46 left who are known to have suffered sexual exploitation and slavery in Japan's military "comfort" system.

individuals occupy different social positions that enable them to exercise different capacities for social agency as well as expose them to different kinds or levels of social vulnerabilities. Colonial rule in the nineteenth and twentieth centuries typically introduced racialized structural injustice into the colonized society but also at times reinforced or exacerbated other existing structural injustices among the colonized. While the vulnerabilities attached to being colonial subjects were collectively shared, the operation of other structural injustices within colonized societies means that not all colonial subjects faced the same structural constraints on agency, nor experienced the same kinds or degrees of vulnerability to marginalization, domination, or exploitation. Being a victim of colonial domination does not translate into equality of domination with all other members of the colonized society. In this sense, a statist or nationalist interactional perspective on colonial injustice distorts the historical record about who were victims and who were perpetrators of colonial injustices. Young's account of structural injustices as social contexts that place "large categories of persons under a systematic threat of domination or deprivation of the means to develop and exercise their capacities, at the same time as these processes enable others to dominate or have a wide range of opportunities for developing and exercising their capacities," allows for a complex array of social positions that individuals and groups may occupy in the social structures that produce injustice.[45]

In other words, a structural analysis of colonial injustice is not likely to support a simplistic division of colonizers and colonized into perpetrator and victim roles. Among colonized populations, individuals and groups occupy different social positions in the structure of colonial domination, and some may use their relatively privileged position and resources to dominate others, and may even derive some benefits from participating in colonial enterprises at the expense of their more socially vulnerable compatriots. Another hallmark of structural injustice, then, is its propensity to produce victim-perpetrators: those in colonial positions of subordination (such as all Korean colonial subjects) nevertheless still occupied different social positions that enabled some (for example, private Korean entrepreneurs engaged in the commercial sex industry or human trafficking) to derive benefits at the expense of their more socially vulnerable compatriots (such as

---

[45] Young, "Responsibility and global justice: a social connection model," 112.

impoverished Korean women and girls). The complexity of structural injustice thus permits more nuanced as well as more expansive judgments about the agents who bear historical responsibility for specific patterns of injustice in colonial contexts. A state-centric interactional approach obscures the fact that colonial practices typically had differential impacts on those within colonial populations. Accounting for this differential impact requires some examination, not only of Korean collaboration, but also of domestic structural injustices operating in colonized societies. I will use the Japanese military "comfort women" system of sexual coercion as an illustrative case.

The anthropologist Sarah Soh has provided a comprehensive examination of the Japanese military "comfort" system as a historical institution "deriving from the dynamics of capitalism, militarism, and a sexual-cultural order." Her study shows that the system had three distinct and overlapping phases of development. A major part of the system operated as a commercial for-profit sex industry, in which women were paid for their sexual services and could leave after paying off their debts. Maki Kimura has also traced the incorporation of Korean, Chinese, and lower-class Japanese women into a licensed and regulated prostitution system, which Japan introduced into its colonies and occupied territories.[46] Another phase of the system that developed as Japan became more deeply engaged in war operated as a paramilitary service organization, in which the enforced prostitution of women's sexual labor served the military objective of maintaining troop morale, thereby supporting the war effort and preventing troops from committing sexual atrocities against civilians in occupied territories. Finally, some parts of the military "comfort" system, especially near the front lines in occupied territories toward the end of the Asia–Pacific war, amounted to a criminal sexual enterprise, involving forced abductions and sexual slavery.[47]

Soh's anthropological study shows that the Japanese military's recruitment of Korean girls did not typically involve large-scale forced abductions or slave-raids but required the cooperation of the Korean colonial government and the collaboration of local Korean elites and entrepreneurs. According to Soh, survivor accounts support the conclusion that civilian "Koreans actually outnumbered civilian Japanese

---

[46] Kimura, *Unfolding the "Comfort Women" Debates*, 90.
[47] Soh, *Comfort Women*, 115 and 107–42.

among those seeking profit by human trafficking, forcing prostitution and sexual slavery upon young female compatriots."[48] She and
scholars such as Pyong Gap Min have demonstrated that "colonization, gender, and class were inseparably tied together" in producing
the heightened social vulnerability of poor, rural, and working-class
Korean women to recruitment into the Japanese military "comfort"
system. Min notes, for example, that because Japanese colonial economic policy devastated Korean agriculture, many young women in
rural areas became vulnerable to pressures to leave home in search
of profitable work, a situation exploited by Korean recruiters for the
Japanese military system of sexual forced labor and slavery. Indeed, the
majority of the Korean "comfort women" (59 percent) were "drafted
through false promises of well-paying jobs in Japan."[49]

A structural injustice approach, by highlighting the differentiated
suffering of Koreans, raises the thorny issue of Korean collaboration under Japanese colonial rule. If we regard the Japanese military "comfort" system in its entirety as one large, "consolidated
wrong" that involved multiple wrongs – including deceptive and/or
forcible recruitment methods; specific targeting of poor rural and
working-class women; and enforced prostitution, rape, confinement,
and/or sexual forced labor and slavery – then the contributory acts
of Korean colonial state officials and police, local elites, and private
entrepreneurs in the recruitment process can be viewed as partially
constitutive of the wrong. Although they had no role in initiating the
wrong, their contributions were central to the operationalization of
the system.[50] In the terminology offered by Chiara Lepora and Robert
Goodin, the Japanese military and state were the "plan-makers," but
the Korean colonial government, local elites, and private entrepreneurs
contributed significantly as "plan-takers" to implementing the plan.[51]

---

[48] Ibid., 140.
[49] Min, "Korean 'comfort women': the intersection of colonial power, gender,
and class," 940, 945, and 951. See also Soh, *Comfort Women*, 116; Kimura,
Unfolding the "Comfort Women" Debates, 92–96.
[50] For an account of measuring an agent's causal and moral responsibility based
on chronological primacy, impact, and multiple causation, see Robert Stover,
"Responsibility for the Cold War – a case study in historical responsibility,"
History and Theory 11, 2 (1972): 145–78 at 166–67.
[51] Chiara Lepora and Robert E. Goodin, *On Complicity and Compromise*
(Oxford: Oxford University Press, 2013).

It is unlikely in the Korean case that the field of those who bear moral culpability for their contribution to such injustices under Japanese colonial rule can plausibly be limited to a handful of politicians, as some Korean nationalists claim, or in fairness be extended to "all those who at some point in time had been in touch with Japan."[52] As discussed in Chapter 3, while judging individual liability for actions committed under conditions of structural injustice is appropriate, the experience of contemporary international criminal tribunals shows that this is a difficult task. In cases of structured and structural injustices that involve organized intentional wrongdoing or mass participation in direct wrongdoing, the attribution of individual guilt is more complicated than in a standard case of individual interactional wrongdoing (where the individual's actions constitute isolated aberrations against a reasonably just background structural condition and violate shared norms, laws or practices).[53] Acknowledging contexts of structural injustice is thus important for making morally reasonable assessments of individual liability for wrongdoing. As Lepora and Goodin suggest, the culpability of plan-takers must be assessed individually, depending on factors such as their motives, their enthusiasm or reluctance in implementing the plan, the existence of excusing circumstances such as duress, and the availability of reasonable opportunities for pursuing alternative courses of action.[54]

The judgment of blameworthy collaboration bases guilt on the degree to which individual Korean agents willfully and intentionally

---

[52] Koen de Ceuster, "The nation exorcised: the historiography of collaboration in South Korea," *Korean Studies* 25 (2001): 207–42 at 230. De Ceuster provides an insightful historiography of the collaboration issue in South Korea, from its taboo status during authoritarian rule to its instrumentalization by a nationalist paradigm in the early period of democratization. Deepening democratization by the late 1990s allowed for historical scholarship on the collaboration issue, at least, to be less hysterical and politicized and more historically contextualized and fair to individual narratives. The public struggle over historical memory and judgment of collaborators, however, remains painful and divisive within South Korea.

[53] See Mark Osiel, *Making Sense of Mass Atrocity* (Cambridge: Cambridge University Press, 2009), for an attempt to improve current legal frameworks for judging individual guilt for mass atrocities such as genocide. These frameworks have been criticized for "missing the collaborative character of genocidal massacre, the vast extent of unintended consequences, and the ways in which 'the whole' conflagration is often quite different from the sum of its parts" (2).

[54] See Lepora and Goodin, *On Complicity and Compromise*, Chapter 3; and Stover, "Responsibility for the Cold War."

participated in wrongdoing that was planned by their Japanese colonial masters. A structural approach, however, raises the question of how structurally unjust social processes within the colonized society might have contributed to producing the negative outcomes of unjust colonial policies. In the case of the military "comfort" system, gender- and class-based structural injustices within Korean society were central to producing the pattern of exploitation and abuse of impoverished rural and working-class women. In one example, in 1941, the Japanese Kwantung Army requested the assistance of the colonial government-general of Korea to recruit twenty thousand Korean women to provide sexual services to Japanese troops preparing to invade the Soviet Union. The colonial government, in turn, relied on local elites or heads of townships to meet the request. These elites proceeded by visiting poor households and persuading the parents "to send their unmarried daughters to work in Japan." This collaborative effort enabled the quick procurement of almost eight thousand recruits, who were then sent to military comfort stations in northern Manchuria.[55]

The moral blameworthiness of the head of the township who recruited the women may be judged according to the factors mentioned above. His decision to approach only indigent households, however, was not unique; the concentration of victims in impoverished and working-class groups indicates that the practice was common, suggesting the influence of unjust social structural processes on the specific distribution of victims. In addition to assessing the moral culpability of individuals for their wrongful acts, acknowledging the role of domestic structural injustices within Korean society in this case raises the question of Korean domestic responsibility for those structural injustices. The contemporary politics of redress for the Japanese military "comfort" system, however, have left "little room for critical self-reflection in South Korean public discourse" on the historical responsibility of Korean elites themselves.[56]

The 2000 Women's International War Crimes Tribunal on Japan's Military Sexual Slavery, organized by human rights activists from Japan, South Korea, and the Philippines, is just one example of a major redress movement that concentrated on indicting Japan – most notably the late Hirohito, posthumously named Emperor Shōwa – for sexual violence against women during the era of Japanese colonialism

---

[55] Soh, *Comfort Women*, 138–39.   [56] Ibid., 237.

and aggressive war, but neglected to make any wider assessments of international responsibility or domestic Korean responsibility.[57] Christine Chinkin has noted that the Tribunal hoped to contribute to the "appropriate attribution of responsibility" away from the victimized women themselves, who were stigmatized, and toward the Japanese government.[58] The stigmatization of survivors, however, was most apparent in postcolonial Korea, where the gender inequalities of strong patriarchal traditions compounded the hardships endured by the women when they returned to Korea.[59] According to Soh's sociological description, for some survivors, it was not their wartime sexual labor but "the humiliation of social stigma and isolation in their postwar lives [in Korea] that made these women despair."[60] A broader structural approach to the question of historical responsibility for the Japanese military "comfort" system would have illuminated the operation of structural injustices that cut across the colonizer–colonized divide, and such an acknowledgment might have helped to prevent the instrumentalization of victims of sexual violence in ethnonationalist politics in South Korea.

Such instrumentalization, to the detriment of victim-survivors, was apparent in the controversy over the National/Asian Women's Fund (AWF), established in 1995 by Japan with "the aim of expressing a sense of national atonement from the Japanese people to the former 'comfort women,' and to work to address contemporary issues regarding the honor and dignity of women." Although the AWF reflected compromises between conservative and progressive forces

---

[57] Ibid., 42 and 108. See Christine M. Chinkin, "Editorial comments: Women's International Tribunal on Japanese Military Sexual Slavery," *American Journal of International Law* 95 (2001): 335–41 at 337, for an account of the Tribunal and an example of a human rights perspective on the experience of women in the Japanese military "comfort" system: "once confined in the facilities, the women were subjected to lives of utter misery, fear, and brutality." Chinkin's characterization of the comfort women experience seems particularly appropriate for the criminal enterprise elements of the system but arguably does not capture counternarratives of women's experiences in the other phases of the military "comfort" system. On counternarratives and their significance, see Soh, *Comfort Women*, 175–96.

[58] Chinkin, "Editorial comments," 341.

[59] Min, "Korean 'comfort women': the intersection of colonial power, gender, and class," 940.

[60] Soh, *Comfort Women*, 140 and 148. Of course, from a normative point of view, these women ought not to have been subjected either to sexual forced labor or to social stigma and isolation upon their return after the war.

within Japanese politics and society, and did not amount to legal state compensation to survivors, it was a "hybrid national public organization," the operation of which was financed and administered by the Japanese government.[61] Instead of supporting such redress efforts as progress toward developing a greater sense of responsibility among Japanese for their colonial and wartime past, critics found fault with the AWF as a "private" fund, through which the Japanese government evaded official and legal responsibility. The Korean Council for Women Drafted for Military Sexual Slavery by Japan (Korean Council), a non-governmental activist organization, lobbied against the AWF and went so far as to denounce the seven Korean survivors who accepted AWF compensation in 1997. In addition, the Korean Council lobbied the South Korean government to offer special support payments to 140 survivors, "with the proviso that survivors sign a pledge not to receive AWF money."[62] What is remarkable about this latter effort is that it did not constitute any acknowledgment by the South Korean government, or society at large, of their responsibility to redress the harms suffered by survivors; rather, the payments instrumentalized the plight of victim-survivors in an ethnonationalist political contest. Not surprisingly, these redress efforts only produced "fissures among the communities of victim-survivors and their supporters."[63]

---

[61] See C. Sarah Soh, "Japan's National/Asian Women's Fund for 'comfort women,'" *Pacific Affairs* 76 (2003): 209–33 at 218, 210, and 221. The AWF distributed a letter of apology from the Japanese prime minister and 2 million yen to each of 285 former comfort women from the Philippines, Korea, and Taiwan. Of this number, only seven Korean women received the letter and compensation, and four others later received "medical welfare support." The AWF also provided 750 million yen from Japanese government funds for "medical welfare support" to affected women in these countries as well as in the Netherlands. In Indonesia, the AWF committed 380 million yen over ten years to build facilities for senior citizens and to support NGO projects and facilities for former comfort women. See Tomiichi Murayama, "The statement by President of the Asian Women's Fund at the final press conference," *Digitial Museum: The Comfort Women Issue and the Asian Women's Fund*, www.awf .or.jp/e3/dissolution.html. For an alternative reading, see Ranjoo Seodu Herr, "Can transnational feminist solidarity accommodate nationalism? Reflections from the case study of Korean 'comfort women,'" *Hypatia* 31, 1 (2016): 41–57.

[62] Soh, "Japan's National/Asian Women's Fund," 229. Furthermore, the eleven women who accepted AWF compensation or medical support were denied the right to apply for South Korean government funds. According to the analysis of structural injustice offered here, it is plausible that survivors should be entitled to reparations from both the Japanese and South Korean governments.

[63] Ibid., 218.

Observing these developments, Soh has criticized the partiality of the "paradigmatic story" of comfort women as a "sex slaves," a war crimes and crimes against humanity issue, which was put forward by both "a transnational women's human rights perspective and South Korean ethnonationalism." Her concern is that the human rights activists' "master narrative has glossed over the more complex, wider-reaching narratives of women's oppression and has thereby failed to generate a sense of societal responsibility among Koreans for their compatriots' lifelong suffering."[64] The critique that contemporary human rights discourse has obscured Korean domestic responsibility reveals a flaw in that discourse's understanding of how human rights violations were produced in a colonial context. Crimes against humanity in such contexts not only involve wrongful actions by colonizers but also typically require various kinds and degrees of complicity among the colonized, as well as the existence of enabling unjust social structures shared by colonizer and colonized groups. Patterns of human rights violations in contexts of colonial rule may result not only from the unjust structural processes introduced by a colonizer state but also from the operation of preexisting structural injustices operating within colonized societies.

When Korean and transnational human rights activists focus their redress efforts only on getting the Japanese state to acknowledge its moral culpability, they miss an important opportunity to bring Japanese and Koreans together to examine and reform shared problematic societal practices and structural processes, leaving unjust social structures in place in both societies that may contribute to recurrences of similar injustices. It is perhaps worth noting that in postcolonial Korea, the Korean military instituted its own "comfort" system, a practice that began in the early 1950s and ended in 1954 with the cessation of the Korean War. Soh notes the parallel rationales offered by Korea's armed forces and Japan's imperial forces: both considered comfort systems to be instrumental to raising troop morale, and a necessary evil to reduce the likelihood of military personnel committing sexual brutality against civilian populations. Although Korea was the victim of Japanese colonial ambitions, Korean society evidently shared with Japanese society debased views of women as sexual objects with only instrumental value for meeting male soldiers' natural urges.[65]

---

[64] Soh, *Comfort Women*, xiii and 237.   [65] Ibid., 215–16.

A structural approach to assessing responsibility for colonial injustices goes beyond the statist interactional approach that dominates international political discourse, admitting a more expansive view of morally responsible agents, as well as a more complex view of the different kinds and degrees of responsibility that attach to individuals' wrongful actions and to their participation in background social structures that produced colonial injustices. Because responsibility for structural injustice is not zero-sum, clarifying the responsibility of the Japanese state or society does not disqualify others, including the Korean state and society, from also bearing some measure of responsibility.[66]

A structural approach exposes gender-based and class-based structural injustices in Korean society that enabled the targeting or vulnerability of poor women for recruitment into the Japanese military system of forced sexual labor and slavery. Identifying the structural bases of colonial injustices that were either shared by colonizer and colonized societies or particular to the colonized society's historical development reveals an illusion underlying contemporary statist and nationalist politics of redress. In such politics, all Koreans can proclaim solidarity with the victims of the military "comfort" system, and may even come to view "comfort women" survivors as the symbols of Korean national victimhood under Japanese colonial rule. This solidarity, unfortunately, is illusory, and comes at the price of glossing over legitimate grievances and claims of redress that victims may hold against their own compatriots and society, as well as obscuring the need for critical collective self-reflection and reform of structural processes within Korean society. To the extent that such reflections are stifled, Korean victim-survivors and vulnerable social groups may experience the reproduction of structural injustice and alienation not only from the Japanese state but also from the Korean state and society.

[66] Similarly, Henry Louis Gates has pointed out that the role of some African leaders in slavery has recently surfaced as a complication in the slavery reparations debate in the US: "Advocates of reparations for the descendants of those slaves generally ignore this untidy problem of the significant role that Africans played in the trade, choosing to believe the romanticized version that our ancestors were all kidnapped unawares by evil white men, like Kunta Kinte was in 'Roots.' The truth, however, is much more complex: slavery was a business, highly organized and lucrative for European buyers and African sellers alike." See his op-ed "Ending the slavery blame-game," *New York Times*, April 22, 2010. Thanks to Yashar Saghai for bringing this case to my attention.

IV Conclusion

On December 28, 2015, the foreign ministers of Japan and the Republic of Korea issued a joint statement, aiming to settle "finally and irreversibly" the issue of the forcible recruitment and enslavement of Korean women in the Japanese military "comfort" system. In the statement, Japanese foreign minister Kishida acknowledged, on behalf of the government of Japan, the "involvement of the Japanese military authorities" and "expresses anew" Japanese prime minister Abe's "most sincere apologies and remorse to all the women who underwent immeasurable and painful experiences and suffered incurable physical and psychological wounds as comfort women." The Japanese government pledged to contribute funds to a foundation, to be established by the Republic of Korea, for the purpose of "recovering the honor and dignity and healing the psychological wounds of all former comfort women." Both governments also agreed to "refrain from accusing or criticizing each other regarding this issue in the international community, including at the United Nations."[67]

Almost immediately, both governments faced internal criticism for making the agreement. Most noticeably on the Korean side, many of the forty-six surviving Korean women of the military comfort system were reported to be against the deal. One survivor, eighty-eight-year-old Lee Yong-su, stated that Prime Minister "Abe has yet to realise what his country has done to us...I am at a loss for words...This kind of irresponsible negotiation is like killing us twice, three times."[68] The surviving women were not consulted on the terms of the agreement, and some of them objected to the fund outlined in the agreement as based on "humanitarian" considerations rather than on an acknowledgment of the Japanese state's legal and moral responsibility for colonial war crimes and crimes against humanity. Another objection is that the payments would be made into a fund rather than as direct compensation to individual survivors. In addition, many found the US$8.3 million sum of the Japanese government contribution – roughly US$180,000 per survivor – to be an inadequate amount of reparation. The Korean Council called the deal "humiliating" and, in

[67] "Full Text: Japan–South Korea statement on 'comfort women,'" *Wall Street Journal*, December 28, 2015, http://on.wsj.com/1QRenU3.
[68] Song Jung-a, "Japan–Korea 'comfort women' deal fails to placate victims," *Wall Street Journal*, December 30, 2015.

particular, objected to the South Korean government's promise to consult with related organizations about removing a statue in front of the Japanese embassy in Seoul that was erected by civil society organizations to commemorate the issue.[69] In the South Korean Parliament, one lawmaker branded the deal "traitorous."[70] One year after the interstate settlement, on December 28, 2016, the continuing resentment it provoked among some parties was apparent as activists installed another statue of protest outside the Japanese consulate in Busan, South Korea.[71]

This chapter has argued that understanding and assessing colonialism as structural injustice reveals the inadequacies of contemporary theories and politics of redress and reconciliation that rely excessively on statist or national frameworks of agency and responsibility. One problem with the statist framing of this recent settlement is the accompanying lack of acknowledgment of individual suffering. While there was an interstate aspect to the Japanese colonization of Korea, the differential class-based and gendered patterns of victimization in the Japanese military "comfort" system indicate that the "nation" is not necessarily the most appropriate subject of redress for this injustice. Indeed, when there are still living individual survivors who experienced an injustice, doing justice requires an interactional settling of accounts with the individual agents subject to wrongful treatment. Although states bear an important responsibility to help such agents seek redress from other states and the international community, it was poor ethical judgment on the part of the two states' officials to come to an

---

[69] Kwanwoo Jun and Alexander Martin, "Japan, South Korea agree to aid for 'comfort women,'" *Wall Street Journal*, December 28, 2015. According to the intergovernmental statement, the ROK government "acknowledges the fact that the Government of Japan is concerned about the statue built in front of the Embassy of Japan in Seoul from the viewpoint of preventing any disturbance of the peace of the mission or impairment of its dignity, and will strive to solve this issue in an appropriate manner through taking measures such as consulting with related organizations about possible ways of addressing this issue." See "Full text: Japan–South Korea statement on 'comfort women,'" *Wall Street Journal*, December 28, 2015.

[70] Jonathan Soble and Choe Sang-hun, "'Comfort women' deal angers some," *New York Times*, December 29, 2015, A7.

[71] "Japan recalls envoy over 'comfort women' statue," *BBC News*, January 6, 2017. Meanwhile, President Park Geun-hye, daughter of Park Chung-hee, who led a military dictatorship in South Korea from 1961 to 1979, was also impeached on December 9, 2016, on charges of corruption and abuse of power.

interstate settlement without having consulted or involved the remaining survivors in the settlement process, and without offering individuated compensation. As I discuss in Chapter 7, the growing salience of the international doctrines of human rights and humanitarian law has supported the development of measures of reparative justice that are focused on individual suffering, and it has become a principle of international law for the accounting of wrongful state conduct to involve direct financial compensation to individual victim-survivors of egregious mistreatment. In addition, the continued nationalist framing of this gendered injustice, which transcended nationality and involved women from several countries, should be of normative concern. The Korean–Japanese settlement has raised concerns of equitable treatment of women from other nationalities who were similarly abused in the same system.[72]

Understanding colonialism as structural injustice should lead us to be critical of much of the contemporary interstate politics of redress, which seem to enforce a simplistic moral coherence on the past in order to stabilize contemporary national identities or shore up states' internal political legitimacy or social cohesion. According to a structural approach, while assigning liability to the Japanese state and military is appropriate, it is insufficient. A structural analysis reveals that the international society of states, in enacting through its rules, customs, and practices a colonial and gendered international order, bears some responsibility for the unjust international social structures that enabled individual, corporate, and state wrongdoing.[73] In addition, a structural approach identifies the contributory role of structural injustices within colonized societies in the production of some colonial injustices, thus raising questions about responsibility *of and among* colonized peoples. Acknowledgment of the transnational structural bases of some colonial injustices – located in international society and the colonizer state

---

[72] According to news reports, as of December 2015, there were twenty-three survivors of the Japanese military system of sexual exploitation and slavery in China, four in Taiwan, and seventy in the Philippines. See Jane McMullen, "The house where the Philippines' forgotten 'comfort women' were held," *BBC News Magazine*, June 17, 2016. "'Comfort women': Taiwan tells Japan to extend compensation," *BBC News*, December 29, 2015.

[73] For an elaboration of how gender norms have contributed to the construction of international hierarchy, see Ann E. Towns, *Women and States: Norms and Hierarchies in International Society* (Cambridge: Cambridge University Press, 2010).

as well as the colonized society – should lead to changes in the way we think about responsibilities for the harms and injuries produced by colonial injustices. In particular, it requires us to examine the nature of the responsibilities of those who participated in unjust social structures but who were not direct perpetrators, as well as identify categories of persons subject to unjust vulnerabilities beyond those who are victims of direct interactional wrongs.[74]

A full accounting of colonial structural injustice thus requires more than an accounting of what individuals or nations did to each other; it must also inquire into the social contexts of their relations, especially the structural processes that shaped social agency and its outcomes. Accounting for the international, transnational, and domestic structural injustices involved in many colonial injustices requires the colonized as well as the colonizer nation to engage in the difficult tasks of critical self-reflection and structural transformation. Revealing the role of transnational structural injustices based on gendered, racialized, and class structures, some of which may be shared by both the colonizer and colonized, in producing specific patterns of victimization among the colonized (as well as among the colonizer population in some cases) may be deeply unsettling and disorienting for contemporary agents steeped in a nationalist or statist discourse and perspective. Yet the willingness of formerly colonized peoples to become partners with their former colonizers in new political relationships defined by morally reciprocal terms of association may depend on their willingness to acknowledge not only their victimization but also their agency and political responsibility. If a new politics of mutual respect is the goal of those societies sharing a colonial past – as colonizer or colonized – it will only be born through a painful labor that forsakes ancestors, avoids soothingly self-serving narratives, and faces the unpleasant, humbling, and complicated, but agency-sensitive and thus potentially liberating, truths revealed by understanding the many faces of colonial structural injustice.

Acknowledging colonial injustices as structural injustices generates a political responsibility to effect structural reforms that ought to be shared by Japanese and Koreans, as well as by the international society of states. This political responsibility is met, and social structures can be considered adequately reformed, only when victims of colonial

---

[74] These questions are discussed in further detail in Chapters 7 and 8.

structural injustices, as well as groups vulnerable to the persistence of similar injustices, achieve the necessary conditions for effective political and social agency within their respective societies. To the extent that this political responsibility is unmet and structural injustice persists, the political responsibility to effect just social structures and conditions is a legacy that those who contributed to the production of structural injustice generate for contemporary agents.

One objection to this conclusion that is skeptical of the applicability of the principle of redress to many cases of colonial injustice has to do with the increasingly historical nature of such claims. What are the moral grounds on which contemporary members of historically colonizing and colonized societies can be said to have any kind of responsibility for historic injustices? After all, contemporary agents are not morally blameworthy for the wrongs committed by past agents, nor were they participants in the social structural processes that produced historical structural injustices and objectionable outcomes. What basis is there, then, to assign to them (or us) any responsibility at all for interactional or structural injustices of the distant past?

5 | *History and Structural Injustice*

If you wish to educate these children you must separate them from their parents during the time that they are being educated. If you leave them in the family they may know how to read and write, but they still remain savages, whereas by separating them in the way proposed, they acquire the habits and tastes – it is to be hoped only the good tastes – of civilized people.

– Canadian Member of Parliament Hector Langevin, 1883[1]

I Introduction

The modern history of international and transnational relations reeks of injustice. Over the course of the past four hundred years – a period that witnessed European-led colonial and imperial expansion into the rest of the world – such relations have been marked by conquest, dispossession, legal exclusion, and unequal treaties, not to mention enslavement, political subjugation, forced labor, violence, and even genocide. Although the institutionalized colonial structure of international and transnational relations was officially repudiated by the society of states in 1960,[2] contemporary international relations continue to be structured by deep inequities.

Stark deprivations and inequalities have fueled a variety of contemporary claims in the international arena for redress, reparation, and compensation for historic injustice. For example, the 2001 Declaration and Programme of Action of the World Conference against Racism,

---

[1] Canada, House of Common Debates, May 22, 1883, 1376. Quoted in Truth and Reconciliation Commission of Canada, *Final Report, Volume 1: Summary* (Toronto: James Lorimer, 2015), 58.

[2] United Nations, "Declaration on the granting of independence to colonial countries and peoples," Resolution 1514 of the United Nations General Assembly, 1960, www.un.org/Depts/dpi/decolonization/declaration.htm.

Racial Discrimination, Xenophobia, and Related Intolerance, held in Durban, South Africa, asserts that "historical injustices," including slavery and colonialism, "have undeniably contributed to the poverty, underdevelopment, marginalization, social exclusion, economic disparities, instability and insecurity that affect many people in different parts of the world, in particular in developing countries."[3] According to Guyanese historian and political activist Walter Rodney, European colonial rule failed to industrialize agricultural production, ensuring that "the vast majority of Africans went into colonialism with a hoe and came out with a hoe."[4] In March 2014, fourteen Caribbean countries agreed on a comprehensive plan that calls upon "the former slave-owning nations of Europe – principally Britain, France, Spain, Portugal, the Netherlands, Norway, Sweden and Denmark – to engage Caribbean governments in reparatory dialogue to address the living legacies of these crimes."[5] These and other calls to acknowledge and compensate historic injustices associated with (mainly) European colonialism and the transatlantic slave trade typically entail the argument that particular contemporary agents have a moral and political responsibility to provide redress, in various forms of reparation, restitution, or compensation, to groups today whose ancestors suffered the historic injustice.

Shifting the burden of responsibility for redressing historic injustice to contemporary agents, however, is controversial. If those who produced or participated in injustice – as architects, perpetrators, victims, and facilitators of injustice – are long gone, in what sense can the attribution of responsibility to contemporary agents still be meaningful or morally justified? Contemporary agents – individual, corporate, or collective – cannot have caused or contributed in any way to

---

[3] The Conference discussed as one its themes "provision for effective remedies, recourses, redress, [compensatory] and other measures at the national, regional and international levels," although consensus could not be reached about the term "compensatory." United Nations, World Conference against Racism, Racial Discrimination, Xenophobia, and Related Intolerance, Durban, South Africa, September 2001, www.un.org/WCAR/e-kit/backgrounder1.htm. For the Declaration: www.un.org/WCAR/durban.pdf.

[4] Walter Rodney, *How Europe Underdeveloped Africa* (Cape Town, South Africa: Pambazuka Press, 1972), 219.

[5] The Caribbean Community (CARICOM) Reparations Commission Press Statement, December 2013, http://caricom.org/jsp/pressreleases/press_releases_2013/pres285_13.jsp. See also "Caribbean nations prepare demand for slavery reparations," *The Guardian*, March 9, 2014.

the production of those past injustices; they cannot have had any control over past events or practices and thus could not have prevented past injustices. The attribution of moral responsibility and liability to contemporary agents for historic injustices seems to violate standard principles of determining moral accountability and responsibility for wrongdoing.[6]

Just as the notion of collective responsibility is controversial because it makes some individuals liable for the acts of other individuals, the claim of contemporary responsibility for historic injustice is similarly controversial for asserting the liability of contemporary agents for the acts of (historic) others.[7] While the pursuit of rectificatory justice in international relations among states has become increasingly resistant to practices of collective punishment,[8] it has been sensitive to the intergenerational limits of reparative responsibilities. For example, in the

---

[6] See Christopher Kutz, *Complicity: Ethics and Law for a Collective Age* (Cambridge: Cambridge University Press, 2000), on the individual difference, control, and autonomy principles that inform the paradigmatic way of determining responsibility for individual wrongdoing. See also Chandran Kukathas, "Responsibility for past injustice: how to shift the burden," *Politics, Philosophy, and Economics* 2 (2003): 165–90, who raises these issues as they pertain to the responsibility of settler societies for historic injustices against indigenous peoples.

[7] See Shane Darcy, *Collective Responsibility and Accountability under International Law* (Leiden: Transnational, 2007), who distinguishes collective responsibility from corporate responsibility (the responsibility of a corporate entity, such as a state) and shared responsibility (the joint responsibility of individuals who share in and contribute to a collective enterprise or goal).

[8] Ibid., 359. The prohibition of collective punishments can be found in the Hague Regulations and the Third and Fourth Geneva Conventions as well as in numerous military manuals and the legislation of many states. See the International Committee of the Red Cross (ICRC), www.icrc.org/customary-ihl/eng/docs/v1_rul_rule103. Charges of collective punishment are rare but were made against Israel in 2014 by a group of international legal scholars in a joint declaration: "The indiscriminate and disproportionate attacks, the targeting of objectives providing no effective military advantage, and the intentional targeting of civilians and civilian houses have been persistent features of Israel's long-standing policy of punishing the entire population of the Gaza Strip, which, for over seven years, has been virtually imprisoned by an Israeli imposed closure. Such a regime amounts to a form of collective punishment, which violates the unconditional prohibition set forth in Article 33 of the Fourth Geneva Convention and has been internationally condemned for its illegality." Richard Falk, "Joint Declaration by International Law Experts on Israel's Gaza Offensive," July 28, 2014, https://richardfalk.wordpress.com/2014/07/28/joint-declaration-by-international-law-experts-on-israels-gaza-offensive/.

conflict-ridden discussions between Allied leaders about war reparations at the Versailles peace conference in 1919, everyone agreed that the burden of reparations assigned to Germany should end "with the generation that made the war."[9]

How then should we think about the responsibility of contemporary agents – as individuals, peoples, and states – for social and political injustices of the distant past? In such cases, where the agents involved are long gone, three particularly contentious kinds of connections need to be established. First, how do past injustices relate to or become contemporary injustices? Second, how are past agents to be connected to contemporary agents, as victims, perpetrators, or otherwise contributors to injustice? Third, what is the relationship that contemporary agents have toward the legacies of past injustices? This chapter evaluates interactional and structural approaches to making these connections, in order to clarify how each approach may conceptualize justice in terms of rectifying historic international and transnational injustices of the distant past, where the original victims, perpetrators and other contributing agents to the injustices are long gone.

The first approach – the *interactional* approach – posits that past perpetrators, typically conceived corporately or collectively as states, nations, or peoples, committed wrongs and produced harms against past victims (also typically conceived as collectives). Without redress, these injustices have endured, creating contemporary beneficiaries as well as contemporary losers of past injustices. Past agents may be related to contemporary agents in various ways, through an ancestor–descendant relationship, or generationally, through some notion of collective identity such as "nationality," or on account of membership in an enduring corporate entity. Finally, the interactional approach posits that contemporary agents relate in different ways to the legacies of historic injustice: some contemporary agents are burdened while others derive a benefit or develop some advantage from past injustice. The unjust interaction approach thus leads to the argument that those today who have benefited from historic injustices committed by others have a responsibility to disgorge those benefits and/or compensate those who have suffered a net loss from historic injustice.

[9] Marc Trachtenberg, *Reparation in World Politics: France and European Economic Diplomacy, 1916–23* (New York: Columbia University Press, 1980), 62. The quotation is from the controversial Fontainebleau memorandum, written by British Prime Minister David Lloyd George on March 25, 1919.

The second approach – the *structural* approach – builds on work by Iris Marion Young.[10] Social structures consist of the normative, institutional, and material resources that together compose the background institutional rules and conditions that enable and constrain agency.[11] The concept of structural injustice focuses not on unjust acts or interactions between agents but on the social structures and processes that condition their interaction, embodied in "institutions, discourses, and practices."[12] In contrast to the interactional approach, the structural approach posits that the past injustices which trigger contemporary responsibilities of redress are those that contribute to the production and reproduction of structural injustices affecting contemporary social relations. While structural injustices are contemporary injustices perpetuated and experienced by contemporary agents, it "is not possible to tell this story of the production and reproduction of structures without reference to the past."[13] In another contrast to the interactional approach, instead of positing a continuous identity between past and present agents, a structural approach posits the continuity and evolution of social structures rather than agents. Under this approach, then, contemporary agents, however they are (or are not) related to past agents, come to share a moral and political responsibility to reform the social structures in which they participate; but since structural injustices are typically historic productions, contemporary agents' responsibility to reform unjust social structures is a responsibility that is derived partly from historic injustices.

Finally, another basic contrast between the two approaches can be seen in the way they understand the relationship that contemporary agents have toward the legacies of past injustice. Whereas the unjust interaction view bases contemporary responsibilities on the idea that contemporary agents have *benefited* from past injustices, the structural injustice approach posits that it is because all contemporary agents are *burdened* by historic injustice – in the form of structural injustice – that they have responsibilities. A structural approach views the legacy

---

[10] See Iris Marion Young, *Responsibility for Justice* (Oxford: Oxford University Press, 2011), Chapter 7.

[11] Young, "Responsibility and global labor justice," *The Journal of Political Philosophy* 12 (2004): 365–88.

[12] Young, "Taking the basic structure seriously," *Perspectives on Politics* 4 (2006): 91–97 at 95.

[13] Young, *Responsibility for Justice*, 185.

of historic injustice not in terms of net benefits or losses to contemporary agents based on the unpaid debts accumulated from past injustice, but in terms of continued patterns of exclusion, domination, subordination, exploitation, and marginalization that are reproduced by contemporary social structures and relations.

While the structural approach is sensitive to the historic sources of structural injustice, it also presupposes that fulfilling the moral and political responsibility to eliminate contemporary structural injustices does nothing to rectify the injustices suffered by historic victims. While contemporary agents have a responsibility to understand and acknowledge past injustice as part of the project of constructing a mutually affirmable and affirmed global order, and to redress contemporary structural injustices, past unjust acts or interactions are not rectifiable by contemporary agents and thus constitute a permanent blight on the historic agents who lived and participated in them.

II Connecting Historic Injustice with Contemporary Deprivation

Problems of Causation

The interactional approach views social and political injustices of the distant past as consisting of a series of unjust interactions or transactions between nations, political communities, states, or peoples, which produced harms and losses to victimized groups. Without compensation, these harms and losses generate distortions or deviations from the scheme of distribution that would have resulted under conditions of just interaction. The duty of contemporary members of perpetrating nations, therefore, is to give up the benefits of past injustice by paying proper compensation to descendants of the victimized group.

Daniel Butt provides the most lucid account of an unjust interaction approach from an "international libertarian perspective," which limits principles of "just international interaction" to respect for national sovereignty or self-determination, and adherence to voluntary treaties and agreements. Even with this minimalist moral account, injustice has been the "dominant characteristic of international relations," producing an unjust distribution of holdings between nations.[14] The unjust

---

[14] Daniel Butt, *Rectifying International Injustice: Principles of Compensation and Restitution between Nations* (Oxford: Oxford University Press, 2009), 73. Butt

interaction approach is agent-centric in that injustice is constituted by what agents have done, intentionally and voluntarily, in violation of principles of justice. Rectificatory justice is based on the principle that one "has a duty to make good the wrong one does."[15] But how do unjust interactions in the past by past agents translate into contemporary injustices?

In Butt's theory of international rectificatory justice, the connection between past and contemporary injustice occurs through the "automatic effects" of past unjust interactions that produce some form of *loss or benefit* to contemporary agents; that is, the past unjust interactions or their effects must in some way be the *cause* of contemporary losses or benefits. Contemporary nations and their members are not morally culpable or blameworthy for historic wrongs perpetrated by their ancestors or past generations, but "when one community is *benefiting*, and another is disadvantaged, as a result of the automatic effects of an act of historic injustice," the benefiting community owes compensation to the disadvantaged community. According to Butt, to determine the effects of historic injustice on the contemporary distribution of holdings between nations, we should ask what kind of distribution would have resulted under conditions of just and consensual interactions between nations. To the extent that the contemporary distribution deviates from such a baseline, we can conclude that some nations have benefited and others suffered harm as a result of historic injustice, triggering interactional rectificatory claims and obligations. Furthermore, current generations in communities that have failed "to fulfill [their] rectificatory duties over time" come to bear responsibility "for an ongoing injustice in relation to another community."[16]

acknowledges additional principles of just international interaction, the violation of which can generate duties of rectification: "1. States should not harm non-nationals. 2. States have duties of reciprocity to non-nationals. 3. States should not exploit non-nationals. 4. States have duties of assistance to non-nationals" (68). See also Robert Nozick's "entitlement theory of justice in distribution," in *Anarchy, State and Utopia* (New York: Basic Books, 1974), 152.

[15] Kok-Chor Tan, "Colonialism, reparations, and global justice," in *Reparations: An Interdisciplinary Inquiry*, Jon Miller and Rahul Kumar, eds. (Oxford: Oxford University Press, 2007), 291.

[16] Butt, *Rectifying International Injustice*, 17, 111, and 115 (italics mine). George Sher, "Ancient wrongs and modern rights," *Philosophy and Public Affairs* 10, 1 (1980): 3–17, raises the problem of tracing automatic effects after many hundreds of years.

Although Butt's account of the baseline is hypothetical and not historical, it still relies on a controversial assumption of a causal connection between past and present distributions of holdings. His account assumes that the distribution of holdings that result over time from just and consensual interactions would be automatically justified, forming the relevant counterfactual baseline by which to assess the legitimacy of actual distributions of holdings that have resulted from a history of unjust and often unconsensual interactions in international relations. It is a feature of John Rawls's domestic and global theories of justice, however, that "unless fair background conditions exist and are maintained over time from one generation to the next, market transactions will not remain fair and unjustified inequalities among peoples will gradually develop."[17] Rawls implies that even voluntary and just interactions do not guarantee the maintenance of structural justice in the form of fair background conditions. This means that the counterfactual hypothetical baseline distribution of holdings derived from just and consensual historic interactions that Butt proposes as a standard by which to judge the contemporary distribution of holdings between nations is implausible. Just interactions do not automatically generate just effects in the distribution of holdings.

In the case of nations that were subject to the wrongs of colonialism, imperialism, and other forms of political domination, showing that historically unjust international interactions can account for disparities in contemporary holdings between nations, or deprivations suffered by contemporary populations, requires a controversial accounting of the causes of contemporary inequalities and deprivation. The unjust interaction approach thus runs into trouble when the causal connections and "automatic effects" of historic international injustice on present-day conditions cannot be established.

China, for example, while never officially colonized, was subject to a century of "unequal treaties" in its interactions with European powers, starting with the Treaty of Nanjing in 1842.[18] This "one hundred years of humiliation" only ended when the Chinese communists won a long civil war under the leadership of Chairman Mao Zedong, who famously declared in September 1949, "The Chinese

---

[17] John Rawls, *The Law of Peoples* (Cambridge, MA: Harvard University Press, 1999), Section 4.5, footnotes 52, 42.

[18] Jonathan D. Spence, *The Search for Modern China* (New York: W. W. Norton, 2001), Chapters 6 and 7.

people have stood up."[19] While it is fairly incontrovertible that Western treatment of China from 1842 to 1945 was marked by various violations of principles of just interaction, it is more difficult to conclude that this period of unjust interaction explains or caused China's national decline, or the deprivations suffered by the Chinese population after the mid twentieth century. Indeed, historians have noted that China was vulnerable to domination by European powers mainly because Imperial China was already collapsing from internal political dysfunctions and internally derived burdensome circumstances. Furthermore, responsibility for Chinese underdevelopment in the following decade can be attributed largely to Mao's poorly conceived economic ideas to transplant Revolutionary Stalinism (1955–1956), and then to launch the Great Leap Forward (1958–1960).[20] After some halting economic progress due to Prime Minister Zhou Enlai's guided modernization policy, Mao unleashed the Great Proletarian Cultural Revolution (1966–1976), which effectively "suspended China's modernization project once more for another decade."[21] After Mao's death, Deng Xiaoping's empirically based economic reforms led to historically unprecedented economic growth and massive social improvements. A 2009 World Bank report notes that between 1981 and 2004, the percentage of China's population "consuming less than a dollar-a-day fell from 65% to 10%, and more than half a billion people were lifted out of poverty."[22] From 1978 to 1989, China's gross domestic product

---

[19] Mao Zedong, "The Chinese people have stood up," September 21, 1949, Mao Zedong, *Selected Works*, vol. 5. (Peking: Foreign Languages, 1977), 15–18.

[20] Revolutionary Stalinism involved the use of large numbers of unskilled laborers to do massive construction projects in a short period of time, "increased collectivization in agriculture, and accelerated nationalization of industry." The Great Leap Forward is estimated to have led to more than 20 million deaths due to starvation. See Lorenz M. Lüthi, "China's Wirtschaftswunder" [China's economic miracle], in Erbe des Kalten Krieges [The legacy of the Cold War], Bernd Greiner, Tim Müller, and Klaas Voss, eds. (Hamburg: Hamburger Edition, 2013), 447–62; and Lüthi, *The Sino-Soviet Split: Cold War in the Communist World* (Princeton, NJ: Princeton University Press, 2008), Chapter 4. For the backstory on China's turn toward agricultural collectivization, which implicates regional and local governments, see Xiaojia Hou, *Negotiating Socialism in Rural China: Mao, Peasants, and Local Cadres in Shanxi 1949–53* (Ithaca, NY: Cornell University East Asia Program, 2016).

[21] Lüthi, "China's Wirtschaftswunder."

[22] World Bank, *From Poor Areas to Poor People: China's Evolving Poverty Reduction Agenda – An Assessment of Poverty and Inequality in China*, Report of the Poverty Reduction and Economic Management Department,

(GDP) increased twofold, from US$214 billion to US$459 billion, and per capita output also nearly doubled, from US$224 to US$413. From 1992 to 2001, the GDP increased from US$500 billion to US$1.316 billion, while per capita output also increased proportionately, from US$432 to US$1,047.[23]

The unjust interaction narrative about the connection between past interactional injustice and present inequalities at the international level makes it difficult to recognize the agency of states or peoples that have been victims of injustice, and the implications of such agency, which is coresponsibility for the domestic determinants of subsequent national wealth and development. In general, it is difficult to sustain the argument that historic colonial injustice has had automatic or uniform effects in colonized societies, given the wide variation in economic performance *among* states that have inheritances of colonial injustice. Indeed, contemporary scholarship on economic underdevelopment in sub-Saharan Africa points to complex interplays between precolonial political institutions, the imported state from colonialism, and postcolonial state formation, which have yielded substantial variations – from economic miracles to disasters – in "development fortunes within Africa."[24]

Of course, showing that historically unjust international interactions did not cause contemporary deprivations in a linear fashion does not mean that contemporary external agents have no responsibility to address contemporary deprivations.[25] Contemporary agents may still have duties to aid those who suffer from deprivation, but the grounds

East Asia Pacific Region, 2009, http://siteresources.worldbank.org/ CHINAEXTN/Resources/318949–1239096143906/China_PA_Report_ March_2009_eng.pdf. The report notes that "by the new international poverty standard of US$1.25 per person per day (using 2005 Purchasing Power Parity for China), the levels of poverty are higher, but the decline since 1981 is no less impressive (from 85% in 1981 to 27% in 2004)."

[23] See Wei Zhang and Liu Xiaohui, "Success and challenges: overview of China's economic growth and reform since 1978," in their edited volume, *China's Three Decades of Economic Reforms* (London: Routledge, 2010), 4–7.

[24] See Englebert, "Pre-colonial institutions, post-colonial states, and economic development in tropical Africa," *Political Research Quarterly* 53, 1 (2000), 7–36 at 7.

[25] Nor does it imply that the return of culturally significant materials that were expropriated in objectionable transactions is not warranted. Where historically unjust interactions involved the expropriation of identifiable specific objects, such as artwork or cultural artifacts, and even human remains, that have endured, contemporary holders of such materials have a duty to return them to

for such duties of assistance would not be the rectification of historic injustices or their effects. Rather, as David Miller has outlined, contemporary agents would have "remedial responsibility," or an obligation to remedy a state of affairs in which people are deprived in a morally unacceptable way: "What matters for remedial responsibility is that the situation is one that demands to be put right: it is morally unacceptable for people to be left in that deprived or needy condition," however the condition came about and whoever or whatever caused it or was morally responsible for it.[26] John Rawls argues that the society of well-ordered peoples has a duty to provide various kinds of assistance to societies burdened by defective domestic institutions so that they can achieve the institutional prerequisites for achieving effective moral and political agency as peoples.[27] Contemporary external agents can have such duties of assistance without any reference to past interactional injustices.

Historicizing Contemporary Structural Injustice

The structural approach, however, opens another way in which contemporary agents' responsibilities may be connected to past injustices. Some structurally unjust social processes and conditions produce and perpetuate social vulnerabilities to deprivation and domination for some, or may entrench arbitrary advantages for others.[28] Different kinds of structural injustice may pervert systems of norms and entitlement; may enable, legitimize, and normalize individual wrongdoing; and, depending on the social structures affected, may produce unjust outcomes ranging from unfair distributions of the burdens and benefits of social cooperation to denials of self-determination to mass violations of human rights or even crimes against humanity against socially and politically vulnerable persons or groups. A generalized social

appropriate representatives or cultural institutions supported by the historically wronged group or agent. This chapter is not concerned with such cases but with how to ground more plausibly reparative and redress claims based on the broad effects of historic social and political injustices on how well or poorly contemporary societies or peoples are faring today.

[26] David Miller, *National Responsibility and Global Justice* (Oxford: Oxford University Press, 2007), 98.

[27] John Rawls, *The Law of Peoples* (Cambridge, MA: Harvard University Press, 1999), 105–12.

[28] See Young, *Responsibility for Justice*, 73.

attitude of racial prejudice, whether in the form of racial privilege for one group or racial derogation of others, is one example of a structural injustice, even if formal laws and institutional rules are not racially discriminatory.

In a structural approach, contemporary agents bear a responsibility to reform contemporary social structures so that they are more just. Part of this task involves halting the reproduction of structural legacies of historic injustice. Past injustices matter in a structural injustice approach because of their role in the historical development of the social structures that condition current social relations. Thus, Young asserts, "it is in the nature of structural causation that one cannot for the most part trace a direct lineal causal relationship between particular actions or policies and the relatively disadvantaged circumstances of particular individuals or groups." In other words, the unjust interaction approach misunderstands the kind of causal analysis that is required for making the connection between past and present injustice. Instead of attempting to trace a linear causal connection between historic agents' acts and their consequences on other agents in the remote future, a structural approach focuses on structural continuity or conditioning, involving a historicized account of the development of contemporary structural injustices.[29] The main way to understand the connection between historic injustice and present injustice lies in uncovering how patterns of historic injustice are reproduced in, or inform the subsequent development of, contemporary social structures.

At the international level, persistent patterns of privilege and disadvantage may reveal structural continuities between contemporary and past international social and political structures. As Thomas McCarthy has put it, "since the most developed countries are disproportionately former colonial powers, and the least developed are former colonies, the [contemporary] neoimperial system of domination and exploitation appears to be, in some considerable measure, a legacy of the five preceding centuries of colonialism and imperialism in their classical modern forms."[30] The various forms of structural injustices at the international level combine to produce several effects, including depriving peoples of the background conditions necessary for effective

---

[29] Ibid., 181–82.
[30] Thomas McCarthy, *Race, Empire, and the Idea of Human Development* (Cambridge: Cambridge University Press, 2009), 4.

moral reciprocity and distorting the operation of principles of mutual advantage and state consent in ways that sustain structural privileges for dominant states at the expense of weaker states and groups.[31] Although formal systems of imperial or colonial domination have been repudiated by the society of states, the existence of contemporary structural injustices in the international system is apparent in the severely impaired ability of poor and weaker countries to enjoy adequate legal and political representation in international negotiations, making them perpetually vulnerable to accepting terms that are generally more partial to the interests of wealthy and powerful countries in a wide range of cases, from access to intellectual property to trade to paying the costs of mitigating and adapting to global climate change.[32]

An interactional account attributes outcomes of unjust interactions purely to the actions of perpetrating agents, obscuring the roles played by social structures at local, domestic, and international levels that organize and mediate agency and its outcomes. As Rainer Forst has observed, however, it is not plausible to draw "a clear separation between internal and external factors of economic and political failures, for these are related in complex ways."[33] A structural account leaves room for both the structural effects of historic international or transnational acts or conditions such as slavery and colonialism on institutional development *and* the significance of contemporary domestic institutions and agents in reproducing problematic domestic structures that yield objectionable outcomes. Focusing on the development of structures, both domestic and international, is crucial to understanding the vulnerabilities, incapacities, and defects of some postcolonial states that produce objectionable outcomes such as poverty or violence. In an interactional account, historic unjust interactions between states produce automatic effects that accumulate over time like debt. Rectificatory justice would simply require the disgorgement of benefits by beneficiary states, to be paid to those that are owed the historic debt.

---

[31] Charles R. Beitz, "Does global inequality matter?," *Metaphilosophy* 32, 1/2 (2001): 95–111 at 107–9; Nancy Kokaz, "Institutions for global justice," *Canadian Journal of Philosophy* 31 (2005): 65–107; and Miriam Ronzoni, "The global order: a case of background injustice? A practice-dependent account," *Philosophy and Public Affairs* 37, 3 (2009): 229–56.

[32] See Joseph E. Stiglitz, *Globalization and Its Discontents* (New York: W. W. Norton, 2002); Lea Ypi, *Global Justice and Avant-Garde Political Agency* (Oxford: Oxford University Press, 2012), 126.

[33] See Rainer Forst, Jeffrey Flynn, trans., *The Right to Justification* (New York: Columbia University Press, 2007), 264.

From a social science perspective, however, unjust acts from the colonial era do not produce automatic effects, though they have affected the development of institutions and structures, which in some cases have contributed to creating contemporary structural conditions that are prone to (re-)producing certain kinds of contemporary social and political problems.

For example, Pierre Englebert has argued that where a postcolonial state is a "reasonable approximation" of precolonial cultures and structures, such as in the case of Botswana, the postcolonial state enjoys greater legitimacy than one that clashes with precolonial cultures or "brings different state systems together while splitting apart long-integrated political cultures" (such as the Democratic Republic of Congo). To the extent that state legitimacy is a precondition for political stability, Englebert shows that this variation can account for the divergent strategies that political elites in postcolonial states employ to maintain power. In particular, in postcolonial states that are configured in less congruent ways with precolonial structures of authority and power, political elites are more likely "to resort to the types of neo-patrimonial policies which lead to poor governance and economic stagnation."[34] While there are alternative plausible explanations, the point is that any plausible explanatory account of the differing developmental capacities of postcolonial states needs to take into account domestic and international agents, institutions, and social structures. Given the importance of institutions, including potentially of precolonial structures, redress of colonial structural injustice is likely to involve structural transformations of the state that can accommodate precolonial governance structures, as well as international structural transformations.

Historicizing a contemporary account of structural injustices also helps to identify what might be objectionable about contemporary social structures. For example, it is not possible to understand why the denial of group self-determination rights to indigenous peoples constitutes any kind of contemporary injustice, without a historic understanding of the forcible incorporation of such groups into contemporary settler colonial and postcolonial states. Why are not all ethnocultural groups, such as Chinese immigrant groups, entitled to similar claims to group self-determination? How can we explain the

---

[34] Englebert, "Pre-colonial institutions, post-colonial states, and economic development in tropical Africa," 13 and 29.

inadequacy of the late Canadian prime minister Pierre Elliot Trudeau's attempt in the late 1960s to resolve the "Indian problem" by unilaterally repealing the Indian Act, extinguishing Indian status, and granting aboriginals equal Canadian citizenship rights? It is only by appreciating the specific nature and quality of historically objectionable political relations between indigenous groups, and settler and colonial groups, that we can arrive at an accurate diagnosis of some contemporary structural injustices.

At the transnational level, the forcible incorporation of indigenous peoples into settler colonial states such as Canada, the US, Australia, and New Zealand, and the entrenchment of their structural indignity vis-à-vis the sovereign state in international law and order, accounts for a distinct kind of contemporary international, transnational, and domestic structural injustice. Rectifying this form of structural injustice may not involve the same measures as rectifying other forms of socioeconomic structural injustice. The latter may be resolvable through more equitable distributive policies, whereas the former may be compounded if equal status or rights are presented as a substitute for the reclaiming of political agency and status as self-determining groups. The argument here does not rely on the view that there are different or special normative grounds or principles distinguishing the rights of indigenous peoples from immigrants or other groups, such as national minorities. These groups, however, have suffered from different historic injustices – from policies of exploitation, exclusion, and discrimination to subjugation and genocide – that may inform the particular shape of contemporary structural injustices; and these differences may require different kinds of remedies. For example, immigrant groups that have experienced policies of discrimination and exclusion may have their claims satisfied in a social/political order that recognizes their equal status and rights and establishes fair background conditions of social and political inclusivity. For indigenous groups that have faced genocide and forcible incorporation, rectifying structural injustice may require supportive measures to enable cultural resurgence and nonalienated agency, as well as constitutional changes in domestic states as well as in international society.[35]

---

[35] See Jennifer Balint, Julie Evans, and Nesam McMillan, "Rethinking transitional justice, redressing indigenous harm: A new conceptual approach," *The International Journal of Transitional Justice* 8 (2014): 194–216.

III Agent versus Structural Continuity and Change

In arguing that contemporary agents bear rectificatory responsibilities for injustices committed by past agents, an unjust interaction approach needs to explain how past and present agents are related to each other. It is common in a statist interactional framework to appeal to the concept of states as corporate agents with enduring identities and personalities that transcend the mortal limits of individuals, or groups of individuals.[36] Focusing solely on the corporate agency and responsibility of states for international and transnational historic injustices, however, may have a distorting effect on the historical record, obscuring the importance of other levels, kinds, and agents of injustices that may require rectification. For example, a state-centric interactional approach that focuses on culpable corporate state agents obscures the wider systemic failings of an imperial and colonial international legal and political order.[37] A corporate statist framework also obscures the claims of indigenous peoples whose forcible incorporation into settler colonial states, such as Canada, may require measures of transformative redress that challenge the statist framework itself.

Similarly, even within domestic contexts, an interactional account tends to obscure other structural dimensions of historic injustice. For example, Jeff Spinner-Halev's theory of "enduring injustice" is focused on certain kinds of injured groups whose historic experiences of injustice merit some kind of political response today.[38] According to Spinner-Halev, the concept of enduring injustice includes three components: (1) the group suffering an enduring injustice must have a collective narrative that dominates other narratives; (2) the group must have been a victim of past injustice; and (3) the past injustice persists and its effects are likely to continue, despite liberal reforms, indicating the inadequacy of liberal justice as a remedy.[39] While groups such as African and Native Americans are the kinds of group agents with

[36] See Tan, "Colonialism, reparations, and global justice."
[37] On the legal framework that constituted an imperial global order, see Duncan Bell, ed., *Victorian Visions of Global Order: Empire and International Relations in Nineteenth-Century Political Thought* (Cambridge: Cambridge University Press, 2007).
[38] See Jeff Halev-Spinner, *Enduring Injustice* (Cambridge: Cambridge University Press, 2012). For my review of this book, see *Notre Dame Philosophical Reviews* (2013), https://ndpr.nd.edu/news/enduring-injustice/.
[39] Halev-Spinner, *Enduring Injustice*, 63.

intergenerational collective narratives that can suffer enduring injustice, Spinner-Halev specifies that other kinds of social groups or categories of persons, such as women and workers, do not: "To the extent that some groups do not have collective narratives, they cannot suffer an enduring injustice."[40]

Spinner-Halev's account of enduring injustice is meant to explain why today, some groups (such as African and Native Americans) are generally considered victims of historic injustice who still need some form of redress, while other groups (such as women and workers) are generally not thought to constitute the kind of group to whom redress is owed for past injustices. To support his claim that gender injustices do not properly constitute enduring injustices, Spinner-Halev argues that the identity of women intersects with other identities, such as ethnicity, race, and nationality, and these latter identities typically trump gender as a social category of identity. In addition, women have made more economic progress than African and Native Americans, so "there is hope that the story of progress for women still holds." With respect to class, he argues that workers do not clearly see themselves as "an intergenerational group with a collective narrative," and class-based injustice does not qualify as enduring injustice because class lines are "often permeable."[41] It is not clear, however, why we should limit the concept of enduring injustice to that suffered by a particular kind of ethnocultural social group. If what unites cases of enduring injustice is a "failure of liberalism,"[42] then the persistence of gender and class violence, discrimination, marginalization and oppression in contemporary liberal societies could make both gender and class qualify as social groups that can suffer from enduring injustice and alienation. One could take Spinner-Halev's account of enduring injustice between cultural groups to describe only one kind or subset of enduring

---

[40] Ibid., 61.

[41] Ibid., 63. In order to make this argument, however, Spinner-Halev needs to tell a more positive and hopeful story about the possibility of liberalism to remedy such structurally based injustices. But surely, just as liberalism was tied to colonial and imperial enterprises, it has also been complicit in the oppression wrought by patriarchy and global capitalism. It is not clear, then, why one should have more faith that liberal justice can remedy structural injustices produced by patriarchy and capitalism but not have a similar faith with respect to structural injustices produced by colonialism and imperialism.

[42] Ibid., 64.

injustices but also acknowledge that the concept of enduring injustice can encompass other kinds of structural injustices.

The inclusion or exclusion of gender- and class-based injustices from Spinner-Halev's concept of enduring injustice is important because of the next step in his argument, which is that the appropriate response of contemporary societies to enduring injustices is acknowledgment and "real understanding of the injustice," along with good-faith efforts to overcome them.[43] Spinner-Halev's arguments here about the importance of acknowledgment in supporting ongoing political efforts to overcome enduring injustices are also useful and pertinent to showing how the stalled progress of liberal domestic societies (and liberal international society) in addressing a variety of unacknowledged structural injustices may be overcome. Perhaps the uniqueness of the injustices suffered by culturally based groups that have intergenerational collective narratives is that the groups' continuous identity allows for extending the rectification of interactional injustices beyond the life spans of individual members. But including gender- and class-based oppression and inequities in thinking about historic injustice and its connections with contemporary structural injustices may also help to expose further the complexity of many enduring structural injustices, especially differentiation in vulnerability to victimization within historically mistreated culturally based communities.

For example, while it would be correct to say that Korea was a victim of Japanese colonialism, this statist or nationalist interactional narrative may not be helpful in accounting for differential patterns of victimization suffered by Koreans under colonialism. As discussed in Chapter 4, Pyong Gap Min has demonstrated that "colonization, gender, and class were inseparably tied together" in producing the heightened social vulnerability of poor, rural, and working-class Korean women to recruitment into the Japanese military system of sexual forced labor and slavery.[44] A structural injustice approach extends our views of responsibility beyond the state-centric and nation-centric perspectives that accompany interactional approaches to accounting for past international and transnational injustices. It helps us to identify categories of victims and vulnerability, based on structures that

---

[43] Ibid., 87.
[44] Pyong Gap Min, "Korean 'comfort women': the intersection of colonial power, gender, and class," *Gender and Society* 17 (2003): 938–57 at 940. See Chapter 4 for a full discussion of this case.

transcend statist or national divides, such as race, class, and gender, opening the possibility of specifying *joint* rectificatory duties of colonizer and colonized states and societies to make reparations to or construct remedies for specific categories of victims as well as to reform different kinds of structural injustices within their own societies as well as in international society. A statist or nationalist interactional view tends to oversimplify the agents involved in producing colonial injustices into a binary colonizer–colonized dichotomy, obscuring the ways in which such injustices required the cooperation of members and groups among both the colonizer and colonized. Our ideas and normative arguments about rectificatory justice for colonialism should be based on empirically plausible, and not oversimplified or distorted, histories of colonialism. As Sandra Halperin has characterized it, "European colonialism and imperialism was a collaborative project that crucially depended for its success on governments, ruling groups, and elites around the world. Colonialism did not disadvantage whole societies. It further enriched or helped create privileged classes." An accurate history of colonialism, and Europe's contribution to its globalization, "reveals the inadequacy of assuming whole nations or regions as the basis for social inquiry," and, we may add, normative inquiry.[45]

Another popular way to connect past and present agents is to posit an ancestor–descendant relationship between them, invoking a familial-type of continuity between past and present perpetrators and victims. Thus, some contemporary agents bear rectificatory duties as descendants of perpetrating nations, just as other contemporary agents are owed compensation as descendants of victimized nations or peoples. As Chandran Kukathas has noted, however, who can claim to be a descendant can be a fraught question: "the more remote the original wrong, the more difficult it is to establish who has cause for complaint and who can rightly be held responsible."[46] The ancestor–descendant framework is sometimes posited as complementary to a corporate statist framework, but in reality, sits uneasily with it. The states that

---

[45] Sandra Halperin, "International relations theory and the hegemony of western conceptions of modernity," in *Decolonizing International Relations*, Branwen Gruffydd Jones, ed. (Toronto: Rowman and Littlefield, 2006), 43–63 at 59–60.

[46] Chandran Kukathas, "Who? Whom? Reparations and the problem of agency," *Journal of Social Philosophy* 37, 3 (2006): 330–41 at 330.

resulted from the decolonization movement of the mid twentieth century contain peoples whose experiences of colonialism may have differed widely. In the case of German colonialism in South West Africa, with which this book began, a corporate statist framework would suggest that Germany may have reparative obligations toward the state of Namibia. Yet Namibia includes the Herero, the Nama, and several other groups, which experienced German colonialism differently. The Herero suffered genocide under German colonialism in 1904–1907, losing three-quarters of its population, while the Nama, some of whom initially helped the German colonial troops to track the Herero, lost half its population. Framing reparations in statist terms would exclude the Herero's particular claim against the German state, in favor of a claim by the Namibian state, which includes the Herero, the Nama, as well as several other groups, including a remnant population of German settlers.[47] Reparative claims based on ancestor–descendant relationships between past and present agents may therefore conflict with those based on a statist interactional narrative of international and transnational historical injustices.

A particular problem for the ancestor–descendant framework occurs in immigration-based societies such as Canada and the US, where such a narrative about the connection between historic and contemporary agents strikes many current citizens as descriptively false, further alienating them from past injustices.[48] Opponents of reparations have referred to the misleading characterization of contemporary agents as "descendants" of past wrongdoers as a ground for dismissing any contemporary responsibilities for redressing such injustice. David Horowitz, for example, included this issue in his list of ten reasons

---

[47] Indeed, the Namibian state refused, until recently, to support the Herero's independent claims for reparations from Germany, on the grounds that all Namibians suffered. One consequence of the 1904 genocide was the political decline of the Herero in the region. See Leonard Jamfa, "Germany faces colonial history in Namibia: a very ambiguous 'I am sorry,'" in *The Age of Apology: Facing Up to the Past*, Mark Gibney, Rhoda E. Howard-Hassmann, Jean-Marc Coicaud, and Niklaus Steiner, eds. (Philadelphia: University of Pennsylvania Press, 2008), 202–15. See Chapter 8 for my view of how contemporary efforts to acknowledge and redress this historic injustice should be framed.

[48] See Young, *Responsibility for Justice*, 176 and 184; Kukathas, "Responsibility for past injustice," 170; and Kukathas, "Who? Whom? Reparations and the problem of agency," 338.

against reparations for African Americans: "America today is a multi-ethnic nation and most Americans have no connection (direct or indirect) to slavery: the two great waves of American immigration occurred after 1880 and then after 1960. What rationale would require Vietnamese boat people, Russian refuseniks, Iranian refugees, and Armenian victims of the Turkish persecution, Jews, Mexicans, Greeks, or Polish, Hungarian, Cambodian and Korean victims of Communism, to pay reparations to American blacks?"[49]

Even in cases of the not-so-distant past, disputes arise about the grounds of responsibility for new agents to contribute to the remedy of past social and political injustice. South Africa, for example, introduced "black economic empowerment laws" as a measure to rectify apartheid-era socioeconomic injustices and human rights violations. In the mining sector, all companies working in South Africa were required to have 26 percent "historically disadvantaged South African" ownership by 2012. Two mining companies disputed the applicability of this law to their firms, on the grounds that the companies purchased the mining operations in 1994, after apartheid. According to Peter Leon, a lawyer representing the Italian mine company owners, they "never benefited from the apartheid system, [so] why are they subject to this form of redress?"[50] Contemporary new agents may claim to have no relationship to past agents (as descendants) and their wrongdoing (as beneficiaries).

According to a structural approach, however, new agents (including new corporations as well as new immigrants) who come to participate in an existing, historically produced social structure acquire responsibilities to contribute to transforming the enduring structural injustice, such as the structure's propensity to place some category of persons in situations of heightened vulnerability to objectionable social relations or outcomes. In short, a structural injustice approach focuses on the continuity and evolution of structures rather than agents. New agents need not be related to past agents as descendants of perpetrators or victims, or as direct beneficiaries of past injustice, in order to acquire a responsibility to reform structural injustices. Rather, new agents –

---

[49] Quoted in Charles P. Henry, *Long Overdue: The Politics of Racial Reparations* (New York: New York University Press, 2007), 113.

[50] See David Kinley, *Civilising Globalisation: Human Rights and the Global Economy* (Cambridge: Cambridge University Press, 2009).

individual, corporate, and collective – come to share this moral responsibility by virtue of their participation in and contribution to the perpetuation of contemporary structural injustices. New agents, such as immigrants, are typically socialized into existing social structures and come to adopt attitudes and beliefs that are supported by such structures. In this sense, participation in a structural injustice can merely involve an uncritical appropriation of problematic dominant national or cultural narratives, or other kinds of social and political narratives that obscure structural injustices and the responsibility for their rectification. For this reason, one of the "calls to action" of the Truth and Reconciliation Commission of Canada is for "the federal government, in collaboration with the national Aboriginal organizations, to revise the information kit for newcomers to Canada and its citizenship test to reflect a more inclusive history of the diverse Aboriginal peoples of Canada, including information about the Treaties and the history of residential schools."[51]

Although I am arguing that the continuity of structural injustice is a more plausible way for understanding the connections between past and present agents, what if structural disruption or radical change occurs? Does the establishment of new social structures and perhaps, with them, new kinds of structural injustices make the claims of those who suffered under the previous structures obsolete? This may be a worry about focusing only on contemporary structural injustices, since this implies that the victims of past injustices may not matter. As the case of contemporary post-apartheid South Africa shows, however, radical structural change is difficult to effect over a short period of time. While political regimes may change, and new constitutions herald new political and social structures, structural injustices may continue to pervade norms, values, and beliefs and shape social practices and habits, fortified by long-standing and obdurate material conditions. For example, as Branwen Gruffydd Jones has pointed out, the marginalization of African scholarship in the study of international relations (and political theory) is not only a product of historical colonialism, but contemporary structural injustices reproduce "internationally uneven material

---

[51] Truth and Reconciliation Commission of Canada, *Calls to Action*, Call to Action 93, www.trc.ca/websites/trcinstitution/File/2015/Findings/Calls_to_Action_English2.pdf.

conditions in the global political economy of social [philosophical and normative] inquiry."[52] There is thus a distinction between acts of injustice being past and structural injustice being a thing of the past. Even if unjust acts or policies end, for example, through defeat of perpetrators in a war, unjust structural processes and conditions may persist. Even in cases of significant structural change, those who continue to occupy social positions of disadvantage or indignity based on the continued reproduction of structural injustices may still have particular rectificatory claims on participants of the contemporary changed structure. To the extent that structural injustices continue to condition the social position of agents, the political responsibility to eliminate such injustices and their effects is a legacy borne by all those who come to participate in and reproduce those structures. Political responsibility thus continues to be reproduced for present and future agents until their social structures become reasonably just.

IV Benefits, Burdens, and the Legacies of Historic Injustice

An interactional approach argues that contemporary agents have rectificatory obligations if they have somehow benefited from past wrongs; in particular, they have compensatory duties toward those who suffer net losses from historic injustices.[53] This accords with a common moral intuition that people should not only refrain from committing injustice themselves, but they should also refrain from benefiting from injustice. The idea of "unjust enrichment" is that one has profited wrongly from injustice. Even if one is not a culpable beneficiary, it is still morally problematic to be a nonculpable beneficiary of injustice; even if I did not rob the bank, it would be wrong for me to keep stolen property from the bank robbery.

---

[52] Branwen Gruffydd Jones, "Conclusion: imperatives, possibilities, and limitations," in *Decolonizing International Relations*, 236.

[53] According to Randall Robinson's *Restatement of the Black Manifesto*, "all Americans and the United States government have benefitted enormously and continue to benefit from the unjust expropriation of uncompensated labor by enslaved Africans, the subordination and segregation of the descendants of the enslaved, as well as from discrimination against African Americans." See Randall Robinson, *Restatement of the Black Manifesto*: TransAfrica Forum, in *Redress for Historical Injustices in the United States*, Martin and Yaquinto, eds., 621. See also Rodney, *How Europe Underdeveloped Africa*, 205–81.

Before examining the difficulties that attend arguments for rectificatory justice based on the claim that contemporary agents benefit
from historic injustice, it is important to note that in terms of moral
description, the claim is morally misleading in describing the relationship between contemporary agents and past wrongs. From a *moral*
perspective, no one benefits from injustice.[54] If it is true that injustice
can be of moral benefit to no one, then talking about benefiting from
injustice is just misguided from the point of view of moral analysis.
In other words, it is problematic to use an *economic* sense of benefit to describe the *moral* relationship of contemporary agents to past
injustices and their legacies.

Putting this argument about moral description aside, particular challenges arise from grounding contemporary rectificatory responsibilities
on the notion of benefiting from past injustice. According to the unjust
interaction approach, when distributions in holdings become uneven
through *just* international interaction, they are justified; compensatory
justice only arises if losses "result from wrongful harm" through unjust
international interaction. To determine how contemporary agents are
benefited or harmed by the effects of past injustice, Butt argues that we
need not compensate for every act of international injustice; rather, we
need to determine the "net effect of historic injustice." Uncompensated
losses that initially resulted from international wrongdoing produce
inequalities between nations that can be compounded and intensify
over time, with the implication that far from fading with the passage
of time, duties of rectification for historic injustice may intensify over
time.[55]

The logic of this route to compensatory duties raises the possibility that some historic injustices may generate no rectificatory obligations because they actually benefited subject populations.[56] In assessing the historic injustices associated with colonialism, disputes may
arise about how to establish the baseline from which to evaluate when
people have been made worse off, giving rise to different judgments
about the positive or negative consequences of colonial policies on a

[54] For a Socratic perspective on the unprofitability of injustice, see Plato, *The
Republic of Plato*, trans. Allan Bloom (New York: Basic Books, 1991), and
Plato, *Gorgias*, trans. James H. Nichols (Ithaca, NY: Cornell University Press,
1998).
[55] Butt, *Rectifying International Injustice*, 99–101.   [56] Ibid., 104.

subject population, with implications for the moral validity of reparative demands. While there are clear cases of exploitation and deprivation, in some cases, there is genuine dispute about the economic and
social legacies of colonialism. Kok-Chor Tan has noted that colonial
powers such as Britain are widely credited in some circles with having
conferred net benefits on their colonial subjects, including parliamentary democracy, the institution of common law, industrial economic
development, and improved economic conditions.[57] Even if colonial
relationships constituted unjust interactions, can they generate contemporary rectificatory duties if a colonial experience results in raising the
standard of living of the colonized population?

These questions are especially pertinent to evaluating the case of
Japanese colonialism in Korea and Taiwan. Atul Kohli has argued that
Japanese colonialism was unique in boosting overall agricultural production in colonial Korea and was a positive contributing factor to
South Korea's "subsequent economic dynamism." Despite the Second
World War and the Korean War, "the knowledge of industrial technology and management, as well as experience of urban living, a modern
educational system and the skills of workers survived, leaving a positive legacy for postwar industrialization." In terms of political development, "Japanese colonial authorities transformed the decrepit Yi
state into a fairly effective state capable of both controlling and mold-
ing the Korean society," although it should be noted that internally
driven reforms were already under way before the Japanese annexation. Kohli nevertheless concludes that "Japanese colonial influence
on Korea, while ruthless and humiliating, was also decisive in shaping a political economy that later evolved into the high-growth South
Korean path to development." On this point, Kohli acknowledges the
uniqueness of the Korean case: "there are hardly any other similar cases
of colonial experience."[58]

Japan's colonial economic policies, however, also created the dire
economic conditions that made so many rural Korean women vulnerable to victimization. Pyong Gap Min notes, for example, that
because Japanese colonial economic policy devastated Korean agriculture, "many young Korean women from farming families" became

[57] Tan, "Colonialism, reparations, and global justice," 281–82. Tan does not
endorse this assessment of British colonialism.
[58] Atul Kohli, "Japanese colonialism and Korean development: a reply," *World
Development* 25, 6 (1997): 883–88.

vulnerable to pressures to leave home in search of profitable work, a situation exploited by Korean recruiters who used deception to lure such women into the Japanese military comfort system.[59] It is likely the case that Japanese colonialism did pave the way for South Korea's economic development *and* also made poor Korean women of the colonial era more vulnerable to abuse, oppression, and exploitation.

Such mixed results are perhaps natural to accounting for the effects of colonialism, given the complexity of social agents, structures, and relations involved. From this examination of an actual historic case of injustice, one might be concerned about a moral theory of rectification that is based on calculating net losses or harms and net benefits for past unjust actions or interactions. For one thing, whatever benefits the Korean social, economic, or political order may have derived from Japanese colonialism do not obviously cancel out other aspects of Japanese colonial practice that enabled some to exercise domination over others, and that imposed independently morally objectionable deprivations or harms on the most vulnerable segments of society, such as poor and working-class women in conquered or colonized territories.[60]

Determining a net benefit or net loss to contemporary agents from past unjust interactions thus may require a dubious moral calculus, in which moral rights and wrongs are compared and weighed against each other. If we base rectificatory duties on an assessment of net losses and benefits to groups such as nations or peoples, we also risk devaluing the wrongs experienced by individuals or nonnational groups, and thus fail to do justice to individual and other socially vulnerable groups. Even if colonialism led to economic improvements for a majority in the future, these good consequences cannot cancel the historic wrongs of colonial domination, oppression, or brutality suffered by specific agents or marginalized groups. It may therefore not be possible

---

[59] Min, "Korean 'comfort women': the intersection of colonial power, gender, and class," 945 and 951; Soh, *Comfort Women*, 116.

[60] See also Lea Ypi, Robert E. Goodin, and Christian Barry, "Associative duties, global justice, and the colonies," *Philosophy and Public Affairs* 37 (2009): 103–35 at 126, arguing that not much follows from claims that colonized peoples might have been worse off without the benefits of "modernization" that accompanied colonialism: "suppose that Tom assaulted Jane. The fact that Dick would have harmed Jane far worse had Tom not assaulted her does not show that Tom did not harm Jane. Indeed, Jane will ordinarily be entitled to seek compensation from Tom for his assault on her."

to come to a morally sustainable accounting of the net losses and benefits of past injustice, or such an account must fail to give past agents and their experiences of injustice their proper due.

Daniel Butt avoids this kind of problematic consequentialist reasoning to determine the net effects of historic injustice on the contemporary distribution of holdings between nations by positing a counterfactual distribution that would have resulted under conditions of just and consensual interactions between nations. I have already argued that this conception of the counterfactual is implausible, given that just interactions do not automatically yield just outcomes over time. In addition, this interpretation of the net effects of historic injustice has difficulty confirming the responsibility of contemporary agents in cases of historic injustices that produced only net losses to all parties, or no net benefits to anyone. In contexts of interstate war, for example, it is possible that members of countries that are morally responsible for starting an aggressive war do not enjoy a net benefit from their own state's past injustice. Jeff Spinner-Halev has put this point rather sharply: "Why should [the obligation of] repairing the injustice turn on whether the perpetrator gained economically from the injustice?"[61]

In a structural account, those who are in a privileged social position do not even necessarily benefit economically in a direct way from historic injustice. Thus, according to Young, "affirming the existence of white privilege does not amount to claiming that white people either as a group or as individuals owe some kind of payment to black people as a group or as individuals." Rather, Young has developed a "social connection model of responsibility" to illuminate the bases of an obligation "to join with others who share responsibility in order to transform the structural processes to make their outcomes less unjust." Her model bases individuals' political responsibility on "the social positions agents occupy in relation to one another within the structural processes they are trying to change in order to make them less unjust." According to a structural approach, it is not because contemporary agents have benefited but because they have inherited burdens of historic injustice – in the form of contemporary structural injustices – that they have responsibilities. Instead of reproducing an implausible victim–perpetrator divide among contemporary agents for distant historic injustices, a structural approach sees all contemporary agents

[61] Spinner-Halev, *Enduring Injustice*, 81.

involved in an unjust social structure as suffering from different kinds of burdens. Those who enjoy privileged social positions that are reproduced by historically rooted structural injustices are uniquely morally burdened by those privileges, whereas those who suffer structural disadvantages that are reproduced from past injustices are burdened in a different way.

The transatlantic slave trade, for example, was in part enabled by ideologies and juridical codifications of white supremacy and by derogatory views of blacks.[62] To the extent that these racialized attitudes of superiority and inferiority persist as contemporary structural injustices, they burden all contemporary agents who participate in the social structures affected. Thus, according to this structural account, it is not only descendants of slave owners who have responsibilities for redressing the structural legacies of historical slavery, nor can the group of people oppressed by such legacies be limited to the descendants of slaves. New agents, including new immigrants, who come to be socialized in and participate in a racially biased society also bear duties to reform such structural injustices, regardless of their lack of connection to the historic injustice. Those who occupy positions of privilege have a political responsibility to eliminate the structural bases of their arbitrary advantage or the structural bases of the variety of injustices suffered by those in structurally vulnerable social positions.[63] Under this account of responsibility, even the oppressed have responsibility for overcoming structural injustice, not in the sense that they are morally blameworthy for their own oppression but in the sense that they have obligations to resist injustice and participate in collective action to transform unjust social structures and processes. The structural injustice approach is thus not focused primarily on beneficiaries rectifying the distribution of holdings between contemporary agents but on all agents in various social positions acting together to rectify the historically developed structurally unjust institutions, discourses, and practices that produce wrongful social practices, or contemporary objectionable relations and outcomes.

The importance of motivating oppressed agents to engage in the struggle for justice and reconciliation is evident in recent works by

---

[62] See Antony T. Anghie, *Imperialism, Sovereignty and the Making of International Law* (Cambridge: Cambridge University Press, 2005).
[63] Young, *Responsibility for Justice*, 187, 96, and 144.

African American scholars. As Melvin Rogers has put it in a call to other African Americans, "we need not look despairingly upon the past because it overdetermines our present; neither do we need to see the past as anchoring a long arc of justice or an inevitable march toward progress. We can instead say simply that there is work to be done and it is ours to do."[64] Indeed, if the elimination of historically rooted racialized injustice is the goal, these struggles themselves must open possibilities for (and engage the capacities of) the oppressed to participate in the overturning of structural injustices and the work of creating a mutually affirmed social/political order, rather than assign to them the passive role of waiting for beneficiaries of historic injustice to produce just distributions by disgorging their benefits.

One worry about this structural approach is that it seems to diffuse responsibility to an amorphous collective, such as all those who participate in a structural injustice, whereas the virtue of an interactional approach seems to be that it puts specific agents on the moral hook for rectifying historic injustices. In Chapter 3, I argued that while the interactional view is a powerful and plausible way to identify which individual agents should be held accountable through punishment or reparations for contemporary individual wrongdoing, its power and plausibility become weaker when the agents involved operate in contexts of structural injustice that enable their wrongdoing, or in other words, in contexts of major social and political catastrophe. In such circumstances, redress needs to be conceived more expansively than holding individual perpetrators accountable through punishment or through assigning reparative obligations to them. The agents who bear responsibility for redressing injustices go beyond direct individual perpetrators to include those who participate in creating the enabling structural conditions that produced the political catastrophe. While states are responsible for establishing such conditions and therefore may be the appropriate corporate agents to institutionalize rectificatory duties with respect to structural injustice, it is often the case that colonial international and transnational injustices involved structural injustices that transcend state boundaries. The argument of this chapter is that the interactional approach is even less plausible as

---

[64] Melvin Rogers, "What good is history for African Americans?," *The Boston Review*, May 17, 2016, http://bostonreview.net/us/melvin-rogers-what-good-history-african-americans.

the wrongdoing becomes more distant, and as more contentious connections cannot be plausibly established between past wrongs and
contemporary inequalities, or between past agents and contemporary
agents.

Perhaps a more serious problem with grounding contemporary rectificatory duties on contemporary agents benefiting from past injustice is
that some of the most egregious harms of colonialism cannot be framed
in the language of benefit, loss, and compensation. One type of harm
not easily assessed in colonial relationships arises from cultural disorientation and forced assimilation. Frantz Fanon has written extensively
on the cultural and psychological damage inflicted by colonial relationships: the colonized are "people in whom an inferiority complex
has taken root, whose local cultural originality has been committed
to the grave," and who must "position themselves in relation to the
civilizing language: i.e., the metropolitan culture."[65] Japan's cultural
policy of "expunging the ethnicity (*minzoku massatsu*)" included forcing Koreans to adopt Japanese names, imposing Japanese as the official language of education, and requiring Koreans to take an oath as
imperial subjects.[66] Although such policies have ended, to the extent
that assimilationist attitudes toward ethnic Koreans or racialized and
other exclusionary conceptions of "Japaneseness" prevail in Japanese
society, the contemporary Japanese state and society share the moral
and political responsibility to redress such contemporary structural
injustices.[67] Assessments of the effects of historic cultural wrongs, however, are complicated when, through the process of colonization, colonized peoples come to adopt and adapt aspects of the colonizer as
their own. If the colonized people continue to adhere to certain "ideas,
values, or social structures of the former colonizer," does this fact signify the perpetuation of colonial oppression or "neocolonialism,"[68] or

---

[65] Frantz Fanon, *Black Skin, White Masks*, trans. Richard Philcox (New York:
   Grove Press, 2008 [1952]), 2.
[66] Yoshimi Yoshiaki, *Comfort Women: Sexual Slavery in the Japanese Military
   during World War II*, trans. Suzanne O'Brien (New York: Columbia University
   Press, 2000), 153.
[67] See Mark E. Caprio, *Japanese Assimilation Policies in Colonial Korea 1910–50*
   (Seattle: University of Washington Press, 2009); and Debito Arudou,
   Embedded Racism: Japan's Visible Minorities and Racial Discrimination
   (Lanham, MD: Lexington Books, 2015).
[68] Ann E. Cudd, *Analyzing Oppression* (Oxford: Oxford University Press, 2006),
   102.

do such developments indicate that historic injustice may have been superseded?

In cases of cultural disorientation and destruction, we can acknowledge that a wrong was committed and even that people today continue to suffer harms stemming from past wrongs, but it is difficult to see how contemporary agents benefit from such harms, nor does the duty not to benefit from injustice provide any guidance on what contemporary agents (or which contemporary agents) should or can do in the way of repair. Indeed, the stance that such harms can be compensated is not obviously emancipatory. To the extent that cultural disorientation, and even destruction, have contemporary structural effects on social agency and relations, for example, through the continued marginalization or cultural disorientation of certain socially vulnerable groups, a structural injustice approach requires reparative responses to reform such structural injustices, even if no contemporary agents really benefit from a group's continued cultural disorientation or diminished social agency.

If the historic destruction of indigenous governance, language, and culture continues to have structural effects for contemporary agents, then redressing such structural injustice requires devoting resources to alleviating these contemporary structural effects of genocide and settler colonialism. Repairing such enduring injustices even justifies departures from liberal neutrality, since the revival of indigenous languages and cultures may be a precondition for indigenous peoples to enjoy fair opportunity for self-determination in contemporary societies. Indeed, Alan Patten argues that the state may be required to provide a proportionately larger share of resources, compared to other cultural groups, to assist such indigenous cultures to revive their languages and cultural practices, whereas for other cultures (that have not experienced similar historic injustices), state provision of resources for cultural flourishing would have to meet a standard of liberal neutrality in order not to favor any particular culture or conception of the good over others.[69] The differential treatment is still justified on the grounds of neutrality, which relies on the claim that the state has an obligation to provide all its citizens with fair opportunity for self-determination. In the indigenous case, special reparative measures, entailing a greater share of resources,

---

[69] Alan Patten, *Equal Recognition: The Moral Foundations of Minority Rights* (Princeton, NJ: Princeton University Press), 2014.

are required to achieve fair equality of opportunity, given the depth of the structural injustice reflected in contemporary conditions.

In addition, decolonizing Canadian society requires a long-term commitment to change the prevailing orientations of most Canadians toward recognizing the structural injustices that persist in shaping Canadian politics, economics, and culture. Whereas compensation for individuals' suffering for serious human rights violations is an important component of justice for victim-survivors of such wrongs, the task of eliminating colonial structural injustice is much more demanding and requires a more comprehensive, forward-looking strategy.

One way that European states have attempted to redress the colonial past is through providing development assistance, especially to their former colonies. For example, while Germany has continued to refuse to accept liability or reparative obligations to Herero descendants for the 1904–1907 genocide, based on the argument that "the international rules on the protection of combatants and civilians were not in existence at the time that war crimes were being committed in Namibia,"[70] Germany has highlighted its development assistance to Namibia as a measure of its acknowledgment of responsibility to help its former colony. According to German government sources, Namibia is the largest per capita "recipient" of German "development cooperation" in Africa, amounting to nearly €800 million from governmental and nongovernmental programs.[71]

Does the commitment of contemporary European states to development assistance for their ex-colonies make reparative demands redundant?[72] One concern raised by Robert Meister about such forms

---

[70] Allan D. Cooper, "Reparations for the Herero genocide: defining the limits of international litigation," *African Affairs* 106 (2006): 113–26 at 117. For a critique of the 2004 apology, see Jamfa, "Germany faces colonial history in Namibia: a very ambiguous 'I am sorry,'" 202–14.

[71] Embassy of the Federal Republic of Germany Windhoek, www.windhuk.diplo .de/Vertretung/windhuk/en/051/__Development__Co-operation.html.

[72] John Torpey, when discussing the issue of reparations for the Herero, suggests that "foreign assistance might nonetheless be viewed as reparations if either government [Germany or Namibia] wanted to call it so; the issue is in part purely terminological." My argument is that the distinctions between reparation, acknowledgment, and assistance are fundamentally normative, and not merely terminological. See John Torpey, *Making Whole What Was Smashed: On Reparations Politics* (Cambridge, MA: Harvard University Press, 2006), 138.

of "reparations" that are not directly connected to an acknowledgment of responsibility for wrongdoing is that they fail to repudiate evil adequately: "There must also be... an element of moral victory for victims – a *judgment* in their favor – without which redress would merely make 'forced transactions' in the past a little more *acceptable* going forward."[73] Meister also raises the challenge of going beyond conventional "loss-based" reparative strategies that require the identification of surviving victims whose documented harms or losses are directly traceable to past wrongs by identifiable perpetrators. Such strategies can severely limit the efficacy and scope of contemporary reparative claims and obligations and typically do not account for the continued structural disadvantages and advantages that have been built upon past social/political injustices. These structural consequences, however, are significant for the projects of justice and reconciliation because their persistence constitutes an objective source of contemporary structural injustice that also provokes the alienation of contemporary agents from the social/political order. In other words, whereas reparation to individuals who suffered directly may be one component for interactional justice for living survivors, contemporary agents also bear a political responsibility to redress the contemporary structural legacies of international or transnational historical injustices. Meister thus advocates a "gain-based approach to reparative justice" that includes the "disgorgement of ill-gotten gains" by "beneficiaries" of past injustice "whether or not victims of the wrong survive and even if successors to their claims could not directly prove individual losses in an equal or greater amount."[74]

I would argue, however, that the main problem with development assistance as it is currently conducted has to do with its reproduction of the civilized–barbarian divide that structured colonial international order. Anghie has observed that in the 1920s, the internationalization of control over mandated territories involved efforts to integrate them into the global economy as a measure of progress toward civilization:

---

[73] Meister, *After Evil*, 243.
[74] Ibid. See also Robert E. Goodin, "Disgorging the fruits of historical wrongdoing," *American Political Science Review* 107, 3 (2013): 478–91. This paragraph also appears in my "Reconciliation and reparations," in *The Oxford Handbook of Ethics of War*, Helen Frowe and Seth Lazar, eds. (Oxford: Oxford University Press, 2015), Chapter 28, doi:10.1093/oxfordhb/9780199943418.013.17.

"Economic penetration can hardly be stopped, and if the native cannot adjust his own culture to meet it, that culture is likely to disappear altogether."[75] The effect of decades of development assistance, however, has not been to support the renewal of the agential capacities of those who continue to face the effects of cultural disruption and devastation but to reproduce the dependency, marginalization, and vulnerabilities to elite corruption and market distortion characteristic of colonial times.[76] If "developed" countries recognized the colonial nature of contemporary structural injustice in the global economy, it would be difficult to uphold the conventional self-congratulatory narrative that "developed" states tell about their aid to "underdeveloped" or "developing" societies.

While the reproduction of structural injustices may have particular features that should inform the kind of appropriate redress policies, in general, such injustices will not have normative priority over other types of contemporary structural justice (that may not have historic roots). The justice of allocating material resources to combat structural injustices that have historic roots must also involve notions of distributive justice that raise questions about how the claims of those vulnerable to particular kinds of structural injustices are to be assessed in relation to wider societal obligations to the generally disadvantaged. In this sense, structural justices that have historic roots may be normatively special or particular but not necessarily enjoy normative priority over other contemporary structural injustices.

V Conclusion

This chapter has identified problematic ways that the interactional approach attempts to answer questions about the responsibility of

[75] Quoted in Anghie, *Imperialism, Sovereignty and the Making of International Law*, 178.
[76] See Dambisa Moyo, *Dead Aid: Why Aid Is Not Working and How There Is Another Way for Africa* (Toronto: Penguin, 2012); and Nicolas Van de Walle, *African Economies and the Politics of Permanent Crises 1979–99* (Cambridge: Cambridge University Press, 2001). In a parallel discussion of the international humanitarian assistance system, Greg Adams, Oxfam America's director of aid effectiveness, notes, "The system by and large perpetuates a lack of local capacity, when we should be doing the opposite." See Howard LaFranchi and Ryan Lenora Brown, 'The humanitarian revolution: reimagining a colonial-era model,' *Christian Science Monitor*, May 20, 2016, www.csmonitor.com/World/2016/0520/The-humanitarian-revolution-reimagining-a-colonial-era-model.

contemporary agents for historic injustices of the distant past. It develops an argument for a structural approach that focuses the responsibility of contemporary agents on rectifying the historically developed structurally unjust institutions, discourses, and practices that are reproduced as contemporary structural injustices. Redressing structural injustice is not less morally demanding than a theory of rectificatory justice for historic unjust interactions, but a structural injustice approach provides a more empirically and normatively plausible account of the moral significance of historic injustice on contemporary inequalities or deprivations, and generates a need to develop alternative remedies for structural injustice other than compensation, restitution, reparation, or disgorgement.

One objection to the structural injustice approach is that it does not really provide redress for or rectify past injustices. The approach requires developing an account of the *contemporary* injustice of social structures and calls on contemporary agents to reform those structures. Sometimes, the worry about present- and future-oriented theories of justice is that they assume just starting points, in effect wiping clean the historic slate, as if the miserable history of human injustice never occurred. It should be clear that the structural injustice approach, while focused on contemporary social relations and conditions, does not posit that past injustices did not occur or are irrelevant to determining what constitutes contemporary structural injustices. The story of how some injustices become structural is an inescapably historic one.

At the same time, the structural injustice approach does require endorsing a bitter, and contentious, claim: whatever contemporary agents may do in response to historic injustices of the distant past, their actions will not wipe the historic slate clean, or make whole what was smashed, or redeem the suffering of victims, or have any punishing or rehabilitative effect on those who participated in or contributed to the wrongs of the past.[77] Indeed, the belief or claim that any contemporary efforts can wipe the historic slate clean fails to respect the distinction between persons, and thus fails to do justice to the moral reality of the past and the present's relation to it.

The structural injustice approach acknowledges that when contemporary agents do what they can do to reform historically rooted

[77] Torpey, *Making Whole What Has Been Smashed.*

structural injustices, fulfilling their political responsibility does nothing to rectify the injustices suffered by the historic victims. However the individual and social identities, status, and relations of contemporary agents may be transformed by acknowledgment and other redress strategies, the lives and experiences of their ancestors or of past agents are not altered. Injustices that have not received a proper response at the time of their occurrence by the agents involved in the injustice thus constitute a permanent blight on those who lived and participated in them.[78] While this view about the relationship between contemporary agents and historic agents is bitter, it may also be motivational, as it concentrates contemporary agents' moral energies on doing justice in our own time. Part of this motivation stems from the recognition that contemporary agents who fail to perform their duties of justice, including their duties to reform unjust social structures in which they participate, cannot hope that the record of their moral failure can be rectified by future generations.

I have also argued that if historic injustices no longer contribute to the production of oppression, exclusion, marginalization, or domination, or sustain social positions of unjustified privilege or disadvantage in contemporary social relations, they would no longer serve as a justification for special reparative measures.[79] One virtue of the structural approach is that it can explain which of the many injustices of human histories should continue to serve as grounds for contemporary reparative responsibilities.

This is not to argue, however, that contemporary societies have no responsibilities whatsoever regarding historic injustices that no longer contribute to contemporary structural injustice. Even with

---

[78] Some kinds of grave injustices endemic to political catastrophes, such as war, oppression, and atrocity, may have no adequate reparation for victims and no adequate measure of accountability that can produce atonement. The aims of accountability and reparation practices in such cases would not be to restore victims to a condition that cannot be recovered, or to mitigate the blight of injustice by trying to balance the moral books, but to build a new condition that repudiates wrongdoing, expresses solidarity with victims, and generates some level of social trust in the social and political institutions that mediate the lives and interactions of agents. See Pablo de Greiff, *The Handbook of Reparations* (Oxford: Oxford University Press, 2006), 466. I thank Sarah Fine for raising this point.

[79] For a conflicting view on this point, see Butt, *Rectifying International Injustice*, 115 and 118.

respect to historic injustices that have no contemporary manifestation, the terms of reconciliation between contemporary agents, or a
mutually affirmable and affirmed social/political order, may include
forthright acknowledgment of such distant historic injustices. This
point is revealed in Atom Egoyan's film *Ararat*, about the problem
of unacknowledged narratives about historic injustice and how such
denials produce alienation and even provoke violence between contemporary agents. In one part of the story, a contemporary Canadian
of Turkish descent tries to move beyond the past in his interactions with
a Canadian of Armenian descent. Both are involved in making a film
about the Armenian genocide. In a conversation after shooting a scene,
the Turkish-Canadian refuses to acknowledge the historic genocide,
and then says, "I was born here. So were you . . . This is a new country.
So, let's just drop the fucking history and get on with it. No one's gonna
wreck your home. No one's gonna destroy your family!" Although he
offers to drink champagne together, he expresses no regret that the
Armenian genocide has been forgotten, at which point the Armenian-
Canadian declines the invitation.[80] In this fictional scene, we can see
that interactional reconciliation between contemporary agents, understood as their mutual affirmation of their contemporary relationship,
involves in part due acknowledgment of the historic record of collective
experiences with which the contemporary agents identify. Contemporary societies have a duty to acknowledge and recognize past injustices,
even if nothing can or needs to be done in the way of repair in contemporary circumstances. Such acknowledgment is, I would argue, the
primary duty that contemporary agents owe to historic agents, and it
is a key condition for developing contemporary and future relations of
mutual respect and political reconciliation among members of groups
or peoples who have experienced historically unjust interactions or
structures.

Even if such acknowledgment was not forthcoming between the historic agents involved in the historic injustice, contemporary agents still
have a duty of acknowledgment. To the extent that "reparations" may
sometimes constitute a form of symbolic acknowledgment or recognition of past wrongs by contemporary agents, their primary justification
is a forward-looking one, to do with the responsibility of contemporary
agents to promote reconciliation or to construct a mutually affirmable

---

[80] See Atom Egoyan's film *Ararat* (Toronto: Miramax, 2002).

and affirmed social/political order between contemporary agents.[81] In this case, the grounds for such "reparations" is not the rectification of historic injustice but a certain conception of reconciliation.

[81] See Leif Wenar, "Reparations for the future," *Journal of Social Philosophy* 37, 3 (2006): 396–405.

6 | *Reconciliation and Alienation*

The black man is not. No more than the white man.

Both have to move away from the inhuman voices of their respective ancestors so that a genuine communication can be born. Before embarking on a positive voice, freedom needs to make an effort at disalienation.

– Frantz Fanon[1]

I Introduction

Reconciliation is a common, as well as controversial, aspiration of people and societies that have experienced political catastrophes.[2] Some hail reconciliation as having great, perhaps even the greatest, moral and political value.[3] At the same time, some find the concept of reconciliation so elusive, confusing, or objectionable that they urge abandoning it entirely.[4] In this chapter, I aim to clarify the project of reconciliation as a response to the alienation revealed or produced by political

---

[1] Frantz Fanon, *Black Skin, White Masks*, trans. Richard Philcox (New York: Grove Press, 2008 [1952]), 206.

[2] Parts of this section, as well as Sections II and III, are drawn from my "Reconciliation and reparations," in *The Oxford Handbook of Ethics of War*, Helen Frowe and Seth Lazar, eds. (Oxford: Oxford University Press, 2015), Chapter 28, doi:10.1093/oxfordhb/9780199943418.013.17.

[3] This is particularly true after civil wars. Since the mid 1970s, of the thirty "truth commissions" established in twenty-eight countries in response to civil war, intrastate violence, or oppression, at least twelve contain the word "Reconciliation" in their titles (Chile, Democratic Republic of Congo, Ghana, Grenada, Indonesia, Liberia, Morocco, Peru, Sierra Leone, South Africa, Timor-Leste, and the Federal Republic of Yugoslavia). See www.amnesty.org/en/international-justice/issues/truth-commissions.

[4] For a lamentation, see Harvey M. Weinstein, "Editorial note: the myth of closure, the illusion of reconciliation: final thoughts on five years as co-editor-in-chief," *International Journal of Transitional Justice* 5 (2011): 1–10.

catastrophes.[5] Contemporary strategies of reconciliation are problematic, however, when (1) they depoliticize the project of reconciliation, by focusing, for example, on a medicalized notion of individual psychological healing from traumatic experiences; (2) they appeal to an unrealistic and undesirable form of conflict-denying social unity that, in reality, serves to pressure the politically weak to accommodate evil and injustice; and (3) they focus too narrowly or superficially on interactional alienation only, foreclosing progressive political struggle to redress deeper structural sources of alienation.

I distinguish between three related forms of reconciliation: (1) *interactional reconciliation*, which responds to alienation arising between agents through their interactions; (2) *structural reconciliation*, which responds to the alienation that arises from the social and political practices and structures that mediate agents' activities and relations; (3) and *existential reconciliation*, which responds to the internal or self-alienation of agents that typically accompanies some forms of relational and structural alienation. Although popular narratives about reconciliation focus on interactional reconciliation between agents – individually, collectively, or corporately conceived – this chapter demonstrates that the project of structural reconciliation is more normatively fundamental for addressing both interactional and existential forms of alienation. Reconciliation in response to political catastrophe should be understood as a regulative ideal that aims not only to reconcile parties relationally to each other, but more fundamentally, to create a mutually affirmable and affirmed social/political order that can support the flourishing of nonalienated agents.

Under what conditions might agents be reconciled to the social/political institutions that enabled or produced social and political injustices, and which still may constitute so many of the options and limits of their lives? With respect to colonialism, this chapter explores

---

[5] Although my account of "structural reconciliation" shares many affinities with Darrel Moellendorf's normative account of reconciliation as a "political value" and Colleen Murphy's understanding of "political reconciliation" as "the process of rebuilding damaged political relationships," neither employs the concept of alienation to explore what reconciliation aims to resolve. Both also confine their arguments to intrastate cases of violent political conflict or oppression, such as South Africa, Argentina, Chile, and Uganda. See Colleen Murphy, *A Moral Theory of Political Reconciliation* (Cambridge: Cambridge University Press, 2010), 1; and Darrel Moellendorf, "Reconciliation as a political value," *Journal of Social Philosophy* 38, 2 (2007): 205–21.

Frantz Fanon's suggestion of the need for a "genuine communication" to take place between colonizers and the colonized about the terms of reconciliation. Two specific challenges arise that help to explain why the politics of reconciliation has been vexed, especially in cases of indigenous peoples' reconciliation with settler colonial states and the international order. These challenges reveal the significance of structural and existential alienation experienced by colonized subjects that complicates the quest for reconciliation involving reparatory dialogue. The problem of structural alienation denotes defects of the social/political structure that hamper the ability of the appropriate agents to engage in reparatory dialogue. Historical colonial relationships may produce a contemporary condition of "structural indignity" for some of the colonized, which undermines the structural prerequisites for a genuine communication to take place. It is not only states that may suffer structural indignity in terms of their social position in relation to a former colonizer state or within the society of states, but structural indignity may also be an "internal" condition of some groups within settler colonial as well as postcolonial states. It is thus an open question whether contemporary postcolonial states are the appropriate representative agents for engaging in reparatory dialogue about colonial injustices. Postcolonial states may need to engage in "internal" reparatory dialogues before or at the same time as they embark on "external" dialogues with ex-colonizer states. In other words, the colonial nature of the decolonization moment in international relations needs to be addressed.

The problem of existential alienation denotes an agent's anxiety and uncertainty about what constitutes authentic agency. Existential alienation may take the form of inauthentic or alienated agency, a condition precipitated by the disruption and collapse of social and moral frames by which agents were socialized and engaged in the activity of self-realization. I criticize some conceptions of authenticity that presuppose a problematic essentialism or that rely on an infeasible recovery of precolonial traditional formative institutions or identities. Instead, I argue that the terms of structural dignity should provide considerable space for creativity, syncretism, and pluralism to facilitate agents' individual and collective struggles to realize nonalienated forms of human flourishing. The criteria of structural dignity and nonalienated flourishing challenge many contemporary postcolonial and settler colonial states' policies of assimilation, integration, state and nation building, as well as the basic constitutional architecture of the contemporary sovereign states system.

II The Case against Reconciliation

Is reconciliation desirable and feasible? Critics worry that reconciliation may be too demanding, psychologically, sociologically, or morally, or not morally demanding enough.

The "excessively demanding" charge may derive in part from Christian interpretations of reconciliation. Dostoyevsky depicts Christian reconciliation in his short story, "The Dream of a Ridiculous Man," which contains a "fantastic" account of "an earth as yet undefiled by the Fall," in which human beings enjoy complete communion with themselves, each other, nature, the celestial realm, and even death.[6] Although this account is religious, the yearning for deep social unity has secular counterparts and is evident when reconciliation signals aspirations for a conflict-transcendent form of social unity. The Institute for Democracy and Electoral Assistance (IDEA)'s *Handbook on Reconciliation after Violent Conflict*, for example, presents reconciliation as "a process through which a society moves from a divided past to a shared future," which depends on "an over-arching process which includes the search for truth, justice, forgiveness, healing and so on."[7] Conflict and disagreement are endemic after political catastrophes involving war, oppression, or atrocity, but they are also endemic to political life in times of relative peace. The dream of reconciliation is problematic if it aims at a kind of social unity that leaves no space for disagreement and dissent.[8] In her critique of philosophical conceptions of alienation from Rousseau to Heidegger, philosopher Rahel Jaeggi also notes that the ideal of reconciliation as a response to alienation is problematic if conceived as an "ideal of a unity free of tension" or

---

[6] Fyodor Dostoyevsky, "The dream of a ridiculous man: a fantastic story," in *A Gentle Creature and Other Stories*, Alan Myers, trans. (Oxford: Oxford World's Classics, 1995), 117–22.

[7] International Institute for Democracy and Electoral Assistance (IDEA), *Handbook on Reconciliation after Violent Conflict* (2003), 12, www.idea.int/publications/reconciliation/.

[8] On problematic conceptions of unity that view difference and dissent as threats to an unmediated social harmony, see Jonathan Allen, "Balancing justice and social unity: political theory and the idea of a truth and reconciliation commission," *University of Toronto Law Journal* 49, 3 (1999): 315–53.

as presupposing the "certainty of a final harmony."[9] Such a fantastical notion of social unity lies behind some of the disappointment with processes of reconciliation and has even led prominent scholars to conclude that reconciliation as a moral/political project comprises "myths and illusions."[10]

This "social unity" conception of reconciliation also makes psychologically and socially infeasible demands on the victims of political catastrophe. As a survivor of the Rwandan genocide put it, "I don't understand this word 'reconciliation.' I can't reconcile with people, even if they are in prison...If a person comes to ask my forgiveness, I will pardon him after he has resuscitated the members of my family that he killed."[11] Psychologically, not even retribution may guarantee sentimental social unity, especially between victims and perpetrators. More generally, individuals respond differently to similar experiences of conflict-driven loss or injury, and there may be many plausible and acceptable answers to how individuals may reconcile or not with those who have caused them grief.

Moreover, such reconciliation is also overdemanding because conflating social and political reconciliation with individual therapeutic models of healing and forgiveness risks sacrificing individual rights, needs, and interests for communal goals. Ultimately, focusing on agents' sentimental transformations (of hatred and resentment against perpetrators, for example) is inappropriate for conceptualizing reconciliation as a political project. Suppose that some "superior" beings suffer a serious social/political injustice or conflict, yet all are extraordinarily resilient, so do not suffer lasting damage or hold negative attitudes toward those responsible. Is the task of reconciliation fulfilled, since such beings hold no resentment against the responsible parties? Should we consider reconciliation achieved if all victims overcome their traumas through counseling? Our negative responses to both cases reveal that personal psychological healing from the traumas of political catastrophes such as war may be worthwhile but cannot account for the moral/political value of reconciliation. When conceptions of reconciliation aim at a deep social unity that depends on such sentimental transformations, they risk depoliticizing the concept

---

[9] Rahel Jaeggi, *Alienation*, trans. Frederick Neuhouser and Alan E. Smith (New York: Columbia University Press, 2014), 2 and 32.
[10] Weinstein, "Editorial note," 9.   [11] Quoted ibid., 8.

and project of reconciliation, thus undermining its moral and political value.

Those who argue that reconciliation is not demanding enough typically view it as a compromise or abdication of justice. Just as reconciliation demands too much from victims (to forgive), it demands too little of the social/political order, letting off punishing perpetrators, compensating victims, and committing to structural transformations. If reconciliation entails affirming evil, it may be better to remain unreconciled. According to progressivists, when governments promote reconciliation as "closure" after civil war, they delegitimate and demotivate continued struggle for moral and political change. In this vein, Robert Meister has criticized the liberal construct of "transitional justice" for focusing only on victims and perpetrators of violence and basic human rights violations. Such practices typically obscure the structural grievances that initially led to violent political struggle, which may not be changed or settled by focusing on retribution or reparations solely for transgressions that arose in the war itself. Meister is also concerned that the beneficiaries of injustice tend to get let off the moral hook in this accounting because reconciliation is deemed to require only punishing and compensating those directly involved in or affected by violent political struggle.[12]

A similar critique is apparent in Kanien'kéhaka scholar Taiaiake Alfred's "Indigenous Manifesto," in which he provocatively argues against reconciliation, positing that reconciliation is a part of the language of the oppressors. To be reconciled is to "trust and accept the world that has been created through the colonization of America," and it is to "yield to the assimilationist demands of the mainstream and abandon any meaningful attachment to an indigenous cultural and political reality."[13] Such a criticism raises the question of what emancipatory potential the political project of reconciliation may have in the context of societies that not only experienced historical colonialism but may also still be burdened by colonial social structures, the contemporary "living legacies" of colonialism.

It would be difficult to understand how reconciliation could be a worthy moral or political value if it requires imposing undue moral

---

[12] Robert Meister, *After Evil: A Politics of Human Rights* (New York: Columbia University Press, 2012).

[13] Taiaiake Alfred, *Peace, Power and Righteousness* (Oxford: Oxford University Press, 1999), xi.

and psychological burdens on individual agents, striving for a conflict-denying form of social unity, accommodating evil, and/or forestalling further progressive social and political change. These critiques expose problematic and implausible conceptions of reconciliation that lie behind many contemporary political strategies and social expectations of these political processes. Only by reconstructing reconciliation as a regulative ideal characterized by agents' mutual affirmation of the social/political order can we explain why so many contemporary reconciliation efforts fail to acknowledge and overcome, in the right way, the alienation to which the concept of reconciliation aims to respond.

III Reconstructing Reconciliation

Calls for reconciliation in conditions of political catastrophe aim to respond to agents' experiences of alienation, a natural corollary to many types of injustice. The concept of alienation refers to experiences of disconnection,[14] disruption, or distortion in "the structure of human relations to self and world" and "the relations agents have to themselves, to their own actions, and to the social and natural worlds." Rahel Jaeggi defines alienation as a "particular form of the loss of freedom" that involves "a relation of disturbed or inhibited appropriation of world and self." Successful appropriation by an agent "can be explicated as the capacity to make the life one leads, or what one wills and does, one's own; as the capacity to identify with oneself and with what one does; in other words, as the ability to realize oneself in what one does."[15] Alienation thus has existential, interactional, and structural aspects.

Relational or interactional alienation pertains to an interaction between individual or group agents. For example, individual victims of torture are alienated from their torturers, and members of a targeted group may be alienated from the police or the military if these government agents were involved in targeting them. Structural alienation may arise from the social and political institutions – both formal

---

[14] On the problem of disconnection, see Kwame Gyekye, "Evolutionary disconnect: a major factor in normative disorientation," paper presented at an international conference on Normative Disorientation and Institutional Instability, University of Ghana, Legon, March 24, 2015.
[15] Jaeggi, *Alienation*, xxi and 22, 2, 36, and 37.

structures and informal practices – that define agents' positional status, rights and agency, and mediate agents' interactions and activities. In civil war, the most relevant structures may be domestic; in interstate and transnational cases of political catastrophe, the pertinent structures may be international and transnational.[16] Whereas the first kind of alienation refers to agents' relational estrangement from each other and from institutional agents, the second form refers to their structural estrangement from the social/political order.

Not every experience of interactional injustice between agents provokes agents' structural alienation from the social/political order. In a recent example, a group of Syrian refugees who just arrived in Vancouver, Canada, were subjected to an assault by a lone male who pepper-sprayed them while riding by on his bicycle. The attack was widely condemned by civic officials and the police treated it as a hate crime. One of the victimized Syrian refugees, Youssef Ahmad al-Suleiman, told Canadian media about "how he and his fellow newcomers were stunned after Prime Minister Justin Trudeau took to Twitter and apologized on behalf of himself and the Canadian people." Another refugee, Hazaa Sahal, explained that although immediately after the attack, some refugees regretted relocating to Canada, the "feeling quickly evaporated when they saw the overwhelming positive response from police, health officials, the government and the Canadian public." According to Sahal, "we felt like nothing bad happens here and goes without being punished, or the actor being held accountable."[17] In this case, the alienating interaction between the victims and the perpetrator did not translate into an experience of structural alienation. In many contexts of political catastrophe, however, war, oppression, and atrocity are symptomatic of a deeper alienation, not only between warring or injured parties, but also typically between agents and the domestic and international social/political orders that mediate their identities, agency, and activities.

These two distinct kinds of alienation produce two different ways of thinking about reconciliation, what it may aim to achieve, and what

---

[16] To the extent that various aspects of civil armed conflicts, including duration, supply of arms, and humanitarian and refugee assistance, may involve external or international agents and structures, alienation from various international structures and practices may also be relevant to many civil wars.

[17] Geordon Omand, "Refugees grateful for response of Canadians after pepper-spray attack," *The Globe and Mail*, January 13, 2016.

methods may be appropriate for realizing its aims. I call these two concepts of reconciliation *interactional reconciliation* and *structural reconciliation*.

While interactional reconciliation responds to alienation between agents, structural reconciliation responds to people's alienation from social and political institutions and practices. If these practices allow some agents to treat others as if they were nothing, then they constitute an objective source of alienation for the victims, independently of the specific harms that they suffer at the perpetrators' hands. Andromache was not only alienated from Achilles, who killed her husband, Hector, or the Greeks who, out of fear of future revenge, killed her infant son, but she and the other captive Trojan women were objectively alienated from a social/political order in which conquered women became the spoils of war, to be made into concubines and slaves according to the whim of the victors.[18] Structural reconciliation aims to remedy agents' alienation from social institutions, processes, and practices; and agents engage in the quest for structural reconciliation by struggling to create a mutually affirmable and affirmed social/political order.[19]

The construction of a mutually affirmable and affirmed social/political order has objective and subjective components.[20] Objectively, structural reconciliation involves constructing a social/political order that establishes a robust scheme of rights and duties for the relevant agents to exercise their appropriative agency against a set of background conditions that ensure agents' reciprocity in their institutional relations and structural conditions. Structural reconciliation also has

---

[18] Euripides, *The Trojan Women*, trans. Nicholas Rudall (Chicago: Ivan R. Dee, 1999). The play was performed in 415 BCE, one year after Athens invaded the island of Melos.

[19] I am taking my inspiration for this concept of reconciliation from Michael Hardimon's interpretation of Hegel's philosophical project of reconciliation. Thanks to Alan Patten for this reference. See Michael O. Hardimon, "The project of reconciliation: Hegel's social philosophy," *Philosophy and Public Affairs* 21, 2 (1992): 165–95. My understanding of reconciliation, and the problem of alienation to which it responds, is also deeply sympathetic to Rahel Jaeggi's reconstruction of alienation in her book *Alienation*.

[20] As will become apparent, my argument does not rely on a strongly objectivistic theory about the content or substance of the good life (see Jaeggi, *Alienation*, 40). Rather, the objective component of structural reconciliation refers to the external normative and material conditions under which agents may successfully exercise their appropriative powers in circumstances of political modernity.

a subjective component: agents' nonalienated affirmation – acceptance or endorsement – of the rules, relations, and conditions of the domestic and/or international social/political order.[21]

In contemporary international relations, human rights and humanitarian law, state sovereign equality and independence, and prohibitions on the use of force by states form the international normative and legal structures that mediate and organize the internal autonomy of states, as well as their external relations with each other and international institutions. These structures lay out the ground rules and produce the background conditions that mediate how various agents interact in international and transnational relations and how they come to create, participate, sustain, and change the structures and terms of their association. The subjective component of structural reconciliation entails that all states (or their representatives) deny the legitimacy of committing mass violations of human rights or humanitarian laws of war in the pursuit of political objectives, as well as political ambitions for world conquest or world revolution. Cultivating agents' commitment to the international order, however, may depend on whether the international order is objectively worthy of reconciliation, and whether the various components of international order successfully combine to acknowledge and support the self-realization and self-determination of various agents, individual and collective, a necessary condition for their nonalienated affirmation of the international order.

International structural reconciliation focuses on the rules and practices that regulate and shape the agency of states in their interactions with each other and with nonstate parties. Insofar as war is a social practice of a sovereign states system, the tasks of postwar structural reconciliation may involve reforming alienating aspects of the international legal and political practice of war. As was evident in the case of the Versailles peace process after World War I (discussed in Chapter 1), the project of international structural reconciliation after war may also involve not only addressing the specific grievances generated directly by the war itself but also resolving sources of alienation from the preexisting order that may have constituted underlying causes of the conflict

---

[21] As Moellendorf rightly points out, the general acceptance of the institutional order indicative of reconciliation can be distinguished from a fuller, more complete endorsement. See Moellendorf, "Reconciliation as a political value," 207.

or its particular brutalities. In this way, a focus on the tasks of structural reconciliation leaves open the need for further political struggle to overcome long-standing structural failings of the international order. Since Versailles, the subsequent conflicts of the twentieth century demonstrate that postwar relational reconciliation is deeply connected to a more fundamental account of structural reconciliation that goes beyond the specific wrongs or damages done during the political catastrophe in question. In this sense, the project of reconciliation in international relations cannot plausibly be interpreted as a project of return to a presumed meaningful and legitimate order.[22]

Although both structural and interactional reconciliation are important, structural reconciliation is normatively fundamental because its components establish the background conditions appropriate for legitimating any negotiated settlement on interactional reconciliation between agents. Neither interactional nor structural reconciliation, as a *political* project, requires changing people's sentimental attitudes toward those who wronged them or contributed to their suffering and losses, although relational reconciliation may aim to recalibrate agents' senses of shame and guilt, as well as repudiate hostile, dehumanizing, and disrespectful attitudes or beliefs about other social groups.[23] Both interactional and structural reconciliation may have an effect on individual psychological healing or sentiments, but changes in these features of agents do not define or fulfill reconciliation understood as a political project.[24]

---

[22] In this sense, the word "conciliation" might be more accurate to describe the project of constructing a mutually affirmed international political order that has not previously existed. However, I have kept the term "reconciliation," as it is the prevailing term in both theoretical and political discourse that I seek to interrogate and reconstruct.

[23] See Lu, "Shame, guilt and reconciliation after war," *European Journal of Social Theory* 11, 3 (2008): 367–83.

[24] This is not to deny the existence and desirability of reconciliation understood as an interpersonal moral project. For example, the memoirs of Eric Lomax provide a powerful story of how a British prisoner of war came to be reconciled with one of the Japanese soldiers who participated in his imprisonment and torture during World War II. See Eric Lomax, *The Railway Man* (London: Vintage, 1996). Brendan Hamber also notes that a growing number of mental health professionals are starting to become aware of the limits of focusing on medical or therapeutic individual interventions and are instead emphasizing the impact of socioeconomic and political contexts on the mental health and recovery of individual victims. See Brandon Hamber, "Does

At the same time, political reconciliation does not need to presuppose a fixed account of a morally ideal social/political order. Rather, reconciliation enables the relevant agents to engage in an open-ended, meaningful, and respectful struggle for a mutually affirmed social/political order. As James Tully has argued with respect to reconciliation between indigenous peoples and the settler colonial societies into which they were forcibly incorporated, "reconciliation is neither a form of recognition handed down to Indigenous peoples from the state nor a final settlement of some kind. It is an ongoing partnership negotiated by free peoples based on principles they can both endorse and open to modification *en passant.*"[25] Given that reconciliation, so understood, does not foreclose continued political struggle over the terms of both structural and relational reconciliation, such a project allows the continuation of moral and political disagreement and does not assume a homogenizing ideal or a conflict-transcendent form of social unity.[26]

IV Conditions for "Genuine Communication": Structural Dignity

The idea that reconciliation involves a genuine communication or reparatory dialogue between the contemporary inheritors of an unjust past has been developing within the contemporary politics of reconciliation in international and transnational relations. In March 2014, for example, fourteen Caribbean countries agreed on a comprehensive plan that calls upon "the former slave-owning nations of Europe – principally Britain, France, Spain, Portugal, the Netherlands, Norway, Sweden and Denmark – to engage Caribbean governments in reparatory dialogue to address the living legacies of these crimes." The plan requests that in formulating a new development agenda for the

the truth heal? A psychological perspective on political strategies for dealing with the legacy of political violence," in *Burying the Past: Making Peace and Doing Justice after Civil Conflict*, Nigel Biggar, ed. (Washington, DC: Georgetown University Press, 2003), 155–76.

[25] James Tully, *Public Philosophy in a New Key: Volume 1, Democracy and Civic Freedom* (Cambridge: Cambridge University Press, 2008), 223–56.

[26] Working from the other end toward the same conclusion, Jaeggi adopts a "qualified subjectivism" and notes that her reconstruction of alienation is "open-ended and not dependent on a closed, harmonistic, model of reconciliation" (*Alienation*, 40).

Caribbean, the involved European nations take into account such a reparatory dialogue, in order to establish a period of "mutual respect, recognition, and conciliation."[27] Similarly, in 2007, the chief of the Herero people, Kuaima Riruako, asserted that the Herero's quest for reparations from Germany for the genocide committed by Imperial Germany in 1904–1907 was, in reality, an appeal "to the government of the Federal Republic of Germany for a dialogue so that we can talk about our colonial experience."[28]

Frantz Fanon argued that one of the aims of contemporary societies marked by a colonial relationship must be "to move away from the inhuman voices of their respective ancestors so that a genuine communication can be born. Before embarking on a positive voice, freedom needs to make an effort at disalienation."[29] Fanon makes it clear that not any communication will do, reminding us of how the politics and discourse of reconciliation has been instrumentalized by governments and elites to evade accountability, force social cohesion, and forestall progressive political change. What, then, are the conditions necessary for a dialogue to be truly reparatory, or for a communication to be truly genuine?[30]

If reconciliation involves a genuine communication about colonialism and its structural legacies between contemporary agents, the problem of structural alienation becomes apparent when we ask the question of who the agents are who should participate in such dialogues. It is conventional to think that the relevant agents in contexts of international and transnational historical injustices such as

---

[27] The Caribbean Community (CARICOM) Reparations Commission Press Statement, December 2013, emphasis mine, http://caricom.org/jsp/pressreleases/press_releases_2013/pres285_13.jsp. See also Ed Pilkington, "Caribbean nations prepare demand for slavery reparations," *The Guardian*, March 9, 2014. Martyn Day, a lawyer at London's Leigh Day who is representing CARICOM, the group of Caribbean states, says the countries' initial aim is to negotiate for reparations. The British law firm Leigh Day recently won compensation for hundreds of Kenyans tortured by the British colonial government during the Mau Mau rebellion of the 1950s.

[28] "German Parliament Debates Compensation for Herero Massacre," *Deutsche Welle*, June 15, 2007. See also http://dw.de/p/1FaC4.

[29] Fanon, *Black Skin, White Masks*, 206.

[30] For an interesting deliberative democratic account, see Sara Amighetti and Alasia Nuti, "Towards a shared redress: achieving historical justice through democratic deliberation," *The Journal of Political Philosophy* 23, 4 (2015): 385–405.

colonialism are representatives of former colonizing states and formerly colonized states.[31] In recent international legal developments regarding state responsibility for reparations for internationally unlawful conduct, it is states that are the primary agents of rectificatory justice in international relations.[32] In his lucid work examining questions of international rectificatory justice, Daniel Butt acknowledges that, while much philosophical literature on rectificatory justice has focused on the claims of indigenous peoples, he explicitly understands "'international' justice in the sense of justice between, not within, modern day self-governing communities," and is thus limited to cases in which "the people of one modern day state have duties to persons who are members of other states."[33] By limiting his analysis of international rectificatory justice in this way, however, Butt effectively excludes indigenous rectificatory claims within settler colonial states, and obscures the pertinence of such claims in constructing a just international and transnational order. Although much of the politics of both justice and reconciliation in international relations today is framed in statist or interstatist terms, it is important to remember that the interstate system, along with the configuration of modern-day settler colonial and postcolonial states, is a product of the global expansion of a Eurocentric society of states and hence is itself a legacy of European colonialism.[34]

---

[31] Kok-Chor Tan emphasizes the injustices of colonialism as wrongs "against a community or *a people*" rather than as harms to individual persons, but he does not discuss other structurally differentiated harms to social groups, based on class and gender. See his "Colonialism, reparations and global justice," in *Reparations: Interdisciplinary Inquiries*, J. Miller and R. Kumar, eds. (Oxford: Oxford University Press, 2007), 283.

[32] For the text of the Articles on "Responsibility of States for Internationally Wrongful Acts," see http://legal.un.org/ilc/texts/instruments/english/draft%20articles/9_6_2001.pdf.

[33] Daniel Butt, *Rectifying International Injustice: Principles of Compensation and Restitution between Nations* (Oxford: Oxford University Press, 2009), 23. According to Butt, taking for granted the statist structure of international relations is necessary "since modern day political agency is typically exercised through the state, and so political questions of duties to others arise primarily at a state level."

[34] G. John Ikenberry states the problem of order as conceptualized by dominant approaches to the study of international relations: "How can a stable and mutually acceptable system of relations be established between strong and weak states?" See Ikenberry, *After Victory: Institutions, Strategic Restraint, and the Rebuilding of Order after Major Wars* (Princeton, NJ: Princeton University Press, 2001).

The society of states, through the 1960 United Nations Declaration on the Granting of Independence to Colonial Countries and Peoples, aimed to rectify the structural alienation of colonized peoples from the international system, grounding decolonization of the international order on an affirmation of "the dignity and worth of the human person," and the recognition of the right of all peoples to self-determination, by virtue of which all peoples have the right to "freely determine their political status and freely pursue their economic, social and cultural development."[35] Reasons employed in colonial contexts to justify the subjugation of peoples were also repudiated: "Inadequacy of political, economic, social or educational preparedness should never serve as a pretext for delaying independence."[36] Decolonization as a political movement repudiated the subjection of peoples to colonial rule, a historically necessary response to the brutal histories of colonial oppression that made "breaking all political relations with their former master . . . the only plausible way forward."[37]

One implication of recognizing the historicity of the decolonization movement is to note that different political circumstances could have generated different forms of political relationships and structures that could be affirmed by colonizer and colonized. As Olusoga and Erichsen note, by 1904, after twenty years of exposure to the German colonial project, the Herero and settlers in the German colonial outpost at Okahandja thrived together (though not equitably) in German South West Africa. The paramount chief of the Herero, Samuel Maharero, built himself a villa in "the fashion of the German settlers. With a vast personal fortune based on cattle and increasingly on the sale of land, his home, furnished with plush velvet sofas and heavy carpets, reflected his social position."[38] Remembering these earlier snapshots of

---

[35] The structural dignity of peoples was tied to human dignity, as the Declaration stated that the "subjection of peoples to alien subjugation, domination and exploitation constitutes a denial of fundamental human rights."

[36] www.un.org/en/decolonization/declaration.shtml.

[37] Ypi, "What's wrong with colonialism," 190.

[38] Olusoga and Erichsen, *The Kaiser's Holocaust*, 123. Unfortunately, when German colonial policies became intolerable, triggering the 1904 Herero uprising, Samuel Maherero's fortunes were tied with his people's. Although he survived the Battle of Waterberg against General von Trotha and his troops, escaping with approximately one thousand Herero to British Bechuanaland (contemporary Botswana) in 1908, the Paramount Chief of the Herero witnessed the destruction of his people and died in 1923, exiled from his homelands.

mutually (though not equally) beneficial relations in colonial contexts, however transitory, allows us to conjecture that the conditions of structural dignity should not be ahistorically conceived to require or be guaranteed by decolonization in the form of granting independent sovereign statehood.[39]

Indeed, historicizing the decolonization process of the mid twentieth century also allows us to recognize its incompleteness, as decolonized states were themselves creations of colonial state-building projects. As Pierre Englebert has shown, the effects of decolonization based on the boundaries drawn by colonial powers were varied, with some precolonial peoples inheriting state structures that were roughly congruent with their previous development, while others were bequeathed postcolonial state structures that clashed with precolonial political and social structures, sometimes with dire consequences for subsequent social and political development.[40] Furthermore, while decolonization conferred the status of equal sovereignty to postcolonial states, precolonial peoples who found themselves within a newly decolonized state or a settler state were denied any international standing as peoples in the interstate order and thus did not enjoy an internationally recognized right to self-determination as peoples, or the freedom to determine their political status or pursue their economic, social, and cultural development. Decolonization thus did not allow for secession or a reconfiguration of territory, or guarantee international standing, or moral and political reciprocity, to peoples and other organized social groups within settler colonial and postcolonial states.[41]

[39] See also Adria K. Lawrence, *Imperial Rule and the Politics of Nationalism: Anti-Colonial Protest in the French Empire* (Cambridge: Cambridge University Press, 2013).

[40] See Englebert, "Pre-colonial institutions, post-colonial states, and economic development in tropical Africa."

[41] The principle of *uti possidetis*, by which new states' territorial boundaries are fixed by the previous colonial administrative borders, was used in the decolonization processes that occurred in Spanish Latin America in the 1800s, in Asia and Africa in the 1950s, and in the breakup of the former Soviet Union, Yugoslavia, and Czechoslovakia in the 1990s. See Steven R. Ratner, "Drawing a better line: *uti possidetis* and the borders of new states," *The American Journal of International Law* 90, 4 (1996): 590–624; Mark W. Zacher, "The territorial integrity norm: international boundaries and the use of force," *International Organization* 55, 2 (2001): 215–50; Brian Taylor Sumner, "Territorial disputes at the International Court of Justice," *Duke Law Journal* 53, 6 (2004): 1779–812.

Decolonization in international relations thus had no emancipatory effect in settler colonial states such as Canada and the US, except to entrench further the "structural indignity" of indigenous peoples who were forcibly incorporated into these states. In the US, for example, before 1849, relations between the US federal government and Indian tribes were managed through the Department of War. In US courts, Indian tribes were considered "domestic dependent nations," akin to "weak states," which were entities that placed themselves under the protection of a more powerful state, without being stripped of the right of government and sovereignty. Starting in 1849, however, the US Bureau of Indian Affairs came to be lodged within the Department of the Interior, a department that manages natural resources and wildlife and not relations between self-governing peoples or governments.[42]

In addition, the colonial form of the twentieth-century decolonization process deprived effective political status and agency to many peoples who were the victims of colonial wars, genocides, dispossession, and exploitation. In the case of German South West Africa, for example, German colonialism involved policies of extermination against the two dominant peoples of the region, the Herero and the Nama.[43] The last colony to achieve independence (in 1990, after the demise of apartheid South Africa), the state of Namibia came to represent all the peoples within German South West Africa. Although the Herero filed a legal case for reparations against the German government (as well as two German companies) in 2001, the Namibian state was, until 2007, reluctant to support the Herero claim, characterizing it as a form of tribalism that hampered the path to development for all Namibians: "The Namibian government argued that *all* Namibians suffered at the hands of German colonizers and that the German government has

---

[42] See N. Bruce Duthi, *American Indians and the Law* (New York: Penguin, 2008), xxviii–xxix; and N. Bruce Duthu, *Shadow Nations: Tribal Sovereignty and the Limits of Legal Pluralism* (Oxford: Oxford University Press, 2013), 12–14. On Indian tribes as "domestic dependent nations," see *Cherokee Nation v. Georgia* (1831), and on the anomalous nature of Indian treaties, given their various deviations from standard international treaties between sovereign, internationally recognized states, see Francis Paul Prucha, *American Indian Treaties: The History of a Political Anomaly* (Berkeley: University of California Press, 1994).

[43] See Sidney L. Harring, "German reparations to the Herero nation: an assertion of Herero nationhood in the path of Namibian development?," *West Virginia Law Review* 104 (2001–2002): 393–417 at 401. See also Olusoga and Erichsen, *The Kaiser's Holocaust*.

since entered into a 'special relationship' with independent Namibia that would be disturbed by litigation for reparations."[44] Although the Namibian government changed its mind and eventually supported the Herero claim, the conflict between the Namibian state-building project and the Herero's desire to make independent political claims in the context of international relations shows that the question of *who* should be involved in any genuine communication aimed at reconciliation may not be appropriately or unconditionally answered in statist terms.[45]

In general, indigenous and other precolonial peoples may experience structural alienation when forced into sovereign state and interstate systems that do not recognize their status as peoples or groups who could have suffered distinct historical wrongs associated with colonialism and who may require particular forms of accommodation. It should be noted that the representatives of the colonized and subjugated who sought an international audience at the League of Nations included Chief Levi General (Deskaheh), leader of the Six Nations, who went to Geneva in 1923 to petition League members to rectify treaty violations and erosions of indigenous sovereignty by the government of Canada, wrongs which constituted, to the Six Nations, "an act of war" and "a menace to international peace."[46] From a historical perspective, we can thus appreciate the necessity of problematizing the modern-day state and states system, and of acknowledging that contemporary conflicts between indigenous peoples and settler colonial states constitute a category of cases that belong in an examination of justice and

---

[44] Allan D. Cooper, "Reparations for the Herero genocide: defining the limits of international litigation," *African Affairs* 106, 422 (2006): 113–26 at 115.

[45] The Namibian Parliament officially changed its position on the Herero's claim for reparations in October 2006. See Uazuva Kaumbi, "Namibia: official support for Herero reparation struggle," *New African*, December 2006, 48. However, in 2016, Herero leaders and activists criticized the framework of negotiations set up between the governments of Namibia and Germany that failed to include them adequately in the dialogue.

[46] Canada was able to block the petition by asserting that the Six Nations suffered from incapacity to assume the responsibilities of statehood, which justified Canada's policy of treating indigenous peoples as "wards of the state in need of both civilizing and federal protection." Great Britain supported Canada by viewing the dispute as a domestic matter within the British Empire. See Mark Pearcey, "Sovereignty, identity, and indigenous-state relations at the beginning of the twentieth century: a case of exclusion by inclusion," *International Studies Review* 17 (2015): 441–54 at 449 and 451–52; and Yale D. Belanger, "The Six Nations of Grand River Territory's attempts at renewing international political relationships," *Canadian Foreign Policy* 13, 3 (2007): 29–43 at 34.

reconciliation in international and transnational relations.[47] The structural alienation of indigenous peoples from the international order has
been largely obscured in contemporary international politics, no doubt
because its acknowledgment challenges the authority and sovereignty
of states that were created in the decolonization process. To acknowledge this structural alienation is to acknowledge that one barrier to
reconciliation involving genuine communication is that some contemporary agents who may legitimately participate in such dialogues do
not only have to deal with the "living legacies" of a colonialism that
occurred in the distant past. Instead, for some of them, in a significant
sense, colonialism is not yet over.

Yet as Glen Coulthard has observed, popular and political discourse
about the project of reconciliation obscures this reality, when "reconciliation takes on a temporal character as the individual and collective process of overcoming the subsequent *legacy* of past abuse, not
the abusive colonial structure itself."[48] From this perspective, to ask
indigenous peoples to be reconciled to a political/legal order that places
them in a continued position of structural indignity is to ask them to
be reconciled to a contemporary injustice. Such reconciliation cannot
be morally desirable or worthy and mirrors historical colonial practices in which indigenous peoples were forced or defrauded into signing
treaties of friendship and protection with European colonizers.[49]

Structural dignity is a fundamental prerequisite of a just social structure and an objective component of structural reconciliation. In part,
it is because agents enjoy structural dignity that they are adequately
enabled to participate in the social/political struggle over what constitutes a just and nonalienating social structure. An agent enjoys structural dignity when the social/political structures in which the agent is
positioned empowers her to participate in the making of meaning in
the social world.[50] Given a certain account of human dignity, social

[47] There was still dispute among international lawyers in the nineteenth century
about the status of "Indian Native States" (South Asia) and their relations with
the British government in international law. See Edward Keene, *Beyond the
Anarchical Society: Grotius, Colonialism and Order in World Politics*
(Cambridge: Cambridge University Press, 2002), 99–100.

[48] Glen Sean Coulthard, *Red Skin, White Masks: Rejecting the Colonial Politics
of Recognition* (Minneapolis: University of Minnesota Press, 2014), 109.

[49] See also Olusoga and Erichsen, *The Kaiser's Holocaust*, 62–64.

[50] For a similar account of this value related to the concept of self-determination,
see Anna Stilz, "The value of self-determination," *Oxford Studies in Political*

systems of slavery or those that produce severe poverty, for example, are ones that place enslaved or impoverished agents in positions of structural indignity. Given a certain account of collective dignity based on the right of peoples to morally reciprocal terms of cooperation and association, a colonial international order that legitimizes the forcible subjugation of some peoples by others (or by an international institution) is one in which the subjugated peoples occupy a position of structural indignity. As the case of indigenous peoples suggests, not only may states suffer structural indignity in terms of their social position in relation to a former colonizer state or within the interstate order but since colonial practices produced differential patterns of victimized groups within colonized states, structural indignity may also be an "internal" condition experienced by some groups within decolonized or settler states. To the extent that the current international society of states suppresses alternative forms of political organization to the sovereign state, it continues to be a colonizing project.[51]

Given that one of the legacies of colonialism and decolonization is the forced integration and subjection of disparate groups or peoples into/by a Weberian state model, achieving structural dignity is not the same as achieving structural equality for all individuals within an existing state. Structural dignity for some colonized substate groups may require structures that enable group self-determination, in addition to (or as an alternative to) guarantees of democratic equality and individual rights that are standard within liberal democracies. Canadian prime minister Pierre Elliot Trudeau's attempt in the late 1960s to resolve the "Indian problem" by unilaterally repealing the Indian Act, extinguishing Indian status, and granting aboriginals equal Canadian citizenship rights is one example of a well-intentioned, but misguided,

---

Philosophy, vol. 2, D. Sobel, P. Vallentyne, and S. Wall, eds. (Oxford: Oxford University Press, 2016), 98–126. The concept of alienation is also central to Stilz's account of the value of self-determination, but she seems mainly to have "structural alienation" in mind, and does not consider the problem of existential or self-alienation of agents that undermines the effective use of any right to self-determination. On dignity, see Jeremy Waldron, *Dignity, Rank, and Rights* (Oxford: Oxford University Press, 2012).

[51] Ironically, in international relations theory, the "international society" or "English" school considers itself "pluralist" because it favors a society of sovereign states over a hegemonic world state. For a critique of the imperial implications of the English school's statist bias, see Pearcey, "Sovereignty, identity and indigenous-state relations."

effort to establish structural justice and reconciliation in response to Canada's colonial history. As Dale Turner has observed, the Liberal government's 1969 White Paper was received by indigenous groups as "yet another manifestation of European colonialism." It ultimately failed to redress Canada's colonial legacy, mainly through its lack of acknowledgment of indigenous claims as distinct from those of other minorities, its absence of critical reflection on the "legitimacy of the initial formation of the Canadian state," and its denial of participation by indigenous peoples themselves in the construction of any policy on indigenous relations with the Canadian state and society.[52] The point here is not that P. E. Trudeau's vision of political equality for indigenous persons was necessarily substantively incorrect; rather, the problem lay in how the one-sided political process accentuated the structural indignity of indigenous groups, and the accompanying alienation of their freedom to engage with others and the world on mutually affirmed terms.

With the introduction of the 2007 United Nations Declaration on the Rights of Indigenous Peoples, the society of states is attempting to extend the decolonization process to indigenous peoples within states. Thus, Article 3 of that Declaration mirrors Article 2 of the 1960 Declaration on the Granting of Independence to Colonial Countries and Peoples: "Indigenous peoples have the right to self-determination. By virtue of that right they freely determine their political status and freely pursue their economic, social and cultural development."[53] In Canada, the Truth and Reconciliation Commission Report on the Indian Residential Schools calls the UN Declaration the "framework for reconciliation." One way to understand the UN Declaration is that it outlines the requirements of structural dignity for indigenous peoples within international and domestic orders. It does so by outlining the "minimum human rights standards for indigenous people around the world and their rights to self-determination."[54] The UN Declaration, when adopted and implemented by governments, would accord indigenous peoples a position of structural dignity in the international order, from which a genuine communication about the terms of both justice and

---

[52] Dale Turner, *This Is Not a Peace Pipe: Towards a Critical Indigenous Philosophy* (Toronto: University of Toronto Press, 2006), 15.

[53] www.un.org/esa/socdev/unpfii/documents/DRIPS_en.pdf.

[54] Haydn Watters, "Truth and Reconciliation chair urges Canada to adopt UN Declaration on Indigenous Peoples," *CBC News*, June 1, 2015.

reconciliation can take place. Significantly, the US, Canada, Australia, and New Zealand – all settler colonial states – initially voted against the UN Declaration in 2007, and while the US has yet to sign the Declaration, the Canadian government did sign in 2010, but considered it an "aspirational" document. In 2015, with the election of the Liberal Party led by Justin Trudeau, the Canadian government has begun to express its commitment to a full adoption and implementation of the UN Declaration, although as of the beginning of 2017, little progress has been made.

The continued structural alienation of indigenous peoples from the international order of states reveals that the decolonization movement in the mid twentieth century was a bittersweet development for those who were forcibly incorporated into empires, and then into settler colonial or newly independent postcolonial states. In addition to recognition of the self-determination of peoples within decolonized states, the struggle for reconciliation of some indigenous peoples may require their participation in the development of international institutions and norms regulating territorial border controls, the development of natural resources, the restrictions on internal state autonomy as it pertains to groups, and even regarding secession. In these ways, we should understand the condition of structural dignity to make potentially radical transformative demands of the current interstate order.[55]

V Existential Alienation: Inauthentic Agency and the Ideal of Nonalienation

In addition to interactional and structural alienation, one legacy of colonial practices of domination and usurpation that fundamentally threatens genuine communication has so far been obscured. This can be characterized as the problem of existential alienation in the form of inauthentic agency. Colonial conditions typically engendered subjects

---

[55] On the refusal of Canadian and American settler citizenship by members of the Mohawks of Kahnawà:ke, in an acknowledgment that "the United States and Canada can only come into political being because of Indigenous dispossession," see Audra Simpson, *Mohawk Interruptus: Political Life across the Borders of Settler States* (Durham, NC: Duke University Press, 2014), 12. See Chapter 8 for a further elaboration of this point. See also Iris Marion Young, *Global Challenges: War, Self-Determination and Responsibility for Justice* (Cambridge: Polity, 2007), 39–57.

who were doubly alienated, from the colonizer's world as well as from their own. Authentic agency in postcolonial contexts must involve overcoming this double alienation.[56] Existential alienation appears when we consider Frantz Fanon's discussion of the cultural and psychological damage inflicted by colonial relationships. The colonized are "people in whom an inferiority complex has taken root, whose local cultural originality has been committed to the grave," and who must "position themselves in relation to the civilizing language: i.e., the metropolitan culture."[57] According to Kok-Chor Tan, those whose identities have been distorted by a colonial experience typically lack the requisite identity resources for engaging in mutually just and cooperative relations: "Victims may internalize the morally inferior status they have in the eyes of their aggressors, while violators may come to have a distorted sense of their own moral superiority, furthering the asymmetry in relationship that makes a just relationship impossible."[58]

Taiaiake Alfred characterizes this form of existential alienation as the problem of living "inauthentic lives."[59] As Alfred notes, "a lot of our Native people imagine themselves to be Canadians. And that's not true ... those Canadianized Indians are 'in the darkness'; they've had their eyes shut to their true being, they can't envision a future in which we are nations. They can't see a positive future; they're wallowing in the pain of being dependent wards of the Canadian state."[60] He takes contemporary indigenous peoples to task for "'mimicking' their traditions, without true understanding of the basic principles ... Too many of our peoples are disoriented, dissatisfied, fearful, and disconnected from each other and from the natural world."[61] According to Alfred, the "underlying cause of [indigenous] suffering is alienation – separation from our heritage and from ourselves."[62] This form of alienation is thus not focused on one's relationship with others, or with the social structures that mediate our relationship with others. Rather, this form of alienation can be termed "self-alienation."

---

[56] For an example of double alienation, see Margaret Kohn and Keally McBride, *Political Theories of Decolonization: Postcolonialism and the Problem of Foundations* (Oxford: Oxford University Press, 2011), 30.

[57] Fanon, *Black Skin, White Masks*, 2.

[58] Kok-Chor Tan, "Colonialism, reparations, and global justice," 287.

[59] Alfred, *Peace, Power and Righteousness*, xi.

[60] Taiaike Alfred, *Wasáse: Indigenous Pathways of Action and Freedom* (Toronto: University of Toronto Press), 34; Alfred, *Peace, Power and Righteousness*, xxi.

[61] Alfred, *Wasáse*, 92.   [62] Ibid., xv.

Understanding the project of reconciliation as involving genuine communication assumes that the agents involved in the dialogue have the capacity to exercise authentic agency. But if indigenous peoples are leading inauthentic lives, then whatever reconciliation is achieved will be illusory. Instead of signaling genuine social unity, dialogues of reconciliation could signal only resignation and dependency. Such reconciliation cannot be considered progressive, and may even amount to a form of false consciousness as well as continued internalized oppression and alienation.

This challenge of existential alienation as inauthentic living appears also in other postcolonial contexts. Pratap Mehta has observed that empire creates "a new existential order," in which the subordinated face a dilemma:

> to assert a difference from the normative hierarchies that imperial powers created was to confirm the very thing the colonizer thought about you. But to assimilate to those demands and fashion yourself in accordance with them was to grant him the ultimate victory. The estrangement that colonialism produced was not so much a substantive estrangement – Am I estranged from my tradition? – but an almost existential one. *Nothing the colonial subject did could be seen to be authentically his own.*[63]

To appreciate how formidable this challenge of existential alienation is to the project of reconciliation, consider that formal decolonization (giving back control or self-determination of formative institutions and processes) does not necessarily give back to those who were colonized authentic agency. In this sense, the problem is not the "impossibility of self-determination," as Mehta put it, but the impossibility of self-realization, despite self-determination. As Anna Stilz has explained, the concept of self-determination has two aspects: "The 'internal' aspects refers to a people's right to choose a government that reflects their

---

[63] Pratap Bhanu Mehta, "After colonialism: the impossibility of self-determination," in *Colonialism and Its Legacies*, Jacob T. Levy and Iris Marion Young, eds. (Lanham, MD: Lexington Books, 2011), 147–70 at 150 and 151. Interestingly, Alfred identifies the struggle for indigenous resurgence with struggles of peoples in Africa and Asia, referring to Albert Memmi, a North African scholar: "One can be reconciled to every situation, and the colonized can wait a long time to live. But, regardless of how soon or how violently the colonized rejects his situation, he will one day begin to overthrow his *unliveable existence* with the whole force of his oppressed personality" ("Wasáse: Indigenous Resurgences," in *Colonialism and Its Legacies*, 84, emphasis mine).

values and priorities, while the 'external' aspect denotes a people's right to be free from outside interference."[64] While Stilz develops a lucid account of the value of self-determination in terms of addressing people's structural alienation from the institutions that govern them, her argument seems to conflate self-determination with self-realization. Her account of self-determination thus presupposes a resolution to the problem of existential or self-alienation, which refers to the problem of inauthentic and alienated agency in forming values and priorities.[65] As Rahel Jaeggi has observed, alienation "is not coextensive with heteronomy" and depends on more than whether agents enjoy self-determination in the negative sense of not being subject to a foreign will.[66] If authentic agency is "impossible," can reconciliation, involving genuine communication, even be possible? And what constitutes authentic agency in postcolonial conditions?

Authenticity is a complicated concept, with a history. The ideal of authenticity developed in the Western history of ideas in the seventeenth and eighteenth centuries: the idea of individuals being true to themselves, rather than the passive inhabitants of roles defined by a prevailing social order.[67] A liberal conception of individual authenticity involves the idea of authorship or self-ownership – of living a life that is fully one's own. The contrast is a life in which one's agenda, decisions, choices, actions, or preferences are imposed by another agent. Robert Nozick's defense of individual liberties appeals to the value of this notion of authenticity: "A person's shaping his life in accordance with some overall plan is his way of giving meaning to his life; only a being with the capacity to so shape his life can have or strive

---

[64] Stilz, "The value of self-determination," 99.

[65] A similar point can be made with respect to Rainer Forst's account of the right to justification as a principle of justice that serves the emancipatory aim of disestablishing domination, or arbitrary social and political power. His conception of justice as an autonomous achievement of political agents presupposes successful resolution of the problem of existential alienation, otherwise structures of justification may themselves become sources of intersubjective domination. See Rainer Forst, Jeffrey Flynn, trans., *The Right to Justification* (New York: Columbia University Press, 2007).

[66] Jaeggi, *Alienation*, 200.

[67] For a review of the concept, see Somogy Varga and Charles Guignon, "Authenticity," in *The Stanford Encyclopedia of Philosophy*, Fall 2014 ed., Edward N. Zalta, ed., http://plato.stanford.edu/archives/fall2014/entries/authenticity/.

for meaningful life."[68] At the same time, according to Charles Taylor, we are social beings, and individual identity is inexorably tied up with intersubjective collective struggles about the good and the meaning of life, and is therefore intimately related to one's membership in a community.[69] Thus, "authenticity is not the enemy of demands that emanate from beyond the self; it presupposes such demands."[70] But an authentic moral agent follows only those "moral sources *outside* the subject [that speak in a language] which resonate[s] *within* him or her," in other words, moral sources that accord with "an order which is inseparably indexed to a personal vision."[71] It is not that authentic agents only look to themselves or to some core or essential idea of their selves to define their own preferences, decisions, choices, or agenda but that the social and moral frames they adopt constitute a "language of personal resonance."[72]

This account of authenticity reveals that the problem of "inauthentic lives," while an affliction affecting individual agents, is fundamentally a social and structural problem. We should understand Alfred's diagnosis of the problem of inauthentic lives as an indication of the alienation of indigenous peoples whose particular social and moral frames have been disrupted, and even rendered inoperable or unintelligible, through colonial settlement, exploitation, genocide, and/or dispossession. In *Radical Hope*, Jonathan Lear recounts how Plenty Coups, the last great chief of the Crow nation, characterized the cultural devastation of the Crow when moved, by force and circumstance created by white settler colonialism in North America, to a reserve: "when the buffalo went away the hearts of my people fell to the ground, and they could not lift them up again. After this nothing happened."[73] Lear interprets this to mean that the cultural context from which individual Crow derived the *telos* and meaning of their actions was no longer intelligible or operable. The problem of authenticity revealed in this case is not just about "who has power to tell the story, or conflicting

---

[68] Robert Nozick, *Anarchy, State and Utopia* (New York: Basic Books, 1974), 50.
[69] Charles Taylor, *Sources of the Self: The Making of the Modern Identity* (Cambridge: Cambridge University Press, 1989), 34–35.
[70] Charles Taylor, *The Ethics of Authenticity* (Cambridge, MA: Harvard University Press, 1991), 41.
[71] Taylor, *Sources of the Self*, 510.   [72] Taylor, *The Ethics of Authenticity*, 90.
[73] Jonathan Lear, *Radical Hope: Ethics in the Face of Cultural Devastation* (Cambridge, MA: Harvard University Press, 2006), 50.

narratives". More fundamentally, it is a problem of the loss of concepts with which to construct any meaningful narrative. Importantly, the physical survival of members of a social group does not mean that the group's existence as a community of meaning survives.

The case of the Crow reveals the interconnectedness between individual authentic agency and collective structural dignity. But the recovery or reinvention of a community of meaning after political catastrophes that entail genocide and cultural devastation is far from straightforward. Conceptions of authenticity that imply a recovery of "traditional" ways or identities can be problematic in presupposing an essentialist view of culture. The appeal to tradition is itself a social, historical, and political construction and serves certain purposes, such as dealing with the existential anxieties provoked by cultural loss through modernity. Indeed, a problematic essentialism underpinned nineteenth- and early-twentieth-century racial ideologies that forecast the inevitable disappearance of all indigenous peoples in the course of human advancement toward civilization. In the US, a belief in the incompatibility of the survival of indigenous peoples and the progress of civilization led Congress in 1913 to plan a monument to the "departed race," to be built on Staten Island, New York. According to President William Howard Taft, the statue to commemorate the expected extinction of indigenous people "tells the story of the march of empire and the progress of Christian civilization to the uttermost limits."[74]

Another stunning example of cultural essentialism was on display at the 1896 Berlin Colonial Show, held in Treptow Park.[75] The intention behind this joint venture between Imperial Germany's Colonial Department and the Colonial Society was to showcase one hundred colonial subjects in their "natural and primitive state," "housed with a series of specially built and ethnologically authentic native villages with an enclosure." The contingent from South West Africa robustly challenged these plans: when the Herero and Witbooi Nama "arrived at

---

[74] "The monument would depict a gigantic figure of a young Indian with hand raised in peace. Had the structure been built as planned, it would have eclipsed the Statue of Liberty in height by fifteen feet." See Duthu, *American Indians and the Law*, xxiii.

[75] Such "showcases for state progress" were a trend, beginning in the 1850s. See Eric Hobsbawm, *The Age of Capital 1848–1875* (London: Abacus, 1975), 49; and Ernst Gellner, *Nations and Nationalism* (Ithaca, NY: Cornell University Press, 1983), 22.

Hamburg, it was clear that the racial expectations of the German public and the proud independence of the South-West Africans were completely at odds. Most of the Herero and all of the Witbooi men wore
European-style military uniforms, bandoliers and side arms...The
women wore bodiced dresses with puffed sleeves and fashionable flo-
ral patterns. They were evidently not the 'pieces of natural savagery'
described in the official report."[76]

Such examples should lead us to reject conceptions of authenticity that rely on a problematic appeal to an essentialist form of traditionalism. They also suggest that the trajectory of the struggle for
an authentic postcolonial identity is not preordained. For Alfred, the
struggle against structural indignity is a crucial component of indigenous peoples' efforts to regain a form of authentic agency. To overcome existential alienation in the form of inauthentic living, there
must be a dismantling of colonial constructions of indigenous political and cultural subjectivity. In the Canadian context, Alfred offers
some resources for this process by noting, for example, that prior to
contact with Europeans, the vast majority of indigenous peoples had
reached "true civilization."[77] In addition, he sketches an image of contemporary Canada as a white settler colonial society that would be
disorienting for a population that considers the injustices of genocide,
dispossession, and forcible incorporation to belong to a distant and
remote past.

Although Alfred advocates a form of indigenous traditionalism to
facilitate reconciling with oneself, or the internal reconciliation of
a community, rather than with others, he conceives of it as involving "creative reinterpretation."[78] Indeed, the regeneration of authentic
agency does not imply a recovery of what has been lost and is irrecov-
erable; thus mourning, the recognition of this loss, is the first step in
regeneration. Furthermore, "regeneration means we will reference ourselves differently, both from the ways we did traditionally and under

---

[76] Olusoga and Erichsen, *The Kaiser's Holocaust*, 93–94.
[77] According to Alfred, they did "not abuse the earth, they promoted communal
responsibility, practiced equality in gender relations, and respected individual
freedom." The basic principles and goals of indigenous forms of life were
respect, balance, and harmony. Decision making was collective, without a
central or coercive authority, and individuals enjoyed freedom to dissent from
collective decisions. Alfred, *Peace, Power and Righteousness*, 22–25.
[78] Alfred, *Wasáse*, 87–88.

colonial dominion. We will self-consciously re-create our cultural practices and reform our political identities by drawing on tradition in a
thoughtful process of reconstruction and a committed reorganization
of our lives in a personal and collective sense. This will result in a new
conception of what it is to live as Onkwehonwe." A genuine communication can only be born when indigenous peoples experience a successful resurgence of their authentic agency, which is predicated on
a successful struggle to overturn the structural indignities of the contemporary domestic and international order: "Fundamentally different
relationships between Onkwehonwe and Settlers will emerge not from
negotiations in state-sponsored and government-regulated processes,
but after successful Onkwehonwe *resurgences* against white society's
entrenched privileges and the unreformed structure of the colonial
state."[79]

At this point, however, a puzzle forms: is there any substantive content that determines what would count as an "authentic" indigenous
life? Indeed, Alfred observes that his call to return to "traditional values" is not universally accepted by native peoples as an objective.[80]
In the context of decolonized states, according to Mehta, anticolonial
nationalist politics already privileges a certain conception of a nation:
"The idea that, through the modalities of a political organization, the
colonized would be restored to an identity from which they are alienated, only invites the by now familiar questions: whose identity are
we talking about? Which cultural groups? Which class? Which gender? And so on."[81] The leaders of decolonization, independence, and
national liberation movements, from Mahatma Gandhi and Jawaharlal
Nehru to Ho Chi Minh, invariably received degrees from universities or
were otherwise socialized in colonial centers of power. In what sense
can their anticolonial politics be considered expressions of authentic
political agency?

Fanon offers a view of what might count as emancipation when he
writes, "The black man is not. No more than the white man. Both

---

[79] Ibid., 93.
[80] Ibid., 6. For some misgivings by another indigenous scholar, see Turner, *This Is Not a Peace Pipe*, 109–10.
[81] Mehta, "After colonialism," 160. He continues, "By what authority does anti-imperialism define its content? Implicit in an anti-imperial politics is an appeal to some idea of emancipation. But then, what counts as emancipation? Who makes this determination?" (166).

have to move away from the inhuman voices of their respective ancestors so that a genuine communication can be born." The struggle for disalienation, for Fanon, should not be understood as a struggle to return to some essentialist and particular traditional way of life but to create our *human* voices. Colonialism distorted those voices – both of the colonized and the colonizer – in a similar way that Rousseau claimed eighteenth-century European civilization had distorted human nature.[82] Yet, as Jaeggi has pointed out, it is no longer plausible to conceive of the realization of human nature as a return to a fixed, essential frame that can distinguish between substantively genuine and inauthentic forms of human flourishing.[83] In this sense, the concern with "authenticity" is misguided if it relies on implausible essentialist or metaphysical presuppositions.

As an alternative, we might conceive of "disalienation" as a process-driven (rather than substantive) concept. As Jaeggi has described it, "not being alienated would refer to a certain way of carrying out one's own life and a certain way of appropriating oneself – that is, a way of establishing relations to oneself and to the relationships in which one lives (relationships that condition or shape who one is)."[84] Instead of conceiving of an authentic self as one that is constant in its commitment to certain substantive or core projects, the "self's continuity" should be conceived as being grounded in the agent's ability "to integrate the succession of changes among projects or commitments."[85] Jaeggi conceives of the "unalienated life" as no longer one that is "reconciled,"[86] but it seems that her account only requires a rejection of harmonistic

---

[82] See Jean-Jacques Rousseau, "Discourse on the origin of inequality," in *The Basic Political Writings*, 2nd ed., Donald Cress, trans. (New York: Hackett, 2011 [1754]), 39.

[83] For her discussion and critique of Rousseau, see Jaeggi, *Alienation*, 7–8 and 30: "How are we to define human nature when its extraordinary variability and malleability appear to be part of human nature itself?" Jaeggi thus develops an account of alienation that "need not be grounded in strongly essentialist or metaphysical presuppositions" or rely on "perfectionist or paternalistic arguments" (32).

[84] Ibid., 33. [85] Ibid., 176.

[86] Ibid., 33. Although Jaeggi observes that "once the phenomenon of alienation has been adequately clarified, a path is opened up for criticizing institutions in so far as they fail to furnish the social conditions individuals need to live a life free of alienation," this critical analysis of institutions and social conditions is "mostly undeveloped" in her book. See Frederick Neuhouser, "Translator's introduction," ibid., xv.

and closed models of reconciliation. Instead, we can reconstruct reconciliation as a regulative political ideal that answers the question of how institutions must be constituted "so that individuals [and other agents] living within them can understand themselves as the (co-)authors of those institutions and identify with them as agents."[87] Such a concept of reconciliation as nonalienation can be contrasted with the false ideals of reconciliation as an overcoming of negative sentiments or the creation of deep social harmony.

Reconciled individuals may still hold resentment against perpetrators, and reconciled societies may still be marked by difference, disagreement and conflict. Indeed, efforts to decolonize existing social structures are likely to generate alienation or disorientation on the part of those whose social positions were predicated on colonial structures of identities, norms, and rules of privilege. As I discuss in Chapter 8, progress toward reconciliation in any society involves addressing the alienation not only of those oppressed in various ways by contemporary structured and structural injustice, but also of those whose identities and beliefs about themselves, others, and the world are called into question in the process of decolonization. While redressing the alienation of the oppressed is part of the duty to rectify structural injustice, the stability and sustainability of structural transformation depends upon strategies of immanent and external forms of critique that can spur the reorientation of those whose alienation stems from the repudiation of problematic identities, beliefs, norms, and other structures. To the extent that these problematic identities, beliefs, norms, and practices persist, the emancipatory potential of practices of reconciliation is undermined.

As a regulative ideal, the project of reconciliation aims to create the social/structural conditions under which all agents may successfully integrate themselves and engage meaningfully in the social worlds they inhabit. A measure of conditions for nonalienated flourishing for indigenous peoples in settler colonial states such as Canada, as well as in the wider world, is not so much whether they have retained the substance of "traditional values" as whether members of indigenous peoples can effectively participate as equals in shaping their terms of association "without giving up who they are as indigenous peoples," and whether they are empowered to return indigenous "ways of knowing

---

[87] Ibid., 220.

the world to their rightful place in the landscape of *human* ideas."[88] It is the capacity of agents to integrate and appropriate the social conditions they inhabit that is important for authentic flourishing, rather than a constancy of substantive orientations or identifications.

Thus the grand chief of the Cree in Quebec, Mathew Coon Come, provides a formulation of disalienated indigenous agency in his comments on how Cree youth, who are successfully flourishing in the Canadian province of Quebec, view their social position: "They can see their own institutions, they can see that they're managing their own affairs, they feel that they're masters of their own destinies." While some indigenous communities suffer from high youth suicide rates, abject poverty, and poor infrastructure, psychologists Michael Chandler and Christopher Lalonde have found little correlation between youth suicide and measures of poverty and isolation. However, youth suicide was "strongly related to measures of cultural continuity, including efforts to regain legal title to traditional lands and to re-establish forms of self-government, to reassert control over education and other community and social services and to preserve and promote traditional cultural practices." The fight to obtain such conditions for disalienated agency for the Cree in Quebec involved engaging in legal battles in the 1970s against Hydro-Québec, which resulted in the landmark 1975 James Bay and Northern Quebec Agreement. Although a political and legal compromise, the Cree agreed to the building of dams for the James Bay hydroelectric project, in exchange for "financial compensation, guaranteed land-use rights and control over local government, including health, education and economic development."[89]

It is by appreciating the importance of nonalienated agency and its social structural conditions that we can begin to comprehend why state and international policies of border control, assimilation and integration in various nation-building and state-building projects continue to generate interactional, structural, and existential alienation. Ultimately, the struggle for reconciliation is a struggle to construct alternatives to colonial modernities. Just as not all colonial modernities have been alienating in the same ways, there is not just one authentic alternative

[88] Turner, *This Is Not a Peace Pipe*, 117, emphasis mine.
[89] Coon Come is also a former national chief of the Assembly of First Nations. For the psychology study, see Michael J. Chandler and Christopher E. Lalonde, "Cultural continuity as a protective factor against suicide in First Nations youth," *Horizons* 10, 1 (2008): 68–72.

but several possible nonalienating alternatives or a plurality of post-colonial modernities that agents may pursue.

VI Conclusion

This chapter has conceptualized reconciliation as a response to different forms of alienation produced by political injustice. In seeking agents' relational reconciliation as well as their affirmation of the social/political order, Fanon's call for "genuine communication" exerts demands on the colonized as well as the colonizer to engage in the difficult tasks of self-reflection and transformation. In some ways, one must surpass oneself, or what one has known about oneself, as well as what one thinks or knows about others, in order to give birth to new forms of political agency, relations, and structures.[90] Reconciliation, understood as a project of nonalienation, involves establishing the relational and institutional conditions for agents' structural dignity and nonalienated agency, which are necessary to facilitate agents' individual and collective struggles to realize nonalienated forms of human flourishing and to engage meaningfully in genuine communications about both justice and reconciliation.

As a process-driven concept that seeks to establish the social conditions in which agents can, in their individual and collective lives, see themselves as the authors of the institutions and practices that organize their activities, it is also quite open-ended in terms of the substantive kinds of social forms or institutionalized relations that agents may come to endorse and pursue. For this reason, such a conceptualization of reconciliation cannot produce a substantive vision of what a reconciled social/political order should look like. This means that engaging in a project of reconciliation in response to settler colonialism in Canada, for example, does not precommit participants to an ideal of inclusion of indigenous peoples within a Canadian constitutional framework. A genuine communication between indigenous and Canadian representatives might instead engage participants in devising

[90] See Ta-Nehisi Coates, "The case for reparations," *The Atlantic*, June 2014, whose reflections on racial injustice in America leads him to conclude, "So we must imagine a new country. Reparations – by which I mean the full acceptance of our collective biography and its consequences – is the price we must pay to see ourselves squarely." www.theatlantic.com/magazine/archive/2014/06/the-case-for-reparations/361631/.

pluralistic social and constitutional reforms, within Canada and within international order, to facilitate rather than hinder different forms of nonalienated flourishing of indigenous peoples.

Some who especially value an ideal of individual autonomous agency might still worry that nonalienation is a problematic ideal for politics. They posit that a consequence of robust individual agency is that some, perhaps most, individuals will be alienated in some way from social/political institutions and structures. Individuals' alienation is in some ways to be praised, since it indicates the lack of a hegemonic agenda on the part of the social/political order to force their conformity. Alternatively, since we are all alienated in one way or another, nonalienation cannot form a plausible regulative political ideal. This libertarian critique of the ideal of nonalienation reminds us of how difficult it often is for individuals in general to negotiate peaceable conditions of social existence. Hobbes noted that people "have *no pleasure*, but on the contrary a great deal of grief, in *keeping company*" with others.[91] And one of Freud's great insights into the human condition is that in addition to our individual physical and internal constitution, and the external natural world that threatens to overwhelm and destroy us, one major less acknowledged source of individual unhappiness stems from our relations with other people.[92]

This libertarian objection, however, overreaches, and cannot distinguish between the ordinary consequences derived from the necessity of living with others in some kind of social/political order in order to achieve any personal goals and the alienation produced by unjust or defective social structures, which distort in a systematic and pervasive fashion individuals' social identities, agency, capacities, aspirations, and achievements. In the context of societies marked by structural injustices, then, this libertarian objection against reconciliation as nonalienation is normatively obscuring if it elides the fact that in practically all societies, not everyone suffers equally from unjust and alienating social structures. In failing to distinguish between general individual alienation, which is a by-product of the development of individual identity, agency, and autonomy, and alienation which stems from structural injustices, which undermines the agential capacities of

---

[91] Thomas Hobbes, *Leviathan*, Chapter 13.
[92] Sigmund Freud, *Civilization and Its Discontents*, trans. David McLintock (Toronto: Penguin, 2002).

specific categories of persons, a libertarian account of individual alienation fails to address structural injustice as a major source of threat against the value of individual autonomy. My conception of reconciliation as nonalienation is antithetical to harmonistic and closed models of reconciliation; thus, the worry that the political project of reconciliation must have homogenizing or conformist tendencies that destroy social pluralism can be avoided.

Now that I have developed interactional and structural conceptions of justice and reconciliation, the remainder of this book turns to the question of redressing interactional and structural injustice and alienation in international and transnational relations. How should we think about the purposes of reparations, the agents responsible for reparations, and the forms that reparative measures should take? And how should acknowledgment of the reproduction of colonial structural injustices – located in international society and the former colonizer state as well as the former colonized society – affect the way we think about reparative responsibilities for the harms and injuries produced by colonial and structural injustices?

7 | *Reparations*

Somebody must suffer for the consequences of the war. Is it to be Germany, or only the peoples she has wronged?

– Allied powers' reply to the German Delegation, 1919[1]

I Introduction

The concept of reparation refers to the redress or remedy of wrongs. In ordinary morality, reparation is entailed by the principle that wrongs should be rectified: one has a duty to make amends for one's wrongs by providing some form of payment or assistance to those who have suffered the wrong.[2] Since the 1990s, there has been a proliferation of calls for reparations for international and transnational injustices, including those associated with colonial rule. One ongoing case involves a lawsuit against several Japanese companies filed by Koreans conscripted into forced labor between 1939 and 1945.[3] In that period, historians estimate that between seven hundred thousand and 1.2 million Koreans were subjected to conscription into skilled and unskilled forced labor by Japanese companies. Corporations disciplined the conscripts with hunger, fear, torture, and other violence resulting in death in some

---

[1] "Reply of the Allied and Associated Powers to the observations of the German Delegation on the Conditions of Peace, and ultimatum," June 16, 1919, in *The Treaty of Versailles and After: Annotations of the Text of the Treaty* (Washington, DC: US Department of State, 1947), 48.

[2] www.oxforddictionaries.com/definition/english/reparation. Aristotle's account of corrective justice refers to the redress of private transactions between citizens in a law-governed political community, whereas his account of distributive justice refers to the public distribution of status, wealth, and other public goods and burdens that are divided among citizens in one polity. See Aristotle, *The Nichomachean Ethics of Aristotle*, 5th ed., trans. F. H. Peters (London: Kegan Paul, Trench, Truebner, 1893), Book V, http://oll.libertyfund.org/titles/903.

[3] "Mitsubishi Company pays Chinese forced laborers," http://uk.reuters.com/article/uk-mitsubishi-ma-compensation-china-idUKKCN0PX2BR20150723.

cases, and could rely on the local police for enforcement of the laborers' corporate subjection. To date, a group of 1,104 Korean survivors have formed the largest class action lawsuit against seventy Japanese firms, including Mitsubishi Heavy Industries (MHI) and Nippon Steel, for forced labor in Japanese munitions factories during World War II, claiming 100 billion won (US$90 million) for unpaid wages and damages.[4]

Until recently, courts in both Japan and Korea have accepted the claim that all wartime accounts between Japan and the Republic of Korea were settled by the 1951 San Francisco Treaty of Peace, as well as by the 1965 normalization treaty between Japan and Korea.[5] In a landmark decision in May 2012, however, the South Korean Supreme Court ruled in favor of the plaintiffs, arguing that denying the reparations claims by individuals against MHI "violated Korea's Constitution and international legal norms."[6] According to the Court, the 1965 interstate Claims Settlement Agreement (Article 2, Clause 1), concerning the settlement of property, rights, and interests of individuals, did

[4] The number of claimants is as of February 2016, but is likely to increase, as the advocacy group, the Asia Victims of the Pacific War Family of the Deceased Association of Korea, is actively seeking more claimants. *Xinhua News*, "100 S. Korean victims of Japan's wartime forced labor join lawsuits against Japanese firms," February 2, 2016. The Special Committee for the Investigation of Forced Labor under Japanese Colonialism was set up by the South Korean government in 2004. For an overview of transitional justice issues in South Korea, both international and domestic, see Hun Joon Kim, "Transitional justice in South Korea," in *Transitional Justice in the Asia-Pacific*, Renée Jeffery and Hun Joon Kim, eds. (Cambridge: Cambridge University Press, 2014), 229–58.
[5] While noting the grave suffering of victims in the forced labor case, the Japanese Supreme Court argued that "settlement of war compensation requires consideration of various factors beyond a particular person's case, such as the policies on economic recovery of the countries involved, the national budget, the nation's economy, and equality of compensation for other people's sufferings." The implication is that "the parliament is better suited to examine these overarching considerations and to decide comprehensive policy." The court has consistently also denied claims for wartime damages by individual Japanese. The only case of Japanese citizens receiving individual compensation was the Hiroshima case, and the award was for the effects of the nuclear bombs, not for conscripted labor. See Sayuri Umeda, "Japan: WWII POW and forced labor cases," *The Law Library of Congress*, September 2008.
[6] Steven Nam, "Revitalized transitional justice and corporate accountability for Korean wartime forced labor in Japan," *Travaux: The Berkeley Journal of International Law Blog*, February 8, 2016. For the South Korean Supreme Court decision, see http://library.scourt.go.kr/SCLIB_data/decision/9–24ohkh2012.5.24.2009Da22549.htm.

not invalidate contemporary claims by individuals for compensation for forced labor:[7] "The 'Agreement between Japan and the Republic of Korea Concerning the Settlement of Problems in Regard to Property and Claims and Economic Cooperation' ('Claims Agreement') did not negotiate for compensation for Japanese colonial rule." Indeed, the court points out that in the agreement, the "Japanese government did not acknowledge colonial rule's unlawfulness and denied legal compensation for forced mobilization victims."[8] Subsequently, in the past four years, South Korean courts have ordered Japanese companies to pay millions in compensation and damages to groups of individual plaintiffs, although the companies involved have so far continued to appeal such decisions.[9]

This legal and political struggle between states, corporations, and individuals raises several general questions about redress of colonial injustices. What are the normative purposes of such practices? Who are the appropriate agents to engage in the processes of settling accounts and reconciliation over these injustices? What is the relationship between interstate processes and civil society processes? What ought to be the role of individual victim-survivors? What constitutes appropriate and adequate reparation? And who should pay? How is the struggle for victim-centric reparations related to struggles for redressing structural injustice, and for distributive domestic and global justice? In addition, are acknowledgment, apology, and compensation by states, corporations, or other entities, such as churches, to individual victim-survivors enough to constitute full redress for colonial injustice?

---

[7] *The Japan Times*, "South Korean court declines to rule on Japanese forced labor agreement," December 23, 2015.

[8] South Korean Supreme Court Decision 2009, Da22549, decided May 24, 2012, http://library.scourt.go.kr/SCLIB_data/decision/9–24ohkh2012.5.24 .2009Da22549.htm.

[9] Choe Sang-hun, "South Korean court tells Japanese company to pay for forced labor," *New York Times*, July 31, 2013. Mitsubishi, however, did apologize and offer compensation to American POWs and Chinese forced laborers in 2015. While the company was willing to pursue similar packages with Korean forced laborers, it is reported that the Japanese government advised the company to resist due to the "different legal situation" of Korea, most likely referring to Korea's colonial status at the time of the violations. See "Mitsubishi to compensate Chinese wartime laborers, ignores Korean victims," *Dong-a Ilbo*, July 25, 2015.

The politically fraught cases stemming from Japanese colonization of Korea, as well as other ongoing cases, such as the redress claims related to German colonialism in South West Africa (Namibia), British colonial injustices in Kenya and Malawi,[10] and participation in the transatlantic slave trade by several European states, point to two significant developments in the politics of reparations in international and transnational contexts: the increasing normative standing of individuals as subjects under international law and the revival of demands for the redress of colonial injustices.[11] Both developments reveal the statist and colonial limits of previous peace settlements, biases which combined to deny colonized subjects avenues of redress and reconciliation that had developed in the wake of the Holocaust and the two world wars. A focus on violations suffered by individuals in international and transnational contexts highlights the growing salience of the international doctrines of human rights and humanitarian law as potential constraints on states' internal and external autonomy and tends to support measures of corrective justice for wrongful conduct, such as financial compensation to individual victim-survivors of egregious mistreatment. The contemporary struggles to extend entitlements to individual compensatory justice from war to cases of colonial violent rule reveal the extent to which colonial, often racialized and gendered, hierarchies have dominated the politics of reparations in the twentieth century.

The rise of colonial reparative claims, in addition, signifies a need to think beyond such forms of reparation in order to redress adequately

---

[10] See Katie Engelhart, "40,000 Kenyans accuse UK of abuse in second Mau Mau case," *The Guardian*, October 29, 2014. On the Malawi case for reparations, see Godfrey Mapondera, "Malawians seek compensation for Nyasaland massacre during British rule," *The Guardian*, April 20, 2015. The claim dates to March 1959 when in British-ruled Nyasaland, now Malawi, thirty-three unarmed demonstrators were killed in a protest against the treatment of detained fighters for independence. On the Mau Mau, see also Tabitha Kanogo, "Mau Mau women: sixty years later," in Shirley Ardener, Fiona Armitage-Woodward, and Lidia D. Sciama, *War and Women across Continents: Autobiographical and Biographical Experiences* (New York: Bergham Press, 2016), 75–93: "There are also plans to sue the Kenyan state."

[11] Demands for compensatory reparations for ex-slaves were made in the nineteenth century, by "freed slaves, Radical Republicans and later the Ex-Slave Mutual Relief, Bounty and Pension Association." Such demands reignited in the 1970s, especially in the US, and in contemporary political and theoretical debates about global justice. See Katrina Forrester, "Reparations, history, and the origins of global justice," presented at the Empire, Race and Global Justice workshop, Cambridge University, April 1–2, 2016.

the structural injustices that enabled widespread and systematic violations of individual human rights, as well as other serious structural inequities, some of which still permeate international and transnational relations. In other words, in addition to backward-looking reparations to individual survivor-victims for serious human rights violations committed in contexts of colonial rule, redressing colonial injustice raises forward-looking challenges of structural reparation and transformation. While an interactional individual-centric account of reparations focuses on the redress of wrongdoing against individual victims, structural reparation refers to the task of redressing structural injustices within contemporary domestic and global orders that reproduce, in modified forms, morally objectionable and alienating relations between larger categories of persons than those who can claim to be individual victims of wrongful acts.

In the following section of this chapter, I trace the development of reparation as a concept and practice in international relations, mainly in response to interstate war, noting that historically, such a concept has only come to prominence as states came to devise and endorse various forms of international law and international institutions attempting to regulate the use of force in their external and internal relations. The persistence of a colonial international structure until the 1960s meant that uses of armed force and other types of repression by colonizing states against the people they subjugated – from disciplinary techniques of "colonial administration" to sexual slavery to genocide – were not considered "wars" or internationally wrongful conduct, and were not generally subject to emerging practices of accountability and reparation between states following the two world wars.

The framework for reparation that did develop was essentially interactional or transactional, in which states deemed culpable for wrongful conduct were obligated to make reparations to their victims and for war damages. While this interactional model of reparation is morally powerful, it is not sufficient in many contexts of political catastrophe, such as war.[12] Thus, if the redress of harms and losses is a natural corollary of the redress of wrongful conduct, then proper redress of political catastrophes requires going beyond the interactional model

[12] It is not even sufficient in many cases of civil war. When the Syrian war ends, it is likely that the Syrian state and society will need extensive international financial support to recover. See Pablo Kalmanovitz, "Sharing burdens after war: a Lockean approach," *The Journal of Political Philosophy* 19, 2 (2011): 209–28.

of reparation, if victims are to receive redress for their losses and damages. In Section III, I focus on how the narrow interactional model must yield to a more structural account of the principle of corrective or reparative justice, which provides structural grounds for victim reparation by other parties, when perpetrators are incapable or unwilling to make such reparation.

The structural account of reparation is pertinent not only for reparations between states after major interstate wars, but also for reparations for individuals who suffer losses and harms in contexts of international and transnational political catastrophes. Section IV focuses on the increased standing of the individual as a subject of international law, and the effects on international practices of reparation in circumstances of armed conflict. In customary human rights and international humanitarian law, various regional and international institutions have legal provisions that entitle individual victims of domestic and international armed conflict to various forms of reparations. While individual-centric reparations highlight the importance of human rights and humanitarian obligations in international law, it is clear that mass reparations programs in response to political catastrophes rely on grounds other than moral responsibility for wrongdoing. While states and international institutions acknowledge that the duty of victim reparation belongs to culpable agents, they have also recognized the need for a more generalized duty of victim reparation and assistance, even in the absence of prosecutions or guilty verdicts. In this sense, practices of redress for major political catastrophes that produce serious violations of international human rights and humanitarian law acknowledge that the responsibility to repudiate such violations and assist individual victims in their social recovery goes beyond the interactional duty of direct perpetrators to provide reparations to their victims. Proper redress of victims' injuries and losses can obligate the victim's state, a liable external state, as well as the society of states and global civil society as a whole.

II War and Justice in Colonial International Relations

Contemporary theorists have conceived of reparations as elemental to notions of "restorative," "reparatory," or "reparative" justice that are formulated as conceptually distinct from both retributive justice and distributive justice. While reparative "justice concerns itself with what ought to be done in reparation for injustice, and the obligation of wrongdoers, or their descendants or successors, for making this repair," retributive justice concerns itself with "the punishment of wrongdoers," and distributive justice with equity, or the question of "how goods should be distributed among individuals or how members of a society should share its benefits and burdens."[13] According to Martha Minow, "the core idea behind reparations stems from the compensatory theory of justice. Injuries can and must be compensated. Wrongdoers should pay victims for losses. Afterward, the slate can be wiped clean. Or at least a kind of justice has been done."[14]

In an interactional framework, reparations may function to settle moral accounts (justice) or make mutually affirmable the relationship (reconciliation) between those agents whose relations have been mired by unjust and alienating interactions. Whether the end is justice or reconciliation, it matters in an interactional account that the agent making reparations is the party that is morally responsible for the loss, harm, or injury that is suffered by the victim, and it is also important that the recipients of the reparative effort are those who experienced the wrong or harm (and/or were alienated by it). This conception of reparations as a component of interactional justice or reconciliation aims to repair an interpersonal or interagent moral relationship between the specific agents involved in a morally objectionable or problematic interaction.[15]

Reparation so conceived is a standard component of corrective justice and is morally powerful for cases of individual interpersonal interactions in contexts of a well-ordered society – that is, a society in which the institutions, structures, and conditions of social life are ordered so as to ensure the structural dignity of agents and to reflect fair and equitable distributions of the burdens and advantages of social cooperation. Although distinct, corrective justice for interactional wrongs presupposes structural and distributive justice, and reparations for wrongdoing are, to a large extent, conditioned by the terms of structural and distributive justice, which enable, shape, and constrain the

---

[13] Janna Thompson, *Taking Responsibility for the Past: Reparation and Historical Injustice* (Cambridge: Polity Press, 2002), xi.

[14] Martha Minow, *Between Vengeance and Forgiveness: Facing History after Genocide and Mass Violence* (Boston: Beacon Press, 1998), 92 and 104.

[15] For example, if Sue deprives Sarah of US$10 in a way that merits compensation, then Sue is the one obligated to make that reparation to Sarah. If Arash, who is uninvolved in the transaction, provides Sarah with the same amount, his action would not constitute reparation, understood in this interactional sense.

reparative claims that wronged agents may make against others or the social/political order. In this sense, any account of reparation as a moral demand in response to interactional injustice is parasitic on a more comprehensive account of the structural terms that mediate and organize the relevant agents' interactions.

In modern domestic contexts, it is typically the state that bears the political task of securing and maintaining fair background structures and conditions, as well as establishing the institutions and mechanisms for enforcing terms of corrective justice upon interacting individual or corporate agents under its jurisdiction. In the case of interactional injustices in which culpable agents are acting in violation of societal norms and laws, the state assumes the power, authority, and responsibility for holding them accountable, and when appropriate, obligating such agents to make reparations, as a way of balancing the moral books between them and their victims. Although victims and perpetrators may never be personally reconciled to each other in a sentimental way, the realization of corrective justice as mediated by social institutions and practices is one way that they may each be reconciled to the social/political order.

The moral power of this interactional account of reparation becomes less coherent where there is no social/political order – a condition of anarchy – or in conditions where the social/political order has a very limited set of terms of interactional and structural justice – a condition of limited justice. Herodotus's account of the conflict between the Persians and the Greeks, which developed into a condition of mutual hostility due to "a series of unjust acts" for which neither side could hold the other to proper account, is an example of an anarchical context, in which the agents involved interacted with each other in the absence of a structure of normative rules or practices to mediate their interactions.[16] Arguably, this was also the condition that characterized the early interactional context of many fledgling settler groups with the indigenous peoples they encountered.[17] In such circumstances, local interacting agents may come to devise ad hoc arrangements for dealing with transgressions, but disagreements over how to settle accounts

---

[16] Herodotus, *The Histories*, trans. Aubrey De Sélincourt (Toronto: Penguin, 1996), 3–4.

[17] See Robert M. Utley, *Indian Wars* (Boston: Mariner Books, 1977); Robert Hughes, *The Fatal Shore: The Epic of Australia's Founding* (New York: Vintage Books, 1988).

for injuries and grievances make such a condition unstable and, as Herodotus observed, prone to fueling chronic conflicts of violent vindication.

As discussed in Chapter 4, the characterization of international relations as a realm of anarchy (or state of nature) is a staple tenet of both realist and liberal international relations theory. I have argued that viewed from a historical political perspective, the depiction of modern international order as an anarchical system of self-help is a normatively obscuring myth. In the nineteenth century, competition between European states for the markers of great-power status led to an increasingly predatory international order, in which the concept of reparations between states, understood as the amends made by a state for wrongful conduct, did not exist. Dominant states in practice enjoyed an unrestricted right to wage war for any reason, including self-aggrandizement and conquest. The settling of accounts after interstate war, involving payment for the costs of waging war, damages caused by war, as well as any other transfers of wealth, people, territory, or other resources, were exacted by victors against vanquished, in accordance with the outcome of the military contest, with the loser incurring the obligation to pay the victor, whatever the moral merits of the victor's case for engaging in war.[18]

Within Europe, in the 1871 Treaty of Frankfurt that concluded the Franco-Prussian War, for example, a defeated France was forced to pay huge "indemnities" to a victorious Germany, despite the fact that Germany, led by Prussian chancellor Otto von Bismarck, was the main aggressor who pushed the French into declaring war.[19] Paying indemnities was the cost of making war, and losing, but did not signify any moral judgment. Material transfers were not guided by considerations of justice but by considerations of relative power advantage, so that "the strong do what they have the power to do and the weak accept what they have to accept."[20]

---

[18] Some portions of the rest of this section, as well as Section III, are drawn from my "Reconciliation and reparations," in *The Oxford Handbook of Ethics of War*, Helen Frowe and Seth Lazar, eds. (Oxford: Oxford University Press, 2015), Chapter 28, doi:10.1093/oxfordhb/9780199943418.013.17.

[19] Michael Howard, *The Franco-Prussian War: The German Invasion of France, 1870–1871* (New York: Macmillan, 1962).

[20] Thucydides, *The Peloponnesian War*, trans. Thomas Hobbes (Chicago: University of Chicago Press, 1989), Book V, paragraph 89.

In Sino-British relations, the 1842 Treaty of Nanjing that concluded the First Opium War between Britain and China (1839–1842), followed by similar treaties between Imperial China and other Western states, such as France and the US, included payments of compensation and indemnities by the Qing to the British for destroyed opium, war costs, and outstanding debts. In addition, the Qing lost the jurisdictional authority to detain or punish prisoners who were British subjects or Chinese subjects who had collaborated with the British; Hong Kong was ceded to Queen Victoria; and five port cities were forcibly opened to European mercantile pursuits.[21] These examples illustrate that although the practice of paying indemnities may have served the prudential function of deterring potential aggressors from initiating wars that they were uncertain of winning, it also provided a material incentive to aggressors who were confident of their military superiority.[22]

At the 1884–1885 Congress of Berlin, European states, as well as Turkey and the US, agreed on the terms of recognizing colonial claims among themselves, thus allowing for a more coordinated "scramble" for Africa as part of a competition among them for resources and national prestige. The colonial wars that ensued, characterized at the time as "small wars," were different from interstate European wars in several ways.[23] The aims of the parties involved were quite expansive compared to those of wars between European states, which were typically more limited in their objectives. Colonizing states engaged in wars of conquest aimed to achieve "total subjection of the population" in a territory to which they had a colonial claim; for those populations resisting colonization, their aim was thus self-determination and sometimes sheer physical survival.[24] David Olusoga and Casper W. Erichsen have observed that, "while colonial wars were undoubtedly small by European standards, they were almost always cataclysmic for the

---

[21] Jonathan D. Spence, *The Search for Modern China* (New York: W. W. Norton, 2001), 159–60.

[22] See Eugene N. White, "Making the French pay: the costs and consequences of the Napoleonic reparations," *European Review of Economic History* 5, 3 (2001): 337–65.

[23] Charles E. Callwell, *Small Wars: Their Principles and Practice* (Champaign, IL: Book Jungle, 2009 [1896]).

[24] H. L. Wesseling, "Colonial wars: an introduction," in *Imperialism and War: Essays on Colonial Wars in Asia and Africa*, J. A. de Moor and H. L. Wesseling, eds. (Leiden: E. J. Brill, 1989), 3.

tribal peoples concerned." Colonial wars did not involve the clash of uniformed armies on a battlefield; rather, those who resisted European colonizers were typically killed in "massacres, ambushes and punitive raids." Because wars of colonial conquest and forced settlement were directed by a professional army against an entire population, the conventional rules of warfare that pertained to interstate wars among European states, including distinctions between civilians and combatants, were not typically applied.[25] Although genocide was not a typical explicit intent of colonial rule, as it was in the case of German South West Africa, many contexts of colonial rule entailed other brutalities against indigenous groups, such as in Kenya during the Mau Mau war in the 1950s, in which Britain's colonial detention system subjected thousands of anticolonial activists and ordinary citizens to detention, torture, maiming, and other abuses.[26]

The international order that emerged after the two world wars of the twentieth century included the development of international institutions and legal mechanisms that aimed to hold states and individual leaders accountable for breaches of international peace, as well as, by the end of World War II, for crimes against humanity. The colonial structure of international order, however, continued to block or distort redress efforts by colonized subjects for colonial injustices. Until recently, the concept of reparations for internationally wrongful conduct did not pertain to colonial wars, oppression or atrocity. In the peace settlements after both world wars, while defeated states were deprived of their colonies, there was starkly different treatment between groups that were subject to colonization and those that maintained independence when it came to reparative claims. For example, in the 1947 Treaty of Peace with Italy, Italy renounced "all right and title" over its colonies in Africa – Libya, Eritrea, and Italian Somaliland. The status of these "possessions" would be determined by the Soviet Union, the US, the UK, and France within a year, but there was no provision in the treaty for the determination of reparative or compensatory claims by peoples – individual, collective, or corporate – in these colonies for losses and damages incurred in war or under colonial rule. In the same treaty, however, compensation for breaches of the peace

---

[25] David Olusoga and Casper W. Erichsen, *The Kaiser's Holocaust: Germany's Forgotten Genocide* (London: Faber and Faber, 2011), 70–71.
[26] Caroline Elkins, *Imperial Reckoning: The Untold Story of Britain's Gulag in Kenya* (New York: Henry Holt, 2005), 97.

and war damages is specified to the states that enjoyed sovereignty: the USSR (US$100 million), as well as Albania (US$5 million), Ethiopia (US$25 million),[27] Greece (US$105 million), and Yugoslavia (US$120 million).

The colonial architecture of modern international relations thus lingered. In 1945, more than a third of the world's population continued to live in non-self-governing, dependent territories ruled by colonial powers or administered through the newly established International Trusteeship System set up under the new United Nations. By 1960, however, the achievements of various anticolonial struggles coalesced into a general repudiation of colonial subjection as a legitimate form of rule in international relations. A decade after the 1960 United Nations Declaration on the Granting of Independence to Colonized Countries and Peoples, the United Nations General Assembly passed Resolution 2621 in 1970, which declared that "the continuation of colonialism in all its forms and manifestations is *a crime*" (Article 1). Focused on the goal of eliminating the colonial subjection of Africans in South Africa and Rhodesia, the resolution did not specify any accountability or reparative measures for past abuses by colonial powers or for colonial rule itself.[28]

III The Duty of Victim Reparation: Interactional and Structural Accounts

In the latter half of the past century, the development of international human rights doctrine and humanitarian law has provided legal imperatives to construct greater institutionalized prohibitions against the use of force by states in their external relations, as well as prohibitions

---

[27] In the unraveling of the Versailles international order in the interwar years, Italy had invaded Ethiopia, a member of the League of Nations, on October 3, 1935, and occupied it militarily by 1936. Other countries, including Britain and France, had recognized Italian sovereignty over Ethiopia by 1938. Because the violation of Ethiopian independence was viewed by the victorious powers as part of the wrongful conduct by fascist Italy, its defeat in World War II entailed rectifying this injustice by reinstating the sovereign status of Ethiopia.

[28] Resolution 2621 (XXV), "Programme of action for the full implementation of the Declaration on the Granting of Independence to Colonial Countries and Peoples," see https://documents-dds-ny.un.org/doc/RESOLUTION/GEN/NR0/ 348/86/IMG/NR034886.pdf?OpenElement. Also quoted in Christian Reus-Smit, *Individual Rights and the Making of the International System* (Cambridge: Cambridge University Press, 2013), 156, emphasis mine.

against genocide, war crimes, and crimes against humanity, in times of war and peace.[29] As a corollary, the cost to a state of engaging in conduct judged to be wrongful under international law includes reparations for wrongful conduct. Under the Articles on the Responsibility of States for Internationally Wrongful Acts (Articles on State Responsibility), adopted by the International Law Commission in 2001 after forty years of debate, an offending state has a duty to cease a wrongful act and to make "full reparation" for any "material or moral" injury or damage caused by the wrongful act (Article 31).[30] As James Crawford and Jeremy Watkins have noted, "by attaching an obligation of repair to acts which it prohibits, international law marks out a certain class of losses – namely those that follow directly from unlawful conduct – as ones which should not lie where they fall."[31] Dinah Shelton identifies two conceptual premises underpinning the obligation of reparation for internationally wrongful conduct in the Articles on State Responsibility. First, requiring reparation for wrongful conduct reflects an attempt to elevate "the importance of upholding the rule of law in the interest of the international community as a whole." Second, reparation highlights the importance of "remedial justice as the goal of reparations for those injured by the breach of an obligation."[32] In these developments, we can see attempts by the society of states, as well as influential participants of global civil society, to calibrate international law and institutions toward regulating and coordinating practices of corrective justice for breaches of international obligation.

As a moral demand, however, the obligation of repair is not unconditional. Viewing the moral entitlements and obligations of victims and

---

[29] On this role of general individual rights in creating a universal international system of sovereign states, and the decolonization era of the 1960s that produced such an international order, see Reus-Smit, *Individual Rights and the Making of the International System.*

[30] Andrea Gattini, "The UN Compensation Commission: old rules, new procedures on war reparations," *European Journal of International Law* 13, 1 (2002): 162. See Dinah Shelton, "Righting wrongs: reparations in the Articles on State Responsibility," *American Journal of International Law* 96, 4 (2002): 833–56 at 845. For the text of the Articles on Responsibility of States for Internationally Wrongful Acts, see http://legal.un.org/ilc/texts/instruments/english/draft_articles/9_6_2001.pdf.

[31] James Crawford and Jeremy Watkins, "International responsibility," in *The Philosophy of International Law*, Samantha Besson and John Tasioulas, eds. (Oxford: Oxford University Press, 2010), 283–98 at 285.

[32] Dinah Shelton, "Righting wrongs," 838.

perpetrators through an interactional framework of corrective justice highlights the right of victims to reparations and the obligation of perpetrators to pay, but tends to obscure the possibility that perpetrators may themselves become materially diminished by their own actions, or that perpetrators have some legitimate entitlements despite their culpability. These issues, however, significantly affect the moral defensibility of victims' reparative claims. Victims have a prima facie entitlement to *some* compensation for their losses, and perpetrators have a prima facie obligation to provide such compensation, but the determination of exactly how much is owed to victims by a culpable agent depends on various other moral considerations beyond those of victims' damages and perpetrators' culpability.

In international contexts, a responsible state may sometimes become an incapacitated state, especially after a major war. In the case of World War I, for example, although a strict settling of accounts might have dictated that Germany alone should pay to rebuild the areas it was responsible for devastating, French leaders were aware that this "would completely crush [Germany] and reduce her to a state of economic bondage which would strip away from humanity all hope of a lasting peace."[33] In the 1951 San Francisco Treaty of Peace with Japan, the principle of reparation for the "damage and suffering" caused by Japan was noted, along with the acknowledgment that "the resources of Japan are not presently sufficient, if it is to maintain a viable economy, to make complete reparation for all such damage and suffering, and at the same time meet its other obligations."[34]

Postwar peace settlements that constitute practices of international justice and reconciliation between states must accommodate the claims of justice of the citizens of the culpable state, thus necessitating limits on the reparative obligations that liable states may have.[35] The extent of a state's reparative obligations to victim parties, whether they are individuals, corporations, or states, must be balanced with its

---

[33] Trachtenberg, *Reparation in World Politics*, 18.

[34] San Francisco Treaty of Peace with Japan, September 8, 1951 (published 1952), https://treaties.un.org/doc/Publication/UNTS/Volume%20136/volume-136-I-1832-English.pdf.

[35] In addition, the Articles on State Responsibility specify that an offending state cannot be required to satisfy a reparative demand in a way that is "out of proportion to the injury" or that takes "a form humiliating to the responsible State" (Article 37.3), http://legal.un.org/ilc/texts/instruments/english/draft_articles/9_6_2001.pdf.

obligations to provide for their own populations.[36] As was discussed in Chapter 3, reparations should not be conceived or justified as punitive measures against the population of a culpable state.[37] Accountability in the form of punishment for wrongful state conduct should be limited to individual political and military leaders, although the responsibility to pay for damages to others resulting from such conduct becomes a liability of the population, along with the political responsibility for any related institutional and structural reforms. Such liability is not based on a collectivized notion of moral responsibility, and whatever the regime type, nothing may justify a level of material reparations that would incapacitate a state from fulfilling its domestic obligations of ensuring domestic security, the effective administration of justice, the provision of a basic and universal level of health care and education, and the maintenance of functional and sustainable economic structures. Thus, Dinah Shelton observes that reparative obligations of wrongful parties are to be determined not only by the claims of injured parties but also by wider community interests.[38]

These wider moral considerations came to be acknowledged in the design of the United Nations Compensation Commission (UNCC) and Compensation Fund, created through Resolution 692 by the UN Security Council in 1992, following the First Gulf War that was ignited by Iraq's invasion of Kuwait.[39] Unlike the Inter-Allied Reparation

---

[36] See John Rawls, *The Law of Peoples* (Cambridge, MA: Harvard University Press, 1999), 95–96, for an argument about accountability for war that precisely aims to leave open conditions of possibility for interactional and structural reconciliation after interstate war. This entails understanding responsibility for war in a way that avoids demonizing and criminalizing entire peoples.

[37] Shelton notes that the aim of "remedial justice" excludes punitive sanctions or penalties from the purpose and scope of reparations claims. In addition, such claims arising from international wrongful conduct are "restricted to provable, proximate losses to avoid excessive recovery," and while there is an insistence on the obligation of full reparation, the Articles on State Responsibility "provide for some flexibility, incorporating proportionality or considerations of equity." See Shelton, "Righting wrongs," 838.

[38] Ibid.

[39] Paragraph 16 of UN Security Council Resolution 687 stated, "Iraq is liable under international law for any direct loss, damage, including environmental damage and the depletion of natural resources, or injuries to foreign Governments, nationals and corporations, as a result of Iraq's unlawful invasion and occupation of Kuwait." See Gattini, "The UN Compensation Commission," 167n27.

Commission formed under Versailles, which was not connected to the League of Nations system, the UNCC was a creature of the UN system, with the implication that it did not "represent the interests of a single state, for example Kuwait, nor of the coalition of states which fought for the liberation of Kuwait, but rather of the whole international community." Andrea Gattini also observes that, as a reparative regime, the UNCC not only efficiently processed the entitlements of victims of Iraqi aggression but also considered "the needs of Iraq's people."[40] The UNCC limited the reparative obligations of Iraq in various ways: the Allied coalition forces were not eligible for compensation for the cost of the forces or their military operations against Iraq and, with some exceptions, members of the Allied coalition force were ineligible for compensation for loss or injury sustained in military operations against Iraq.

The Iraqi civilian population, however, came to suffer significant deprivations in the postwar context. In the course of the forty-three-day aerial campaign of the First Gulf War, ninety thousand tons of bombs were dropped, devastating Iraq's civilian infrastructure, including most electricity-generating plants and water-pumping and sanitation systems. While Saddam Hussein retained power in Iraq, comprehensive trade sanctions against his regime hampered postwar reconstruction and compounded the toll of the war on the civilian population. Infectious disease spread as untreated sewage contaminated drinking water, but sanctions led to medical shortages and the scourge of hunger and malnutrition. At the same time, funding for the UNCC fund to compensate external victims of the war amounted to 30 percent of the annual Iraqi oil export revenue (later reduced to 25 percent in 2000 and 5 percent in 2010).[41] And although the United Nations attempted to alleviate the plight of the Iraqi civilian population through the Oil-for-Food program, its poor design left the system open to widespread corruption, perverting its purposes. It is now well established that the hardships suffered by the Iraqi population in the 1990s, following the First Gulf War, were partly a result of internationally imposed sanctions and partly due to domestic policies of Saddam Hussein's government, which distributed the impact of the sanctions and reparations in a way that produced objectionable

[40] Ibid., 164, 167.   [41] www.uncc.ch/compensation-fund.

deprivations among the most vulnerable members of Iraqi society.[42] As was evident in the case of post–World War I Germany, the imposition of accountability measures, such as reparations and sanctions, on unreconciled regimes can create perverse outcomes, as such regimes tend to create or exaggerate domestic crises as a strategy in their "propaganda war" with external opponents.[43] If the populations suffering under such regimes can also be considered victims of the regime's wrongful conduct, then it is more difficult to justify the imposition of reparations against such a regime to compensate external victims, since doing so foreseeably involves distributing the economic burden of reparations to the internal victims of the regime. In such cases, an interactional account of responsibility for reparations becomes morally vexed.

But what about the external victims of an incapacitated or unreformed state's wrongful conduct? If such victims' reparative claims may be limited, not only practically but also morally, by the obligations of culpable states to provide for their own populations, does this mean that their losses have to lie where they fall, despite being the product of a state's wrongful conduct? The Articles on State Responsibility only obligate culpable states to repair losses arising from their misconduct, but such an interactional account of reparation that focuses solely on the obligation of wrongdoers will be inadequate in circumstances when wrongdoing results in losses, burdens, or other objectionable consequences beyond the capacity of culpable states to compensate or repair.

---

[42] On the controversy surrounding responsibility for Iraqi civilian malnutrition and mortality from sanctions, see David Cortright, "A hard look at Iraq sanctions," *The Nation*, December 2001. See also David Rieff, "Were sanctions right?," *New York Times*, July 27, 2003. For a devastating assessment of the diplomacy behind the sanctions regime, from the perspective of a British diplomat involved in the process, see Carne Ross, *Independent Diplomat: Dispatches from an Unaccountable Elite* (Ithaca, NY: Cornell University Press, 2007), 50–70. On punitive sanctions, see Anthony F. Lang Jr., *Punishment, Justice and International Relations: Ethics and Order after the Cold War* (New York: Routledge, 2008), 78–106.

[43] Pablo Kalmanovitz notes the problem of perverse incentives when the duty of reparations is conditional on the satisfaction of a baseline of sufficiency for the civilian population of the culpable state. See his "Sharing burdens after war: a Lockean approach," 223. On the exaggeration of child mortality and medical shortages following the First Gulf War, see Rieff, "Were sanctions right?"

If we return to the principle of corrective justice, that wrongs should be rectified, we can see that it consists of two parts: one is that those responsible for wrongs have a particular obligation to make reparations to their victims, and the other is that those who have suffered wrongs have a particular claim to some form of redress for their losses or injuries. In an interactional account, these two parts are connected, so that it is uniquely wrongdoers who hold the obligation to repair their victims' suffering. However, if wrongdoers are incapacitated or if their compliance cannot be enforced, this interactional account of reparation becomes thwarted and is insufficient to realize the end of corrective justice as it relates to victims, which is to repair the harms or losses they suffered as a result of others' wrongdoing. While an interactional account of the reparative obligation owed by culpable agents to their victims is morally cogent, it is not sufficient in many contexts of international and transnational political catastrophes, such as interstate war.

This insufficiency of interaction-based grounds for reparations reveals that adequate redress of wrongs must include additional grounds that obligate other agents and forms of remedy for victims. As Pablo Kalmanovitz has argued, while it is "natural to think that those responsible for an unjust war" should pay for the material burdens of the war, "additional criteria will be needed when destruction is so vast that those responsible cannot shoulder the burdens all by themselves."[44] In Chapter 1, I noted that when the goal of victim reparation is beyond the capacity of the responsible state(s) to fulfill alone, then the obligation to repair the losses and damages resulting from war may have to be distributed beyond the directly responsible state, "through a system of international loss-spreading which extends across the community of nations."[45] Such a collective system of victim reparation was essentially what France hoped for from its allies in the aftermath of World War I, but such a system failed to materialize due to a lack of agreement among the other Allied powers on how to distribute

---

[44] Kalmanovitz, "Sharing burdens after war," 210. Kalmanovitz criticizes Locke's "individualized liability" view of attributing liability for the material burdens of war and argues that using Locke's construction of the moral agency of the state, not only are individual citizens responsible for their own acts or omissions but they can also "be made liable *through* their state's responsibility" (213).

[45] Crawford and Watkins, "International responsibility," 298.

the costs associated with fighting the war and with the postwar economic reconstruction of Europe.

To illuminate the grounds for extending victim reparation beyond perpetrators, we need to locate the principle of corrective justice in a structural framework. The rehabilitation of victims is not only a demand against wrongdoers but is also a demand of structural justice. In one form, victim reparation is an obligation of structural justice because social structures were implicated in the wrongdoing. The interactional account of reparative obligations does not adequately capture the responsibility of agents involved in producing and reproducing structural injustice, where social structures are unjust or are implicated in wrongdoing or morally objectionable outcomes, as is typical for most cases of political catastrophe involving colonial domination. The interactional account of reparations that emphasizes the responsibility of direct wrongdoers to make reparation becomes less sufficient as wrongful conduct or morally objectionable interactions or conditions are enabled or in other ways mediated by social and political structures and institutions, discourses, processes, and practices. In cases where structural injustice enables widespread, coordinated, legalized, and normalized individual, collective, or corporate wrongdoing – a typical defining feature of most major political catastrophes – a narrow account of reparation that aims to settle accounts only between the particular agents involved is no longer appropriate for determining the field of responsible agents for victim reparations.

In another form, victim reparation is an obligation of structural justice because social structures have the general task of effecting or maintaining structurally just conditions. The demand to work collectively toward structural justice is a presentist or forward-looking claim that entails forms of victim reparation to ensure their structural dignity and effective moral and political agency. If all belligerents are economically exhausted, it is possible from the point of view of structural justice that even culpable states will require assistance in order to meet their domestic obligations and make the necessary institutional and structural reforms. One way to think about this ground for an obligation of victim reparation is to extend John Rawls's concept of a "duty of assistance" toward "burdened societies" to include societies devastated by armed conflict, international or domestic.[46] Such a duty of

[46] See Rawls, *The Law of Peoples*, 106.

assistance is not only an obligation of the responsible state toward its own or another state's population but the obligation can and must be extended to the international community if the ends of the duty of assistance (to support groups to achieve effective moral and political agency and to create or maintain a society of well-ordered peoples) are to be realized. In the context of civil wars, Pablo Kalmanovitz has posited "an imperfect international duty of development aid, so that wealthy-enough neighboring states, or international organs, ought to invest in . . . economic reconstruction" of states devastated by war. But if the duty of assistance is a component of international and transnational justice, then it may be perfect, requiring the creation of an international agency to coordinate and distribute fairly the duty of (reparative) assistance between states. From both structural points of view, the end of victim reparation is to rehabilitate or assist victimized agents to a condition of structural dignity and justice. The end or target of such a duty of victim reparation would not be full restitution of the victimized state to a prewar baseline but to secure sufficient structural support and conditions for the state to meet its domestic obligations to its own citizens, as well as to protect itself from predatory or exploitative interactions and to be able to engage in mutually advantageous forms of international cooperation and exchange.[47]

In both forms, structural accounts of reparative duties would take us beyond the interactional victim–perpetrator framework for thinking about reparations. Without the institutionalization and internationalization of principles of corrective justice beyond the interactional model, it is not surprising that ad hoc attempts by states to validate a moral principle of reparation for internationally wrongful conduct falter in the face of their lack of commitment to establishing the structural conditions for an equitable system of corrective justice among states in international relations.

Indeed, it is significant that all of the above examples of reparation by states for wrongful conduct involved the defeat of states in armed

---

[47] According to Kalmanovitz, "when responsibility-based liability runs out and there are people below the natural baseline or unable to put themselves to work, charity and the sufficiency condition provide further bases for liability, in all types of war." The aim of international development aid in such contexts "is to secure subsistence or to re-establish access to employment, not to re-establish or approximate the pre-war distribution of property." See Kalmanovitz, "Sharing burdens after war," 225.

conflict. Powerful states, however, can still largely escape accountability and duties of reparation to their victims, due to the lack of robust international institutions that can enforce judgments of wrongdoing. The Articles on State Responsibility affirm a state duty of reparation in the context of forwarding a principle of interactional corrective justice, but the enforcement of such a principle requires international structural support. Without such support, those who are victimized by powerful states that cannot be forced to comply with obligations derived from international law will continue to live in a world without remedy.

IV The Turn to Reparations for Individual Victims of Political Catastrophe

A structural account of reparative obligations is especially pertinent to realizing justice for individual victims of international and transnational political catastrophes. In international relations, the agents that have historically been the claimants of reparations for international political catastrophes, such as interstate war, have been states. A number of interstate agreements concluded in the aftermath of the Second World War did contain provisions for the restitution or reallocation of various kinds of "identifiable property," such as jewelry, household goods, and cultural property, to individuals and civil society organizations.[48] As Christine Evans has noted, however, "claims for individual compensation could be lodged only through inter-state complaints. There was no obligation on the state whose nationals had been injured to present claims against other states. In fact, there was no impediment against states being able to waiver their claims without any consultation with the [individual] victims concerned." Since the end of the Second World War, individuals have gained status as subjects of international law, and the current international order contains a variety of mechanisms by which individuals may make reparative

---

[48] This included the restitution or reallocation of property seized by the National Socialists "from co-operative societies, trade unions, charitable organizations and other democratic organizations." See the Convention on the Settlement of Matters Arising Out of the War and the Occupation, *The American Journal of International Law* 49, 3 (Supplement: Official Documents, July 1955): 69–120. In a more recent example, the judgment of the Eritrea-Ethiopia Claims Commission, established by the 2000 Peace Agreement between the two countries, included US$2 million for claims by individual Eritreans (August 2009), see http://legal.un.org/riaa/cases/vol_XXVI/505–630.pdf.

claims against their own states, as well as other states, for wrongful conduct or conduct that constitutes serious violations of human rights or humanitarian law, namely, genocide, crimes against humanity, and war crimes.[49] In customary international law, based on the 1907 Hague Convention (IV) and Additional Protocol I, a state that violates international humanitarian law acquires a duty to pay compensation.[50] Evans argues that there is an "emerging customary right for individuals to receive reparations for serious violations of human rights and the corresponding responsibility of states," based on the UN General Assembly's (nonbinding) adoption in March 2006 of the UN Basic Principles and Guidelines on the Right to a Remedy and Reparation for Victims of Gross Violations of International Human Rights Law and Serious Violations of International Humanitarian Law ("Basic Principles on the Right to Reparation for Victims").[51] The concept of reparation in contemporary international law is also quite expansive and includes "restitution, compensation, rehabilitation, satisfaction, and guarantees of non-repetition" in response to wrongdoing.[52]

The concern with redressing individuals for the harms of interstate war was evident in the work of the United Nations Compensation Commission (UNCC), following the 1990–1991 First Gulf War.[53] The UNCC's decisions ranked the urgency of different types of claims, creating a classification of victims from individual to corporate to governmental claims.[54] The category of cases considered most urgent by the

[49] Articles referring to victims' rights to effective remedies, fair and adequate compensation, compensatory damages, full rehabilitation, and just satisfaction can be found in various international human rights documents, including the Universal Declaration of Human Rights (Article 8), the International Covenant on Civil and Political Rights (Article 9), the Convention against Torture (Article 14), the European Convention (Article 50), and the American Conventions (Article 10). See Evans, *The Right to Reparation in International Law*, and De Greiff, *The Handbook of Reparations*.

[50] International Committee of the Red Cross (ICRC), Customary IHL Database, www.icrc.org/customary-ihl/eng/docs/v1_cha_chapter42_rule150.

[51] Evans, *The Right to Reparation in International Law*, 7.

[52] Ibid., 17 and 13. Other terms that cover this concept of reparations are "remedy" and "redress." The denial of individuals as claimants did not mean that interstate reparations never benefited individuals, only that individuals could not directly make reparative claims against states.

[53] The Governing Council of the UNCC was based on the composition of the Security Council, while claims were assessed by independent panels of Commissioners.

[54] See www.uncc.ch/.

UNCC were almost 1 million cases of mostly migrant workers from Africa and Asia, as well as Kuwaitis, who were forced by the circumstance of the Iraqi invasion, and then the bombing by the Allied coalition forces, to flee Kuwait and parts of Iraq.[55] Category A claimants were considered by the UNCC Governing Council to be "urgent claims" and had priority to compensation (between US$2,500 and US$4,050), which was paid to "any person who, as a result of Iraq's unlawful invasion and occupation of Kuwait...departed from Kuwait or Iraq during the period of 2 August 1990 to 2 March 1991."[56] While most individuals had to submit their claims through their governments, some three thousand, including stateless persons, were able to submit claims through international organizations, including the UN Development Program, the UN High Commissioner for Refugees, and the UN Relief and Works Agency for Palestinian Refugees (UNRWA).[57] In addition to this compensation for forced exodus arising from the circumstance of interstate war, individual claimants who qualified in Categories B and C, for serious personal injury and death or for pain and anguish, received additional payments.[58]

While Gattini is right that the UNCC was "the first collective relief system organized by the international community in response to an aggression," the funding for the system of compensation was not borne by the international community, only the decision to organize such a compensation committee to assess reparative claims.[59] The obligation to fund the system of compensation lay solely with the defeated power, Iraq, and was based on a percentage of the "proceeds generated by the

---

[55] According to the UNCC Secretariat, the number of Category A claims was 923,158, with most claimants coming from Egypt, India, and Sri Lanka. See Iñigo Salvador-Crespo, "Making good for forced exodus: compensation for departure from Iraq or Kuwait – claims of individuals: 'A' claims," in *War Reparations and the UN Compensation Commission: Designing Compensation after Conflict*, Timothy J. Feighery, Christopher S. Gibson, and Trevor M. Rajah, eds. (Oxford: Oxford University Press, 2015), 221–41. Salvador-Crespo was a legal advisor at the UNCC and in charge of the Category A claims (fixed sum claims submitted by individuals for departure from Kuwait and Iraq).
[56] Ibid., 222.
[57] Evans, *The Right to Reparation in International Law*, 141. See also D. Caron and B. Morris, "The UN Compensation Commission, practical justice, not retribution," *European Journal of International Law*, 13, 1 (2002): 183–99.
[58] For claimants in Category B (personal injury or death), the total family-based compensation amount was US$10,000. Categories D, E, and F were large-scale claims from corporations, governments, and international organizations.
[59] Gattini, "The UN Compensation Commission," 166, 181.

export sales of Iraqi petroleum and petroleum products."[60] In many other cases of political catastrophe, however, redress for individual victims is unlikely to be achieved through reparations made by perpetrators or culpable states alone.

When genocide, war crimes, and crimes against humanity became subject to international legal prohibition, it became possible to conceive of state responsibility to provide reparation for such crimes. But the development of international law and institutions reveals that victim reparation has not been limited to culpable states or domestic political structures. Guarantees of nonrepetition, for example, not only involve a state adopting domestic laws but such adoption is often spurred by international laws that support the prohibition and punishment of such crimes. Mechanisms for victims to obtain satisfaction, including holding perpetrators accountable, have also been internationalized to include ad hoc, hybrid, and international courts, including the International Criminal Court, that judge individual criminal liability for such acts.

The need for a structural account of reparative duties toward victims of internationally recognized wrongful conduct has become apparent in the evolution of the mandate of the Trust Fund for Victims (TFV), a fund that is part of the International Criminal Court (ICC). As discussed in Chapter 3, the ICC is an institution of international criminal justice that aims to uphold humanitarian law by holding natural persons accountable for genocide, war crimes, and crimes against humanity. In addition to this retributive function, many have noted the significance of the provision for victim reparation in the Rome Statute (Article 79) that established the International Criminal Court:

1. A Trust Fund shall be established by decision of the Assembly of States Parties for the benefit of victims of crimes within the jurisdiction of the Court, and of the families of such victims.
2. The Court may order money and other property collected through fines or forfeiture to be transferred, by order of the Court, to the Trust Fund.
3. The Trust Fund shall be managed according to criteria to be determined by the Assembly of States Parties.[61]

---

[60] www.uncc.ch/compensation-fund.
[61] http://trustfundforvictims.org/legal-basis.

Rule 98 (1–4) of the ICC Rules of Procedure and Evidence specifies that individual and collective awards for reparations can be made against a convicted person. In addition, Rule 98 (5) specifies that "other resources of the Trust Fund may be used for the benefit of victims."[62] Over time, the TFV has recognized the need for such other resources in order to provide generalized assistance to victims, even in the absence of prosecutions or convictions. Indeed, victims of grave injustices in contexts of political catastrophe often have an immediate need for assistance. The TFV has developed a mission "to provide physical, psychological, and material support to victims and their families. By assisting victims to return to a dignified and contributory life within their communities, the TFV contributes to the realization of sustainable and long-lasting peace through the promotion of restorative justice and reconciliation."[63] Even if those who committed wrongdoing are never punished, or are not able to provide any compensation, the rehabilitation of victims is a matter of structural justice and reconciliation.

The function of the TFV accords largely with the understanding of reparations in the literature on "transitional justice," which has focused mainly on the responses of newly democratizing governments to mass or systematic serious human rights violations perpetrated under previous regimes of rule. "Reparations" in this context refer specifically to "measures that provide benefits to victims directly," distinguishable from other measures that may have "reparative effects . . . (such as the punishment of perpetrators or institutional reforms), but which do not distribute a direct benefit to victims themselves." As Pablo de Greiff has put it, "the most general aim of a program of reparations is to do justice to victims."[64] It is important to note that while restitution in the form of returned territories, resources,

---

[62] Adopted September 2002, www.icc-cpi.int/iccdocs/PIDS/legal-texts/RulesProcedureEvidenceEng.pdf.

[63] "Since 2004 to October 2014, the accumulated total of contributions from countries has amounted to over €20.4 million euros. In 2014 alone, the total amount of contributions from countries was over €5 million euros." See www.trustfundforvictims.org/financial-information. The ICC 2016 budget is €153.32 million. Of this amount, the Secretariat of the Trust Fund for Victims ("the Fund" or "TFV") is proposing a budget for 2016 of €2.48 million to cover staff and other costs of administering the fund.

[64] De Greiff, *The Handbook of Reparations*, 453 and 455. De Greiff distinguishes between "material" (cash payments, or services including education, health and housing) and "symbolic" (official apologies, public commemorations)

and people, as well as cultural property, has been a common feature of peace settlements, symbolic and material reparations for victims of certain kinds of harms and losses produced by political catastrophes such as war cannot meet the principle of *restituio in integrum*, or restoration to a prior condition, as if the injustice had not occurred. In many cases, it is impossible to cancel out the losses and suffering of victims, or to restore lives to the way they were before, and the idea that one can do so is perverse. What form or amount of reparations would be adequate for redressing wrongs such as genocide, enslavement, torture, rape, and other crimes against humanity? What price can be put on the loss of one's husband or children? The problem with the kinds of losses and suffering endemic to war, oppression, and atrocity is their fundamental irreparability and the inescapable inadequacy and arbitrariness of any amount of material compensation. These problems are compounded by the mass extent of injuries and harms produced by major political catastrophes. Thus, German reparations to Jewish victims of the Holocaust, as negotiated by the Conference on Jewish Material Claims against Germany, noted that reparations "were not intended to have a moral purpose. 'Moral' and 'material' claims were kept separate."[65]

In the interactional account, "reparations" refer specifically to what is owed by wrongdoers to their victims as remedy for wrongdoing. In a structural account of victim reparation, "reparations" may refer to what the relevant social structures owe to victims in relation to their rehabilitation as full participants in those social structures. Using Henry Shue's account of "basic rights,"[66] we can see that the recognition of victims' rights to reparation under international law entails correlative duties on the part of member states and international institutions. One correlative duty is that agents must avoid depriving victims of such reparation. States establish and maintain systems of corrective justice, as well as conflict mediation and resolution mechanisms

reparations, but this distinction can be somewhat misleading, since all measures require some devotion of material resources, and some forms of "material" reparation, such as cash compensation for the death of loved ones or for suffering, can only be symbolic.

[65] See John Authers, "Making good again: German compensation for forced and slave laborers," in De Greiff, *The Handbook of Reparations*, 424.

[66] Shue argues that basic rights are "everyone's minimum reasonable demands on the rest of humanity," specifically, rights to security and subsistence. See Henry Shue, *Basic Rights: Subsistence, Affluence, and US Foreign Policy*, 2nd ed. (Princeton, NJ: Princeton University Press, 1996), 19.

precisely to ensure that victims' right to reparation is realized. Within contemporary liberal democracies, states have in fact assumed responsibility for realizing some form of remedial justice for victims of interactional wrongs, following the rise of social movements for victims' rights and restorative justice since the 1970s. Most Canadian provinces, for example, have compensation and financial assistance programs for victims of violent and personal crimes.[67] In these domestic contexts, the state bears the responsibility of reconciling the duty of victim reparation with general duties of distributive justice. The societal obligation of victim reparation in liberal democratic contexts can be justified, according to Pablo de Greiff, based on the political aims of enhancing recognition, civic trust, and social solidarity.[68]

Another correlative duty is structural support for the right, so that social structural processes do not create strong incentives to violate the duty of reparation.[69] For example, in a society that exhibits structural racism or discrimination against a racialized group, social solidarity may not extend to members of the group. Institutions and processes of guaranteeing public safety and the administration of justice, including the police and the courts, may operate in biased ways and be less diligent in protecting members from such communities or pursuing accountability and reparation for their victimization. In such a context of structural injustice, wrongdoers may victimize members of such marginalized communities, knowing that they are more likely to escape accountability for their wrongdoing. This, unfortunately, describes the situation faced by indigenous women in Canada, who are four times more likely to go missing or be murdered than their non-indigenous counterparts.[70] Christine Evans has thus argued that a state may bear reparative obligations to victims of serious human rights violations,

---

[67] Such programs were "created to acknowledge the harm done to innocent victims and to help ease the financial burden that often accompanies victimization. The compensation/financial assistance program is seen as the payer of last resort, therefore all other coverage must be exhausted prior to claims for compensation." Awards vary, with provincial maximums ranging from CAN$2,000 to CAN$127,000. See the Canadian Resource Centre for Victims of Crime: http://crcvc.ca/for-victims/financial-assistance/.

[68] De Greiff, *The Handbook of Reparations*, 466.   [69] Shue, *Basic Rights*, 60.

[70] See the Inter-American Commission on Human Rights, *Murdered and Missing Indigenous Women in British Columbia*, Canada (Organization of American States, December 21, 2014), www.oas.org/en/iachr/reports/pdfs/Indigenous-Women-BC-Canada-en.pdf.

even when it is not the direct perpetrator of such wrongs, if it is has been derelict in its duties and has "omitted or failed to demonstrate due diligence to prevent violations."[71] In interstate contexts, the social guarantee of basic individual rights recognized at the international level, such as a right to reparation for serious violations of human rights or humanitarian law, entails duties, not only on the part of direct perpetrators, but on the part of international society as a whole to establish institutional and structural support for effective realization of victims' rights to reparation.

Thus, Evans argues that in cases of genuine state incapacity, "while the obligation to provide reparations is that of the state, in certain instances it is clear that the international community bears positive obligations to assist poorer states in fulfilling their responsibilities."[72] Evolving practices of redress for major political catastrophes involving human rights and humanitarian law, as well as international criminal justice, contain the acknowledgment that the responsibility to assist victims and redress the losses and harms they suffered often goes beyond direct perpetrators. The duty of victim reparation can obligate the liable state, the victim's state, as well as the society of states as a whole. Individual victims may claim reparations from those who committed injustice against them and from those who participated in structural injustices that enabled their victimization.

In addition, victims of international wrongful conduct may make general claims based on distributive justice as it relates to the fair distribution of humanitarian obligations to the victim's home state, other states, and the international community. As in the interstate case, victim reparations programs, when distributed to the international community or to member states as well as to international nongovernmental organizations such as the Red Cross, Oxfam, CARE, and Doctors without Borders, ought to be connected to notions of distributive justice that raise questions about how victims' reparative claims are to be assessed in relation to the international community's wider obligations to those in need of humanitarian and social assistance. In some cases, victims may need special types of assistance; thus feminist activism has highlighted the special needs of victims of sexual violence in constructing reparative programs in contexts of settling armed conflicts.[73] But

---

[71] Evans, *The Right to Reparation in International Law*, 126.
[72] Ibid., 230.   [73] Ibid., 117–27.

while victim reparation programs may be distinct from general humanitarian programs funded by the international community, they do not necessarily enjoy normative priority over humanitarian needs that arise, for example, as a result of natural disasters, as opposed to internationally recognized wrongful conduct.[74] Civilian victims of armed conflict may suffer from loss of income and food insecurity, but these deprivations also afflict those who suffer from drought, and the international community's duty of victim reparation and assistance must be balanced with its duties of humanitarian assistance in general.

Currently, such an "equity approach" is lacking not only in general humanitarian assistance but also in victim reparation. In contemporary international and transnational realms, the duty of reparation to victims of serious violations of human rights and humanitarian law is currently imperfect in most regions of the world. Some regional human rights systems – most notably in Europe and the Americas – have developed effective and comprehensive regimes of victim reparation, with robust supervisory and follow-up mechanisms.[75] In other regions, however, the sustainability of various victim trust funds at national and international levels, including the TFV of the ICC, largely depends on voluntary funding by states, corporations, organizations, and individuals. Thus, as Evans notes, "victims of ordinary crimes are still more likely to receive redress than those who have suffered serious human rights violations, in particular, when the victims are numerous in the context of an armed conflict."[76] In the recent case of separatist conflict in eastern Ukraine that began in March 2014, causing widespread infrastructural damage and population displacement and injury, the United Nations released its Ukraine Humanitarian Response Plan for

---

[74] On issues of equity in the work of humanitarian INGOs, see Jennifer Rubenstein, *Between Samaritans and States: The Political Ethics of Humanitarian INGOs* (Oxford: Oxford University Press, 2015). Discussing the tendency of armed conflicts in Syria, the wider Middle East, and eastern Ukraine to dominate the humanitarian agenda and eclipse the drought in southern Africa that threatens the food security of 31.6 million people, Elhadj As Sy, Secretary-General of the International Federation of Red Cross and Red Crescent Societies, called for an "equity approach" at the 2016 World Humanitarian Summit in Istanbul. See "Competing crises could push African drought down humanitarian summit agenda," *The Globe and Mail*, May 17, 2016. To the extent that more extreme weather conditions are caused by human-made global climate change, it is possible to describe those who suffer from such adverse climate conditions to be victims of global structural injustice.

[75] Evans, *The Right to Reparation in International Law*, 126.   [76] Ibid., 2.

2017, requesting states to contribute US$214 million to assist people who have to cope with various dire hardships due to the conflict, such as injury, displacement, food insecurity, and loss of income. As of June 2017, international donations totaled US$33 million, or 15.4 percent of what the UN requested for its humanitarian program in Ukraine for the year.[77]

In another case from the global "war on terror," troop contributing nations of the International Security Assistance Force (ISAF) in Afghanistan[78] do offer *ex gratia* (out of kindness) payments for death, injury, and property damage arising from their actions, sometimes accompanied by apologies. Even in this one conflict, however, ISAF members have failed to construct uniform policies for compensation, leading to widely varying rewards given for similar losses and harms; have not been diligent in gathering information about civilian harm caused by ISAF actions; and have not taken up the challenge of helping affected civilians to gain access to compensation programs by removing foreseeable formidable barriers.[79]

More fundamentally, this case raises the concern that compensation payments serve not as a measure that signifies the end of an unjust condition or act but as a means for its perpetuation. Significantly, in agreements signed with the Afghan government, ISAF forces "are not liable for damage to civilian property or civilian injury or death as a result of lawful operations," and "ISAF members are explicit that these payments do not represent acceptance of responsibility or liability. Instead they are considered expressions of sympathy – a tangible symbol of condolence to persons harmed in the midst of war." Robert Meister has criticized such forms of "reparations" that are not directly connected to an acknowledgment of responsibility for wrongdoing as inadequate,

---

[77] See www.humanitarianresponse.info/system/files/documents/files/ukraine_ humanitarian_snapshot_20170619_en.pdf. Of the US$23.5 billion requested by the United Nations for 25 Humanitarian Response Plans affecting 37 countries, donors had funded $6.2 billion, or just 26 percent. See www.unocha .org/sites/unocha/files/GHO-JuneStatusReport2017.pdf.

[78] ISAF forces that have made some form of payment to civilians for death, injury, or property loss include the US, the UK, Germany, Italy, the Netherlands, Canada, Australia, Poland, and Norway.

[79] See Chris Rogers, "Addressing civilian harm in Afghanistan: policies and practices of international forces," Campaign for Innocent Victims in Conflict (CIVIC) White Paper, 2010.

since they fail to repudiate the wrong.[80] Normatively, such payments do not constitute "reparations," or even "acknowledgment payments," but could be termed "denial payments," since they are predicated on a denial of a right to acknowledgment and reparation of wrongdoing or objectionable harm. Such systems of denial reveal a condition in which justice has no place and confirm that, in some contexts of domination, "kindness" is the utmost limit of demands that the weak can make against the powerful.

V Conclusion

This chapter has examined the development of reparative practices for interstate war, as well as traced one of two contemporary developments in the politics of reparations in international and transnational relations: the recognition of individuals as direct claimants of reparations. This latter development supplants a previous statist bias in the politics of reparations in international relations. In both cases, however, reparations programs or schemes in response to political catastrophes rely on grounds other than individual or corporate moral culpability for wrongdoing. Redress of victims' injuries and losses from major political catastrophes must entail going beyond the interactional duty of perpetrators to provide reparations to their victims. Thus reparations as a component of structural justice can obligate the victim's state, a liable external state, as well as the society of states and global civil society as a whole. The next chapter explores the implications of this view for assessing contemporary reparative claims for colonial injustices.

[80] See Robert Meister, *After Evil: A Politics of Human Rights* (New York: Columbia University Press, 2012), 243.

8 | *Beyond Reparations*
Toward Structural Transformation

"When you gets to the North," [Sarah] said, "they invites you to the dining room, and they asks you to sit at the table. Then they offers you a cup of tea, and they asks, 'Does you want cream and sugar?'"

I was dumbfounded . . . She had changed; she'd gone mad. I took a swallow of my coffee. "And this appealed to you?" I asked.

"Yes," she said, raising her eyes very coolly to mine. "It appeal to me."

– Valerie Martin, *Property*[1]

I Introduction

In the closing scene from Valerie Martin's *Property*, set in Louisiana in 1828, Manon Gaudet, the wife of a sugar plantation owner, is questioning Sarah, an enslaved woman who managed to escape for a time but has been recaptured and returned to Manon. While Sarah is serving Manon breakfast, she shares the recollection of her short experience of freedom. Manon considers Sarah's desire, to have a seat at the table and be served tea herself, to be "perfectly ridiculous," as she cannot imagine a slave warranting such treatment by herself.[2] Although slavery entails many outright brutalities, one of its features as a structural form of domination is that those who enslave as well as those who are enslaved often cannot imagine things otherwise, even in the absence of direct abuse, force, or coercion.[3] For some, it may seem difficult to grasp the

---

[1] Valerie Martin, *Property* (New York: Vintage, 2003), 192.
[2] Ibid., 193.
[3] As Kevin Bales has noted, slavery has incorporated "the most horrible crimes known – torture, rape, kidnap, murder, and the willful destruction of the human mind and spirit." On the persistence of slavery in diverse forms in contemporary contexts, afflicting 27 million people worldwide, see Kevin Bales, *Understanding*

depth of Manon's unresponsiveness to Sarah's experience of freedom. One hallmark of normalized and naturalized structural injustice is that it may distort or disable the moral and cognitive capacities of agents who participate in its perpetuation, making them "morally deaf and dissociated" from the testimonies, experiences, and claims of others.[4] Although over 150 years have passed since the end of the transatlantic slave trade and the abolishment of slavery, normalized and naturalized ideas, discourses, and practices of racial superiority and supremacy still condition contemporary social structures and relations in many domestic and international contexts, constituting one of the main structural injustices in contemporary international and transnational order. As Jade Larissa Schiff has noted, one of the challenges of working through just what political responsibility for structural injustice entails for each of us, in our individual and social lives, is the challenge of cultivating responsiveness. Such responsiveness is a prerequisite for assuming responsibility in an appropriate way, which is easily undermined by thoughtlessness, bad faith, and misrecognition in the narratives that we construct to define ourselves, others, and our social relations in the world.[5]

This book has argued that practices of justice and reconciliation in contemporary world politics suffer from shortcomings that stem from a failure to acknowledge and respond adequately to the persistence of structural injustice and alienation in the development of modern international order. Conceptualizing the tasks of justice and reconciliation in interactional *and* structural terms provides for a more normatively robust and complete response to the types of injustice and alienation

Global Slavery: A Reader (Berkeley: University of California Press, 2005), 6–7. In the republican tradition, a condition of slavery is denoted by domination, or being subject to the arbitrary will of another, whether or not there is any direct interference or violent method of control. See Philip Pettit, *Republicanism: A Theory of Freedom and Government* (Oxford: Oxford University Press, 1997), 31–35. See also Steven Lukes, *Power: A Radical View* (London: Macmillan, 1974).

[4] Judith Shklar, *Faces of Injustice* (New Haven, CT: Yale University Press, 1990), 48. On epistemic injustice in the forms of testimonial and hermeneutical injustice, both of which are on display in Manon's incredulity when presented with Sarah's account of her experience of freedom, and her conclusion that Sarah had gone mad, see Miranda Fricker, *Epistemic Injustice: Ethics and the Power of Knowing* (Oxford: Oxford University Press, 2007).

[5] Jade Larissa Schiff, *Burdens of Political Responsibility: Narrative and the Cultivation of Responsiveness* (Cambridge: Cambridge University Press, 2014).

that attend international and transnational political catastrophes. In particular, the identification of structural injustices in the production of most major political injustices, including those associated with historical colonialism, requires us to go beyond conventional interactional accounts of both justice and reconciliation that focus on individual or corporate victims and perpetrators of wrongful acts. The persistence and reproduction of such structural injustices in contemporary social relations and orders mean that the backward-looking tasks of settling accounts and coming to terms with past unjust acts or interactions are deeply related to the forward-looking tasks of redressing contemporary structural injustice and alienation. Acknowledging the centrality of structural injustice in the production of political catastrophes is important for making appropriate normative judgments about the responsibility of culpable agents for wrongdoing, as well as about the responsibility of a broader group of agents for transforming unjust or alienating features of contemporary global and international social structures.

In Chapter 5, I established that as the individual agents involved in a historic injustice pass into history, the concept of reparation, understood as a rectification between agents of such injustice, becomes less and less appropriate as a framework for conceptualizing the responsibility of contemporary living agents. While contemporary agents have a duty to understand and acknowledge past injustice as part of the project of constructing a mutually affirmable and affirmed global order, the distinction between persons means that contemporary agents are largely incapable of rectifying unjust acts of the distant past. In addition to acknowledgment, however, contemporary agents have a moral and political responsibility to eliminate unsurpassed structural injustices that contributed to, or resulted from, the production of past injustice and that continue to pervade contemporary social relations and structures, though fulfilling this task does nothing to rectify the injustices suffered by historic victims.

The claims of the Herero and the Nama, with which this book began, constitute one such historic case, where more than one hundred years have now passed since the 1904–1907 genocide by Imperial Germany. Under my account, the lack of living survivors and perpetrators from the time of the genocide makes the concept of reparation, understood as the redress of wrongs by perpetrators to their victims, largely inoperable. When agents involved in wrongdoing have passed, any payments made by contemporary agents cannot be understood as reparations, properly understood, that serve the backward-looking function of rectifying or repairing the original injustice to the victims. Although no historic agents involved as victims or perpetrators in the genocide are still alive, Germany still has a duty of acknowledgment of the genocide against the Herero and the Nama. Furthermore, since no reparations were paid at the time, "acknowledgment payments" from Germany to the Herero and the Nama can act as a form of symbolic acknowledgment or recognition of past wrongs by contemporary agents. The primary justification of contemporary acknowledgment payments is a forward-looking one, to do with the responsibility of contemporary agents to promote reconciliation or to construct a mutually affirmable and affirmed social/political order between contemporary agents.[6] The grounds for such so-called reparations is not the rectification of historic injustice but a certain conception of reconciliation that entails the non-alienation of contemporary agents in their social relations with each other and with the social/political order that organizes and mediates their activities.

In this case, since acknowledgment of past injustice is the purpose of acknowledgment payments, they need to be specified between Germany and those groups that were the explicit targets of genocidal policies and therefore should be distinct from any "development assistance" that Germany pays to the postcolonial state of Namibia. The insistence of German officials on categorizing any financial transfer as "development assistance" further obscures the proper role of such payments, which is to fulfill Germany's responsibility to acknowledge forthrightly its historic responsibility for the injustice.[7] In addition, the contemporary German state and society have a particular responsibility to acknowledge this wrong if they aim to construct a mutually affirmable political relation with the Herero and Nama. The process of acknowledgment should also be conducted in a way that does not reproduce the structural injustices that contributed to the original

---

[6] See Leif Wenar, "Reparations for the future," *Journal of Social Philosophy* 37, 3 (2006): 396–405. See the conclusion in Chapter 5.

[7] On the Herero's continuing quest for redress in an interstate order, see *The Guardian*, "Germany sued for damages of 'forgotten genocide' in Namibia," January 5, 2017. In addition to acknowledgment payments, other measures may also be required to redress structural injustices that still pervade Germany's contemporary relations with the peoples of Namibia.

wrong. While the rectification of historic justice is no longer possible, contemporary agents bear a political responsibility to redress structural aspects of the historic injustice that have persisted. The current inter-state process of acknowledgment, however, reflects the structural bias of a statist order that essentially denies the standing and agency of the Herero to negotiate the terms of acknowledgment of the historic injustice committed against their social group. Such denial shares similarities with the historic denial of Herero entitlements to political standing and self-determination that attended German settler colonialism, which culminated in genocide. Thus, although the postcolonial state of Namibia should facilitate this acknowledgment process, it ought not to assume for itself the position of the subject of the acknowledgment or of the recipient of acknowledgment payments.

In this chapter, I examine contemporary claims of a right to reparation for colonial injustices. Where there are still individual survivors of colonial wrongs that amount to violations of human rights and humanitarian law, either in the routine course of colonial rule and administration or in colonial responses to episodes of violent revolt, reparation in the forms of official acknowledgment, apology, and financial compensation to individual victims is one important component of international reparative justice, as well as of victims' reconciliation with domestic and international social/political orders. Given the many levels of structural injustice that needed to obtain for systematic and pervasive violations to occur, victim-survivors may have reparative claims against a variety of different types of corporations, churches, colonizing states, as well as their own states. Politically and legally, many such redress claims have followed the development of individual rights to reparation for genocide and other serious human rights violations. At the same time, redress for individual survivors who suffered such violations does not adequately redress political catastrophes involving structural injustices, such as colonialism.

While morally significant, an interactional approach to redressing colonial injustice is still quite limited, not only because victim-survivors of colonial injustice are passing into history but because redress of interactional injustices associated with colonial rule are not adequate for redressing the structural injustices that mediated, conditioned, or enabled interactional harms and wrongs. Redressing structural injustices implicated in, constitutive of, or produced by colonial injustice entails recognizing that (1) colonialism did not only produce genocide, and serious human rights violations against specific individuals, and that (2) colonial injustice was not only a wrong between colonizer states and colonized nations or peoples. The structural injustices implicated in colonial wrongdoing were and are often international and transnational and affect larger categories of persons than those who can claim to be historic individual victims of egregious human rights violations. Redressing colonial structural injustice that has persisted thus requires thinking beyond a conventional interactional account of reparations between perpetrators and victims.

By taking the task of redress out of the interactional frame between victims and perpetrators or their associated social collectives and highlighting the centrality of political responsibility to transform persisting unjust contemporary social structures, this book puts contemporary legal and political reparations settlements and policies in perspective and advances the need to go beyond such reparations. A normative focus on the social stratifications of contemporary international order that reproduce structural injustice generates new ways to think about and engage in transformative politics of redress. The chapter concludes by exploring three interrelated strategies that can help to reorient redress efforts in response to the colonial structural injustices that continue to pervade contemporary international and transnational relations: decolonization, decentering, and disalienation.

II Responsibility for Reparations

With the rise of individuals as subjects of international law and the growing validation of a right to reparation in international law for victims of armed conflict and serious human rights abuses, those who have suffered colonial injustices that constitute similar abuses have begun to seek and win successful redress. For example, although international legal experts did not expect such a case to be legally viable, the British government did, in June 2013, conclude a "full and final settlement" of a high court action brought by five living victims of the Mau Mau war who suffered extreme physical violence during the state of emergency declared by the British colonial administration in its attempts to thwart an anticolonial insurgency between 1952 and 1960.[8] The settlement saw 5,228 Kenyans receiving compensation payments of

[8] Ninety thousand Kenyans were killed or injured in the eight-year period, and over 1 million were held in detention facilities. Some of the abuses were committed by the Kenya Police and Kenya Home Guard. The state of emergency was lifted in 1960.

£2,600 each, for a total of £19.9 million.[9] Although the British foreign secretary at the time, William Hague, claimed that this settlement would not establish a precedent, historian Caroline Elkins has argued that "Britain's acknowledgement of colonial era torture has opened as many doors as it has closed... The Mau Mau detention camps were but one site in a broader policy of end-of-empire incarceration, torture and cover-up."[10]

Indeed, a further legal claim has been launched against the British Foreign and Commonwealth Office (FCO) by a group of more than forty-one thousand Kenyans for physical abuse, false imprisonment, forced labor, and other deprivations that occurred in relation to Britain's attempts to stifle resistance against colonial rule in the 1950s. The successful 2013 Mau Mau reparations case also inspired the current lawsuit by the families of thirty-three people who were killed by British colonial forces while peacefully demonstrating against the detention of pro-independence activists during a state of emergency declared in the spring of 1959 in Malawi. In these cases where the claimants are living victims, or victims' immediate family members, claims for reparation for colonial injustice fit into an interactional framework of rectificatory justice.

The senior counsel on the Kenyan case, Paul Muite, who represented Mau Mau war veterans in the successful case for compensation from the UK, however, has advocated that the Kenyan government enter into interstate negotiations with the UK to work out a comprehensive reparations package. Muite notes that "justice in London was limited to those who were able to produce evidence of torture acceptable in law."[11] The exacting requirements of meeting the legal standard make it likely that large categories of people who suffered under British colonial rule will receive no compensation. Similarly, Pablo de Greiff has argued that in domestic or intrastate cases of major political and social injustices, political settlements for comprehensive reparations programs administered by the state serve victims better than ad hoc

[9] *The Guardian*, "UK to compensate Kenya's Mau Mau victims," June 6, 2013.

[10] Caroline Elkins, "Britain has said sorry to the Mau Mau. The rest of the empire is still waiting," *The Guardian*, June 7, 2013. See also my "Reconciliation and reparations," in *The Oxford Handbook of Ethics of War*, Helen Frowe and Seth Lazar, eds. (Oxford: Oxford University Press, 2015), Chapter 28, doi:10.1093/oxfordhb/9780199943418.013.17.

[11] Mazera Ndurya, "State asked to seek all-inclusive 'final settlement' with UK over Mau Mau case," *Daily Nation* (Kenya), September 15, 2015.

case-by-case litigation processes. The latter suffer from inequitable outcomes, given differential access to courts by people who have suffered similar violations, are costly and time consuming, and may even yield contrary decisions because of insufficient evidence. As de Greiff puts it, "a well designed reparations program may distribute awards which are lower in absolute terms, but comparatively higher than those granted by courts, especially if the comparison factors in the faster results, lower costs, relaxed standards of evidence, nonadversarial procedures, and virtual certainty that accompanies the administrative nature of a reparations program."[12]

Legal efforts, however, have been effective at stimulating the initiation and coordination of unilateral and interstate political redress efforts. For example, starting in the 1990s, German companies and the German state began to face numerous class action lawsuits filed in US courts by groups of individuals who were subjected to slave labor and forced labor under the National Socialist regime. In response, in 2001, the German parliament approved the creation of a foundation, Remembrance, Responsibility, and the Future, that compensated a total amount of €4.4 billion to 1.66 million people, located in almost one hundred countries, for slave and forced labor.[13] The capital of €5.2 billion for the foundation (German acronym EVZ) was provided in equal amounts by the German Industry Foundation Initiative and the German federal government. In the negotiated settlement, the Federal Republic of Germany and German companies accepted "moral and historical responsibility arising from the use of slave and forced laborers, from property damage suffered as a consequence of racial persecution and from other injustices of the National Socialist era and World War II."[14] The material compensation was accompanied by a

---

[12] Pablo de Greiff, *The Handbook of Reparations* (Oxford: Oxford University Press, 2006), 459. See also Christine Evans, *The Right to Reparation in International Law for Victims of Armed Conflict* (Cambridge: Cambridge University Press, 2012), 235.

[13] "Slave laborers" were mostly Jewish and had worked in the concentration camps in conditions of extreme cruelty, while "forced laborers" were mostly Slavic young women who were forced to work for the war effort of the National Socialist regime, but in more humane conditions. See John Authers, "Making good again," in De Greiff, *The Handbook of Reparations*, 421. After a contentious negotiation, the parties agreed that individuals subject to "slave labor" would receive awards of US$7,500 each, whereas those subject to "forced labor" would receive US$2,400 each. The payments were concluded in 2007. See www.stiftung-evz.de/eng/the-foundation/history.html.

[14] Authers, "Making good again," 427.

letter of apology from the president of Germany. In praising such a political settlement that included the German state over an alternative successful legal case that might have compelled German companies to pay compensation, John Authers argues that "apologizing and admitting that any amount of money could never be enough had a much more positive effect on its recipients than checks for much larger amounts of money paid by banks or insurance companies."[15] Significantly, a condition of the agreement required by the German state was "legal peace," or the dismissal of all lawsuits against German companies.

The involvement of companies and other agents of civil society in international and transnational injustices should remind us that many colonial injustices were enabled, supported, or perpetuated by participants of various forms and levels of structurally unjust social structural processes and background conditions. This book has shown how practices of justice and reconciliation for political catastrophes in twentieth-century international relations have been limited, mediated, and distorted by prevailing structural injustices that define a colonial international order. What does acknowledging the persistence of these structural injustices entail for thinking about redressing and addressing colonial injustice?[16]

With respect to individuals, states, and other corporate agents that are direct perpetrators of wrongdoing, the acknowledgment of structural injustice does not displace the requirement to assign moral blame for wrongdoing to them, although, as argued in Chapter 3, the structural context of wrongdoing is an important factor in assessing appropriate accountability mechanisms, including the liability of agents to punishment and/or reparations. For individuals acting in extreme cases of structural domination, such as that faced by interns in National Socialist concentration camps, judgment may be impossible. Thus, as Primo Levi noted about judging prisoners who helped to run such concentration camps and sometimes committed brutalities against fellow inmates, "the condition of the offended does not exclude culpability, which is often objectively serious, but I know of no human tribunal to

---

[15] Ibid., 440.

[16] The rest of this section is drawn from my "Colonialism as structural injustice: historical responsibility and contemporary redress," *The Journal of Political Philosophy* 19, 3 (2011): 261–81.

which one could delegate the judgment."[17] States acting under extreme cases of domination may also be denied the structural conditions of effective state agency and responsibility; for example, given that Korea was a colonized entity of Japan and enjoyed no formal or effective sovereignty over its own internal and external affairs, it would be difficult to assign to it moral culpability as a perpetrator state, despite Korean human and material contributions to Japan's aggressive war efforts.[18]

In addition to complicating judgment about the moral culpability of perpetrators, be they individuals, corporations, or states, a structural analysis raises the question of what kinds of responsibilities are incurred by agents who are not direct perpetrators in relation to a set of victims but who participated in the production of unjust structural social processes that enabled or supported the increased vulnerability of members of a group to objectionable social and political relations. At the level of international society, for example, states enacted and legitimated through their norms, laws, and practices a colonial international system in which dominant (mainly European) states competed for colonial possessions, each pursuing dreams of empire by subjugating weaker states, peoples, or territories. Korea fell victim to Japanese imperial ambitions, but do other state participants in a structurally unjust colonial international system bear any responsibilities in relation to Korea's victimization? More generally, what responsibilities do agents who participate in producing unjust structures and structural conditions, but who may not be direct perpetrators of wrongdoing, have toward the resulting harms and damages suffered by vulnerable others? Furthermore, with the passage of time, what responsibilities do contemporary agents who participate in reproducing unjust structures have toward those structural injustices?

---

[17] Primo Levi, *The Drowned and the Saved*, trans. Raymond Rosenthal (New York: Vintage International, 1989), 44.

[18] The judgment that Korea as a state was not morally culpable does not preclude judgments of culpability against individual Koreans whose collaboration with Japan's aggressive war aims might have been blameworthy. For example, while most Koreans conscripted to fight for the Japanese were victims of circumstance, South Korea's governing elites before democratization in the 1980s included more blameworthy collaborators, with some having risen to officers in the Imperial Japanese Army. See E. Taylor Atkins, *Primitive Selves: Koreana in the Japanese Colonial Gaze, 1910–45* (Berkeley: University of California Press, 2010), 191.

In her account of responsibility for global structural injustice, Iris Marion Young proposes a "political" or "social connection" model of responsibility, whereby all those participating in a social structural process that produces, even indirectly and unintentionally, unjust outcomes bear responsibilities to reform their activities, practices, and institutions to prevent the reproduction of similarly unjust outcomes. Young distinguishes two types of responsibility. The function of the "liability model" of responsibility is chiefly to hold culpable individual agents accountable for their wrongful actions, through punishment, redress, or compensation, while the main function of political responsibility is to stimulate collective action to transform social structures so as to avoid further injustices and injuries. Both types of responsibility are important in response to structurally based injustices, but they are distributed differently.[19] Those who participate in unjust social structural processes are not morally liable for other individuals' wrongful acts, even if those acts were conditioned by those unjust structures. According to Young, to accept political responsibility is not to accept moral blame for the harms and damages caused by others' wrongdoing.[20]

As the previous chapter noted, however, one implication of the structural supports for interactional colonial wrongs is that the agents who participate in the establishment and perpetuation of the structural injustice can become liable for the effects of wrongs, even though they are not morally culpable for an interactional wrong. I therefore agree with Young that nonculpable agents who contribute to the production of unjust structural conditions bear political responsibility to reform their social practices so that they are more just. Young, however, seems to think about compensation for victims only within the framework of a liability model of responsibility and argues that her conception of political responsibility "seeks not to reckon debts, but aims rather to bring about results," namely, structurally just social relations and conditions. She also argues that political responsibility avoids blaming agents and is mainly concerned with mobilizing "collective action for the sake of social change and greater justice."[21]

---

[19] Iris Marion Young, "Responsibility and global justice: a social connection model," *Social Philosophy and Policy* 23, 1 (2006):102–30 at 118.

[20] For a differing view, see Larry May, *Sharing Responsibility* (Chicago: University of Chicago Press, 1992).

[21] Young, "Responsibility and global labor justice," 379, 381.

My argument, however, attributes moral responsibility (and blame-worthiness) to agents who fail to fulfill their political responsibility to redress unjust social structures, although the correlative duties of redress and accountability mechanisms cannot be conceived in terms of liability to individual punishment. My argument does make the concept of political responsibility more controversial, because such responsibility can include reparative obligations to victims of wrong-doing. This is because the causal implication of structural injustice in contemporary wrongful conduct makes those who perpetuate such structural injustice partially liable for the harms or injuries that result from wrongful conduct. Agents who perpetuate structural injustice implicated in wrongdoing are not morally responsible or blamewor-thy for the wrongful conduct of others, but they are morally respon-sible (and blameworthy) for failing to redress structural injustice and its consequences. Furthermore, the justness of the outcomes or social conditions that result from structural reform must include the elimina-tion of disadvantages in social standing that identifiable victims as well as vulnerable social groups may suffer as a result of injustice, and may thus include some measure of victim reparation or compensation. As discussed in the previous chapter, for example, indigenous women in Canada are four times more likely to go missing or be murdered than their non-indigenous counterparts.[22] Given the myriad race-based, class-based, and gender-based structural injustices that are implicated in this heightened vulnerability of indigenous women to victimization, the Canadian state (or province) bears reparative obligations to the vic-tims and their families, even though the state is not the direct perpetra-tor of such wrongs.[23] Victim compensation therefore may be required

---

[22] Joanna Jolly, "Red River women," *BBC News*, April 8, 2015. See also the Inter-American Commission on Human Rights, *Murdered and Missing Indigenous Women in British Columbia*, Canada (Organization of American States, December 21, 2014), www.oas.org/en/iachr/reports/pdfs/Indigenous-Women-BC-Canada-en.pdf.

[23] As Christine Evans has put it, the state has been derelict in its duties and has "omitted or failed to demonstrate due diligence to prevent violations." See Evans, *The Right to Reparation in International Law*, 126. Of course, the Canadian state is responsible for much more than paying compensation to victims or their families, since making progress on reducing the vulnerability of indigenous women to victimization will require more fundamental structural revisions of political, economic, and social policies that affect the social position of indigenous peoples and persons, women, and the poor in Canadian society.

as a measure of moral and political responsibility for structural injustice.

I argued in Chapter 5 that in contexts of injustices of the distant past, acknowledgment is the primary duty that contemporary agents owe to historic and contemporary agents, as it is a key condition for developing contemporary and future relations of mutual respect and political reconciliation among members of groups or peoples who have experienced historically unjust interactions or structures. While victims are still alive, acknowledgment is also an additional function of special reparative measures to such survivors, which are required not only as rectificatory measures but because, as Kok-Chor Tan has noted, victims' experiences of injustice produce "spillover unjust effects in an indirect way . . . by tainting present relations that make justice between the affected parties difficult to achieve."[24]

Although Tan is referring to relations between a colonizer and its colonized peoples, his observation is also pertinent to thinking about the relationship between colonial victims and their own state and society, given that colonial injustice typically resulted in part from structural injustices that involved domestic political and social institutions and practices. Those who experienced political and social injustices may develop a profound sense of mistrust of and alienation from political and social institutions that linger even after general political and social transformations. Reparations, in a political responsibility framework, constitute measures to clear out "an undergrowth of disrespect and distrust" left by injustice, "so that trusting relations can take root."[25] And while such reparations may not do anything to reconcile victims with the perpetrators of injustice, the reparative measures of social and political institutions contribute to the task of reconciling victims to the social/political order.

Although reparation is not the appropriate conceptual framework for conceiving of contemporary obligations in response to historic injustices, the recognition of enduring structural injustices requires us to think more seriously about how all those whose current relations involve or rely on unjust social processes that supported historic

---

[24] Kok-Chor Tan, "Colonialism, reparations and global justice," in *Reparations: Interdisciplinary Inquiries*, J. Miller and R. Kumar, eds. (Oxford: Oxford University Press, 2007), 280–306 at 287.

[25] Wenar, "Reparations for the future," 403 and 404. A moral concern for political reconciliation is pertinent not only between former colonized and colonizer societies but within and among each of these societies.

injustices, and continue to reproduce similar inequities in contemporary social structures, may need to engage in transformative projects as part of their moral and political responsibility to realize just and nonalienating social relations and conditions.[26]

At the level of international society, some might argue that this political responsibility has been met by the society of states through measures such as the 1960 Declaration on the Granting of Independence to Colonial Countries and Peoples and the ensuing decolonization period. Such changes in the formal rules of international law and society, while promising, are not adequate for meeting Young's or my conception of political responsibility. According to Young, structural injustice refers not only to unjust formal laws but is characterized mainly by unjust social processes and practices that bring about certain unjust social conditions, such as inhumane working conditions for factory workers or a disproportionate percentage of single mothers living under the poverty line. Young describes structural injustice as involving "large categories of persons" being dominated or deprived, while others enjoy benefits in the form of greater opportunities to develop and exercise their capacities, and as "structural social processes with unjust outcomes."[27] A political responsibility to correct structural injustice is thus concerned with changing the formal laws and societal norms underlying social institutions and practices, but political responsibility is fulfilled only when these changes bring about or realize just structural or social processes and conditions.[28]

In the global context, just social conditions in the face of enduring structural injustice would, at a minimum, require not only formal but also effective and fair opportunities for self-determination of previously colonized peoples. Although colonialism has been repudiated in international law, we are still far away from a world order that is mutually affirmable and affirmed by previously colonized peoples.

---

[26] See Christian Barry, Robert E. Goodin, and Lea Ypi, "Associative duties, global justice, and the colonies," *Philosophy and Public Affairs* 37, 2 (2009): 103–35 at 134, for an argument that distributive justice obligations among those sharing a past colonial relationship may also not be unidirectional (from colonizer to colonized) but multilateral.

[27] Young, "Responsibility and global justice: a social connection model," 112, 118, emphasis mine.

[28] As Miriam Ronzoni has argued, "a basic structure is just not when each of its institutions (whatever they are) respects certain principles, but when, taken as a whole, it brings about certain social conditions." See Ronzoni, "What makes a basic structure just?," *Res Publica* 14 (2008): 203–18 at 205.

Thus contemporary international society continues to bear political responsibility for reforming international economic, social, and political structures, institutions, and practices in ways that would result in a fairer and more inclusive international order, especially for colonized groups and other social groups that suffer from structural injustices in a socially stratified international order. As I argued in Chapter 6, this responsibility extends to transforming international order in ways that can accommodate the nonalienated agency of indigenous groups, a point that challenges not only settler colonial states and some post-colonial states but the very constitutional terms of contemporary statist international order. In this sense, recognizing that we are still far away from a world order that is mutually affirmable and affirmed is a critique not only of former colonizer states but also of settler colonial as well as many postcolonial states that have perpetuated colonial structural injustices that undermine the conditions for structural dignity and nonalienated agency of formerly colonized peoples, including indigenous peoples such as the Herero.

The moral and political responsibility to redress structural injustice in international order is distinct from John Rawls's "duty of assistance" to "burdened societies." Although both share the aim of enabling peoples to develop the appropriate social structures and conditions necessary for realizing human dignity and exercising effective collective political and moral agency, the project of redress for structural injustice understands that one source of burdened societies' "unfavorable conditions" is international structural injustices.[29] While legal changes can go a long way toward establishing just social conditions, other strategies of redress for structural injustices are also necessary for realizing, in practice, the patterns of social relations that define a just and nonalienating international and world society.

III Strategies of Transformative Redress: Decolonization, Decentering, Disalienation

Redressing structural injustices implicated in and constitutive of colonial injustice entails recognizing that colonialism as a wrong did not only produce genocide, and serious human rights violations against

---

[29] John Rawls, *The Law of Peoples* (Cambridge, MA: Harvard University Press, 1999), §4.1, 37 and §15.1, 106.

specific individuals, and that colonial injustice was not only a wrong between colonizer states and colonized nations. The structural injustices implicated in colonial wrongdoing affected larger categories of persons than those who can claim to be victims. To suffer from structural injustice is not necessarily to be a victim but to be more vulnerable to victimization than others. Acknowledging the moral and political responsibility to correct structural injustices thus requires moving beyond the victim–perpetrator framework for identifying and redressing injustice. While reparative measures to redress interactional wrongs focus on repairing wrongs committed and suffered by distinct agents, measures to correct or rectify structural injustice aim to have a wider impact than the redress of specific wrongs suffered by specific victims.

For example, if structural racism leads to episodes of racialized violence between agents, specific victims of such violence may be entitled to compensation, and specific perpetrators may deserve to be held accountable, but the existence of racism as a structural injustice also means that the wider societies involved (1) share reparative obligations to the survivors or their immediate families, since the structural injustice causally enabled the interactional wrong, and (2) also have a political responsibility to formulate and implement appropriate and effective measures to counter racialized forms of structural injustice in social relations. Even if wrongs that were conditioned by structural racism occurred in the distant past, contemporary agents bear a moral and political responsibility to redress racialized structural injustice to the extent that it continues to pervade contemporary social structures.

Combating structural racism is an important structural corrective for racially motivated wrongful conduct, in the sense of correcting the background conditions that make some people more vulnerable to wrongful acts than others. Redressing racialized structural injustice is not mainly for the victims of direct wrongful acts, who may be long gone, but for the whole category of persons who are vulnerable to suffering wrongs and inequities stemming from structural racism, as well as for all those whose identities are distorted by the structural injustice. In this sense, all agents have a moral stake in eliminating structural injustice, not just direct victims and perpetrators of wrongdoing. Even if the victims and perpetrators of a past unjust act or episode are long gone, if the relevant structural injustices have endured, political responsibility endures. Contemporary agents do not incur a debt for past agents' wrongdoing, but unsurpassed structural injustice creates a condition in which the responsibility of agents to redress that enduring injustice is *re*-produced in a contemporary context. If structural injustices implicated in the production of past colonial injustices have not been eliminated, then there is a significant sense in which colonialism is not yet over, even if particular unjust acts have ended or particular forms of wrongful practices have been changed. To the extent that such structural injustices continue to pervade our social structures and relations at domestic, international and transnational levels, the moral and political responsibility to eliminate them constitutes the unfinished work of the political struggles for justice and reconciliation in international and transnational relations, especially as they relate to the legacies of empire, slavery, and colonialism.

Contemporary agents bear moral and political responsibility to correct persisting structural injustices, and reparative measures that enable the victimized and the vulnerable to exercise effective political and social agency constitute one requirement for contemporary social structures to be considered just and nonalienating. At the international level, the duty of reparation by states for contemporary internationally wrongful conduct thus needs to be supplemented by a wider political responsibility of states (that are not directly involved in a specific wrongdoing) to combat international and transnational structural injustices that enable internationally wrongful conduct. Acknowledging structural injustices in contexts of international and transnational political catastrophes thus requires a fuller account of reparative obligations for a wider set of agents than the interactional view demands.

To say that states share a moral and political responsibility to eliminate international and transnational structural injustices does not involve the assumption that such injustices can be adequately captured by interactional statist models of wrongdoing. Structural injustices do not only pertain to interactions or relations between social groups that have been incorporated into states, or that form an intergenerational collective narrative. In this sense, my account of structural injustice is more expansive than Jeff Spinner-Halev's concept of "enduring injustice," which he argues pertains only to intergenerational groups with collective narratives. Significantly, according to Spinner-Halev, "to the extent that some groups do not have collective narratives, they cannot suffer an enduring injustice." In my account, however, the injustices suffered by national, racialized, or ethnic groups constitute only one framework for analyzing social and political injustice, and it is not clear why we should limit the concept of enduring injustice only to such social groups. Indeed, the persistence of gender and class discrimination, marginalization, and oppression could qualify as enduring structural injustices for women and workers.

As Chapter 4 demonstrated, recognizing gender- and class-based structural injustices complicates the nationalist and statist premises of redress politics in domestic and international relations and opens the possibility of constructing joint reparative efforts by colonizing and colonized societies, as well as by international society.[30] Gender- and class-based structural injustices are likely to cut across state, national, racial, and ethnic groupings, and redressing such structural injustices may require not only international and transnational efforts but also national and group efforts of the colonized. In many contexts, the political responsibility to eliminate structural injustice in modern conditions may involve the state. Whereas Young understood the political responsibility to redress structural injustice to be shared by individuals, Serena Parekh has argued that states can also be "politically responsible" for eliminating structural injustice. According to Parekh, "states are responsible not in the sense that they are to blame for having caused the harm; rather, states are responsible in that they can discharge the duties that are associated with it in a more systematic way because of their privileged position vis-à-vis unjust social structures."[31]

While the state may be central to coordinating political responsibility at the domestic level to combat such structural injustices, by adopting and enforcing national legislation for gender equality or labor rights, or by providing political opportunities for projects for disalienation among the oppressed and marginalized, for example, the state cannot fulfill the task of eliminating structural injustice alone. Rather, political responsibility must typically go beyond political institutions and structures and become embedded in social institutions and practices, such as the family, civil society, institutions of knowledge production, educational and religious institutions, as well as other realms of public discourse and practice. Furthermore, the political

---

[30] For a critique of David Miller's nation-based theory of redress and an elaboration of the complexity of colonial injustice, see Sara Amighetti and Alasia Nuti, "David Miller's theory of redress and the complexity of colonial injustice," *Ethics and Global Politics* 8 (2015), doi:10.3402/egp.v8.26333.

[31] See Serena Parekh, "Getting to the root of gender inequality: structural injustice and political responsibility," *Hypatia* 26, 4 (2011): 672–89 at 673.

responsibility to combat structural injustice must be shared by international and transnational institutions, given the globalized nature of contemporary gender and labor structural injustices. Thus, at the international level, eliminating colonial structural injustices, mediated by race, class, gender, and other consequent categories of social stratification, will likely require transnational cooperation through international institutions and give rise to the joint responsibility of states, including of postcolonial states, to identify and address problems of structural injustice within the myriad of institutions that constitute international order.

In "postcolonial" international conditions, however, the disconnection of international institutions and the postcolonial state from local, more traditional and consequent structures of authority and power means that state-based agents are not likely to be the most suitable agents to coordinate and install desirable structural changes. As Margaret Kohn and Keally McBride have noted, "the postcolonial state was also structured by colonial ideas and institutions that were designed to enforce subordination and exploitation. This meant that the postcolonial state was a divided state."[32] As a matter of international policy, to the extent that international organizations continue to channel their efforts to promote models of state building that do not engage constructively with local or indigenous social and political structures of authority and power, even good-faith efforts to combat internal structural injustice may generate alienation as well as domination, while also failing to empower and motivate domestic actors to engage meaningfully in struggles to transform domestic social structures.[33]

Acknowledging the moral and political responsibility of contemporary agents to redress structural injustices that mediated colonial

---

[32] Margaret Kohn and Keally McBride, *Political Theories of Decolonization: Postcolonialism and the Problem of Foundations* (Oxford: Oxford University Press, 2011), 5.

[33] For a critique of the liberal democracy promotion practices developed since the 1990s by Western governments as well as international organizations, see Milja Kurki, *Democratic Futures: Re-visioning Democracy Promotion* (New York: Routledge, 2013). See also Antony Anghie, "Decolonizing the concept of 'good governance,'" in *Decolonizing International Relations*, Branwen Gruffyd Jones, ed. (Lanham, MD: Rowman and Littlefield, 2006), 109–30; and Pierre Englebert, "Pre-colonial institutions, post-colonial states, and economic development in tropical Africa," *Political Research Quarterly* 53, 1 (2000): 7–36.

injustice and continue to pervade international order requires new normative and political reorientations. Contemporary theorists and practitioners must think beyond frameworks of "accountability" and "reparations" to construct innovative practices of justice and reconciliation in ways that respond more appropriately to the contemporary reproduction of a structurally unjust international order. What strategies of redress might transform structural injustice? In closing, I would like to highlight three interrelated strategies to develop new normative and political reorientations: decolonization, decentering, and disalienation.

Politically, decolonization involves continuing the process of creating international political conditions that support structural dignity and nonalienated agency for those who continue to suffer from structural injustices. Historical decolonization in the form of the granting of political independence to colonized states was the beginning, not the end, of the decolonization process. Full implementation of the 2007 United Nations Declaration on the Rights of Indigenous Peoples (UNDRIP) would entail great transformations of state sovereignty as well as the standards of internationally legitimate political authority. According to Article 43, the Declaration constitutes "the minimum standards for the survival, dignity and well-being of the indigenous peoples of the world." These standards include domestic and international political and financial support for indigenous self-government (Article 4); control over relevant political boundaries and territories (Articles 10 and 26–8); natural resource exploitation and environmental protection (Articles 29 and 32); and social, economic, educational, and cultural development.

In addition, the Declaration recognizes that the configuration of sovereignty in postcolonial conditions has resulted in indigenous peoples being divided by international borders, thus it provides for such indigenous peoples to "have the right to maintain and develop contacts, relations and cooperation, including activities for spiritual, cultural, political, economic and social purposes, with their own members as well as other peoples across borders" (Article 36).[34] Indeed,

[34] United Nations General Assembly, *United Nations Declaration on the Rights of Indigenous Peoples*, 2007, www.un.org/esa/socdev/unpfii/documents/DRIPS_en.pdf. For a discussion of struggles by peoples of the Iroquois Confederacy (Mohawk, Oneida, Onondaga, Cayuga, Seneca, and Tuscarora) to traverse the US-Canada border, involving challenges directly connected to the denial of indigenous self-determination by the contemporary interstate order,

many postcolonial states also include peoples or social groups divided by international borders. The boundaries of African states, for example, are results of negotiations between European powers at the Berlin Conference of 1884–1885 to fix their various spheres of influence.[35] Given limited knowledge of patterns of human settlement or even physical geography, European powers typically used straight lines or astronomical lines; thus about 30 percent of boundary lines in Africa are straight lines. On the African continent, boundaries were "dehumanized": there are 177 "partitioned culture areas," with all African states incorporating several distinct culture areas as well as several partitioned culture areas.[36] While theorists of self-determination have aimed to determine the conditions under which the principle of self-determination may justify how political boundaries should be redrawn or internal governance structures reconfigured, I would argue that both the strategies of redrawing boundaries and reforming internal governance are insufficient for accommodating the self-determination claims of transboundary peoples and groups.[37] In this sense, the UNDRIP's assertion of the rights of indigenous peoples requires more radical revisions of the international organizing principle and discourse of sovereignty: "The question of the colonial history of sovereignty discourse ... goes to the heart of considerations about structural injustice – the subordination of indigenous peoples and cultures

see Audra Simpson, *Mohawk Interruptus: Political Life across the Borders of Settler States* (Durham, NC: Duke University Press, 2014), 115–45.
Meanwhile, the Tohono O'odham Nation, which occupies a reservation that traverses the US-Mexican border, stands to come into conflict with the US President Donald Trump's plan to build a 1,954-mile border wall in the name of national security. See Fernanda Santos, "Border wall would cleave tribe, and its connection to ancestral land," *New York Times*, February 20, 2017.

[35] The European colonial powers that participated in the drawing of boundaries included Britain, France, Germany, Belgium, Portugal, and Italy. Ethiopia emerged as an empire builder in 1896 when it defeated Italy at Adowa.

[36] Ieuan Griffiths, "The scramble for Africa: inherited political boundaries," *The Geographical Journal* 152, 2 (1986) 204–16 at 207. Griffiths also notes that negotiations between European colonial powers did admit of more locally sensitive boundaries in some cases (209).

[37] On self-determination and boundaries, see Steven R. Ratner, *The Thin Justice of International Law: A Moral Reckoning of the Law of Nations* (Oxford: Oxford University Press, 2015), 143–83; and Anna Stilz, "The value of self-determination," *Oxford Studies in Political Philosophy*, vol. 2, D. Sobel, P. Vallentyne, and S. Wall, eds. (Oxford: Oxford University Press, 2016), 98–126 at 119–25.

through the process of European expansion is embodied in the very concept that underpins both nation-states and the international order they constitute."[38] In particular, I would argue that one significant revision of state sovereignty entails limiting the coercive rights of states to control the application of territorial borders to transboundary groups, in order to rehumanize such borders to facilitate the nonalienated agency of transboundary peoples and groups to move and travel, to trade and exchange, and to engage in various sorts of social relations across international boundaries.[39]

In the Canadian context, the UNDRIP accords with calls to action made by the Truth and Reconciliation Commission of Canada, including a call to the government of Canada to repudiate "concepts used to justify European sovereignty over Indigenous lands and peoples such as the Doctrine of Discovery and *terra nullius*."[40] What does such a call demand in the way of institutional reform? I suggest that the best way to understand this task is that even though historic injustices of indigenous dispossession, cultural destruction, and genocide cannot be rectified by contemporary agents, processes of reconciliation between contemporary agents cannot be predicated on the continued acceptance of these concepts that made such historic injustices possible. Mutual affirmation of contemporary social structures thus requires the repudiation of problematic concepts, and the transformation of institutional arrangements, both within settler colonial states, such as Canada, as well as of international order, so that they provide political space for constructing alternative, less alienating, structures of governance compatible with indigenous legal and political traditions and practices.

---

[38] See Jennifer Balint, Julie Evans, and Nesam McMillan, "Rethinking transitional justice, redressing indigenous harm: a new conceptual approach," *The International Journal of Transitional Justice* 8 (2014): 194–216 at 204. See also Avigail Eisenberg, Jeremy Webber, Glen Coulthard, and Andrée Boisselle, *Recognition versus Self-Determination: Dilemmas of Emancipatory Politics* (Vancouver: University of British Columbia Press, 2014).

[39] It should be noted that this argument for transboundary rights for transboundary peoples and groups is focused on rectifying colonial-based international structural injustice, and is distinct from an argument that endorses a universal or general right to freedom of movement for all individuals, or a world without borders.

[40] Truth and Reconciliation Commission of Canada, Calls to Action, number 45 (Winnipeg, Manitoba: TRC Canada, 2012), www.trc.ca/websites/trcinstitution/File/2015/Findings/Calls_to_Action_English2.pdf.

Progress toward further political decolonization of international
order also entails progress in normative decolonization, which partly
involves the destruction of legitimating, obscuring, or excusing myths
that sustain illusory and distorted views of contemporary international
order. The image of international anarchy, discussed in Chapter 4,
is normatively obscuring because it precludes the image of international order as a structurally unjust hierarchy. The efforts of indigenous
scholars, such as Taiaike Alfred, to revitalize indigenous conceptions
of civilization, and to identify the continuation of settler colonialism in
contemporary Canadian politics and society, also contribute to erod-
ing the myths that historical colonialism brought civilization to those it
subjugated, and that colonial dispossession is an injustice of the distant
past.[41] Understanding the structural injustices that organize and mediate the historical and contemporary normative development of international order allows us to view struggles for justice and reconciliation as
raising central political and normative questions about contemporary
international and transnational order.

In Chapter 4, I noted that colonial legality was a hallmark of the
structural nature of colonial injustice, since typically, structural injustices occur "as a consequence of many individuals and institutions
acting in pursuit of their particular goals and interests, *within given
institutional rules and accepted norms.*"[42] Thus, the British foreign
secretary who announced the settlement with the Mau Mau fighters
in 2013 continued to insist that "Britain still did not accept [that] it
was legally liable for the actions of what was a colonial administration
in Kenya."[43] Although contemporary British political leaders clearly
acknowledge the "abuses" of the Kenyan colonial administration, they
do so in a similar way that they condemned, in 1919, the abuses of
German colonial rule in South West Africa. Such acknowledgments,
however, imply that there is a morally legitimate form of colonial rule
or authority, properly carried out, which can be distinguished from

---

[41] See Chapter 6 for a fuller discussion of Taiaike Alfred, *Peace, Power and
Righteousness* (Oxford: Oxford University Press, 1999). For Gandhi's
observations about the pathologies of Western civilization, see Mahatma
Gandhi, *"Hind Swaraj" and Other Writings*, ed. Anthony Parel (Cambridge:
Cambridge University Press, 1997).
[42] Young, "Responsibility and global justice: a social connection model," 112
(emphasis mine), 114, 115.
[43] *BBC News*, "Mau Mau torture victims to receive compensation – Hague,"
June 6, 2013.

abuses of such rule. Although it is difficult to judge whether politicians have the intention of doing so, their discourse leaves open the possibility of endorsing colonial rule as a largely legitimate enterprise, while condemning certain flagrant abuses that entailed severe human rights violations. In other words, by instrumentalizing the historical legality of colonialism to avoid contemporary reparative and redress obligations, Hague evades the judgment that colonialism in itself is an objectionable structure of political relation that requires certain forms of political and structural redress. While it is true that individual compensation is not the appropriate form of reparation for colonialism as a structural injustice, the lack of acknowledgment that the legality of colonialism itself was wrong and that the persistence of structural injustices associated with colonial rule requires structural forms of redress is normatively evasive.

In addition, decolonization involves repudiating the marginalization of non-European modes of knowledge, discourse, and political practice; it is not only a matter of inclusion, but there is also a need to relinquish and repudiate normatively obscuring myths about the origins of modern international order. As Fanon revealed, a major weapon of colonizers is to impose their image of the colonized on those they subjugate.[44] Decolonizing knowledge and discourse are fundamental to transforming how we think about justice and how we engage in political practice to reform institutions in ways that open conditions of possibility for progress toward a more equitable and truly universally inclusive global community of humankind. As Robbie Shilliam has noted, however, strategies of decolonization can be assessed as better or worse, depending on how their repudiation of problematic frameworks help those who suffer under them to engage in "meaningful re-humanization and reclamation of personhoods." He thus argues that while the 1950–1951 United Nations Education, Scientific, and Cultural Organization (UNESCO) attempted to repudiate "scientific racism" by substituting race with the neutral and ahistoric category of "ethnicity," it not only debunked doctrines of supremacist hierarchy but also depoliticized the race-based struggles to resist them.[45]

---

[44] Frantz Fanon, *The Wretched of the Earth*, trans. Richard Philcox (New York: Grove Press, 2004).

[45] In contrast, the fourth UNESCO statement of 1967 provided a more politically constructive statement on race that recognized the historically developed roots

The result of decolonizing our images of our selves, others, and the world is that we develop a clearer view of contemporary political realities, deeply marked not only by historic wrongs but also by contemporary structural injustices. For those who enjoy privileges that stem from structural injustice, such as racial or gender or class privileges, decolonization will reveal such privileges and their effects as moral burdens that need to be eradicated.[46] Campaigns to remove public recognition and valorization of historic figures who were active perpetrators of historic wrongs can be viewed as symbolic attempts to acknowledge past injustice and commit to overcoming contemporary structural injustice.[47] In addition, decolonization means understanding and appreciating the agency of the colonized and the decolonized, which can help to ground an awareness and respect for contemporary efforts by those who suffer from structural injustice to participate effectively in the struggles for justice and reconciliation, both against their own states as well as against international institutions and other external agents.[48] As I have argued in this book, this clearer vision

of racial injustice and allowed for the valorization of the contemporary struggles of those with racialized identities to reestablish their humanity and personhood. See Robbie Shilliam, "Race and research agendas," *Cambridge Review of International Affairs* 26, 1 (2013): 152–58; and Robbie Shilliam, *The Black Pacific: Anticolonial Struggles and Oceanic Connections* (London: Bloomsbury Press, 2015).

[46] Thus, while Rawls is right to presuppose that most people want more rather than less of social primary goods, the reasonableness of this desire is tied to assessments about the justness of the social structures and conditions that generate inequalities in social primary goods. Most people would not want more if they thought that it was the result of injustice.

[47] In an announcement, President Peter Salovey of Yale University provided the reason that the university would rename one of its twelve undergraduate residential colleges, Calhoun College: "The decision to change a college's name is not one we take lightly, but John C. Calhoun's legacy as a white supremacist and a national leader who passionately promoted slavery as a 'positive good' fundamentally conflicts with Yale's mission and values." See "Yale to change Calhoun College's name to honor Grace Murray Hopper," *Yale News*, February 11, 2017. For an ongoing case, see the controversy surrounding the Rhodes Must Fall campaign, which calls on Oriel College at Oxford to remove a statue of the British imperialist Cecil Rhodes. Even though this latter case did not result in removal of the obscure statue, the campaign itself promoted greater critical reflection of Britain's imperial legacy. For a historical analysis of the intrinsically fraught and contentious nature of "Pax Britannica," see Antoinette Burton, *The Trouble with Empire: Challenges to Modern British Imperialism* (Oxford: Oxford University Press, 2015).

[48] See Rahul Rao, *Third World Protest: Between Home and the World* (Oxford: Oxford University Press, 2010).

of contemporary social and political reality entails recognition of the differentiated impact of many colonial injustices, organized not only between states or nations but between different, intersecting social categories of persons, defined prominently by race, gender, class, majority-minority, and core-periphery hierarchies.

Politically, decentering is a relevant task in the movement to reform and create more legitimate international and domestic governance institutions, processes, and practices that can respond effectively and appropriately to the demands of marginalized and oppressed agents and perspectives.[49] Formal inclusion of the oppressed in decision-making structures and cooperative schemes, however, is not enough, since under unjust background conditions of structural domination, the principles of consent and mutual advantage are not sufficient for overcoming structural domination and injustice.[50] As Vincent Pouliot has illustrated, the social stratification that defines the "pecking order" among states is not substantially mitigated but persistently reproduced due to its practical logic, even in contexts of multilateral diplomacy.[51] Multilateralism may thus only be the starting point, rather than the final point, of institutional reform at the global level and cannot operate effectively to yield morally legitimate decisions in conditions of structural injustice.

More important than multilateralism may be decentralization, which would create space for a greater variety of agents to be heard,

[49] See Barry Buzan, and George Lawson, *The Global Transformation: History, Modernity and the Making of International Relations* (Cambridge: Cambridge University Press, 2015), 275–304, on the material and ideational conditions for "decentred globalism," and its potential implications for world order.

[50] As Nancy Kokaz (Bertoldi) has argued, in addition to mutual advantage and consent, moral reciprocity must define the background structural conditions, understood as conditions which the participants reasonably affirm for mutual acceptance, and which no party considers to be a condition in which they are taken advantage of, or forced to give in to claims that they do not accept as legitimate. See Kokaz, "Institutions for global justice," *Canadian Journal of Philosophy* 31 (2005): 65–107. See also Vincent Pouliot, "Against authority: the heavy weight of international hierarchy," in *Hierarchies in World Politics*, Ayşe Zarakol, ed. (Cambridge: Cambridge University Press, forthcoming).

[51] See Vincent Pouliot, *International Pecking Orders: The Politics and Practice of Multilateral Diplomacy* (Cambridge: Cambridge University Press, 2016). Pouliot criticizes David Lake's contractualist notion of hierarchy in international relations as producing "too light a notion of social domination," because it implies voluntarism and choice based on agents' rational calculation of the costs and benefits of hierarchy (259). See David Lake, *Hierarchy in International Relations* (Ithaca, NY: Cornell University Press, 2009).

and which would support the development of pluralistic practices, an important aspect of self-development of historically oppressed groups as well as a source of restraint for dominant agents. For example, as outlined in Chapters 1 and 6, the petition process of the Permanent Mandates Commission of the League of Nations provided a forum for the internationalization of some colonial conflicts but, at the same time, also deprived some agents, such as indigenous groups and other displaced peoples, from receiving a hearing for the injustices they suffered. Unfortunately, the contemporary structures of international diplomacy, as found in the United Nations, continue to deny such peoples, as well as other nonstate representatives, any standing to make claims or participate in making decisions regarding international or transnational disputes related to territorial claims, governance, or resource use that profoundly affect them. As the former British diplomat Carne Ross observed about the world of international diplomacy, "often those with most at stake are not even allowed into the room where their affairs are being discussed."[52] Ross provides the example of the Sahrawis of the Western Sahara, nomadic peoples who have been seeking international support for a political process to substantiate their right to self-determination against Morocco, which invaded and occupied the territory upon the retreat of Spanish colonial power in 1975.[53] The Sahrawis' representative, the Polaris Front of Western Sahara, has no standing to make claims in international settings, a significant reason for the ongoing international failure to settle the territorial dispute between Morocco and the Polaris, with the result that 70 percent of the Sahrawi population continue to live in refugee camps.

In the study and practice of international relations, decentering may also take the form of assessing political institutions from several vantage points. The multiparty political systems developed in Western modern democratic states may look and operate quite differently in non-Western and postcolonial contexts.[54] A decentering strategy

---

[52] See Carne Ross, *Independent Diplomat: Dispatches from an Unaccountable Elite* (Ithaca, NY: Cornell University Press, 2007), 190–91.

[53] Ibid., Chapter 6.

[54] Kwasi Wiredu, "Democracy and consensus in African traditional politics: a plea for a non-party polity," in *Postcolonial African Philosophy: A Critical Reader*, Emmanuel Chuckwudi Eze, ed. (Cambridge: Blackwell, 1997), Chapter 14. According to Wiredu, "indigenous African systems of politics, at least in some well-known instances, offered examples of democracy without a multiparty mechanism."

also leads us to raise critical questions about disjunctures between international, domestic, and local receptions of dominant practices and discourses of human rights, self-determination, good governance, transitional justice, humanitarian intervention, development, and even sustainable development and climate adaptation.[55] In refocusing political inquiry and action away from the powerful or dominant modes of inquiry and political engagement, decentering practices may also assist the process of decolonization.[56] For example, Shilliam has argued that the research agenda on race "is dominated by one story – what the master does unto the sufferers – and addressed to one politics – can the master redeem the detritus of his humanity? What of the sufferers and their stories and politics? Are they merely fragments of raw data? Or do they have an epistemic part to play in the research agenda on race and racism?"[57]

Similarly, the kind of ethnocentricity that Charles Taylor has criticized shows that one task of decentering is to expand the horizons from which being human can be imagined, expressed, and practiced.[58] Decentering leads to new avenues of intellectual inquiry into the foundations of contemporary global order and may show that "much worldwide historical and contemporary lived experience is excluded and made invisible for a unilinear narrative that implicitly takes a hermetically sealed Europe to be both the motor and destination of the modern political subject."[59] Decentering thus serves to correct a

---

[55] On the latter, see Isabelle Anguelovski, Linda Shi, Eric Chu, Daniel Gallagher, Kian Goh, Zachary Lamb, Kara Reeve, and Hannah Teicher, "Equity impacts of urban land use planning for climate adaptation: critical perspectives from the Global North and South," *Journal of Planning Education and Research* 36, 3 (2016): 333–48, which finds that climate adaptation strategies pursued by city planners typically fail to protect the interests of vulnerable, indigenous, and poor populations from negative consequences such as displacement, while disproportionately prioritizing the protection of elite group interests. The authors conclude that climate "adaptation interventions can reinforce historic trends of socioeconomic vulnerability, compound patterns of environmental injustice, and create new sources of inequity" (345).

[56] See Kwasi Wiredu, *Conceptual Decolonization in African Philosophy: Four Essays* (Ibadan: Hope, 1995); and *Cultural Universals and Particulars: An African Perspective* (Bloomington: Indiana University Press, 1996).

[57] Shilliam, "Race and research agendas," 156.

[58] Charles Taylor, *Multiculturalism: Examining the Politics of Recognition* (Princeton, NJ: Princeton University Press, 1994).

[59] Robbie Shilliam, "What about Marcus Garvey? Race and the transformation of sovereignty debate," *Review of International Studies* 32, 3 (2006): 379–400 at 385.

common human tendency to project one's own institutional experiences or social and political histories onto others, as if those others were blank forms with no social and political histories, sciences, and experiences. Coupled with disalienation, decentering practices enable the epistemic agency of marginalized participants to engage as equals in a joint enterprise to construct a mutually affirmable and affirmed international and transnational social/political order.

The normative function of decentering is to ensure that the process of constructing and revising the terms of global justice for differentially situated agents in conditions of structural injustice can make progress toward a morally reciprocal order. If the project of global justice involves mutual affirmation of principles of global justice between the relevant moral agents, it becomes clear why enduring structural injustices need to be resisted and redressed. In contexts of structural injustice that produce structural indignity and alienated agency for some categories of persons, negotiations between agents about the terms of global justice are likely to reproduce rather than overcome structural injustice. While some theorists have adopted a statist framework for contextualizing duties of cosmopolitanism and global justice in modern conditions, I would argue that the construction and realization of such duties require much more critical distance from, and scrutiny of, statist and interstate institutions, practices, and frameworks of governance.[60]

In her "statist cosmopolitan" account of global justice, Lea Ypi argues that a "progressive interpretation of the function and purpose of existing institutional practices should integrate both normatively fundamental and causally fundamental principles." While she focuses on relative inequalities in state power as causally fundamental to the production of global injustice, including severe deprivation, she also acknowledges that reducing such interstate inequalities does not

---

[60] See Charles Beitz, *The Idea of Human Rights* (Oxford: Oxford University Press, 2011); Daniel Butt, *Rectifying International Injustice: Principles of Compensation and Restitution between Nations* (Oxford: Oxford University Press, 2009); Mathias Risse, *On Global Justice* (Princeton, NJ: Princeton University Press, 2012). Similarly, critics have identified a conceptual constraint of the transitional justice literature, "namely its focus on strengthening, rather than challenging, the state," and its invocation of past harms as a tool of nation building. See Balint, Evans, and McMillan, "Rethinking transitional justice, redressing indigenous harm," 201–2.

address issues related to decolonization.[61] My argument is that if the configuration of state sovereignty in international order and processes of postcolonial state formation are interacting in causally fundamental ways to reproduce oppressive structured and structural injustices – including the disproportionate vulnerability of some groups to usurpation of decisional agency, dispossession, severe human rights violations, as well as poverty – then the problems of global justice cannot be wholly divorced from the challenge of decolonization. The global justice literature thus needs to engage more systematically with theorizing postcolonial justice in contexts of alternative and more pluralistic social, legal, and political structures that constitute the basic structure of postcolonial societies, politics, and economies, as well as how to conceptualize principles and agents of global justice in light of alterity and pluralism.[62] The quest for structural justice, measured by the structural dignity and nonalienated agency of all relevant moral agents, may entail truly revolutionary structural transformations of world order that involve pluralizing the agents that can have political standing in international and transnational institutions and structures, as well as fundamental modifications of the coercive architecture of the modern sovereign states system.[63]

Disalienation is a political strategy for the oppressed and marginalized to build up capacities of nonalienated agency, a necessary condition for their participation in genuine communication about global justice and reconciliation with the terms of international and transnational order. The struggle for nonalienated agency requires more than acknowledgment of alienating past injustices, since the persistence of structural alienation in contemporary contexts produces a need for measures that address contemporary forms of structural alienation. Frantz Fanon understood the process of shedding the

---

[61] See Lea Ypi, *Global Justice and Avant-Garde Political Agency* (Oxford: Oxford University Press, 2012), 129.

[62] See Margaret Kohn, "Postcolonialism and global justice," *Journal of Global Ethics* 9, 2 (2013): 187–200.

[63] For an elaboration, see my "Cosmopolitan justice, democracy and world government," in *Institutional Cosmopolitanism*, Luis Cabrera, ed. (Oxford: Oxford University Press, forthcoming). Iris Marion Young formulated "a postsovereign alternative to the existing states system," consisting of a "decentred diverse democratic federalism." See Young, *Global Challenges: War, Self-Determination and Responsibility for Justice* (Cambridge: Polity, 2007), 16 and 32–38.

colonial construction of the identity of the colonized to be part of the agenda for disalienation: "Before embarking on a positive voice, freedom needs to make an effort at disalienation."[64] As discussed in previous chapters of this book, disalienation involves the difficult struggle to construct alternatives to colonial modernities. Just as not all colonial modernities have been alienating and unjust in the same ways, there is not just one authentic alternative but several possible nonalienating alternatives or a plurality of postcolonial modernities that agents may pursue.

Indigenous peoples in North America have been at the forefront of this struggle, as their extinction was the predicted correlate of the advance of modern civilization. As Glen Coulthard has noted, indigenous scholars worry that focusing on the redress of historic injustice has obscured the political responsibility of contemporary agents "to address structural injustices that continue to inform our settler-colonial present."[65] The examination of Kohn and McBride of various strategies of disalienation, from negritude to nationalism to land-based claims, shows that processes of disalienation cannot be understood as taking place "outside of the trajectory of history."[66] In this vein, it is understandable that some current disalienation politics in contemporary circumstances of globalization and climate change have targeted capitalism, positing a remedy of "radical sustainability" that requires capitalism to die.[67] At the same time, an acknowledgment of the historicity of disalienation politics may lead to a worry that disalienation, and hence any genuine structural transformation, is largely infeasible. Pouliot's account of the "weightiness" of international hierarchy leads him to hold a pessimistic view of the practical feasibility of agents' resistance capacities to engage in disalienation. Given that agents are embedded within a practical order, even if involuntarily, the "practical logic of competence" tilts "towards social reproduction" of the hierarchies that infuse that order.[68]

---

[64] Frantz Fanon, *Black Skin, White Masks* (New York: Grove Press, 2008 [1952]), 206.

[65] See Coulthard, *Red Skin, White Masks*, 155. See also Leanne Simpson, *Dancing on Our Turtle's Back: Stories of Nishnaabeg Re-Creation, Resurgence and a New Emergence* (Winnipeg: Arbeiter Ring Press, 2011).

[66] See Kohn and McBride, *Political Theories of Decolonization*, 33.

[67] See Coulthard, *Red Skin, White Masks*, 172–73.

[68] Pouliot, "Against authority: the heavy weight of international hierarchy" (forthcoming).

While I agree that disalienation is a difficult task of destruction and creation, historical analysis tends to reveal a much more varied landscape of potential for agency, even for those oppressed and marginalized by structural domination. As Adria Lawrence's examination of resistance to French imperial rule demonstrates, to the extent that local elites pursued political equality within the French republic as a viable and serious remedy for the defects of French *authoritarian* rule over its colonies, the subsequent turn to "nationalism was not inevitable." In this sense, the project of decolonization was not linked in an intrinsic, deterministic, or teleological way to the development of nationalist identity, mobilization, or violence. Acknowledging the historical indeterminacy of struggles for justice and reconciliation in conditions of domination opens intellectual and political space for conceptualizing and developing in practice alternative institutional futures to contemporary international hierarchies.[69]

Disalienation is important in shaping the course of struggles for justice and reconciliation, because without it, the results of such struggles will likely create false remedies and resolutions. First, alienation may engender futility and resignation, which demotivate many among the alienated from exploiting the available constructive avenues afforded by the social structure to struggle for justice. Alienation can generate all sorts of attitudes, dispositions, and acts that are not conducive to constructive approaches to struggling for justice; these span from apathy to cynicism to (self-) destructive acts. Second, even when alienated agents participate in struggles for justice, their identities, interests, and visions may still be constructed by dominant social structures and practices. According to Coulthard, for example, while engagement with Canadian law, state, and society is necessary due to the minority position of indigenous peoples, disalienation is important for such engagement to serve emancipatory ends rather than merely contributing to the reproduction of structural domination. In this vein, he argues for a "resurgent politics of recognition that seeks to practice decolonial, gender-emancipatory, and economically nonexploitative alternative structures of law and sovereign authority grounded on a critical refashioning of the best of Indigenous legal and political traditions."[70] Disalienation

[69] See Adria K. Lawrence, *Imperial Rule and the Politics of Nationalism: Anti-Colonial Protest in the French Empire*(Cambridge: Cambridge University Press, 2013).
[70] Coulthard, *Red Skin, White Masks*, 179.

serves to promote the achievement of reconciliation as nonalienation, a condition that helps to motivate the oppressed to engage constructively in shaping the content and course of struggles for justice. In this sense, the importance of disalienation cannot be overstated, as it is foundational to the project of reconciliation as nonalienation, a project that is central to establishing conditions in which agents can engage meaningfully in constructing terms of global justice that are free from the distortions produced by enduring structural injustice.

Through engaging in these strategies separately and simultaneously, contemporary agents may begin to imagine and create new forms of social relations. Like the prisoners in Plato's cave allegory, contemporary agents must struggle to turn away from the images of themselves and each other produced through objectionable social and political structures and relations and effect a turning around or reorientation of their vision.[71] To decolonize, decenter, and disalienate is to bring all agents to "a state of waking,"[72] conscious of our joint responsibility to work together to create mutually affirmable and affirmed social and political orders for nonalienated human flourishing.

IV Conclusion

Justice and reconciliation in response to political catastrophe are complex moral and political strivings in world politics. In this book, I have argued that practices of justice and reconciliation in contemporary world politics suffer from shortcomings that stem from a failure to acknowledge and respond adequately to the persistence of structural injustice and alienation in the development of modern international order. In making this argument, I have challenged two dominant approaches to conceptualizing international justice and order. First, positing that international order is structurally unjust implies a rejection of images of international relations as a realm of anarchy. I have argued that the concept of international anarchy is a normatively obscuring myth that is implausible in light of the actual historical development of international order. Second, in revealing the failure of contemporary international practices of justice and reconciliation to

---

[71] Plato, *The Republic of Plato*, 2nd ed., trans. Allan Bloom (New York: Basic Books, 1991), Book VII, 514a–518d.
[72] Ibid., 520d.

redress the structural injustice and alienation of the international order, I call into question the liberal progressive narrative of the development of practices of "transitional justice" since Nuremberg. The inadequacy of contemporary practices of justice and reconciliation is most apparent on the issue of redressing colonial international order, and this inadequacy betrays serious challenges to the legitimacy and stability of a liberal international order.

I have attempted in this book to convince contemporary theorists and scholars of international relations, law, justice, and reconciliation, of the necessity to think beyond frameworks of "accountability" and "reparations" when devising responses to political catastrophes. Justice and reconciliation as moral/political projects must be conceived not only interactionally, but also structurally, raising questions about the moral and political responsibility of agents other than perpetrators and victims to respond to the challenges posed by different, but often intersecting, forms of structural injustice in domestic and international orders. With new orientations gained through decolonization, decentering, and disalienation, variously situated contemporary agents can begin to imagine differently the ways that agents may relate to each other and the social worlds they inhabit and to recognize the practical necessity of embarking on the political projects of justice and reconciliation. In acknowledging this moral responsibility to engage in the political struggle to overcome the structural injustices that pervade our social norms, habits, and processes, contemporary agents can only make progress by working together to disalienate the agency of the oppressed; to decenter narratives and practices of politics; and to decolonize the structures of normative, social, and political thought and practice. Paradoxically, the greater contestation prevailing practices of justice and reconciliation provoke, the greater potential they may reveal for transforming domestic, international, and transnational orders toward achieving nonalienation and structural justice for all.

Epilogue

Antigone's Escape

Tragedians know all too well how to
dig – beneath the docile Eumenides,
past layers upon layers of bodies –
'til they find the Furies, still furious
at Orestes, Athena, and us all;
or Antigone, staring at three walls
of necessity, a familial crypt,
awaiting her end in a well-known script.
Only, something swells below the structure,
Shifting, cracking, old certainties rupture.
Upon pushing, the walls recede from view –
give way to something unfamiliar, new.
Wind brushes her cheeks, open landscapes
stretch before her. Antigone escapes.

References

Abdel-Nour, F. (2003). National Responsibility. *Political Theory*, 31 (5), 693–719.

Aeschylus, R. Lattimore, trans. (1953). *Oresteia: Agamemnon, The Libation Bearers, The Eumenides*, Chicago: University of Chicago Press.

Akhavan, P. (2013). The Rise and Fall, and Rise of International Criminal Justice. *Journal of International Criminal Justice*, 11 (3), 527–36.

Alfred, T. (1999). *Peace, Power and Righteousness*, Oxford: Oxford University Press.

   (2005). *Wasáse: Indigenous Pathways of Action and Freedom*, Toronto: University of Toronto Press.

Allen, D. S. (2000). *The World of Prometheus: The Politics of Punishing in Democratic Athens*, Princeton, NJ: Princeton University Press.

Allen, J. (1999). Balancing Justice and Social Unity: Political Theory and the Idea of a Truth and Reconciliation Commission. *University of Toronto Law Journal*, 49 (3), 315–53.

American Historical Review Forum. (2009). Truth and Reconciliation in History. *American Historical Review*, 114 (4), 899–977.

American Society of International Law. (1955). Convention on the Settlement of Matters Arising out of the War and the Occupation. *The American Journal of International Law*, 49 (3), 69–120.

Amighetti, S. & A. Nuti. (2015). David Miller's Theory of Redress and the Complexity of Colonial Injustice. *Ethics and Global Politics*, 8, 1–13.

   (2015). Towards a Shared Redress: Achieving Historical Justice through Democratic Deliberation. *The Journal of Political Philosophy*, 23 (4), 385–405.

Anghie, A. (1996). Francisco de Vitoria and the Colonial Origins of International Law. *Social and Legal Studies*, 5 (3), 321–36.

   (2004). *Imperialism, Sovereignty and the Making of International Law*, Cambridge: Cambridge University Press.

   (2006). Decolonizing the Concept of "Good Governance." In B. G. Jones, ed., *Decolonizing International Relations*, Lanham: Rowman and Littlefield, 109–130.

Anguelovski, I., L. Shi, E. Chu, D. Gallagher, K. Goh, Z. Lamb, K. Reeve, and H. Teicher (2016). Equity Impacts of Urban Land Use Planning for Climate Adaptation: Critical Perspectives from the Global North and South. *Journal of Planning Education and Research*, 36 (3), 333–48.

Aristotle (1984). *The Politics*. C. Lord, trans. Chicago: University of Chicago Press.

(1998). *Aristotle's Poetics*. S. Halliwell, trans. Chicago: University of Chicago Press.

(2000). *Nicomachean Ethics*. R. Crisp, ed. Cambridge: Cambridge University Press.

Arudou, D. (2015). *Embedded Racism: Japan's Visible Minorities and Racial Discrimination*, Lexington Books.

Asselin, P. (2013). *Hanoi's Road to the Vietnam War 1954–65*, Berkeley: University of California Press.

Atkins, E. T. (2010). *Primitive Selves: Koreana in the Japanese Colonial Gaze, 1910–45*, Berkeley: University of California Press.

Bales, K. (2005). *Understanding Global Slavery: A Reader*, Berkeley: University of California Press.

Balint, J., J. Evans, and N. McMillan. (2014). Rethinking Transitional Justice, Redressing Indigenous Harm: A New Conceptual Approach. *The International Journal of Transitional Justice*, 8, 194–216.

Barkan, E. (2000). *The Guilt of Nations: Restitution and Negotiating Historical Injustices*, New York: W. W. Norton.

Barkawi, T. (2004). On the Pedagogy of "Small Wars." *International Affairs*, 80 (1), 19–37.

Barkawi, T. and M. Laffey (2006). The Postcolonial Moment in Security Studies. *Review of International Studies*, 32, 329–52.

Barry, C., R. E. Goodin, and L. Ypi (2009). Associative Duties, Global Justice, and the Colonies. *Philosophy and Public Affairs*, 37 (2), 103–35.

Bass, G. J. (2002). *Stay the Hand of Vengeance: The Politics of War Crimes Tribunals*, Rev. ed., Princeton, NJ: Princeton University Press.

Beitz, C. (1999) [1979]. *Political Theory and International Relations*, Rev. ed., Princeton, NJ: Princeton University Press.

(2001). Does Global Inequality Matter? *Metaphilosophy*, 32 (1–2), 95–112.

(2011). *The Idea of Human Rights*, Oxford: Oxford University Press.

Belanger, Y. D. (2007). The Six Nations of Grand River Territory's Attempts at Renewing International Political Relationships. *Canadian Foreign Policy*, 13 (3), 29–43.

Bell, C. (2009). Transitional Justice, Interdisciplinarity and the State of the "Field" or "Non-Field." *International Journal of Transitional Justice*, 3 (1), 5–27.

Bell, D., ed. (2007). *Victorian Visions of Global Order: Empire and International Relations in Nineteenth-Century Political Thought*, Cambridge: Cambridge University Press.

(2016). *Reordering the World: Essays on Liberalism and Empire*, Princeton, NJ: Princeton University Press.

Berg, M. and B. Schaefer, eds. (2009). *Historical Justice in International Perspective*, Cambridge: Cambridge University Press.

Bianchi, H. (1986). Abolition: Assensus and Sanctuary. In H. Bianchi and R. van Swaaningen, eds., *Abolitionism: Towards a Non-Repressive Approach to Crime*, Amsterdam: Free University Press, 113–26.

Biermann, W. (1998). Epilogue. In W. Szpilman, ed., A. Bell, trans., *The Pianist: The Extraordinary Story of One Man's Survival in Warsaw, 1939–45*, Toronto: McArthur, 209–20.

Biersteker, T. J., J. G. Blight, R. K. Brigham, R. S. McNamara, and H. Y. Schandler, eds. (1999). *Argument without End: In Search of Answers to the Vietnam Tragedy*, New York: Public Affairs.

Bowden, B. (2009). *The Empire of Civilization: The Evolution of an Imperial Idea*, Chicago: University of Chicago Press.

Braithwaite, J. (2000). Survey Article: Repentance Rituals and Restorative Justice. *The Journal of Political Philosophy*, 8 (1), 117.

Branscombe, N. R. and B. Doosje, eds. (2004). *Collective Guilt: International Perspectives*, Cambridge: Cambridge University Press.

Bull, H. (1977). *The Anarchical Society: A Study of Order in World Politics*, London: Macmillan.

Burton, A. (2015). *The Trouble with Empire: Challenges to Modern British Imperialism*, Oxford: Oxford University Press.

Buruma, I. (2004). The Destruction of Germany. *The New York Review of Books*, 51 (16), 8–12.

Butler, J. (2005). *Giving an Account of Oneself*, New York: Fordham University Press.

Butt, D. (2009). *Rectifying International Injustice: Principles of Compensation and Restitution between Nations*, Oxford: Oxford University Press.

Buzan, B. & G. Lawson (2015). *The Global Transformation: History, Modernity and the Making of International Relations*, Cambridge: Cambridge University Press.

Callwell, C. E. (2009). *Small Wars: Their Principles and Practice*, 3rd ed., Champaign, IL: Book Jungle.

Caprio, M. (2009). *Japanese Assimilation Policies in Colonial Korea 1910–50*, Seattle: University of Washington Press.

Caron, D. and B. Morris (2002). The UN Compensation Commission, Practical Justice, Not Retribution. *European Journal of International Law*, 13 (1), 183–99.

Carr, E. H. (1965). *International Relations between the Two World Wars (1919–1939)*, London: Macmillan.

Chandler, M. J. and C. E. Lalonde (2008). Cultural Continuity as a Protective Factor against Suicide in First Nations Youth. *Horizons*, 10 (1), 68–72.

Chapman, J. M. (2013). *Cauldron of Resistance: Ngo Dinh Diem, the United States, and 1950s Southern Vietnam*, New York: Cornell University Press.

Chinkin, C. M. (2001). Editorial Comments: Women's International Tribunal on Japanese Military Sexual Slavery. *American Journal of International Law*, 95 (2), 335–41.

Clark, A. and S. MacIntyre (2004). *The History Wars*, Melbourne: Melbourne University Press.

Cole, E. A., ed. (2007). *Teaching the Violent Past: History Education and Reconciliation*, Lanham, Maryland: Rowman and Littlefield.

Comaroff, J. and J. L. Comaroff, eds. (2006). *Law and Disorder in the Postcolony*, Chicago: University of Chicago Press.

Cooper, A. D. (2006). Reparations for the Herero Genocide: Defining the Limits of International Litigation. *African Affairs*, 106 (422), 113–26.

Coulthard, G. S. (2014). *Red Skin, White Masks: Rejecting the Colonial Politics of Recognition*, Minneapolis: University of Minnesota Press.

Craig, G. A. and A. L. George (1990). *Force and Statecraft: Diplomatic Problems of Our Time*, 2nd ed., Oxford: Oxford University Press.

Crawford, J. and J. Watkins (2010). International Responsibility. In S. Benson and J. Tasioulas, eds., *The Philosophy of International Law*, Oxford: Oxford University Press, 283–98.

Crawford, N. C. (2002). *Argument and Change in World Politics: Ethics, Decolonization, and Humanitarian Intervention*, Cambridge: Cambridge University Press.

Cudd, A. E. (2006). *Analyzing Oppression*, Oxford: Oxford University Press.

Daase, C., S. Engert, M.-A. Horelt, J. Renner, and R. Strassner, eds. (2016). *Apology and Reconciliation in International Relations: The Importance of Being Sorry*, London: Routledge.

Darcy, S. (2007). *Collective Responsibility and Accountability under International Law*, Leiden: Transnational.

De Ceuster, K. (2001). The Nation Exorcised: The Historiography of Collaboration in South Korea. *Korean Studies*, 25 (2), 207–42.

De Greiff, P. (2006). *The Handbook of Reparations*, Oxford: Oxford University Press.

(2012). Theorizing Transitional Justice. In M. Williams, R. Nagy, and J. Elster, eds., *Transitional Justice*, New York: New York University Press, 31–77.

Dickinson, L. A. (2003). The Promise of Hybrid Courts. *The American Journal of International Law*, 97 (2), 295–310.

Digeser, P. E. (1994). *Political Forgiveness*, Ithaca, NY: Cornell University Press.

Dostoyevsky, F. (1995). The Dream of a Ridiculous Man: A Fantastic Story. In A. Myers, trans., *A Gentle Creature and Other Stories*, Oxford: Oxford World's Classics, 117–22.

Dower, J. (1996). The Bombed: Hiroshimas and Nagasakis in Japanese Memory. In M. J. Hogan, ed., *Hiroshima in History and Memory*, Cambridge: Cambridge University Press, 116–42.

Drumbl, M. A. (2007). *Atrocity, Punishment, and International Law*, Cambridge: Cambridge University Press.

Dudden, A. (2005). *Japan's Colonization of Korea: Discourse and Power*, Honolulu: University of Hawai'i Press.

(2008). *Troubled Apologies among Japan, Korea and the United States*, New York: Columbia University Press.

Duff, R. A. and D. Garland, eds. (1994). *A Reader on Punishment*, Oxford: Oxford University Press.

Duiker, W. J. (1994). *US Containment Policy and the Conflict in Indochina*, New York: Oxford University Press.

Duska, R. F., B. S. Duska, and J. A. Ragatz (2011). *Accounting Ethics*, 2nd ed., Malden, MA: Wiley-Blackwell.

Duthu, N. B. (2008). *American Indians and the Law*, New York: Penguin.

(2013). *Shadow Nations: Tribal Sovereignty and the Limits of Legal Pluralism*, Oxford: Oxford University Press.

Edmonds, P. (2016). *Settler Colonialism and (Re)conciliation: Frontier Violence, Affective Performances, and Imaginative Refoundings*, Basingstoke: Palgrave Macmillan.

Eisenberg, A., J. Webber, G. Coulthard, and A. Boisselle, eds. (2014). *Recognition versus Self-Determination: Dilemmas of Emancipatory Politics*, Vancouver: University of British Columbia Press.

Eley, G. and B. Naranch, eds. (2014). *German Colonialism in a Global Age*, Durham, NC: Duke University Press.

Elkins, C. (2005). *Imperial Reckoning: The Untold Story of Britain's Gulag in Kenya*, New York: Henry Holt.

Englebert, P. (2000). Pre-colonial Institutions, Post-colonial States, and Economic Development in Tropical Africa. *Political Research Quarterly*, 53(1), 7–36.

Erichsen, C. W. and D. Olusoga (2010). *The Kaiser's Holocaust: Germany's Forgotten Genocide,* London: Faber and Faber.

Erskine T., ed. (2003). *Can Institutions Have Responsibilities? Collective Moral Agency and International Relations,* New York: Palgrave Macmillan.

(2011). Kicking Bodies and Damning Souls: The Danger of Harming "Innocent." In T. Isaacs and R. Vernon, eds., *Accountability for Collective Wrongdoing,* New York: Cambridge University Press, 261–86.

Euben, P. (1990). *The Tragedy of Political Theory,* Princeton, NJ: Princeton University Press.

Euripides (1999). *The Trojan Women,* N. Rudall, trans., Chicago: Ivan R. Dee.

Evans, C. (2012). *The Right to Reparation in International Law for Victims of Armed Conflict.* Cambridge: Cambridge University Press.

Fanon, F. (2004). *The Wretched of the Earth,* R. Philcox, trans., New York: Grove Press.

(2008) [1952]. *Black Skin, White Masks,* R. Philcox, trans., New York: Grove Press.

Finch, G. A. (1919). The Peace Negotiations with Germany. *American Journal of International Law,* 13 (3), 536–57.

Forst, R. (2007). J. Flynn trans. *The Right to Justification,* New York: Columbia University Press.

Fowler, C. and J. Sarkin (2008). Reparations for Historical Human Rights Violations: The International and Historical Dimensions of the Alien Torts Claims Act Genocide Case of the Herero in Namibia. *Human Rights Review,* 9, 331–60.

Franck, T. (2003). Interpretation and Change in the Law of Humanitarian Intervention. In J. L. Holzgrefe and R. O. Keohane, eds., *Humanitarian Intervention: Ethical, Legal, and Political Dilemmas,* Cambridge: Cambridge University Press, 204–31.

French, P. A. (1984). *Collective and Corporate Responsibility,* New York: Columbia University Press.

Freud, S. (2002). *Civilization and Its Discontents,* D. McLintock, trans., Toronto: Penguin.

Fricker, M. (2007). *Epistemic Injustice: Ethics and the Power of Knowing,* Oxford: Oxford University Press.

Gaeta, P. (2004). Is the Practice of "Self-Referrals" a Sound Start for the ICC? *Journal of International Criminal Justice,* 2 (4), 949–52.

Galtung, J. (1969). Violence, Peace, and Peace Research. *Journal of Peace Research,* 6 (3), 167–91.

Gandhi, M. (1997). *"Hind Swaraj" and Other Writings,* Anthony Parel, ed., Cambridge: Cambridge University Press.

Gattini, A. (2002). The UN Compensation Commission: Old Rules, New Procedures on War Reparations. *European Journal of International Law*, 13 (1), 161–81.

Gellner, E. (1983). *Nations and Nationalism*, Ithaca, NY: Cornell University Press.

Gewald, J.-B. (1999). *Herero Heroes: A Socio-Political History of the Herero of Namibia 1890–1923*, Oxford: James Currey.

Gewald, J.-B. and J. Silvester (2003). *Words Cannot Be Found: German Colonial Rule in Namibia: An Annotated Reprint of the 1918 Blue Book*, Leiden: Brill.

Gilabert, P. (2012). *From Global Poverty to Global Equality: A Philosophical Exploration*, Oxford: Oxford University Press.

Goldsmith, J. and S. Krasner (2003). The Limits of Idealism. *Daedalus*, 132 (1), 47–63.

Gong, G. (1984). *The Standard of "Civilization" in International Society*, Oxford: Clarendon Press.

Goodin, R. E. (2013). Disgorging the Fruits of Historical Wrongdoing. *American Political Science Review*, 107 (3), 478–91.

Goodin, R. E. and C. Lepora (2013). *On Complicity and Compromise*, Oxford: Oxford University Press.

Griffiths, I. (1986). The Scramble for Africa: Inherited Political Boundaries. *The Geographical Journal*, 152 (2), 204–16.

Griswold, C. L. (2007). *Forgiveness: A Philosophical Exploration*, Cambridge: Cambridge University Press.

Halev-Spinner, J. (2012). *Enduring Injustice*, Cambridge: Cambridge University Press.

Halliwell, S. (1984). Plato and Aristotle on the Denial of Tragedy, *Proceedings of the Cambridge Philological Society*, 30, 49–71.

Halperin, S. (2006). International Relations Theory and the Hegemony of Western Conceptions of Modernity. In B. G. Jones, ed., *Decolonizing International Relations*, Toronto: Rowman and Littlefield, 43–63.

Hamber, B. (2003). Does the Truth Heal? A Psychological Perspective on Political Strategies for Dealing with the Legacy of Political Violence. In N. Biggar, ed., *Burying the Past: Making Peace and Doing Justice after Civil Conflict*, Washington, DC: Georgetown University Press, 155–76.

Hampton, J. (1988). The Retributive Idea. In J. G. Murphy and J. Hampton, eds., *Forgiveness and Mercy*, Cambridge: Cambridge University Press, 111-61.

Hampton, J. & J. G. Murphy (1988). *Forgiveness and Mercy*, Cambridge: Cambridge University Press.

Hardimon, M. O. (1992). The Project of Reconciliation: Hegel's Social Philosophy. *Philosophy and Public Affairs*, 21 (2), 165–95.

Harring, S. L. (2001–2002). German Reparations to the Herero Nation: An Assertion of Herero Nationhood in the Path of Namibian Development? *West Virginia Law Review*, 104, 393–417.

Harrison, B. (1971). Violence and the Rule of Law. In J. A. Shaffer, ed., *Violence*, New York: McKay, 139–76.

Hartmann, W. (1999). Funerary Photographs: The Funeral of a Chief. In W. Hartmann, J. Silvester, and P. Hayes, eds., *The Colonizing Camera: Photographs in the Making of Namibian History*, Athens: Ohio University Press, 125–31.

Hedges, C. (2003). *War Is a Force That Gives Us Meaning*, New York: Anchor Books.

Henry, C. P. (2007). *Long Overdue: The Politics of Racial Reparations*, New York: New York University Press.

Herman, J. L. (1997). *Trauma and Recovery: The Aftermath of Violence – From Domestic Abuse to Political Terror*, New York: Basic Books.

Herodotus (1996). *The Histories*, A. de Sélincourt, trans., J. Marincola, ed., Toronto: Penguin.

Hobbes, Thomas (1962). *Leviathan: Or the Matter, Forme and Power of a Commonwealth Ecclesiastical and Civil*, M. Oakeshott, trans., New York: Collier Books.

Hobsbawm, E. (1975). *The Age of Capital 1848–1875*, London: Abacus.

Hochschild, A. (1998). *King Leopold's Ghost: A Story of Greed, Terror, and Heroism in Colonial Africa*, New York: Houghton Mifflin.

Homer (2011). *The Iliad of Homer*, R. Lattimore, trans., Chicago: University of Chicago Press.

Howard, M. (1962). *The Franco-Prussian War: The German Invasion of France, 1870–1871*, New York: Macmillan.

Hou, X. (2016). *Negotiating Socialism in Rural China: Mao, Peasants, and Local Cadres in Shanxi 1949–53*, Ithaca, NY: Cornell University East Asia Program.

Hughes, R. (1988). *The Fatal Shore: The Epic of Australia's Founding*, New York: Vintage Books.

Hurrell, A. (2003). Order and Justice in International Relations: What Is at Stake? In R. Foot, J. L. Gaddis, and A. Hurrell, eds., *Order and Justice in International Relations*, Oxford: Oxford University Press, 24–48.

Ikenberry, G. J. (2001). *After Victory: Institutions, Strategic Restraint, and the Rebuilding of Order after Major Wars*, Princeton, NJ: Princeton University Press.

Isaacs, T. (2011). *Moral Responsibility in Collective Contexts*, Oxford: Oxford University Press.

Isaacs, T. and R. Vernon, eds. (2011). *Accountability for Collective Wrongdoing*, Cambridge: Cambridge University Press.

Jacobson, J. (1983). Is There a New International History of the 1920s? *The American Historical Review*, 88 (3), 617–45.

Jaeggi, R. (2014). *Alienation*, F. Neuhouser and A. E. Smith, trans., New York: Columbia University Press.

Jahn, B. (1999). IR and the State of Nature: The Cultural Origins of a Ruling Ideology. *Review of International Studies*, 25 (3), 411–34.

(2000). *The Cultural Construction of International Relations: The Invention of the State of Nature*, Basingstoke: Palgrave.

Jamfa, L. (2008). Germany Faces Colonial History in Namibia: A Very Ambiguous "I Am Sorry." In J.-M. Coicaud, M. Gibney, R. E. Howard-Hassmann, and N. Steiner, eds., *The Age of Apology: Facing Up to the Past*, Philadelphia: University of Pennsylvania Press, 202–15.

Johanningsmeier, E. (2004). Communist and Black Freedom Movements in South Africa and the US: 1919–50. *Journal of Southern African Studies*, 30 (1), 155–80.

Kalmanovitz, P. (2011). Sharing Burdens after War: A Lockean Approach. *The Journal of Political Philosophy*, 19 (2), 209–28.

Kanogo, T. (2016). Mau Mau Women: Sixty Years Later. In S. Ardener, L. D. Sciama, F. Ardener, S. Armitage-Woodward, and L. D. Sciama, eds., *War and Women across Continents: Autobiographical and Biographical Experiences*, New York: Bergham Press, 75–93.

Karnow, S. (1983). *Vietnam: A History*, New York: Viking Press.

Keene, E. (2002). *Beyond the Anarchical Society: Grotius, Colonialism and Order in World Politics*, Cambridge: Cambridge University Press.

Keynes, J. M. (1963). *Essays in Persuasion*, New York: W. W. Norton.

Kimura, M. (2016). *Unfolding the "Comfort Women" Debates: Modernity, Violence, Women's Voices*, Basingstoke: Palgrave Macmillan.

Kinley, D. (2009). *Civilising Globalisation: Human Rights and the Global Economy*, Cambridge: Cambridge University Press.

Kohli, A. (1997). Japanese Colonialism and Korean Development: A Reply. *World Development*, 25 (6), 883–88.

Kohn, M. (2013). Postcolonialism and Global Justice. *Journal of Global Ethics*, 9 (2), 187–200.

Kohn, M. and K. McBride (2011). *Political Theories of Decolonization: Postcolonialism and the Problem of Foundations*, Oxford: Oxford University Press.

Kokaz, N. (2005). Institutions for Global Justice. *Canadian Journal of Philosophy*, 31, 65–107.

Kolko, G. (1994). *Anatomy of a War: Vietnam, the United States, and the Modern Historical Experience*, New York: The New Press.

Kosinski, J. (1976). *The Painted Bird*, 2nd ed., New York: Grove Press.

Kraut, R. (2002). *Aristotle: Political Philosophy*, Oxford: Oxford University Press.

Krog, A. (1998). *Country of My Skull: Guilt, Sorrow, and the Limits of Forgiveness in the New South Africa*, New York: Three Rivers Press.

Kukathas, C. (2003). Responsibility for Past Injustice: How to Shift the Burden. *Politics, Philosophy, and Economics*, 2 (2), 165–90.

(2006). Who? Whom? Reparations and the Problem of Agency. *Journal of Social Philosophy*, 37 (3), 330–41.

Kurki, M. (2013). *Democratic Futures: Re-visioning Democracy Promotion*, New York: Routledge.

Kutz, C. (2000). *Complicity: Ethics and Law for a Collective Age*, Cambridge: Cambridge University Press.

Lake, D. (2009). *Hierarchy in International Relations*, Ithaca, NY: Cornell University Press.

Lawrence, A. (2013). *Imperial Rule and the Politics of Nationalism: Anti-Colonial Protest in the French Empire*, Cambridge: Cambridge University Press.

Lear, J. (2006). *Radical Hope: Ethics in the Face of Cultural Devastation*, Cambridge, MA: Harvard University Press.

Leebaw, B. (2011). *Judging State-Sponsored Violence, Imagining Political Change*, Cambridge: Cambridge University Press.

Levi, P. (1989). *The Drowned and the Saved*, R. Rosenthal, trans., New York: Vintage International.

Lightfoot, S. (2016). *Global Indigenous Politics: A Subtle Revolution*, New York: Routledge.

Lind, M. (1999). *Vietnam, the Necessary War: A Reinterpretation of America's Most Disastrous Military Conflict*, New York: The Free Press.

List, C. and P. Pettit (2011). *Group Agency: The Possibility, Design, and Status of Corporate Agents*, Oxford: Oxford University Press.

Lomax, E. (1996). *The Railway Man*, London: Vintage.

Lu, C. (2002). Justice and Moral Regeneration: Lessons from the Treaty of Versailles. *International Studies Review*, 4 (3), 3–25.

(2006). The International Criminal Court as an Institution of Moral Regeneration: Problems and Prospects. In J. Harrington, M. Milde, and R. Vernon, eds., *Bringing Power to Justice: The Prospects of the International Criminal Court*, Montreal: McGill-Queen's University Press, 191–209.

(2008). Shame, Guilt and Reconciliation after War. *The European Journal of Social Theory*, 11 (3), 367–83.

(2011). Colonialism as Structural Injustice: Historical Responsibility and Contemporary Redress. *The Journal of Political Philosophy*, 19 (3), 261–81.

(2011). The Politics of Legal Accountability and Genocide Prevention. In R. Provost and P. Akhavan, eds., *Confronting Genocide*, Dordrecht: Springer, 295–303.

(Forthcoming). Cosmopolitan Justice, Democracy and World Government. In L. Cabrera, ed., *Institutional Cosmopolitanism*, Oxford: Oxford University Press.

Lukes, S. (1974). *Power: A Radical View*, London: Macmillan.

Lüthi, L.M. (2008). *The Sino-Soviet Split: Cold War in the Communist World*, Princeton, NJ: Princeton University Press.

(2009). Beyond Betrayal: Beijing, Moscow, and the Paris Negotiations, 1971–1973. *Journal of Cold War Studies*, 11 (1), 57–107.

(2013). China's Wirtschaftswunder [China's Economic Miracle]. In B. Greiner, T. Müller, and K. Voss, eds., *Erbe des Kalten Krieges [Legacy of the Cold War]*, Hamburg: Hamburger Edition, 447–62.

MacMillan, M. (2001). *Paris 1919: Six Months That Changed the World*, New York: Random House.

Manela, E. (2007). *The Wilsonian Moment: Self-Determination and the International Origins of Anticolonial Nationalism*, Oxford: Oxford University Press.

Martin, M. T. and M. Yaquinto, eds. (2007). *Redress for Historical Injustices in the United States: On Reparations for Slavery, Jim Crow, and Their Legacies*, Durham, NC: Duke University Press.

Marks, S. (1978). The Myths of Reparations. *Central European History*, 11 (1), 231–55.

Martel, G. (1998). A Comment. In M. F. Boemeke, G. D. Feldman, and E. Glaser, eds., *The Treaty of Versailles: A Reassessment after 75 Years*, Cambridge: Cambridge University Press, 615-636.

Martin, V. (2003). *Property*, New York: Vintage.

May, L. (1992). *Sharing Responsibility*, Chicago: University of Chicago Press.

McCarthy, T. (2009). *Race, Empire, and the Idea of Human Development*, Cambridge: Cambridge University Press.

McMahon, R. J. (1999). Vietnam War (1960–75): Changing Interpretations. In J. W. Chambers, ed., *The Oxford Companion to American Military History*, Oxford: Oxford University Press, 767–68.

Mégret, F. (Forthcoming). International Justice. In J. d'Aspremont and S. Singh, eds., *Fundamental Concepts of International Law*, Cheltenham: Edward Elgar Press.

Meister, R. (2012). *After Evil: A Politics of Human Rights*, New York: Columbia University Press.

Mihai, M. (2016). *Negative Emotions and Transitional Justice*, New York: Columbia University Press.

Mihai, M. and M. Thaler, eds. (2014). *On the Uses and Abuses of Political Apologies*, Basingstoke: Palgrave Macmillan.

Mill, J. S. (2008). *Considerations on Representative Government* [1861], in *On Liberty and Other Essays*, Oxford: Oxford University Press.

Miller, D. H., ed. (1928). *The Drafting of the Covenant*, vol. 1, New York: Putnam.

Miller, D. (2001). Distributing Responsibilities. *The Journal of Political Philosophy*, 9 (4), 453–71.

(2004). Holding Nations Responsible. *Ethics*, 114 (2), 240–68.

(2007). *National Responsibility and Global Justice*, Oxford: Oxford University Press.

Miller, E. (2013). *Misalliance: Ngo Dinh Diem, the United States, and the Fate of South Vietnam*, Cambridge, MA: Harvard University Press.

Miller, J. and R. Kumar, eds. (2007). *Reparations: Interdisciplinary Inquiries*, Oxford: Oxford University Press.

Miller, M. C. (2013). *Wronged by Empire: Post-Imperial Ideology and Foreign Policy in India and China*, Stanford, CA: Stanford University Press.

Min, P. G. (2003). Korean "Comfort Women": The Intersection of Colonial Power, Gender, and Class. *Gender and Society*, 17 (6), 938–57.

Minow, M. (1998). *Between Vengeance and Forgiveness: Facing History after Genocide and Mass Violence*, Boston: Beacon Press.

Moellendorf, D. (2007). Reconciliation as a Political Value. *Journal of Social Philosophy*, 38 (2), 205–21.

Mommsen, H. (1996). *The Rise and Fall of Weimar Germany*, E. Forster and L. E. Jones, trans., Chapel Hill: University of North Carolina Press.

Morefield, J. (2004). *Covenants without Swords: Idealist Liberalism and the Spirit of Empire*, Princeton, NJ: Princeton University Press.

(2014). *Empires without Imperialism: Anglo-American Decline and the Politics of Deflection*, Oxford: Oxford University Press.

Morris, B. (2001). *Righteous Victims: A History of the Zionist-Arab Conflict 1881–2001*, New York: Vintage Books.

Moyar, M. (2006). *Triumph Forsaken: The Vietnam War, 1954–1965*, Cambridge: Cambridge University Press.

Moyo, D. (2012). *Dead Aid: Why Aid Is Not Working and How There Is Another Way for Africa*, Toronto: Penguin.

Müller, J.-W., ed. (2002). *Memory and Power in Post-War Europe: Studies in the Presence of the Past*, Cambridge: Cambridge University Press.

Murphy, C. (2010). *A Moral Theory of Political Reconciliation*, Cambridge: Cambridge University Press.

(2016). A Reply to Critics. *Criminal Law and Philosophy*, 10 (1), 165–77.

(2017). *The Conceptual Foundations of Transitional Justice*, Cambridge: Cambridge University Press.

Murphy, J. G. (1973). Marxism and Retribution. *Philosophy and Public Affairs*, 2, 217–43.

(2003). *Getting Even: Forgiveness and Its Limits*, Oxford: Oxford University Press.

Mutua, M. (2001). Savages, Victims, and Saviors: The Metaphor of Human Rights. *Harvard International Law Journal*, 42 (1), 201–45.

(2002). *Human Rights: A Political and Cultural Critique*, Philadelphia: University of Pennsylvania.

Nguyễn, K. V. (1978). *The Long Resistance: 1858–1975*, 2nd ed., Moscow: Foreign Languages.

Nguyen, L.-H. T. (2012). *Hanoi's War: An International History of the War for Peace in Vietnam*, Chapel Hill: University of North Carolina Press.

Nino, C. S. (1996). *Radical Evil on Trial*, New Haven, CT: Yale University Press.

Nisbet, R. (1982). *Prejudices: A Philosophical Dictionary*, Cambridge, MA: Harvard University Press.

Nouwen, S. and W. Werner (2010). Doing Justice to the Political: the International Criminal Court in Uganda and Sudan. *European Journal of International Law*, 21 (4), 941–65.

Nozick, R. (1974). *Anarchy, State and Utopia*, New York: Basic Books.

Olusoga, D. and C. W. Erichsen (2010). *The Kaiser's Holocaust: Germany's Forgotten Genocide*, London: Faber and Faber.

Orr, J. J. (2001). *The Victim as Hero: Ideologies of Peace and National Identity in Postwar Japan*, Honolulu: University of Hawaii Press.

Osiel, M. (2009). *Making Sense of Mass Atrocity*, Cambridge: Cambridge University Press.

Parekh, S. (2011). Getting to the Root of Gender Inequality: Structural Injustice and Political Responsibility. *Hypatia*, 26 (4), 672–89.

Parrish, J. M. (2009). Collective Responsibility and the State. *International Theory*, 1 (1), 119–54.

Pasternak, A. (2011). Sharing the Costs of Political Injustices. *Politics, Philosophy and Economics*, 10 (2), 188–210.

(2013). Limiting States' Corporate Responsibility. *The Journal of Political Philosophy*, 21 (4), 361–81.

Patten, A. (2014). *Equal Recognition: The Moral Foundations of Minority Rights*, Princeton, NJ: Princeton University Press.

Pearcey, M. (2015). Sovereignty, Identity, and Indigenous-State Relations at the Beginning of the Twentieth Century: A Case of Exclusion by Inclusion. *International Studies Review*, 17 (3), 441–54.

Pedersen, S. (2015). *The Guardians: The League of Nations and the Crisis of Empire*, Oxford: Oxford University Press.

Peskin, V. (2008). *International Justice in Rwanda and the Balkans: Virtual Trials and the Struggle for State Cooperation*, New York: Cambridge University Press.

Pettit, P. (1993). *The Common Mind: An Essay on Psychology, Society and Politics*, Oxford: Oxford University Press.

Philpott, D. (2012). *Just and Unjust Peace: An Ethic of Political Reconcilia-tion*, Oxford: Oxford University Press.

Plato (1988). *The Laws of Plato*, T. Pangle, trans., Chicago: University of Chicago Press.

(1991). *The Republic of Plato*, A. Bloom, trans., New York: Basic Books.

(1998). *Gorgias*, J. H. Nichols, trans., Ithaca, NY: Cornell University Press.

Pouliot, V. (2016). *International Pecking Orders: The Politics and Prac-tice of Multilateral Diplomacy*, Cambridge: Cambridge University Press.

(Forthcoming). Against Authority: The Heavy Weight of International Hierarchy. In A. Zarakol, ed., *Hierarchies in World Politics*, Cambridge: Cambridge University Press.

Qiang, Z. (2004). *China and the Vietnam Wars*, Chapel Hill: University of North Carolina Press.

Radzik, L. (2009). *Making Amends: Atonement in Morality, Law, and Poli-tics*, Oxford: Oxford University Press.

Ramsbotham, O. and T. Woodhouse (1996). *Humanitarian Intervention in Contemporary Conflict: A Reconceptualization*, Cambridge: Polity Press.

Rao, R. (2010). *Third World Protest: Between Home and the World*, Oxford: Oxford University Press.

Ratner, S. R. (1996). Drawing a Better Line: *Uti Possidetis* and the Borders of New States. *The American Journal of International Law*, 90 (4), 590–624.

(2015). *The Thin Justice of International Law: A Moral Reckoning of the Law of Nations*, Oxford: Oxford University Press.

Rawls, J. (1999). *The Law of Peoples*, Cambridge: Harvard University Press.

Reidy, D. and J. von Platz (2006). The Structural Diversity of Historical Injustices. *Journal of Social Philosophy*, 37 (3), 360–76.

Reus-Smit, C. (2013). *Individual Rights and the Making of the International System*, Cambridge: Cambridge University Press.

Ridge, M. (2003). Giving the Dead Their Due. *Ethics*, 114 (1), 38–59.

Risse, M. (2012). *On Global Justice*, Princeton: Princeton University Press.

Robertson, G. (1999). *Crimes against Humanity: The Struggle for Global Justice*, New York: New Press.

Robinson, R. (2000). Restatement of the Black Manifesto. In Martin and Yaquinto, eds., *Redress for Historical Injustices in the United States*, 621–24.

Rodney, W. (1972). *How Europe Underdeveloped Africa*, Cape Town, South Africa: Pambazuka Press.

Ronzoni, M. (2008). What Makes a Basic Structure Just? *Res Publica*, 14 (3), 203–18.

(2009). The Global Order: A Case of Background Injustice? A Practice-Dependent Account. *Philosophy and Public Affairs*, 37 (3), 229–56.

Ross, C. (2007). *Independent Diplomat: Dispatches from an Unaccountable Elite*, Ithaca, NY: Cornell University Press.

Rotberg, R. I. and D. Thompson (2000). *Truth v. Justice: The Morality of Truth Commissions*, Princeton, NJ: Princeton University Press.

Rousseau, J.-J. (1927). *Project of Perpetual Peace*, E. M. Nuttall, trans., London: Richard Cobden-Sanderson.

Rubenstein, J. (2015). *Between Samaritans and States: The Political Ethics of Humanitarian INGOs*, Oxford: Oxford University Press.

Salvador-Crespo, I. (2015). Making Good for Forced Exodus: Compensation for Departure from Iraq or Kuwait – Claims of Individuals: "A" Claims. In T. J. Feighery, C. S. Gibson, and T. M. Rajah, eds., *War Reparations and the UN Compensation Commission: Designing Compensation after Conflict*, Oxford: Oxford University Press, 221–41.

Scarry, E. (2003). *The Body in Pain: The Making and Unmaking of the World*, Oxford: Oxford University Press.

Schaap, A. (2005). *Political Reconciliation*, New York: Routledge.

Scheff, T. J. (1987). The Shame-Rage Spiral: A Case Study of Interminable Quarrel. In H. B. Lewis, ed., *The Role of Shame in Symptom Formation*, Hillsdale, NJ: LEA, 109–49.

Schiff, J. L. (2014). *Burdens of Political Responsibility: Narrative and the Cultivation of Responsiveness*, Cambridge: Cambridge University Press.

Schivelbush, W. (2003). *The Culture of Defeat: On National Trauma, Mourning and Recovery*, J. Chase, trans., New York: Metropolitan Books.

Shakespeare, W. (1998). *The Tragedy of Othello*, New York: Signet Classics.

Shelton, D. (2002). Righting Wrongs: Reparations in the Articles on State Responsibility. *American Journal of International Law*, 96 (4), 833–56.

Sher, G. (1980). Ancient Wrongs and Modern Rights. *Philosophy and Public Affairs*, 10 (1), 3–17.

Shilliam, R. (2006). What about Marcus Garvey? Race and the Transformation of Sovereignty Debate. *Review of International Studies*, 32 (3), 379–400.

(2013). Race and Research Agendas. *Cambridge Review of International Affairs*, 26 (1), 152–58.

(2015). *The Black Pacific: Anticolonial Struggles and Oceanic Connections*, London: Bloomsbury Press.

Shimazu, N. (1998). *Japan, Race and Equality: The Racial Equality Principle of 1919*, New York: Routledge.

Shklar, J. N. (1964). *Legalism: Law, Morals, and Political Trials*, Cambridge, MA: Harvard University Press.

(1984). *Ordinary Vices*, Cambridge, MA: Harvard University Press.

(1990). *The Faces of Injustice*, New Haven, CT: Yale University Press.

Shue, H. (1996). *Basic Rights: Subsistence, Affluence, and US Foreign Policy*, 2nd ed., Princeton, NJ: Princeton University Press.

Sikkink, K. (2011). *The Justice Cascade: How Human Rights Prosecutions Are Changing World Politics*, New York: W. W. Norton.

Simpson, A. (2014). *Mohawk Interruptus: Political Life across the Borders of Settler States*, Durham, NC: Duke University Press.

Simpson, L. (2011). *Dancing on Our Turtle's Back: Stories of Nishnaabeg Re-Creation, Resurgence and a New Emergence*, Winnipeg: Arbeiter Ring Press.

Slaughter, A.-M. (2004). *A New World Order*, Princeton, NJ: Princeton University Press.

Sliedregt, E., van (2012). *Individual Criminal Responsibility in International Law*, Oxford: Oxford University Press.

Smyth, M. (2003). Putting the Past in Its Place: Issues of Victimhood and Reconciliation in Northern Ireland's Peace Process. In N. Biggar, ed., *Burying the Past: Making Peace and Doing Justice after Civil Conflict*, Washington, DC: Georgetown University Press, 125–53.

Snyder, J. and L. Vinjamuri (2003–2004). Trials and Errors: Principle and Pragmatism in Strategies of International Justice. *International Security*, 28 (3), 5–44.

(2015). Law and Politics in Transitional Justice. *Annual Review of Political Science*, 18 (1), 303–27.

Soh, C. S. (2003). Japan's National/Asian Women's Fund for "Comfort Women." *Pacific Affairs*, 76 (2), 209–33.

(2008). *The Comfort Women: Sexual Violence and Postcolonial Memory in Korea and Japan*, Chicago: University of Chicago Press.

Spence, J. D. (2001). *The Search for Modern China*, New ed., New York: W. W. Norton.

Spinner-Halev, J. (2012). *Enduring Injustice*, Cambridge: Cambridge University Press.

Stiglitz, J. E. (2002). *Globalization and Its Discontents*, New York: W. W. Norton.

Stilz, A. (2011). Collective Responsibility and the State. *The Journal of Political Philosophy*, 19 (2), 190–208.

(2016). The Value of Self-Determination. In D. Sobel, P. Vallentyne, and S. Wall, eds., *Oxford Studies in Political Philosophy, Volume 2*, Oxford: Oxford University Press, 98–126.

Stover, E. and H. M. Weinstein (2004). *My Neighbor, My Enemy: Justice and Community in the Aftermath of Mass Atrocity*, Cambridge: Cambridge University Press.

Stover, R. (1972). Responsibility for the Cold War – A Case Study of Historical Responsibility. *History and Theory*, 11 (2), 145–78.

Subotic, J. (2009). *Hijacked Justice: Dealing with the Past in the Balkans*, Ithaca, NY: Cornell University Press.

Sumner, B. T. (2004). Territorial Disputes at the International Court of Justice. *Duke Law Journal*, 53 (6), 1779–812.

Suzuki, S. (2005). Japan's Socialization into Janus-Faced European International Society. *European Journal of International Relations*, 11 (1), 137–64.

(2009). *Civilization and Empire: China and Japan's Encounter with European International Society*, New York: Routledge.

Tan, K.-C. (2007). Colonialism, Reparations and Global Justice. In J. Miller and R. Kumar, eds., *Reparations: Interdisciplinary Inquiries*, Oxford: Oxford University Press, 280–306.

Taylor, C. (1989). *Sources of the Self: The Making of the Modern Identity*, Cambridge: Cambridge University Press.

(1991). *The Ethics of Authenticity*, Cambridge, MA: Harvard University Press.

(1994). *Multiculturalism: Examining the Politics of Recognition*, Princeton, NJ: Princeton University Press.

Teitel, R. G. (2000). *Transitional Justice*, New York: Oxford University Press.

Thompson, J. (2002). *Taking Responsibility for the Past: Reparation and Historical Injustice*, Cambridge, MA: Polity Press.

Thucydides (1989). *The Peloponnesian War*, Thomas Hobbes, trans., Chicago: University of Chicago Press.

Torpey, J. (2006). *Making Whole What Has Been Smashed: On Reparations Politics*, Cambridge, MA: Harvard University Press.

Totani, Y. (2008). *The Tokyo War Crimes Trial: The Pursuit of Justice in the Wake of World War II*, Cambridge, MA: Harvard University Press.

Towns, A. (2010). *Women and States: Norms and Hierarchies in International Society*, Cambridge: Cambridge University Press.

Trachtenberg, M. (1980). *Reparation in World Politics: France and European Economic Diplomacy, 1916–1923*, New York: Columbia University Press.

Truth and Reconciliation Commission of Canada (2015). *Final Report of the Truth and Reconciliation Commission of Canada, Volume 1: Summary*, Toronto: James Lorimer.

Tully, J. (2008). *Public Philosophy in a New Key*, vol. 1 of Democracy and Civic Freedom, Cambridge: Cambridge University Press.

Turner, D. (2006). *This Is Not a Peace Pipe: Towards a Critical Indigenous Philosophy*, Toronto: University of Toronto Press.

Utley, R. M. and W. E. Washburn (1977). *Indian Wars*, Boston: Mariner Books.

Valentini, L. (2011). *Justice in a Globalized World: A Normative Framework*, Oxford: Oxford University Press.

Vernon, R. (2011). Punishing Collectives: States or Nations? In T. Isaacs and R. Vernon, eds., *Accountability for Collective Wrongdoing*, Cambridge: Cambridge University Press, 287–306.

Vinjamuri, L. (2015). The International Criminal Court and the Politics of Peace and Justice. In C. Stahn, ed., *The Law and Practice of the International Criminal Court*, Oxford: Oxford University Press, 13–29.

Waldron, J. (2012). *Dignity, Rank, and Rights*, Oxford: Oxford University Press.

Walker, M. U. (2006). *Moral Repair: Reconstructing Moral Relations after Wrongdoing*, Cambridge: Cambridge University Press.

Walle, N. (2001). *African Economies and the Politics of Permanent Crises 1979–99*, Cambridge: Cambridge University Press.

Wallerstein, I. (2011) [1976]. *The Modern World-System: Capitalist Agriculture and the Origins of the European World-Economy in the Sixteenth Century*, Berkeley: University of California Press.

Walzer, M. (1977). *Just and Unjust Wars: A Moral Argument with Historical Illustrations*, New York: Basic Books.

Webster, D. (1988). *Aftermath: The Remnants of War*, New York: Vintage Books.

Weinstein, H. M. (2011). Editorial Note: The Myth of Closure, the Illusion of Reconciliation: Final Thoughts on Five Years as Co-Editor-in-Chief. *International Journal of Transitional Justice*, 5 (1), 1–10.

Weitz, E. D. (2007). *Weimar Germany: Promise and Tragedy*, Princeton, NJ: Princeton University Press.

Welch, D. A. (1993). *Justice and the Genesis of War*. Cambridge: Cambridge University Press.

(2017). The Justice Motive in East Asia's Territorial Disputes. *Group Decision and Negotiation*, 26 (1), 71–92.

Wenar, L. (2006). Reparations for the Future. *Journal of Social Philosophy*, 37 (3), 396–405.

Wendt, A. (1992). Anarchy Is What States Make of It: The Social Construction of Power Politics. *International Organization*, 46 (2), 391–425.

(1999). *Social Theory of International Politics*, Cambridge: Cambridge University Press.

Wesseling, H. L. (1989). Colonial Wars: An Introduction. In J. A. de Moor and H. L. Wesseling, eds., *Imperialism and War: Essays on Colonial Wars in Asia and Africa*, Leiden: E. J. Brill, 1–12.

Wheatley, N. (2015). Mandatory Interpretation: Legal Hermeneutics and the New International Order in Arab and Jewish Petitions to the League of Nations. *Past and Present: A Journal of Historical Studies*, 227 (1), 205–48.

White, E. (2001). Making the French Pay: The Costs and Consequences of the Napoleonic Reparations, *European Review of Economic History*, 5 (3), 337–65.

Winter, S. (2014). *Transitional Justice in Established Democracies: A Political Theory*, Basingstoke: Palgrave Macmillan.

Wiredu, K. (1995). *Conceptual Decolonization in African Philosophy: Four Essays*, Ibadan: Hope.

(1996). *Cultural Universals and Particulars: An African Perspective*, Bloomington: Indiana University Press.

Wolf, R. (2011). Respect and Disrespect in International Politics: The Significance of Status Recognition. *International Theory*, 3 (1), 105–42.

Xiaohui, L. and W. Zhang (2010). Success and Challenges: Overview of China's Economic Growth and Reform since 1978. In L. Xiaohui and W. Zhang, eds., *China's Three Decades of Economic Reforms*, London: Routledge, 3–14.

Yoshimi, Y. (2000). *Comfort Women: Sexual Slavery in the Japanese Military during World War II*, S. O'Brien, trans., New York: Columbia University Press.

Young, I. M. (1990). *Justice and the Politics of Difference*, Princeton, NJ: Princeton University Press.

(2004). Responsibility and Global Labor Justice. *The Journal of Political Philosophy*, 12 (1), 365–88.

(2006). Responsibility and Global Justice: A Social Connection Model. *Social Philosophy and Policy*, 23 (1), 102–30.

(2006). Taking the Basic Structure Seriously. *Perspectives on Politics*, 4 (1), 91–97.

(2007). *Global Challenges: War, Self-Determination and Responsibility for Justice*, Cambridge: Polity.

(2009). Structural Injustice and the Politics of Difference. In T. Christiano and J. Christman, eds., *Contemporary Debates in Political Philosophy*. Malden, MA: Wiley-Blackwell, 362–83.

(2011). *Responsibility for Justice*, Oxford: Oxford University Press.

Ypi, L. (2012). *Global Justice and Avant-Garde Political Agency*, Oxford: Oxford University Press.

(2013). What's Wrong with Colonialism. *Philosophy and Public Affairs*, 41 (2), 158–91.

Zacher, M. W. (2001). The Territorial Integrity Norm: International Boundaries and the Use of Force. *International Organization*, 55 (2), 215–50.

Zarakol, A. (2011). *After Defeat: How the East Learned to Live with the West*, Cambridge: Cambridge University Press.

Zedong, M. (1977). *Selected Works of Mao Tsetung*, vol. V, Peking: Foreign Languages.

Zunino, M. (2016). Subversive Justice: The Russell Vietnam War Crimes Tribunal and Transitional Justice. *International Journal of Transitional Justice*, 10 (2), 211–29.

Index

Cambridge Studies in International Relations: 144

CPSIA information can be obtained
at www.ICGtesting.com
Printed in the USA
LVHW032051081118
596444LV00016B/258/P

9 781108 413053